Praise for *The Face in the Window: Haunting Ohio Tales:*

"Deserves the largest possible public...M.R. James with footnotes...".
–Dr. Beachcombing,
Beachcombing's Bizarre History Blog, strangehistory.net

Praise for *The Ghost Wore Black: Ghastly Tales from the Past:*

"'*The Ghost Wore Black*' is highly enjoyable reading, but even more importantly, these newspaper reports serve as a cache of primary source material dealing with an often-ignored aspect of American cultural history."
–Undine, Strange Company, strangeco.blogspot.com

"An accomplished historian...she sees connections that others don't see. Elegant, thought out, novel and surprising..."
–Dr Beachcombing's Bizarre History Blog

"A great book for the enthusiasts of the uncanny and one that should be read with caution in the wee small hours."
–*Fortean Times*

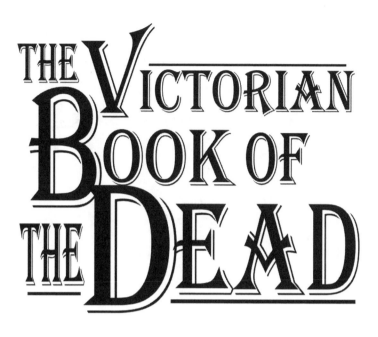

THE VICTORIAN BOOK OF THE DEAD

SELECTED AND EDITED BY CHRIS WOODYARD
AUTHOR OF THE GHOSTS OF THE PAST SERIES

Kestrel
Publications

ALSO BY CHRIS WOODYARD

Haunted Ohio: Ghostly Tales from the Buckeye State
Haunted Ohio II: More Ghostly Tales from the Buckeye State
Haunted Ohio III: Still More Ghostly Tales from the Buckeye State
Haunted Ohio IV: Restless Spirits
Haunted Ohio V: 200 Years of Ghosts
Spooky Ohio: 13 Traditional Tales
Ghost Hunter's Guide to Haunted Ohio
The Wright Stuff: A Guide to Life in the Dayton Area
A Spot of Bother: Four Macabre Tales (Fiction)
The Face in the Window: Haunting Ohio Tales
The Headless Horror: Strange and Ghostly Ohio Tales
The Ghost Wore Black: Ghastly Tales from the Past
When the Banshee Howls: Uncanny Tales of the Past

See the last page of the book for how to order your own copy of this book or other books by Chris Woodyard

Second Printing (October 2016)

Printed in the United States of America

Design and Typesetting by Rose Island Bookworks
Cover Art and Chapter Heads by Jessica Wiesel

Woodyard, Chris
The Victorian Book of the Dead / Chris Woodyard
SUMMARY: A compilation of 19th- and early 20th-century newspaper and journal articles on death, mourning practices, widows, ghosts, and horrors with commentary and annotations by Chris Woodyard.

ISBN 978-0-9881925-2-2

1. Death—Social aspects—19th century
2. Mourning customs—19th century
3. Funeral rites and ceremonies—19th century
4. Bereavement
393.3 W663 Vi
GT3243|b.W663 2014

To those who are not lost, but gone before.

Acknowledgments

The Anomalist: Patrick Huyghe, Melanie Billings, and Chris Savia, www.anomalist.com

Dr Beachcombing, http://www.strangehistory.net/

Rowan Gibbs

Marsha Hamilton

Elizabeth Hertenstein, Bowling Green State University Libraries

Susan Leonard, Rose Island Bookworks

Susan Longo

Beth Marshall, Archivist, Logan County [OH] Historical Society

Samantha McCarty

Michael Robinson

Jessica Wiesel

Strange Company, http://strangeco.blogspot.com/

Table of Contents

Introduction
A Deathbed, by Dickens

We begin, as many books end, with a deathbed. It is a Victorian deathbed, so often the sensational centerpiece of three-volume novels, fraught with secrets, repentance, and revelations, or simply with sorrow.

They were all about her at the time, knowing that the end was drawing on. She died soon after daybreak. They had read and talked to her in the earlier portion of the night, but as the hours crept on, she sunk to sleep.... Waking, she never wandered in her mind but once, and that was of beautiful music which she said was in the air. God knows. It may have been.

Opening her eyes at last, from a very quiet sleep, she begged that they would kiss her once again. That done, she turned to the old man with a lovely smile upon her face—such, they said, as they had never seen, and never could forget—and clung with both her arms about his neck. They did not know that she was dead, at first.

The Death of Little Nell, *The Old Curiosity Shop*, Charles Dickens, 1841

It was a beautiful deathbed. The still white figure lies in the coffin in the parlor. A lamp casts dim shadows.
Did an eyelid flicker? Did the bosom stir?
It is a long time until dawn.

I grew up with the stories and artifacts of Victorian death. Stored away in my grandmother's attic was a portrait of a nameless dead baby in a large gilt frame, its eyes painted open beneath stiff, veined eyelids. When my great-great-grandfather was killed at the Battle of Chickamauga, his body was never identified. It was whispered that his head had been blown off. One of his daughters would never turn away a tramp, thinking that it might be her father, come back.

In scanning my shelves of books on post-mortem photographs, ghosts, and graveyards, it struck me that many books describe royal and upper-class mourning rituals, or specific subjects like famous corpses,

Spiritualism, cemeteries, and burial alive. Bodysnatching has been done, so to speak, to death....

But the humbler figures in respectable black trudging behind the hearse have been often overlooked. This book will try to draw back the dark veil from lesser-known nineteenth-century funereal fads and fancies.

The purpose of *The Victorian Book of the Dead* is threefold. It is an historical look at the ephemera and material culture of mourning; a reflection of some popular Victorian attitudes towards death and the bereaved; and a macabre scrapbook of ghoulish anecdotes reported by the press.

This book is by no means a complete encyclopedia of Victorian death or a scholarly dissertation. There is no overarching sweep of funerary history. Rather it is an idiosyncratic collection of the morbid and the mournful. It is not representative of all classes, places, or ethnic groups. Many subjects had to be omitted due to space limitations. The majority of stories are from the United States and the British Isles and were written between 1840-1920. The term "Victorian" in the title is one of cultural attitudes, rather than strict chronology.

These stories rarely contain the elevated sentiments of the etiquette books. They are not the individual experiences recorded in diaries and letters, but reflect familiar beliefs and fears of the Victorian public.

Here you will find ghosts who haunt cemeteries, an electric corpse, a table made of human flesh, grisly post-mortem photography tips, exploding coffins, a maggot-ridden morgue, and many other tales from the crypts of the Victorian era. You will also read interviews with undertakers and gravediggers and find stories of widows merry and mournful. There are handy tips on renovating crape, the essential mourning fabric, and for ensuring that one is not buried alive. Everything in this book is drawn from primary sources: the books, newspapers, and magazines read by ordinary people. Much of this odd and ephemeral material has not been seen since it was first published. Here it is given new life, resurrected from newspaper morgues. The illustrations are Victorian photographs as well as antique book and newspaper illustrations, while many of the chapter headings were drawn by Jessica Wiesel from Victorian originals.

How we mourn our dead says something about who we are. The twenty-first-century fragmentation of the family has led to a detachment from death. The care of the dying and dead is, for the most part, in the hands of trained professionals rather than family members.

Today the happy funeral is commonplace. It is a "celebration of life," a phrase which would have raised Victorian hackles, and which usually involves brightly-colored clothing for mourners, the deceased's favorite tunes, and perhaps a release of balloons.

The Victorians memorialized lives both well-lived and ill-spent, but they also knew how to mourn. They cherished their funeral rituals and understood the grieving of the bereaved, particularly that of the widow. They would have been appalled at the notion of urging the bereft to "smile" or to move on from their losses in a matter of weeks. There was a reason that deep mourning lasted a full year.

The Victorian Book of the Dead is not a handbook on how to express grief, but it offers some insights into a time when people knew that death was inevitable. Recently there has been a renewed interest in death and dying, the so-called "Death Acceptance Movement," in reaction to the separation of death from normal human experience. There is also an interest in "green" funerals, just as nineteenth-century burial reformers urged shroud-only burials, wicker coffins, and cremation. Death as a concept, as a fit object for study, is once again in fashion. I think the Victorians would have approved.

Death comes to all of us, sometimes in the darkest of garments, sometimes in celebratory red. The symbols of loss and the rituals of mourning may alter over the centuries, but death, with its attendant sorrow, is unchanging.

Tonight the wind plays against the parlor windows. The candles flicker around the coffin.
We have the whole night before us.
Let us watch by the dead.

Notes on editing, spelling, and formatting.

I started life as an historian and I have tried to keep my intrusions to a minimum because these historic tales need to be told in their own voices. I have tried to provide some context, annotation, and backstories because the past really is a different country and topical references can be obscure. After each story you'll find a citation for that story, the state or country where the story took place, and notes or comments on the story. Newspapers often reprinted stories from other papers; that is why the name of another newspaper often appears at the end of an article. Some citations omit page numbers if the book is available online.

I have kept most of the spelling as found in the original newspaper article except for obvious spelling errors. Period newspapers often inserted headlines into the text of an article for emphasis and I have kept these intact. This is dense language and sometimes difficult to read without such divisions. I have censored only one inflammatory word. The rest of the language is as it came from the pencil of the reporter. It should be understood that the sentiments expressed in these articles, no matter how odious or bigoted, are not my own, but those of the original journalist or newspaper in which they appeared.

The Victorian Book of the Dead

1.

"I Am the Death Angel:"
Victorian Personifications of Death

What did death look like to the Victorians? The literary personification of Death was a conventionally tender-hearted one—the bright angel, the friend and healer, or the apparition of a dear relative ready to bear away the soul to bliss.

Death fluttered in the crape on the door or arrived in a black-bordered envelope. Death bent over the bed in the shape of an old woman—Atropos, poised to snip the thread of life. Death might flit about darkened streets as a veiled woman in black, be glimpsed in a white bird battering at the window, or be heard in the wail of the banshee. Yet the sinister, skeletal figure with the scythe was never far from the consciousness of the Victorians.

About this period I went to live in the East End of London, Haggerston and Whitechapel, where I had a night shelter of my own. There I saw into what surroundings children were born, how they grow up, and how their parents live and die. I have seen so much of the lives of the outcast poor that I can feel nothing but the most passionate pity for them, even though I can now look upon them as souls just beginning to climb the ladder of evolution.

My night shelter was for women only, and was purposely of the roughest description. The floor was bare concrete, and round the walls were heaps of millers' sacks I had bought cheap, owing to mice having eaten holes in them.

According to our laws the legal age at which a girl can marry is thirteen, and I used to get many of these girl wives in for the night, as their lawful husbands used to turn them out of doors. I discovered that it was no uncommon practice for a man to buy one of those children from the parents for a few pence, the parents' consent being necessary. The marriage was solemnized, and the child wife was used only as a drudge to slave for the husband and his mistress, who was of a more suitable age to become his mate.

I used to be very much troubled by women in the throes of delirium tremens. They would come in quite quietly when the shelter opened, strip, pick up a sack and get into it, and then lie down and at once go to sleep. After a few hours' dead slumber they would get up, raving mad, and disturb all the other sleepers. The reason of this peculiar form of D. T. was explained to me by a doctor in the neighborhood. The publicans kept a pail behind the bar, into which was thrown the dregs of every species of liquor sold during the day. This concoction was distributed cheap at closing time, and its effects were cumulative.

One night I had a curious experience. The room was unusually quiet, and I had closed my eyes, but I was not asleep. I opened them, and, in the bright light of one unshaded gas jet, I saw a dark figure moving. Its back was towards me, and I instantly thought a plain clothes policeman had entered, no unusual occurrence, without my hearing him. In these days detectives used often to escort the West End ladies on slumming expeditions, and they usually called on me. Then I saw this figure was clad in dark robes, and was very tall. Again I thought, this is some old Jew who has crept in, and I was just about to rise and eject him, when something suddenly stopped me.

I saw through him and beyond him. I then and there realized that feeling of hair of one's head rising on one's scalp is no mere figment of speech.

The figure moved softly round the room, it made no sound whatever, and as it came to each sleeper it bent down, as if closely scrutinizing each face. It occurred to me that it was looking for some one. I began to dread the moment when the search was over, and the figure would turn its face towards me. I felt that my hair had turned into the quills of a porcupine. I wanted to shut my eyes, but dared not. Then before that quest was over, the figure straightened itself and turned full towards me. My fears instantly fell away from me like a fallen mantle, for though I knew the visitor had come from the other side, there was something so profoundly sad in the pale weary face, that compassion quite eclipsed fear. Another second and it had vanished.

Ghosts I Have Seen: And Other Psychic Experiences, Violet Tweedale, (New York: Frederick A. Stokes Company, 1919) ENGLAND

Poor and rich alike could be visited as shown in this well-known, but still chilling, story of the Dart of Death as told by Victorian raconteur Augustus Hare. It begins with Lord Somers paying a visit to Lord Warwick, the narrator.

> When [Somers] got to Lymington, he found Lord Warwick ill in bed, and he said, "I am so glad to see you, for I want to tell you such an odd thing that has happened to me. Last night I was in bed and the room was quite dark (this old-fashioned room of the inn at Lymington which you now see). Suddenly at the foot of the bed there appeared a great light, and in the midst of the light the figure of Death just as it is seen in the Dance of Death and other old pictures—a ghastly skeleton with a scythe and a dart: and Death balanced the dart, and it flew past me, just above my shoulder, close to my head, and it seemed to go into the wall; and then the light went out and the figure vanished. I was as wide awake then as I am now, for I pinched myself hard to see, and I lay awake for a long time, but a last I fell asleep. When my servant came to call me in the morning, he had a very scared expression of face, and he said, 'A dreadful thing has happened in the night, and the whole household of the inn is in the greatest confusion and grief, for the landlady's daughter, who slept in the next room, and the head of whose bed is against the wall against which your head now rests, has been found dead in her bed.'"

"The Poor Man's Friend," John Leech, Punch, February 1845.

The Story of My Life, Vol. IV, Augustus J.C. Hare,
(London: George Allen, 1900) ENGLAND

NOTE: Hare, in a footnote, says that he also heard the story from Lord Warwick himself: George Guy Greville, 4th Earl of Warwick [1818-1893]. Lord Somers was Charles, 3rd Earl of Somers [1819-1883].

This story of Death as a deadly little old lady comes from the terrible time of the Influenza Pandemic of 1918-1919.

Near Boissevain, Manitoba, a minister's wife, Flora Oke, had as strange a delusion as any. As sick as her own four children, Mrs. Oke wanted nothing more from life but to close her eyes and rest—yet each time she did so a little old lady appeared. She was bent and ugly, leaning with difficulty on a cane, always approaching nearer to the bedside. Once she bent almost close enough to kiss Flora Oke. At once Flora opened her eyes—and the old woman disappeared.

Now it became a battle. Again Flora closed her eyes—and all at once the old woman was hovering again. With half her being, Flora wanted desperately to surrender to that embrace, which she knew well enough was the kiss of death. Then, though sleep was a drowsy torment, the thought of the children forced her yet again to open her eyes and keep them open; to stare the little old lady who was death out of countenance.

The Plague of the Spanish Lady: The Influenza Pandemic of 1918-1919, Richard Collier, (New York: Atheneum, 1974), 267-8 CANADA

Curiously, none of the next two Angel of Death stories in this chapter report standard winged angel imagery. The shipboard Angels of Death in the account below appear in the guise of strapping young men.

THE ANGEL OF DEATH.

The ship *Raven*, bound from New York to the East Indies, was crossing the Southeast trades, with all drawing sail set. It was the last dog watch, the time between six and eight o'clock, and several of the watch who ought to have been on deck were below, listening to a yarn which Tom Gray was spinning.

"Catch that pigeon," said Bill Graves, interrupting the yarn, and springing from his seat, "catch that beautiful pigeon before it flies on deck again!" "What pigeon?" demanded half a dozen voices, "we don't see anything." In the mean time, before the sailors could make further inquiry, an order was issued from the quarter deck, to haul the main to mast staysail down. This brought the stragglers of the watch on deck, and those below requested Tom to continue his yarn; but Tom, apparently unconscious of their request, said, in a sorrowful tone, "Poor Bill, he is not long for this world. The white pigeon which he saw was *the angel of death*, who appeared to me as he has done before, like a young man with an hour-glass in his hand, the sands of which had nearly run out. He was rigged in white, fastened round the waist with a band like fire, and the name of Bill Graves on it." Hardly had he finished his description, when the thrilling cry rang fore and aft. "A man overboard!" In an instant all hands were on deck, the ship hove to, and the lee-quarter boat lowered. But all in vain. Poor Bill Graves, who had been thrown overboard by the staysail sheet, sank to rise no more. By the time the boat was hoisted up, and the sails trimmed, the dog watch was out. After the exchange of sorrowful regrets the watches separated, but the fate of Graves was the theme of their conversation; even after the watch below had turned into their hammocks, they spoke of him, and his many fine qualities as a seaman for he was a general favorite. The watch on deck formed a group around Tom Gray, who said that he had frequently seen the Angel of Death before. "The first time, shipmates, I saw him, was when I belonged to the British ten gun pelter *Vulture*, lying in the harbor of Sierra Leone. We had the fever on board, and over thirty men were down with it. I was sick at the time myself. The Angel of Death came down the main hatchway, and walked deliberately forward, among the hammocks. He was then dressed in a long flowing robe of orange yellow, and in his right hand he held a scroll with the

---

In the way that the Inuit are said to have many different words for snow, there are multiple descriptors for Death in the Victorian lexicon.

There are the references to personifications of Death:

- The Angel of Death's relentless hand has wielded its sickle in our midst, 1897
- Those upon whom the death angel laid his hand, 1871
- Called by the Angel of Death, 1884 and 1906
- The call of the minister of death, 1895
- Ringing up the black messenger, 1899
- The white robed messenger of death, 1873 and 1902
- Visited by the cold icy hand, 1901

There are images of sleep:

- That slumber from which there is no waking, 1880
- Last sleep, 1824
- Fell asleep, 1808
- The sleep that apparently has no waking this side of eternity, 1869

And of Heaven as another country:

- The Bourne from which no man returns, from *Hamlet*.
- Summerland, 1862 and after
- Gates of pearl, 1871
- The dark and narrow house, 1903
- The Great Beyond, 1871
- Land of shadows, 1837
- Passed into the spirit land, 1847

Some phrases refer to mourning in the earthly sphere:

- The shadow of the long, mournful crape, 1886
- The empty chair, 1870
- There is crape on the door, 1890s

Others are more whimsical:

- Joined the Choir Invisible, 1867
- Pushing up daisies, 1910s
- Six feet under, 1871

The dates note a representative, rather than the earliest, appearance of a word or phrase.

names of a dozen men on it, and in his left was the same hour glass that I saw this evening. He was very beautiful, had long, curly hair, of raven black, encircled by a band on which the words "Angel of Death" seemed to blaze and burn. He looked at me as he passed. Our eyes met, and I thought I knew him. He smiled, and said "not yet." Then passing from hammock to hammock, he retraced his steps toward the main hatchway, followed by the men whose names were on the scroll. A dozen men died that night. He paid us a visit almost every day, sometimes taking one or more from our number, until we had lost twenty-five men. The next time I saw him was in a church in Bermuda. He entered the pulpit, and stood beside the minister full five minutes, looking at the hour-glass. I could see the sand distinctly running, and when it was out, the parson staggered and fell. I was the first to rush to his assistance, and as I raised him in my arms, I saw his form follow the Angel of Death down the broad aisle, and disappear. The minister died in my arms. The last time I was in New York. I saw him take a poor suffering child from its mother's arms into his own, and kiss it and disappear. The child died a few minutes afterwards, which makes me think that the soul leaves the body before life is extinct. The angel was then robed in green." Tom told many other strange stories of the Angel of Death and his doings, which left a deep impression on the minds of his hearers, who believed his every word. *Boston Traveller.*

The National Era [Washington DC] 8 December 1859 ATLANTIC OCEAN

The angels in this next story have wing-like rays of light coming from their shoulders and seem to have taken a detour on their way to the dying woman.

AN APPARITION OF ANGELS.

The following incident, which was mentioned to me in September last, occurred to Mrs. Nolan-Slaney's sister, a healthy, bonny girl of eighteen.

"I gave her description," Miss Slaney writes, "exactly as she wrote it a few days after the death of our neighbour, and I may add that, although she has told the story many times in my hearing, it has never varied from the original version.

"The neighbour mentioned was a charitable, honest, God-fearing woman, plain-spoken and practical, and an invaluable nurse. She was taken ill with influenza, in February, 1895, and had been ailing since, but my sister did not know that she had been taken worse, and played and sung with my brother the evening before, as usual, in a room almost beneath the one in which the sick woman lay—which, of course, they would not have done had they had the faintest idea that she was worse than usual.

"I append to my sister's description of her 'vision' the questions I put to her when she first told me of it, and have asked her to sign the whole.

"I went to bed as usual on the night of August 30th (1895), and fell asleep. I became quite suddenly wide awake, and heard a rustle in the room. Then it seemed to me that the ceiling and walls of our house and the next one were moved away, and I saw five beautiful angels floating above me. I was frightened, and cried out, 'What do you want?' I said, 'Oh, don't take me!' One of them answered, 'No, we shall not take you,' and then they all passed on. The angels came in a peculiar manner. First, there was one by itself, a little boy it looked like, then three altogether, then another, and, I think, another behind that. There seemed to be a lot of other angels in the background. Those I saw looked most beautiful, and had wings on the top of their shoulders, instead of on their backs, as I always thought they were. They had not any bodies, but long rays of light seemed to come from them. When they had gone I was dreadfully frightened, and called for my mother and ran into her room. My father (who usually calls everything of this kind 'nonsense') said to her, 'You had better go to the child if she is frightened, for I feel nervous myself. I feel as though someone were in the house;' then looking at his watch he remarked that it was half-past twelve. My brother then joined us, and asked what was the matter. I told him what I had seen, and he said, 'Mrs. M. is dead.'

"'What made you count the angels?'

"'I don't know, but I was struck by the peculiar way they were arranged, and thought they would look better two and two.'

"'Did the angel actually speak to you?'

"'No, it seemed as though someone inside me spoke to my brain.'

"'What did the angel's wings look like?'

"'Like bright light coming out of them.'

"'(Signed) Francis Claire Burns.'"

"The following is the daughter's account of what took place at the death-bed. Two daughters were present. The one who related to me what passed said:—

"'My back was towards the corner where Tom's box stood, but my sister faced it. She said, 'If you look towards that corner you'll see three rays like half-moons, coming up from behind Tom's box. They are shaped like half-moons, but shine like the sun.' I looked but I could not see anything. They disappeared as my mother passed away. 'Lord Jesus!' she said several times, then she sat upright in bed and stretched out her arms, saying, 'Clara, Tom,' and fell back and died.

"'At what time?'

"'About a quarter-past five, but she was taken for death at half-past twelve.' "'What date?' "'August 30th.'

"'How many of your mother's children have died?"'

"'Two babies—boys (they would be nearly fifty if living), then Clara, then Rose, then Mrs. T., and then Tom—six.'

"'(Signed) M. A. MORRIS....'

Borderland: A Quarterly Review and Index, Volume 3, edited by William Thomas Stead, 1896

Where exactly did the term "Grim Reaper" come from? The imagery of the skeleton with the scythe goes back to the Middle Ages—there is a fourteenth-century image of a skeleton reaping victims of the Black Death. The skeleton in the hooded robe dates to about the fifteenth century, but the "classic" Grim Reaper we know is primarily a nineteenth-century image. A striking example is found in the illustrations by John Leech of the Ghost of Christmas Yet to Come in *A Christmas Carol* by Charles Dickens. Although the creature does not carry a scythe, "It was shrouded in a deep black garment, which concealed its head, its face, its form, and left nothing of it visible save one outstretched hand."

The actual term "Grim Reaper" is first found in US newspapers in the 1840s. It is used only in the context of nineteenth- and early-twentieth-century death reports or obituaries. While hooded apparitions appear in Victorian ghost literature, they are not specifically described as the Grim Reaper, as in this singular story about a man's fight with a hooded figure of Death.

When I was living in Calcutta in an old house near the heart of the city, I was leading juvenile man in a theatrical company.

One night I awoke in my bed with a feeling that something strange was about to happen. I looked about the great apartment, but saw nobody. The room, a large one, was fairly well lit from a lamp burning on a table by the wall, about four yards from the bed and nearly facing it. On the right of the bed and distant perhaps eight yards were the windows—three, very large, very lofty and all wide open. There was no moon, so the trees and building were outlined in inky-black silhouettes against the star-studded sky. From a window to the apex of the angle formed by the return wall was 3 feet. My bed was in the opposite angle, the wall to my left.

My eyes wandered to the windows and onto the angle referred to. There was something in the corner! I tried to see.

After awhile something moved. I felt menaced and was compelled to watch that corner. There was something there! It looked like an ample black crape veil hung on a peg and moved by a gentle breeze. But there was no peg in that corner and not a breath of air stirring. Now it became plainer. Unmistakably a figure, tall and broad, clad in a black garment like a monk's robe, with a wide, loose cowl, which hung over the head down just below the throat, thus completely hiding the features. The sleeves hung six inches over the hand.

The figure hardly moved for some time, just seeming to vibrate at times as if shivering. At length it undulated out of its corner towards me. I began to feel uneasy; it wasn't craven fear, but an increased apprehension. Presently the figure had so far advanced into the room as to be standing between me and the window; its opaque outline was distinctly visible. Most ghosts are quoted as being transparent—mine was not. I scruddled myself back in the bed towards the wall; at last I touched it. The figure was within three yards of the bed. I felt certain if that shade came on and touched me I was a dead man. By the Lord, I wasn't going to die without a fight. I sat up in bed, feeling for the support of the angled walls with my back, and prepared for a fight. Oddly enough, I didn't feel there was going to be any battle of muscles, but a fight of wills. The figure came on. I audibly addressed it in a sort of hoarse whisper—I couldn't find any voice.

"Get back, will you?"

It advanced. I stiffened my arms, dug my hands into the bed-clothes.

"Go back! Go back!"

It still advanced. I felt rage at being defied. I had no sense of fear of any kind now, only frantic anger. I raged till I perspired. I cursed and swore at the figure till the arm in its wide, overhanging sleeve, which was advancing, stopped. I continued my abuse in the most violent language at my command till the figure, recurving, backed right into its corner.

"Oh, you beast; I've beaten you this time!"

This was my parting shot and I tumbled over tired and went to sleep.

But that is not all. I had another meeting with that grim phantom!

Thirteen months after I went to Bombay I was very ill, and was carried on the Peninsular and Oriental boat to Nepal dying. Three days out we were driving through the monsoon. I was lying weak, helpless in my bunk, the ship rolling terribly. I had the same premonition. The figure was outside the cabin door. I got out of the bunk, jammed myself down in a corner and, holding onto the washing-bowl with one hand and the raised-wood ornamentation round the porthole with the other, I most unwillingly rehearsed that scene again, and it was no walk-through. I worked as hard as I knew how. But Dr. Ferris and the Nepal doctor tacitly agreed that if I had caved in on either of these occasions I should not now be spoiling paper in an attempt to edify newspaper readers. H. St. Maur [Actor and author Harry St. Maur]

Idaho Falls [ID] Times 18 February 1892: p. 7 INDIA

NOTE: One wonders if M.R. James ever read this account of a bedroom intruder and incorporated the notion of "if that shade came on and touched me I was a dead man" for his 1904 story, "Oh, Whistle, and I'll Come to You, My Lad." The narrator tells of Parkins's reactions when faced with the Thing with the "face of crumpled linen." "Somehow, the idea of getting past it and escaping through the door was intolerable to him; he could not have borne—he didn't know why—to touch it; and as for its touching him, he would sooner dash himself through the window than have that happen."

2.

A Baby's Coffin in the Air:
Banshees, Black Dogs, and Other Harbingers of Death

Despite the era's great scientific advances, the Victorians lived in a world of strange premonitions, death omens, and tokens of mortality. One of the leading Spiritualist publications was called the *Spiritual Telegraph*, suggesting that if messages could fly along telegraph wires, this modern electrical magic might even bridge the chasm between life and death itself.

That gap was as wide as that between the Victorian distaste for "superstition" and people's experiences and family lore. No matter how often science explained the supernatural, people continued, perversely, to have prophetic dreams, see ghosts, and hear the cry of the banshee. Yet to believe in such things was to be ignorant and quite out of fashion. The struggle between these irreconcilable positions forms a common theme in many Victorian reports of supernatural events.

As for Scripture, it is crystal clear on the point: "Watch therefore: for ye know not what hour your Lord doth come." Faithful Victorians kept an anxious watch for omens of that dread hour, listening for the wings of the approaching dark angel.

It was a Victorian custom to hang crape on the doorknob or door knocker of a bereaved household. Black crape ribbons announced the death of an adult, while white told of the passing of a child. Observers often wrote of how terrifying the sight of crape on the door could be. In this case, a vision of phantom crape foreshadowed coming sorrow.

IN A VISION

A Dying Woman Foresaw the Death of Herself and Child

Mr. Kroger's Heavy Affliction

Three times within a very short period death laid its cruel hand on the family of Mr. Henry Kroger, converting his once happy home at No. 2237 Flora place, Clifton Heights, into a desolate and dreary house of mourning and sadness. The first victim of the grim reaper was Alma, the bright little daughter of Mr. Kroger. Like a flower in the bud she was cut down at the tender age of 1½ years. This was about a month ago, and on the day of the funeral the bereaved mother, while weeping at the grave of her darling, contracted pneumonia, of which she died Monday afternoon. The funeral was to have taken place yesterday morning, but a few hours before the appointed time Mr. Kroger's three-year-old daughter, Henrietta, also succumbed to the same dread disease which had carried off his wife.

On account of this additional death the burial of Mrs. Kroger was postponed until this morning, when the double funeral of mother and daughter will take place. A peculiar feature of these two deaths was a strange presentiment that Mrs. Kroger had. A few hours before she passed away she called her husband to her bedside and asked him why he had not arranged the crepe on the door properly. He replied that he had not put any there and did not expect to. Thereupon she insisted that he was mistaken, as she could distinctly see two separate pieces of crepe on the door—a white one and a black one. Mr. Kroger, thinking that his wife was delirious, paid no attention to her words, but now that both she and their daughter are lying in the house dead, the ill-omened words have come back to him with full force, clearly showing that the dying woman had had a prophetic vision of the death of herself and child.

The sorrow-stricken husband and father is prostrated with grief and he has the sympathy of kind friends and neighbors, who are doing all they can to console him.

The *Cincinnati [OH] Enquirer* 15 August 1895: p. 5 OHIO

Visions of coffins are one of the most sinister and unmistakable tokens of death in the Spiritualist literature.

A DREAM OF DEATH

A writer in a late number of the *Philosophical Journal* is responsible for the following dream story which he notes was told by the dreamer to her husband before its fulfillment:

Mrs. Hiram Hammond, of Winthrop, Me., dreamed that there came to the house of her nearest neighbours (a French-Canadian family named Ratier) a little white coffin bearing the picture of a cross, such as she had never seen before, and which impressed her as a novelty. She also dreamed that she placed in the coffin the body of a little child belonging to the Ratiers.

A few days later a little child of the family came to its death by accidental drowning in a tub of water, and Mrs. Hammond's dream as to the coffin, and her assistance in the preparations for burial, was fulfilled in every particular.

Borderland: A Quarterly Review and Index, Vol. 2, William Thomas Stead, 1895 MAINE

A friend of mine, Elizabeth Graham, during the cholera year of 1849, bringing a pail of water from a neighbor's well, beheld a baby's coffin in the air. It rushed so swiftly toward her that she leaped aside lest it should strike her face. That night her baby was attacked with cholera and died before the dawn.

Again: Calling upon her in October, 1860, I found her sunk in deep depression. "I am going to lose another of my children," she averred. "How can you say so?" I demanded. "All three are well and happy."

"Yesterday," she told me, "passing through my parlor and glancing round, I saw upon two chairs, across the north-east corner, the coffin of a child," and she related once again her vision of eleven years before. "*That* was prophetic; why not *this*?" I could not reason her belief away.

Upon the day that followed her recital, after a sickness of but half a day, Abby, her baby, died of virulent diphtheria. My mother and myself were with her when the sexton came, bringing the little coffin. He went alone into the parlor, coming out a little later to invite the mother in, lest she might disapprove of his arrangements. He had placed the coffin on a table set between the two west windows. After he had gone the half-distracted mother sobbed: "I knew that I should lose a child, for I was shown a coffin—only not so small as this and not so placed. *That* one was in the further corner, set across two chairs."

On the way home my mother said: "It seems very strange Elizabeth does not understand! It was not Abby's coffin that she saw, but Martha's. She must lose another child, that's evident."

Three days later Martha had also died, and we were there again. Another sexton (the former having been objected to), drove up with Martha's coffin, entered the front door and parlor, remained a little while, and went away without a word. Soon after we went in to see what he had done in preparation for the funeral. On two chairs lay

Martha's coffin, placed diagonally, in the north-east corner. Elizabeth cried out: "That is exactly what I saw...."

A Psychic Autobiography, Amanda Theodocia Jones, (New York: Macoy Publishing Co., 1910)

Clocks have a dual role in the folklore of death. They may tick like a "death watch," or, stop on the death of the owner as in the song, "My Grandfather's Clock," which includes the lines, "It stopp'd short—never to go again, when the old man died."

Church Farm, Gorleston.
September, 17th, 1885.

DEAR SIR, Seeing your advertisement in the *Times* it occurred to me to send you the particulars of an event which took place 5 years ago.

In the June of 1880, I went to a situation as governess. On the first day of my going there, after retiring for the night I heard a noise which was like the ticking of a watch. I took no particular notice of it, but I noticed that every time I was alone I heard it, more especially at night. I even went so far as to search, thinking there must be a watch concealed somewhere in the room. This continued until I grew quite accustomed to it. It was on the 12th of July that I was coming from the dining-room with a tray of glasses that I saw what appeared to me to be a dark figure standing just outside the door, with outstretched arms. It startled me, and when I turned to look again it was gone.

On the 23rd of September I received news that my brother was drowned on the 12th of July. I heard the ticking up to the time I had the letter, but never once afterwards.

There is nothing very startling in this narrative, but it is very vivid in my memory. Hoping it will be of some use to you. I am sir, yours faithfully,
F[lorence]. A. BALE.

The Journal of the Society for Psychical Research, Vol. II, 1885-6, p. 65 ENGLAND

NOTE: The SPR was quite thorough and asked for corroboration of all published cases. The original article includes letters, appropriately dated, from her brother's captain, informing the family of his death, as well as a letter from a friend recalling Miss Bale telling her on 12 July, 1880, of seeing the apparition and another relating the story of hearing the ticking.

BURIAL GOWN
Donned Two Hours Before She Died
Family Clock Stopped.

Whitesburg, Ky., Nov. 20. Mrs. Mary Adams, 35, wife of Isaac Adams, a young farmer of Colly, three miles above here, died last night. She prepared her burial gown two months ago. Two hours before she died she arose, went to her trunk and dressed in her burial robe, telling her husband she wanted no change made in her dress. Her last words were: "Thank the Lord I'll soon be gone; my suffering is over," and died. Directly over her bed the clock ceased to tick as the last breath left her. All efforts to start the clock have proved futile. Owing to this strange coincidence the husband will leave his once happy home.

Jackson [MI] Citizen 23 November 1900: p. 3 KENTUCKY

There is an inevitable quality to some premonitions that suggests a nightmare where the dreamer tries to call out a warning, but cannot.

PRESENTIMENT
Of Death He Sought to Forget Was Strangely Fulfilled.

Upper Sandusky, Ohio, July 26. Fireman Douglass, of the Pennsylvania [Railroad], attended the funeral of an aunt at Crestline [OH] several weeks ago. Since that time he was in constant fear of a tragic death. Every time he was called out he had a presentiment that he would be brought back dead. A day or so ago he asked a lay off, so that he could return home and forget the presentiment. He returned home, and was assisting in unloading hay. Lightning struck the barn and he was instantly killed.

Jackson [MI] Citizen Patriot 26 July 1901: p. 1 OHIO

A Strange Presentiment.

The Scranton (Penna.) *Republican* tells the following sad story of one of the victims of the late Pittston disaster:

William James expired about three o'clock on the afternoon of the Tuesday following the catastrophe, and was the last added to the list of those upon whom the death angel laid his hand in that awful havoc. He was a Welshman, and had been in this country about seven months.

On the morning of the dreadful day in question he had taken his breakfast, and his wife had made ready his dinner and set the pail beside him. For some time he sat wrapped in thought, his arms folded, his eyes fixed vacantly upon the stove, and a deep melancholy apparently brooding over him. He was aroused from his reverie by his wife telling him that his dinner was ready and that he would be late as the bell had rung.

He started to his feet and, gazing upon her for a moment with a look full of tenderness and significance said to her, "If I should not come back alive would you be in such a hurry getting me out?" The wife answered "No," but remarked that "if he was going at all it was time he was gone." He lifted his pail without saying a word, and, after kissing his wife, kissed his four little children, who were sitting playing on the doorstep.

When he had got about fifty yards from his home he returned again, and kissed his wife and children once more with great fervency. His wife noticed that he was the victim of gloomy forebodings and as he turned away she was about to entreat him not to go to work if he apprehended any danger. But hope and courage and the pressing necessities of their family overcame her intention and she let him go.

"She stood in the door and watched him on his way to the fatal pit. When at a point where he turned out of her sight, he paused and cast a wistful look toward his home and little ones and seeing his wife, waved with his hand a last adieu. He parted with his loved ones forever."
Philadelphia [PA] Inquirer 8 June 1871: p. 8 PENNSYLVANIA

NOTE: The West Pittston, Pennsylvania coal mine fire, 27 May 1871, killed 20 men by suffocation and fire.

The rise of Spiritualism made the Afterlife seem only a rap or a table turn away from this world. Helpful spirits, speaking through Spiritualist mediums sometimes gave accurate warnings of death so that the living could prepare for death. In 1856, a horrifying case suggested that medium Hattie Eager had taken steps to insure that her prophetic utterances came true.

Suicide by a Spiritualist. A short time since it was stated in the newspapers that a young lady, Miss Hattie A. Eager, of Boston, had died under peculiar circumstance—being a spiritual medium, she had predicted her own death at a certain time, being at the time of the prediction in good health. She was buried with ceremonies peculiar to the spiritualists, and since the event, her case has been mentioned by spiritualists as a clear and convincing proof of the truth of their theory. It has come out now that she committed suicide. The examining physicians say that 20 grains of antimony was found in her stomach after death.

Lowell [MA] Daily Citizen 15 December 1856: p. 2 MASSACHUSETTS

NOTE: The day after she died, Miss Eager was said to have appeared at a Spiritualist circle and proclaimed, "It is all true!" According to a caustic letter from psychic investigator and one-time Spiritualist La Roy Sunderland, printed in the *Daily Democratic State Journal* [Sacramento, CA] 20 January 1857: p. 1, "one of her friends, fearing, 'all was not true,' obtained the assistance of two physicians, who, unknown to the 'circle' aforesaid, took the stomach and a portion of the bowels for future examination," which is how the poison came to be discovered. Some Spiritualists said that Miss Eager was too fine a soul to have killed herself merely to prove the Truth of their religion; others said she killed herself under the influence of evil spirits or had ingested the poison while in trance; still others insisted she had earthly troubles that had led to her suicide.

These points were addressed in the newspapers and in medical journals.

Death of a Spiritualist

The Boston Correspondent of the Springfield *Republican* writes, on the 18th ult:

I don't know whether or not you have recorded the singular death of Miss Hattie Eager of this city. It has been the subject of a great deal of talk as well as of newspaper comment. Miss Eager was a spiritual medium, and foretold her demise with so much particularity and directness that the event was regarded by the more enthusiastic and impulsive spiritualists, as the literal fulfillment of a spiritual prophecy. A post mortem examination, however, established the fact that she died of poison, administered, without any doubt, by her own hand. There is no reason to suppose that she destroyed herself for any such impotent purpose as the vindication of her character as a prophetess, although there are enough to assign that. But weariness of life was doubtless the ruling motive. She was in ill health, comparatively friendless, and had been recently disappointed in an affair of the heart. The case, taken all together, is certainly a very melancholy one.

Boston [MA] Recorder 1 January 1857: p. 3 MASSACHUSETTS

A Spiritualist correspondent of *The Medical World*, had harsh words for "modern" Spiritualism, calling it a "mania" and a "mental epidemic" leading to fanaticism and insanity. He was in line with medical journals and newspapers, which frequently reported on madness and suicides among the Spiritualists. He also censured Miss Eager's supposed "guardian spirits."

Modern Spiritualism tends to suicide (in certain cases) inasmuch as, more than any other subject, it removes the fear of committing self-murder. This is done, as in the case of Miss Eager, when the spirits render their mediums "unconscious," while they induce them to swallow the poison. But Hattie, it seems, came to consciousness before she died, as the spiritual editor tells us that her "struggles *were violent and distressing.*" And I have it from eye witnesses that her sufferings were intense beyond the power of language to describe.

So it seems the spirits which had predicted her death (and who indeed must have caused it), these "guardian spirits," it seems, could not keep poor Hattie sufficiently "unconscious" to prevent the most horrible state of suffering in her death struggles. Let all mediums remember these facts.

L. Sunderland
Boston, June 8th, 1857.

The Medical World: A Journal of Universal Medical Intelligence,
Volumes 1–2, 1857

In a still more horrifying case, a young girl "medium" named Alma or Almira Bezeley or Bezely predicted the death of her baby brother.

Almira Bezely, a medium in Providence, R. I., predicted that her infant brother would die at a specified time, and then bought arsenic, with which she poisoned him! On her trial for murder, Samuel B. Holliday testified: "It was in evidence before the [coroner's] jury, that the death of the child was predicted by the rappings. My impression is that the child died at about the time predicted. I do not think she could have committed the crime without this influence."—*Providence Journal,* October 22, 1851.

This case illustrates the mode by which the spirits sometimes verify their predictions!

Spiritualism versus Christianity: or, Spiritualism Thoroughly Exposed,
J. W. Daniels, (New York: Miller, Orton & Mulligan, 1856)
RHODE ISLAND

NOTE: Miss Bezely was acquitted on the grounds of insanity. She was 14 years old and while she had shown great calculation in purchasing the arsenic and asking if doctors could detect poison in a corpse, the jury believed two physicians who testified that "the constitutional changes at her period of life, and the mental excitement occasioned by the rappings had impaired her reason."

Our traditional view of ghosts in sheets arises from the practice of burying the dead in winding sheets or shrouds. Shrouded spirits could also prove prophetic of a coming death. This account is from Dr. George J. Romanes, F. R. S. He is writing to Mr. Myers, the secretary of the Society for Psychical Research:

> "Toward the end of March, 1878, in the dead of the night, while believing myself to be awake, I thought the door at the head of my bed was opened, and a white figure passed along the side of the bed to the foot, where it faced about and showed me it was covered, head and all, with a shroud. Then with its hands it suddenly parted the shroud over the face, revealing between its two hands the face of my sister, who was ill in another room. I exclaimed her name, whereupon the figure vanished instantly. Next day (and certainly on account of the shock given me by the above experience) I called in Sir W. Jenner, who said my sister had not many days to live. She died in fact very soon afterwards.
>
> "I was in good health, without any grief or anxiety. My sister was being attended by our family doctor, who did not expect anything serious; therefore I had no anxiety at all on her account, nor had she herself. I have never, either before or after this, had such an experience."
>
> *Science and a Future Life*, James Hervey Hyslop,
> (London: G. P. Putnam's Sons, 1906) ENGLAND

NOTE: Dr. Romanes [1848–1894] was an evolutionary biologist and friend of Charles Darwin and Sir William Jenner, the noted epidemiologist. Mr. Myers was Frederic William Henry Myers, one of the founders of the Society for Psychical Research.

Birds, that symbol of the soul, were one of the most widespread tokens of death. White birds or doves—interpreted by some as the dove of the Holy Spirit—or the ominous owl were the most common visions. Other ill-omens were a bird in the house, a bird flying against a window, or a mysterious bird appearing where no bird should be.

On the morning of the battle of El Caney, a mourning dove (the omen of death) alighted on the shoulder of J. J. Bampton, a soldier in the Twenty-second Regiment, as he was entering the ranks. "I guess that settles me," said he, when his attention was called to the bird. He was the first man in the regiment to be killed and the only one in his company.

New York [NY] Evening Journal 16 July 1898: p. 4 CUBA

NOTE: The Battle of El Caney, 1 July 1898, on the outskirts of Santiago de Cuba, during the Spanish-American War, was also known as the Battle of San Juan Hill. Private Bampton was disinterred from his grave and returned for reburial in Cleveland, Ohio in 1899. [Source: *Cleveland (OH) Leader* 27 March 1899: p. 10]

Dove True Death Omen

New York, Nov. 20. A white dove was the true omen of death to good old James McGuire, who was buried from his residence, No. 786 Columbus avenue yesterday. Seventy-four years old, McGuire worked for the Park Department for forty-six years; he was foreman of the drivers in the Central Park stables latterly.

Many of these companions were at his funeral. They said the dove flew in the stable and circled McGuire's head.

"I don't like to see that bird here, it means somebody's going to die soon," said the old man. A few minutes later he dropped dead of heart disease.

The dove is in the stable still, although it was never seen around there before, the drivers said.

Evening News [San Jose, CA] 20 November 1907: p. 8 NEW YORK

The custom of planting a tree when a child is born links the tree to the infant and turns its fate into an omen of life or death.

Bad Omen of Death of Tree.

At Rome, N.Y., last Sunday, in conversation with a friend, David Jenkins spoke of his trouble in raising trees which had been set out about his home, several of them having died. He said he felt worst over the death of an apple tree while it was in blossom, for it meant death in the family.

On Wednesday following the above remark, Mr. Jenkins, who was a boss roller at the Rome copper mill, received injuries which resulted in his death in a few hours. He was feeding into the rolls a copper sheet weighing 250 pounds, 12 feet long, half an inch thick and 27 inches wide. The plate went over into the neck of the rolls and caught Mr. Jenkins and pinioned him to the standard of the rolls, the sheet sawing off his right leg and mangling the other so that it would have had to be amputated had he lived.

Jackson [MI] Citizen Patriot 30 June 1903: p. 6 NEW YORK

OMENS AND TOKENS OF DEATH

Mr Ponting, a tailor, now residing in Bedfordbury, leading from New street to Chandos street, Covent Garden, was, in the autumn of the year 1819, accompanied by Mrs Ponting, at Turnham Green, when they called on a friend of the name of Smith, who still resides there. They walked into the garden attached to the house, and their attention was fixed on an apple tree which carried a good show of fruit. Mrs Ponting was in a thriving way, and, from fatigue or some other cause, was induced to lean against the tree which she and her husband had been looking at. Whether she fell against it, or otherwise shook it with violence, we are not informed, but the tree was shaken, and all the fruit, with the exception of a single apple, was the next moment strewed on the ground. Though vexed at the accident, Mr and Mrs Ponting attached no vast importance to it, nor did their friends at the moment, but in the course of the day Mrs Smith took an opportunity of communicating with Mr Ponting on the subject.

The lady spoke to this effect—that she was much disturbed at what had happened, and it was her fear that the accident was nothing less than an omen of death. Her impression, which she could not get rid of, was that Mrs Ponting would not get well through her expected confinement. From one apple being left on the tree uninjured, she concluded that the child would live, but the mother she mournfully predicted would not recover.

A few months set the question at rest. Mrs Ponting gave birth to an infant and died; the child lived to grow up. But this is not all. Our informant goes on to add that the tree, though up to that period it had in most years brought a good crop, since the year 1819 has never in any season borne more than a single apple. The tree, which was named

"Elizabeth," after the lady whose early departure it was supposed to shadow forth, is still standing, and may be seen by the curious.

The Mirror of Literature, Amusement, and Instruction, Volume 4, 1843
ENGLAND

One would think that a warning of death would cause panic, but some discerning souls merely busied themselves with prudent preparations for their burial.

Woman Foretold her Death, Arranged Flowers for Her Coffin, and Died.

Mrs. Catherine Ault, aged 44, of Kokomo, Ind., the other day told her friends that her time had come to die. She was afflicted with asthma, but her case was not considered at a dangerous stage. Mrs. Ault had a collection of flowers on exhibition in The Knights of Pythias hall, at Galveston, eight miles northwest of Kokomo. She took the flowers from the hall to a church, remarking that a funeral would occur there during the week, and those particular chrysanthemums would be appropriate for the casket. She arranged the collection near the pulpit in an oblong square the size and form of a coffin. On leaving the church she said to a friend: "Those are for my coffin, and I will be there this week." She then closed various business matters with neighbors and went home. She retired early, saying to the family, "Do not call me for breakfast." In the morning she was found dead in bed. Death was from natural causes. The funeral took place the next day, just as she had arranged, the flowers she took to the church adorning the casket. She was a widow, and a daughter of George Stanley, a well-known resident of Galveston.

Marietta [OH] Daily Leader 20 December 1900: p. 8 INDIANA

The butterfly, although a symbol of the soul, is not often found as a death omen. When it does come as a token of death, it usually hovers in the sick-room.

THE WONDERFUL BUTTERFLY.

In connection with death many beautiful incidents have occurred, the most peculiar of which will be given. The Jersey City *Journal* speaks of a physician who resided in that city at one time, who had won considerable fame from the successful cures he had made in medicine and surgery. Whenever one of his patients died, no matter where he was, what time of day or night, a small white butterfly came to him, and flitted about until it attracted his notice, when it departed. The moment the Doctor saw the little winged messenger of death, he was at once made aware of the demise of the patient; and if at night the warning came to him, he invariably remained in his office in the morning in order to give a certificate of death. The first time the Doctor ever saw this butterfly, was while he was looking at the form of a deceased child; the butterfly alighted on its breast, and there remained, slowly raising its wings up and down until the body was closed in its little coffin. On one occasion, while the Doctor was attending a patient in Park Place, the butterfly entered the window and commenced flitting about his head. He looked up at it, and one of the ladies in the room, thinking it annoyed him, said: "Oh! let it alone; it will soon burn its wings by the blaze of the gas." "No, it won't," replied the Doctor. "It has come on a mission, and will soon disappear. I have just lost a patient, and in the evening I will be called upon for a certificate of death." Sure enough, the next morning the father of the child that had died the night before called, and notified him of the loss of his little one. This is only one of the many instances where the Doctor has received this strange visitation, and kept a record of the circumstances, besides that of calling the attention of those present to the fact of the butterfly's warning of death among his patients. Premonitions of death are of common occurrence, being usually impressed upon the mind through the instrumentality of dreams or visions.

The Encyclopaedia of Death and Life in the Spirit-world, John Reynolds Francis, (Chicago: The Progressive Thinker Publishing House, 1906) NEW JERSEY

Just as apparitions of coffins and crape presaged death, so did visions of tombstones.

My Aunt Elizabeth's Vision of Her Own Tombstone

My mother's sister, Mrs. Elizabeth Higgins...never left her bed at night to visit scenes about to transpire, but nearly everything of importance was foreshadowed in her dreams. She would frequently relate them on the morning following...I will only add the last sad fulfilment of a dream which she had some years previously to its fulfilment. She was then in her nineteenth year. She said, "I dreamed I was in a new country, walking alone, when suddenly I came to a small cemetery, and, walking up to one of the most prominent head-stones, read the inscription, which was this:

IN MEMORY
OF
ELIZABETH SMITH,
Wife of H____
Who departed this life
In the year of our Lord 18—,
Aged 27 years, 8 months and 26 days.

She was deeply impressed by this dream, and could not rest. She left her bed, and went into her mother's sleeping-room, sobbing, and related the dream. Her father and mother both endeavored to disabuse her mind of any belief in this unhappy dream. He tenderly folded her in his arms and quoted from Scripture many beautiful sayings, such as: "Of that day and hour knoweth no man: no, not even the angels in Heaven." She was comforted and seldom referred to her dream. The gentleman to whom she was affianced died. Her father purchased a home, and moved to Sodus, Wayne County, N. Y., where she became acquainted with Mr. C. Higgins. They were married, and enjoyed five years of uninterrupted happiness. The time was drawing near when she expected to become a mother. Uncle Charles was a devoted husband, and regretted that duty called him from home at this time. (He was engaged in Albany on public business.) He could not rest; he must return to his darling little wife, and spend a few days with her, and arrange with his brother, Dr. Higgins, to remain as a protector and physician in his house, until all danger had passed. He came (to her) unexpected, and she was delighted to see him.

The doctor came to remain as long as it was necessary. Her husband had already overstaid his time; and, as it was important for him to be in Albany, he was obliged to leave. There were many anxious hearts that feared, and silently prayed that their hopes of happiness might be realized. (I really do think that she had been reasoned out of belief in *that* dream.) She rejoiced and was happy when he promised her he would never again accept an office which would take him from home.

It was a bright, lovely morning. The team stood waiting at the gate, to take him to Newark (ten miles), the nearest point from which he could reach the canal packet boat for Albany. Bessie walked with him to the gate (about two hundred feet from the door), where he tenderly embraced her and kissed her again and again, promising that he would refrain from leaving home on business in the future. He alluded in glowing terms to their prospects of happiness, in the birth of their expected child, and warned her of the danger of yielding to superstition. He begged her not to repeat her dreams, as they were the result of a disordered condition of health. Then, taking her in his arms, he carried her back to the house, saying: "My darling, I cannot part with you here at the gate; permit me to remember you as seated in your pleasant room, surrounded by loving friends, and happy again." He held her in a long, fond embrace, kissing her with tears and sobs, and gently seating her in her easy-chair, bade her farewell, and rushed to the conveyance, fearing to look back, lest he should see her weeping at the door.

She wept some time after he was gone, but soon felt more cheerful, and frequently repeated what he had promised—that he would never leave home again after that season.

A week had passed, and a little voice was heard. She fondly clasped her babe to her breast and called it "My little Charles, my darling baby! Oh! how happy I am." They were both doing well. Letters were sent to her husband by every mail, which were duly received by him. She wished the child would resemble his father, who was a splendid man in every sense. She too was perfect in form and feature.

It was the day on which she had attained her age of twenty-seven years, eight months, and twenty-six days, *the age marked on the tombstone she had seen in her dream of about nine years before.* All the family knew of it, though she gave no sign of thinking of it, and seemed entirely cheerful and happy.

The little one was two weeks old; a letter was received that morning saying, "I shall be at home the last of this week. I shall say farewell to Albany." Words cannot express her joy at this unexpected announcement. She directed everything, how to dress the baby, and arranged for them to go after her husband's mother and sister, who had not seen the little one, as they had been absent on a visit. They were delighted to find Bessie and the baby so well, and the little Charles looking "so exactly like his father, except that he had his mother's curly hair." The mother seemed perfectly happy, but there were anxious hearts that silently prayed to God to avert the fearful calamity, which they feared might now be hanging over them. The day was passing away. She was well and cheerful. Her family were near her, doing all they could to divert her thoughts from *the date.* Her minister, Rev. Mark Johnson, and his wife called to spend an hour with the family. She was pleased to see them, and united with them in prayer. She called Mrs. Johnson to see how sweetly the infant nestled in her bosom. Then, turning to the minister she said, "Mr. Johnson, we shall have the baby christened Charles Smith Higgins as soon as his father comes home."

The last rays of the setting sun shone on the tree tops. Once more she called attention to the child, smiling on it the while; when suddenly she exclaimed, "Oh!" and placed one hand upon her breast, while with the other pressing the babe closer to her bosom.

Mother caught her in her arms, her sister Catharine ran to call the doctor; but before they could enter the room, her spirit had taken its flight to the immortal world.

Her tombstone now records her dream, verbatim, in the old cemetery in Sodus...

The Missing Link in Modern Spiritualism, A. Leah Underhill, (New York: Thomas R. Knox & Co., 1885) NEW YORK

NOTE: Anna Leah Underhill was the eldest of the Fox sisters of Spiritualistic fame, the other two being Kate and Maggie.

Phantom funerals are a particularly well-known motif in European ghost lore. These mysterious visionary processions are either seen or heard by the viewer, but never both at once. The actual funeral is always found to be identical to the one foreseen.

A CASE OF "SECOND SIGHT."

We are indebted to Lord Bute for the following narrative of second sight, communicated by Sister Illtyd of the Boys' Home, at Treforest, Pontypridd. Sister Illtyd heard of it from Sister Catherine, but not till after the child's death. Sister Catherine's own narrative is as follows:

On Sunday the 14th August, 1898, when I was taking the boys for a walk to the Rocking Stone, old Mrs. Thomas (who lives in one of Dr. Price's cottages on the road to the common), came out to speak to me and asked if one of the Home children had died that week. I said "No," and asked why she wanted to know. She said, "Because I saw a child's funeral going down the hill from the Home, but not the way you go down with the children, but to the left, and I thought it must be one of the Home children because of the boys who were carrying the coffin and walking. I thought at first it was a school." I enquired if any of the neighbours in Tower Road just below the

Home had lost a child. None of them had, nor had any child's funeral passed that week, but on the Wednesday of the following week, a little girl of three belonging to one of the neighbours in Tower Road was accidentally drowned.

The child's mother came up to ask Sister Illtyd if our boys could carry the little one to the grave, as, on account of the strike, and nobody having any tidy clothes, she could not get anyone else. Sister Illtyd agreed to let the boys go though it is against our rule for them to attend any funerals except our own, and the procession went down the hill to the left just as Mrs. Thomas had seen a fortnight before. Mrs. Thomas's house overlooks this side of the valley and is nearly on a line with the Home.

I did not tell Sister Illtyd what Mrs. Thomas had seen till after she had given permission for the boys to carry this child to the grave. Pontypridd, February, 1899.

The Journal of the Society for Psychical Research No. CLX. Vol. IX, June 1899, 263. WALES

There is the famous English story told by one John Ovens, a farm laborer, who met a phantom funeral which was the replica of that of one of his friends who had been buried some thirty years or more. There was the hearse, with the same wreaths and crosses, drawn by a pair of coal-black horses. Following it was a long procession of carriages and carts pulled by horses of every description, decked with mourning ribbons, and in the carriages sat the very mourners who had followed their dead to the grave so long ago, many of them themselves on the farther side.

The memory of this ghostly procession haunted John to his death, some twenty-five years later, and he is said to have been unable to speak of it without trembling.

The Ogden [UT] Standard-Examiner 18 November 1923: p. 26 ENGLAND

Phantom funerals were very rarely seen in the United States, but here is one of the few, a rainbow-colored cemetery procession from Georgia.

A DEATH FORETOLD

A gentleman from Georgia relates the following curious story:

Some years ago, when I was a school boy, attending school at Calvary, Ga., I, in company with one of my cousins, witnessed one of the most wonderful of spirit processions.

'Twas on a Friday afternoon, in the spring of the year, and we were on our way from school. We came down the road, laughing and talking together. We were just opposite the grave yard, at the Primitive Baptist Church (Piedmont), where we witnessed one of the grandest burials imaginable. Just in front of us, as silent as moonlight, came the burial procession. On, on, it came. First the corpse in a blue wagon drawn by two white mules. Then the mourners in black. Then the rest of the procession in all the colors of the rainbow, moving with silent tread to the grove which surrounds the yard.

Coming to the grave they halted, lifted the coffin from the wagon, lowered it into the grave and filled it. Then re-entering their wagons and buggies, all of them moved off, passing over graves, trees and everything else in the way. The whole procession then disappeared like a mist. We knew all of the people, and knew whom they buried. When it disappeared we went home in a hurry and told my mother about it. She would not let us tell Uncle J. and his wife, because it was their little girl that we saw buried. She was at the time, to my certain knowledge, well and hearty. Before Saturday night she was a corpse, and she was carried to the grave in exact accordance with the scene we had witnessed.

Logansport [IN] Pharos Tribune 2 April 1889: p. 3 GEORGIA

There was a surprising variety in other omens:

A Presentiment.

A lady, who does not pretend to be a medium, nor to have any well-established faith in Spiritual Manifestations, has just informed us of the following fact in her experience: While engaged in cutting a garment for a little girl, an interior voice seemed to say to her, "Cut it two fingers' breadths larger, and then it will do for the next elder child; for the one you are cutting it for will never wear it." The child for whom she was cutting the garment was then in perfect health; she had not previously entertained a thought that its death might be approaching, and strove to banish this impression from her mind; but, as it were in spite of herself, she obeyed the monition of the voice, and cut the garment two fingers' breadths larger than she had intended. The child for whom she intended it accordingly died a few days after, and the next elder child wore the dress.

Spiritual Telegraph, Vol. 3, 1854

DEATH FORETOLD BY PHONOGRAPH

Mrs. Howard McGrail, of Bendersville, Became Suddenly Ill Following Crumbling of Favorite Phonograph Records.

The death of Mrs. Howard McGrail a former resident of Bendersville, which occurred in Harrisburg on Sunday morning was foretold by a peculiar phonograph incident. Mrs. McGrail visited in Adams County last week returning to her home in Harrisburg last Thursday.

Mr. McGrail has a large phonograph and on Saturday evening took it into the rear yard of his home and began running off several new records which neighbors had given him. During the playing his wife came out to listen while the instrument played her favorite hymn, "Holy, Holy, Holy." At its conclusion she requested her husband to repeat it.

As he was about to accede to her request the record suddenly broke in two in his hands. He was startled, as the record was perfectly new, but in order not to alarm her he said: "O, no, I'll try something else. I never did like that myself," and going over to the cabinet he selected a little catchy song that had always been one of her favorites. He carried this one over to the machine and was about to put it on when that record also crumbled in his hands. Mr. McGrail was visibly startled, and having a feeling that something was wrong, turned around to put the machine away when his wife gave a little scream and he saw that she was ill.

Simultaneously with the breaking of the second record she had become critically ill. She was helped into the house and her little 6-year-old daughter, Beryl looked after her until medical aid was summoned, but the breaking of the records had been death's token. She died several hours afterward.

Neither of the records had ever been used and no reason could be given for the breaking, as they were not cracked. Mr. McGrail said he felt the moment the second had broken that something was to befall her.

Adams County News [Gettysburg, PA] 14 August 1909: p. 1
PENNSYLVANIA

SINGULAR STORY.

The death of Mr. F. H. Wiggin, proprietor of the Northumberland Arms, Bermondsey, took place on Thursday morning, the 8th inst. Mr. Wiggin retired to bed the previous night in his usual health and spirits, but at 5 o'clock in the morning he ruptured a blood-vessel, and in six hours he expired from exhaustion. It seems a remarkable presentiment of his death was made known to him two months previously, when, to amuse his children, he drew upon a slate a coffin, and wrote an inscription, a verbatim copy of which was inscribed on his coffin plate on his interment, as follows:—"Frederick H. Wiggin, died October 8th, 1868, aged 40." This sketch and inscription he showed to his wife, and others who happened to be present. The remains of the deceased, who was much respected, were, on Monday, taken from London to Horton, for interment by the side of his father's grave.—*Daily News,* 19 October.

The Spiritual Magazine, Vol. III, 1 November, 1868 ENGLAND

Saw a Ghostly Hearse.

Valparaiso, Ind., Oct. 4. Elijah Priest, a farmer residing near this city, was returning home Saturday night, and a short distance from his home there appeared an apparition of a buggy. He was considerably surprised on looking a second time to see a hearse driving around a haystack. After putting up his team he went to the spot, but could find nothing. He went into the house, but became worried over the matter and again went out, but could see nothing. Just before he reached the house he happened to look across the field and again plainly saw the hearse going in a southeasterly direction. He stood watching it for several minutes when it vanished from sight. Sunday he received word that his nephew had died Saturday night at Bryan, O.

The Daily Democrat [Huntington, IN] 4 October 1894: p. 1 INDIANA

Perhaps because of the extreme danger of their work, miners believed in a variety of death tokens: usually rappings and knockings made by the spirits known as "kobolds" or "knockers," and mysterious lights. However, in the mining communities of nineteenth- and early twentieth-century Pennsylvania, the apparition of the "Woman in Black" was a harbinger of death by disease or mining disaster. These apparitions (see Chapter 12 of *The Ghost Wore Black*) became linked with the black-robed banshee.

A BLACK GHOST

The apparition of a Woman Dressed in Black Has Been Seen in Carbondale, Pa.

People Have Chased the Ghost, But She Disappears Suddenly and Mysteriously.

Superstitious People Regard it as the Harbinger of a Mine Disaster.

A Ghostly Visitor.

Carbondale, Pa., Feb. 11 Superstitious people in this city and neighborhood—and there are many among the large mining population—are greatly disturbed over the appearance in this city of what they call a black ghost. This mysterious apparition has been seen three times within the past fortnight, each time just after midnight, and in different parts of the town. It is in the form of a woman dressed in black from head to foot. A "caller" in the employ of the Erie Railroad company, whose duty it was to awaken their men who go out on the trains, was the first to see it. The woman in black was standing in the street near the railway depot. The caller approached her and she moved slowly away toward the city. The caller and another railroad man wondering what could have brought a woman alone to that part of the town as such an unusual hour, followed her. She seemed to be moving slowly along the street, but although the men walked as rapidly as they could, and then broke into a run, they could not overtake the figure in black, she keeping a few yards in advance with the same apparent slow movement, and finally suddenly disappearing from sight entirely. A few nights later the woman in black appeared again in another part of the city, led two citizens a similarly weird chase and then disappeared in the same uncanny way. Early on Friday morning she was seen and disappeared under the same mysterious circumstances, near the old Coal Brook mine entrance. Miners say that a short time before the disastrous cave-in at the Delaware and Hudson Canal company's old No. 1 mine in this city, fifty years ago, a black ghost, just like the one that is prowling about the town now appeared under the same circumstances three times. Twenty-eight years ago this winter, the same woman in black, or one with the same habits, appeared three times, just as this one has done, and the memorable plague of black fever, which carried away scores of men, women and children in Carbondale and vicinity, followed her appearance. Superstitious people hereabouts are greatly disturbed over the reappearance of this black ghost.

Bismarck [ND] Daily Tribune 12 February 1892: p. 1 PENNSYLVANIA

The lore of the British Isles is rich in black dogs, phantom funerals, and wailing banshees, yet it is surprising how few of those beliefs traveled across the Atlantic and become rooted in American soil.

When a Black Dog appears, it is usually a harbinger of death, as in these two stories.

A young woman named Jane had come to America and wanted to marry a man outside her faith. She wrote her mother back in Ireland, asking for her blessing. That letter crossed in the mail with one announcing her mother's death.

She felt that she had failed her mother and the failure plunged her into regret for her rebelliousness. She regretted that she had left home. She did not, perhaps, regret the justification of her success, but it became void to her. It became tasteless and valueless. In this mood she broke off her engagement. She wrote to her fiancé that she was now prevented from marrying him. She explained that she could have fought the living to get him. She could not fight the dead. The cause and the argument both died on her. She refused to see him. For her the whole matter of her love came to a definite end. She entered into possession of her house in a state of mourning.

A curious thing happened to her. There was a night in which she was unable to sleep. She rose from her bed and turned on the light and there was a large black dog upon her threshold. When she looked at him he vanished. She went into the corridor and there was no sign of him. There was no sign of him at the head of the stairs. There was nowhere he could have gone. He had simply disappeared. The next morning news was brought to her that her fiancé had committed suicide. She always associated this with the black dog. The image added to her woe. She was convinced that she had helped to damn this young man's soul.

The Magical Realm, Kathleen Coyle, (New York: E.P. Dutton, 1943), 248-9
NEW YORK

NOTE: Jane was author Kathleen Coyle's sister. Their mother was a devout Catholic and Jane felt intense guilt about abandoning her mother's church by wanting to marry a Protestant.

To another family, living in the East of England (of the rank of gentle people), appears an Omen, equally, if not more disagreeable. The appearance of a spectral Black Dog is also a portent of death. About twenty years ago, A.D. 1853, the then head of the family married, and though he himself (by no means superstitious) could not reject the tradition of the unpleasant omen, having heard so much about it on its previous appearance, he said nothing to his wife. Some years afterwards, in 1861, their eldest child was taken ill. The illness, however, (as the physician asserted) was slight, and not at all likely to prove dangerous; so little, in truth, was this anticipated that there were several persons staying in the house at the time. Just before dinner was announced one evening, the wife of the head of the family asked to be excused for a moment or two, while she looked into the night nursery to see how the sick child was. She went, but returned almost immediately, saying, "Darling ___ is fast asleep; but there's a large black dog lying under the bed; go and drive it out." The father, at once calling to mind the omen, was sorely terrified. He went at once to the sick room. Neither under nor near the bed, nor (as was afterwards discovered) on the premises, was there, or had there been, any dog, but the poor child's sleep was found to be the sleep of death.

Glimpses of the Supernatural, Frederick George Lee,
(New York: G.W. Carleton & Co., 1875) ENGLAND

Black dog stories are quite rare in the United States. This is one of the few America stories about these portents of death.

In an Oklahoma stope several years ago, thirteen miners died as a result of a cave-in. Survivors told of the apparition of a black dog which dashed back and forth supposedly to warn the workers of approaching danger. In connection with this disaster there is supposed to be the spectre of a woman attired in black, who patrols the path from the scene of the mishap to the undertaking parlors where the bodies of the dead miners were taken.

The Morning Sun [Yuma AZ] 4 March 1923: p. 2

NOTE: A stope is an open place in an underground mine where ore has been removed. Here we again find the miner's omen of death, The Woman in Black.

The banshee was, of course, the Irish messenger of death. Some banshees were known for the "Death Knock," a mysterious knock on a door or window, sounding for the death of one within. The banshee might also sing or shriek of doom, as in this traditional manifestation.

On the night preceding my father's death, my mother was sitting in the dining-room, which overlooked the back garden, reading. It was a windy but fine night, and, save for the rustling of the leaves, and an occasional creaking of the shutters, absolutely still. Suddenly, from apparently just under the window there rang out a series of the most harrowing screams. Immeasurably startled, and fearing, at first, that it was some woman being murdered in the garden, my mother summoned the servants, and they all listened. The sounds went on, every moment increasing in vehemence, and there was an intensity and eeriness about them that speedily convinced the hearers that they could be due to no earthly agency. After lasting several minutes they finally died away in a long, protracted wail, full of such agony and despair, that my mother and her companions were distressed beyond words.

As soon as they could summon up the courage they went out and scoured the gardens, but though they looked everywhere, and there was little cover for anyone to hide, they could discover nothing that could in any way account for the noises. A dreadful fear then seized my mother. She believed that she had heard the Banshee which my father had often spoken about to her, and she was little surprised, when, in a few days' time, the news reached her that my father was dead. He had died about dawn, the day after my mother and the servants had heard the screaming. I sent an account of the incident, together with other phenomena that happened about the same time, signed by two of the people who experienced them, to the Society for Psychical Research, who published it in their journal in the autumn of 1899...

The Banshee, Elliott O'Donnell, (London, UK: Sands & Company, 1920)
IRELAND

NOTE: O'Donnell was well-known for embellishing his narratives. Harrowing screams do not appear in his account in the *Journal for the Society for Psychical Research* of October, 1899, although other "strange noises" do. http://www.archive.org/stream/journalofsociety09sociuoft/ journalofsociety09sociuoft_djvu.txt

The Cry of the Banshee

There is now living in Bristol a Mrs. Linahan, an old Irish woman, who has not seen her own country for forty years. She is old, poor, bed ridden and suffering, but patient and cheerful beyond belief. Her strongest feeling is love for Ireland, and she likes talking to me because I am Irish. Many a time, sitting in her little, close room, above the noisy street, she has told me about banshees and phookas and fairies, especially the first. She declares solemnly she once heard the cry, or caoin of a banshee.

"It was when I was a little young child," she told me, "and knew nothing at all of banshees or of death. One day mother sent me to see after my grandmother, the length of three miles from our house. All the road was deep in snow, and I went my lone – and didn't know the grandmother was dead, and my aunt gone to the village for help. So I got to the house, and I see her lying so still and quiet I thought she was sleepin'. When I called her and she wouldn't stir or speak, I thought I'd put snow on her face to wake her. I just stepped outside to get a handful, and came in, leaving the door open, and then I heard a far away cry, so faint and yet so fearsome that I shook like a leaf in the wind. It got nearer and nearer, and then I heard a sound like clapping or wringing of hands, as they do in keening at a funeral. Twice it came and then I slid down to the ground and crept under the bed where my grandmother lay, and there I heard it for the third time crying, 'Ochone, Ochone,' at the very door. Then it suddenly stopped; I couldn't tell where it went, and I dared not lift up my head till the women came in the house. One of them took me up and said: "It was the banshee the child heard, for the woman that lies there was one of the real old Irish families – she was an O'Grady and that was the raison of it.'"

Aberdeen [SD] Daily News 18 May 1887: p. 4 IRELAND

NOTE: Irish funerals were noted for the keening or wailing of the mourners. The cry "ochone," from the Irish Gaelic *ochōn*, is an exclamation of grief. Mourners often threw up their hands and clapped them together, as the child heard the banshee do. Some believed that only the "old Irish families" would be warned by their banshee.

Sometimes, the dead could part the veil and return, if only briefly, to warn of death or to escort the newly dead into the Great Beyond. A recurring theme in death omens is a loved one coming in ghostly form to "fetch away" the dying. In this touching case, the ghost was seen literally carrying off his wife.

A Danbury Ghost Story

Woman Saw Dead Father Carry Her Mother Away – The Mother Found to Have Died at the Same Time.

Danbury, Mass., March 19. As Mrs. C. W. Lee of 55 Jefferson Avenue, this city, lay on a bed of sickness, it is declared that she saw the apparition of her father, Oliver B. Pettit, formerly of Brooklyn, who died sixteen years ago, enter the room across the hall, where her mother was, and carry her out in his arms.

Mrs. Lee avers that she distinctly saw her father walk through the hall, and heard him call his wife by name, and ask her to go away with him, pleading with her until she consented. At first, the wife, Mrs. Margaret Pettit of 39 Grove Street, Brooklyn, refused, but her love for her husband evidently overcame her fear, and the daughter saw the stalwart form of her father emerge from the room and disappear with his wife in his arms.

Mrs. Pettit had been visiting her daughter, and, although not ill, was in the habit of spending the morning hours in bed. Yesterday she remained in her bed later than usual, and it was at noon that her daughter saw the vision. Calling for her husband, Mrs. Lee told him what she had seen, and Mr. Lee, hurrying to the room of his wife's mother, found her dead. Her death must have occurred at exactly the moment when Mrs. Lee saw her father enter the room. A physician later said that Mrs. Pettit died from heart failure.

The New York Times 20 March 1900: p. 1 MASSACHUSETTS

Even stranger was the sequel.

HER FATHER'S SPIRIT

Beckoned to Her, and Though Recovering, She Soon Died.

When Mrs. Charles Lee died, at Danbury, Mass., last week, it was in peaceful resignation and with the conviction that her father's spirit was bearing her away.

She had been waiting for five days for his coming—ever since she saw the ghostly visitor bear away her mother in that strange vision. That it was not the malady from which she had been suffering that caused Mrs. Lee's death there is the testimony of the doctors. She was convalescing from an operation, and, so far as it was concerned, was out of danger.

That Mrs. Lee became conscious in some mysterious way that her mother, Mrs. Margaret Pettit, was dying, there can be no doubt. Mrs. Pettit left her home at No. 39 Grove Street, to go to nurse her daughter in Danbury. When Mrs. Pettit went to bed on Saturday night she was apparently in excellent health.

Her daughter gave the first news of the mother's death. She told her husband that something had happened—that her mother was dead—and then Mrs. Lee swooned.

When Mrs. Lee had partly recovered she told those about her of her vision. She said she had seen the spirit of her father, who has been dead for 16 years, enter her mother's room and say:

"Margaret, come with me."

She had seen her father take her mother in his arms, and, as they moved away they paused before Mrs. Lee, she said, and her father paused and beckoned to her, saying she would soon follow them.

Since that vision Mrs. Lee has hovered on the borderland between life and death. A great part of the time she has been delirious or in a state of coma. But in her lucid intervals she talked constantly of the vision and of her own summons.

Nothing could shake her conviction that her father's spirit would return for her. When she was perfectly sane she said she was only waiting. She knew she would never get well.

She spoke of it when her husband and son were called to her bedside, and she said good bye to them. She told them she believed that they would soon join her, that the summons was for all of them, and that the family would be united in the beyond.

She died with her mother's name on her lips.

Jackson [MI] Citizen Patriot 28 March 1900: p. 3 MASSACHUSETTS

Some of the most touching death omens are visions of loved ones gone before. It is one thing for a sick child to see a vision of his mother on his deathbed; such things can be dismissed as hallucinations. Yet it's quite another to find multiple witnesses who recognize the ghost.

Saw His Mother's Spirit

[Hull (Mass.) Cor. *Globe-Democrat*.]

The following story is vouched for by ten or twelve of the most respectable citizens of the place: Harvey Samson, the 15-year-old son of R. B. Samson, prominent in commercial circles, died of lingering consumption at his father's residence in the suburbs on last Tuesday night. He was fully conscious up to the time he drew his last breath, and several times on the day before he died expressed his fear of death, always adding that this arose from no dread of the hereafter, but from a purely physical shrinkage from the Unknown, and that if he could only have had his mother with him he would lose all such fear. Mrs. Samson, to whom Harvey had been devoted and enjoyed an even unusual degree of companionship with, has been dead for over two years.

On Tuesday morning he said to his aunt, Mrs. Josephine Burwell, that he had prayed that his mother might be allowed to come for him and guide him into the spirit land, and that he believed she would come. That evening about the twilight hour, and a short time before the end, the dying boy sprang up in bed with a glad cry turned toward the door, which had just blown open, and, with outstretched arms, appeared the next moment to clasp some one ardently to his breast.

Dr. Osborne, who was attending him, and who was alone with him at the moment, inquired of him what is was.

"It is my mother," the boy replied, with a tender smile at the chair close beside his bed. "She's come for me."

The doctor then advanced and felt the lad's pulse, only to find him perfectly free from fever and wholly unexcited, but sinking fast. He called the family, who came to bid Harvey good-by. The boy then requested them to take away the light, except the small night lamp burning on a table near, as he said the glare kept him from seeing his mother plainly. When this wish was carried out, the afflicted family, Drs. Osborne and Cunningham, with the nurse and a friend or two, declare that they saw sitting beside Harvey, holding his hand and smiling on him, a woman clad in snowy garments, and in whom they had no difficulty in recognizing Mrs. Samson, who had been personally and well known to each and all of them. She remained distinctly visible for two hours and more, when she suddenly vanished, and on approaching the bed they found that the boy was dead.

The Cincinnati [OH] Enquirer 18 January 1891: p. 6 MASSACHUSETTS

3.

Died of Lizards:

Strange Deaths from Poisoned Stockings to Self-Decapitation

There were entirely too many ways to die an unnatural death in the nineteenth century. Without x-rays, vaccines, or antibiotics the young died of teething and the old of pneumonia. Blooming mothers died in childbirth; hearty farmers were kicked by their horses or fell under combines. Husbands hurled flaming oil lamps at their wives; wives fed their husbands strychnine. Some newspapers made a custom of running round-ups of the previous year's news on December 31. The bulk of these news items were violent deaths, which is suggestive either of the fragility of life or the morbid tastes of the newspaper-reading public.

Alimentary amphibians in the news were a perennial favorite. A shocking number of people enjoyed ill health, believing that they had a live frog, snake, lizard, mouse, or bird in their stomachs. However, few of them died, unlike the unfortunate Miss Herman.

LIZARDS FOUND IN GIRL'S STOMACH

Cleveland, O., Dec. 16. Two live lizards three and a half inches long, several smaller ones, and a number of lizard eggs, were taken from the stomach of Lovel Herman, nineteen, four days before she died, according to Dr. A. J. McIntosh. A post-mortem examination showed that the wall of the stomach had been attacked by the animals, the doctors say. The heart had enlarged to three times its normal size.

For several years she had been ill, complaining that something was clawing at her stomach. Specialists were puzzled until finally Dr. McIntosh, working on the theory that it was a tapeworm, found the lizards.

Miss Herman drank water from a spring in which there were lizards, when she lived at Millersburg, twelve years ago, and it is believed that she swallowed the eggs or the young animals at that time and that they grew while in her body. She craved meat and eggs during the four months of her illness and it is believed she demanded such animal food because the lizards, as well as her body, had to be fed. She ate ravenously, but weighed only eighty pounds.

Incidentally, the health officials refuse to accept the certificate of death based upon the lizard theory, declaring that no such case has been reported since the days of primitive medicine.

Fort Wayne [IN] News 16 December 1910: p. 28 OHIO

NOTE: Her name was actually Lovie L. Herman [1890–1910]. She is buried in Fryburg Cemetery, Holmes County, Ohio.

The animal kingdom was responsible for some truly unnatural deaths.

Swallowed a Spider

A spider swallowed by Katherine Degen, the 6-year-old daughter of H.C. Degen, of Louisville, Ky., is believed to have caused the little girl's death which occurred early in the morning. At dinner she ate a saucer of strawberries and while eating the fruit remarked at the table that she "thought she had swallowed something." Two hours later she was taken ill and died despite all the efforts of physicians to save her. The latter believe the poisonous insect caused her death.

According to the child's grandmother, the strawberries were being prepared for the table when she discovered a spider in the fruit. The berries were washed several times, but the spider was not found. The grandmother believes the insect was among the berries served to the little girl.

St. Johns Review [St. Johns, OR] 2 July 1909: p. 1 KENTUCKY

What One Can Go Through

A Queer Story from Canada

An extraordinary occurrence was brought to light at an inquest held on the body of a man in South London. In a workroom, where many young girls were at work, a mouse suddenly made its appearance on a table, causing, of course, considerable commotion, and a general stampede. The intruder was seized, however, by a young man who happened to be present, but the mouse slipped out of his hand, and, running up his sleeve, and coming out between his waistcoat and shirt at the neck. The unfortunate man had his mouth open, and the mouse, on the lookout for some convenient place of concealment, entered the man's mouth, and he, in his fright and surprise, swallowed it. That a mouse can live for a considerable time without much air has long been a popular belief, and was unfortunately proved to be a fact in the present instance, for the mouse began to tear and bite inside the man's throat, and chest, and the result was that the fellow died after a little time in horrible agony. Several witnesses corroborated the above facts and medical testimony as to the cause of death having been given, a verdict of "accidental death" was returned. *Toronto Globe*

The Milan [TN] Exchange 9 March 1876: p. 1 CANADA

The gas-fiend parrot perches alone in the annals of strange deaths.

PARROT WAS A GAS FIEND.

At Last Killed His Owner by Tearing Off Burner While She Slept.

Special to *The New York Times.*

Washington, Sept. 13 Alice Knott, twenty-three years old, of 803 Twelfth Street, came to her death yesterday through the instrumentality of her pet parrot, an evil-dispositioned bird, who was cordially detested by everybody except his mistress, but who seemed to have a strong affection for her. He would follow her from room to room, and was never happy except in her presence. He was generally regarded as a devil by the negroes and as a bird of ill-omen by the whites. His unpopularity was increased by an uncanny habit of pulling the tips off the gas burners with his strong beak and inhaling the gas until it stupefied him. He was a gas fiend, a feathered victim of the gas habit.

While his young mistress was sleeping yesterday the parrot took off the lava tip in her room and started on a gas debauch. This time there was no one near to avert the consequences of his deed. When Miss Knott's relatives, alarmed by her long silence, broke open the door they found her dead. Her little murderer was found half-unconscious by the door. When he found himself succumbing to the gas and was not rescued as usual by his mistress, he realized that something was wrong, and had wit or instinct enough to make for the door and shove his bill as far as he could underneath it. He recovered, and while the Coroner was in the house the malignant little bird was caught trying to turn on the gas again.

The New York Times 14 September 1899: p. 1 WASHINGTON D.C.

Many fashion victims sleep in the graveyards of the Victorian era. Medical men and journalists spoke of "The Crinoline Holocaust," where thousands of women were roasted to death by wearing hoop petticoats or were otherwise stabbed or disemboweled by the metal frames. Other sartorial perils were poisoned stockings and gloves, lethal arsenic dyes, and flaming celluloid collars.

Crinoline fire cartoon, perhaps by John Leech, c. 1869.

Open fires for light, heat, and cooking made death by flaming crinoline a horribly familiar story in the Victorian newspapers. These are just two stories from a lengthy and impassioned article titled "A New Kind of Wilful Murder."

More deaths are caused by the skirt catching fire behind than in front. It was but the other day that a poor young collier's wife, M. A. R, was stooping to her baby's cradle, when her large hoop drove her dress behind against the bars. Then followed the useless endeavours of neighbours, with their blankets and wet towels; useless in these days, because the hoops prevent any effectual compression of the dress, and admit air within the burning garment. The poor babe has lost its young mother. She lingered through several days of agony, and then died at the age of twenty.

In another case a little boy of ten appeared at the inquest on his mother, and told what he had tried to do to save her. Her skirt went into the wood fire behind, without her being aware of it. The boy squeezed her clothes, and knocked out some of the flames with a stick. When a man came in to help, the boy called the neighbours: but in a minute or two she was seen in the road with her cotton-dress in flames, the canes preventing their being put out. There was a piece of steel hoop also left in the road. " For mercy's sake! for mercy's sake! put it out!" she cried, till she fell: but not till she fell could anything be done. She was just thirty-three—old enough to have dressed herself more wisely.

Once a Week, Volume 8, Eneas Sweetland Dallas, editor, 1863 ENGLAND

KILLED BY GLOVES

One of the Most Singular Cases of Poisoning Ever Recorded.

Rarely, it may be thought, has a more singular case of accidental death been recorded than that which recently threw a much-esteemed family residing in the environs of St. Petersburg into mourning. A young lady in perfect health, and with the brightest of futures before her, was among the guests invited to a ball, and, her toilet completed, she drew on a pair of long gloves, reaching above the elbows. Scarcely half an hour afterwards she felt considerable irritation and pain in her arms and hands, to which, however, for the moment—taken up with pleasures of the evening—she paid but little attention. On returning home her suffering increased, and the following day her hands and arms became covered with sores, which were attributed by the doctor called in to blood poisoning. A week later the poor girl died, after severe suffering and despite the efforts made to save her. The fatal gloves have been handed over for analysis, the conjecture being that the animal with the skin of which they were made was in some way or other diseased, and that the skin used had been imperfectly cleansed. In any case, if this conjecture prove correct, measures will doubtless be taken to ascertain, if possible, whether other gloves, similarly contaminated, are on sale. *London Standard.*

Kalamazoo [MI] Gazette 1 March 1890: p. 9 RUSSIA

NOTE: It is said that people who sorted wool or worked with animal bone, bristles, or hides were susceptible to inhalational anthrax. There was also the possibility of arsenic being used in processing some skins.

Poisoned stockings are the surprise candidate for "most lethal accessory." There are dozens of cases reported, although relatively few ended in death.

Gertrude Thornton, aged six years, daughter of A.G. [sic, actually G. Alfred] Thornton, of Port Jarvis, N.Y., recently died of pyaemia, or blood poisoning, resulting from the wearing of stockings colored in "old gold" and brown. Over a month ago the child was coasting, and, being thickly clad, her feet became warm, and when her shoes were taken off it was found that the coloring of the "old gold" and brown in the feet of the stockings had been absorbed into the warm flesh of the feet, leaving the stockings almost white. The girl soon began to show symptoms of poisoning. Her limbs became swollen and discolored, and she suffered the most excruciating agony for thirty-eight days. She would scream at times with pain, and during the whole time of her sickness there was hardly a day without the keenest suffering. As the end drew near, her limbs and hips grew swollen and mortified, and all the body except the face showed the deadly poison. A half hour before her death she sank into a comatose state, and never regained her consciousness. The utmost skill of Dr. Van Etten could not check the ravages of the poison.

Owyhee Avalanche [Silver City, ID] 18 March 1882: p. 1 NEW YORK

The early plastic known as celluloid was seen as a perfect, lightweight product for shirt collars, jewelry, and other ornaments. Unfortunately it was also highly flammable and explosive.

EXPLODING COMBS KILL HER

Celluloid Ornaments Set Afire and Woman's Death is Sad Result.

Lancaster, Pa., Jan. 3. Mrs. Mazie McLane, wife of Deputy Recorder McLane, was fatally burned. She arose at 3 a.m. to take medicine, and after lightning the gas threw the match into a tray. The burning match caused the celluloid combs to explode and the flames ignited Mrs. McLane's night dress and she died several hours later.

The Alliance [NE] Herald 6 January 1910: p. 3 PENNSYLVANIA

Even holidays had their signature fatalities: Christmas tree fires and clothing ignited by festive candles made the winter holiday deadly. Noxious egg dyes marred Easter. Fireworks and firearms were the lethal agents of Independence Day, while Halloween saw deaths from poisonous candy colors and from masks.

KILLED BY PAPIER MACHE MASK

Paint Melted and Caused Girl's Death by Blood Poisoning.

ORANGE, N.J., Nov. 13. Little Freda Henke, the fourteen-year-old daughter of Mr. and Mrs. Otto Henke of 24 Church Street, this city, is dead at her home as a result of blood poisoning contracted by wearing a papier mache mask at a Hallowe'en party she recently gave a number of her young friends.

At the party all the children wore masks, and there was much romping. The perspiration on the girl's face melted the paint on the mask and this contaminated an abrasion on her upper lip.

New York Times 14 November 1902: p. 1 NEW JERSEY

Stories involving dynamite fatalities are startlingly common. The explosive seems to have been treated rather casually, as just another handy household product for use around the farm. One man memorably stored several sticks in his stove and, forgetting about it, lit the stove. This Ohio farmer chose dynamite as a novel form of self-destruction.

IN THE BUCKEYE STATE
FARMER'S SUICIDE

He Took a Quantity of Dynamite to a Field and Blew Himself to Atoms.

Payne, O., March 23 Samuel Haggerty, a prosperous and wealthy farmer living three miles south of town, committed suicide in a most shocking manner Friday. He took a quantity of dynamite and went to the field, announcing his intention to blast stumps. Later a violent explosion alarmed the neighbors and on investigation they found a few scattered remnants of the despondent man. Esquire Rubin was called and held an inquest which established the fact that the deceased had placed several pounds of the explosive in a large stump, sat thereon and deliberately lighted the fuse. Despondency over the loss of his wife is thought to be the cause.

Spirit of Democracy [Woodsfield, OH] 28 March 1901 OHIO

Like Farmer Haggerty's dynamite suicide, this next story, unless a macabre fiction, seems an unnecessarily painful and public way to go.

A Singular Suicide

The *People* gives the following account of a most singular suicide which occurred near Philadelphia a short distance east of the city Thursday week.

A farmer was threshing his grain by steam power, near the road side, when a well-dressed stranger drove up in a buggy, got out tied his horse and came up to the machine. He first went to the engineer and asked the privilege of feeding the machine awhile, and was referred to the feeder. The feeder seeing no reason to refuse letting him try his hand, yielded his post, which the stranger filled with ability. After running a short time he looked to the engineer for more steam, which the engineer put on, and then, while the machine was going at lightning speed, he motioned to the man handing sheaves to stop, and as soon as the teeth were clear he doubled up his arms and threw himself head-foremost into the thresher, before the horror stricken observers had an idea of his intention. He was literally torn all to pieces in an instant. No clue to his identity could be discovered, his pocket book containing $30 but nothing in the way of papers. The citizens of Philadelphia are still in the dark as regards the name of the man or the cause of his making away with himself.

Elyria [OH] Independent Democrat 30 August 1871: p. 2 PENNSYLVANIA

Freakish accidents were a popular newspaper category. The grave's a fine and private place, but you can be sent there by an embrace...

RECEIVES FATAL WOUND WHILE EMBRACING GIRL
Singular Accident Which Led to the Death of
Thomas M. Dougherty
Had Sweetheart in His Arms When a Needle She Wore Fatally
Stabbed Him.

Philadelphia, Nov. 12. Tonight, after a day spent in the investigation of the death of Thomas M. Dougherty of Dunsmore, who was killed by being pierced in the heart by a long needle, the local police and County Detective Phillips decided to withdraw the warrant that had been issued for the arrest of Katie Burke, the girl who was suspected of having caused Dougherty's death. The authorities are of the opinion that the girl is innocent of murderous intent. She says that she had been mending her brother's clothing with a long needle, used hereabouts in mending miners' heavy outer clothing and that on going down town in the evening she stuck the needle in the bosom of her dress. Dougherty, who had been her sweetheart, hailed her and asked her to take a walk with him. He attempted to embrace her and the point of the needle that was in her dress caught in his vest while the "eye" or blunt end rested against her corset.

In the embrace the needle was forced into his body, through the fifth rib and into the cavity between the pericardium and the heart. Hemorrhages resulted that caused death.

Omaha [NE] World Herald 13 November 1906: p. 1 PENNSYLVANIA

A Coroner's jury might well have rendered a verdict of "Visitation of God" for this next singular death.

The Death of a Priest at the Altar

An extraordinary accident happened yesterday morning in the Roman Catholic parish church of Kildare. As the Very Rev. Dr. Kavanaugh, parish priest, was standing in front of the altar with his hands on the chalice to raise it, at the close of 7 o'clock mass, and was about to descend the altar steps to recite the altar prayers, the marble figure of a cherub over the altar fell and struck him with great force on the head. He fell back heavily, murmured the words, "My God!" twice, and then became insensible. A cry of horror and anguish was raised by the congregation who witnessed the accident. Some persons rushed forward to lift him up, while others ran for medical help. Three doctors were soon in attendance, and Dr. Kavanagh was carried into the adjoining convent, where, having never recovered consciousness, he died soon afterwards. The altar is a new marble one which was consecrated about a year ago by Archbishops Croke and Walsh. The tabernacle was surmounted by a spire-shaped canopy. The four pillars which support the canopy have corresponding short pillars above them, springing from each angle of the canopy and on these are forty cherubs. The one which fell weighed over forty pounds. *St. James Gazette,* August 6th.

The Salt Lake [UT] Herald 31 October 1886: p. 11 IRELAND

NOTE: The Very Rev. James B. Kavanagh, D.D. was eulogized in an obituary headed "Priest and Patriot" as "one of the most notable

Irish ecclesiastics...theologian, philosopher, and scientist." *Donahoe's Magazine*, Volume 17, 1887

Then there are the nineteenth-century versions of the Darwin Awards, like these two, with heartless headlines.

The Same Old, Old Story.

Peoria, Ill., May 3 Yesterday Miss Jessie Benning, aged 18, while in the office of William Scott, a real estate agent to whom she was engaged to be married, pointed at herself a revolver supposed to be unloaded, and remarking, "I wonder if I can kill myself?" pulled the trigger. The weapon was discharged, killing her instantly.

Newark [OH] Daily Advocate 3 May 1889: p. 1 ILLINOIS

Took Poison "For Fun."

Just for fun, Carrie Mattison, aged twenty and pretty, took a dose of strychnine at the farm house of Frank Richardson, in the eastern part of Woodbury county. "I took it just for fun," was her only explanation. "I saw it there and thought I'd take some just for fun." The young woman climbed from the cellar where she took the drug to the kitchen where she told Mrs. Richardson of her act. Before anything could be done to relieve her she was dead. The poison was kept to kill rats. It is believed the young woman thought a small portion would not hurt her, as no excuse for the act can be learned. She was the daughter of Mr. and Mrs. Mattison of Battle Creek, Ia.

Spencer [IA] Herald 1 May 1907: p. 1 IOWA

Some deaths seem unbelievably bizarre, like the stuff of urban legends.

STRANGLED WITH HER OWN HAIR
Strangled With Her Own Hair
Madeline Messner Commits Suicide in a Novel Manner.

Toledo, Ohio, Jan. 30. Madeline Messner of Gibsonburg, Ohio, a melancholy patient at the insane asylum here committed suicide this afternoon in a peculiar manner. While sitting in a chair she fastened her hair around her neck and to the back of the chair and leaned forward. When found some minutes later she was dead.

Daily Inter Ocean [Chicago, IL] 1 February 1896: p. 6 OHIO

NOTE: Mrs. Mary Magdalena "Lena" Messner was 44 when she died. She had eleven children with her husband.

READ NOVEL, WENT CRAZY AND DIED

Boston, April 13. After reading Sir Conan Doyle's "House of the Baskervilles," [sic] which tells of the ghostly dog that tears the throat of a man and leaves him dead on the moor, Marcus J. Long, 65, chopped to pieces all the keys and strings of the piano, smashed a $1,000 violin, then committed suicide by inhaling illuminating gas.
The Spokane [WA] Press 13 April 1909: p. 6 MASSACHUSETTS

A circus in a town or village inoculates [inculcates?] the lad with a passion for throwing summersaults and for standing on their heads or hands. Master [Jesse] Pratt, aged 11, of Lanesboro, Mass., spent a whole forenoon in summersaulting, in consequence of which his bowels became so twisted and tied into knots that in ten days the derangement proved fatal.
Jackson [MI] Citizen 16 September 1873: p. 1 MASSACHUSETTS

A little girl named Alice [Emma] Brown died at Mt. Gilead, a week ago, from the effect of "skipping the rope." This is the second death at that place from the same cause.
Athens [OH] Messenger 5 May 1881: p. 1 OHIO

Singular circumstance. A Baltimore paper states, that a girl died recently in Virginia from having bitten a thread with which she had sewn up a rent made by the bite of a mad dog, in her apron.
Ohio Monitor [Columbus, OH] 29 June 1831: p. 2 VIRGINIA

Some papers took a strange glee in recounting multiple fatalities: horror piled upon horrors.

Strange Fatality

Erie, PA., June 13 Mrs. Mary Kreshner suicided to-day under peculiar circumstances. A few weeks ago her husband's dead and mangled body was brought home and the hearse containing the corpse ran over and killed her only child while enroute to the cemetery. She was about to return to her father in Germany when news came that he was drowned. Then Mrs. Kreshner resorted to laudanum for relief from further fatalities.

Marion [OH] Star 17 June 1885 PENNSYLVANIA

The strangest succession of ill fortunes, a short time ago, made Mrs. Bennett Kyle, of Decatur, Tenn., a childless widow. She was doing the family washing at a short distance from her home, when the infant with her was bitten by a rattlesnake. She killed the snake, but she picked up her babe only to see it die. Clasping it in her arms she hurried to the house, and there found her other child drowned in a tub of water. Then came the crushing blow of fate. Her cries of agony, as she beheld this second bereavement, so startled her husband, who was repairing the roof, that he slipped and fell, and was instantly killed.

San Francisco [CA] Chronicle 5 July 1874: p. 1 TENNESSEE

Death and Birth Together

A baby was born to Mrs. Walter Jones, at Newark, N.J., Monday night under peculiarly tragic circumstances. Mrs. Jones was in bed and a midwife was in attendance, the birth of the babe being expected hourly. The bedroom getting cold, her husband started to carry a small stove upstairs. A woman named Mrs. Agnes was assisting Mr. Jones by holding a lamp for him. When he reached the top of the stairs he tripped and dropped the stove, which crashed down the stairs and struck the woman knocking the lamp out of her hand, breaking it and sending the burning oil over her. The wretched woman ran screaming into Mrs. Jones' room. The husband followed and tried to smother the flames with blankets, but the fire had gained such headway that she died in terrible agony. When the fiery apparition appeared in the room the midwife left Mrs. Jones and jumped out of the window, breaking her right leg. Mrs. Jones got out of bed and would have followed the midwife, but was caught by her husband, who carried his wife to a neighbor's house where a healthy boy baby was born. The house was partially destroyed by fire. In the same house the body of a brother was lying awaiting burial.

Jackson [MI] Citizen Patriot 21 April 1894: p. 2 NEW JERSEY

Rats were a nineteenth-century scourge, in city and countryside. There are horrifying stories about rats attacking babies left alone in tenement rooms. Just as shocking are these deaths by rats in institutions.

Child Killed by Rats.

In the Bellevue Hospital at New York, on Monday night, a poor Irish woman was admitted to the lying-in Ward. She gave birth to a babe, and so little attention was paid to the patient, that the infant was literally devoured by rats before morning, its suffering mother being too weak to drive them off the bed which they swarmed over. The baby's feet and head were nearly separated from its body.

The Daily Dispatch [Richmond, VA] 27 April 1860: p.1 NEW YORK

EATEN BY RATS

Fate of Baby Twin Sisters in an Ohio City.

Springfield, O., Feb. 6. Eizabeth Black, an orphan was found dead in her bed yesterday at the Logan County Children's Home. She followed her little twin sister to the grave, the other having died a few days before.

They were mere babies and were taken to the home from Kenton. Last week they were attacked by a swarm of rats in their miserable home and virtually eaten alive. The children suffered terribly.

Kalamazoo [MI] Gazette 7 February 1904: p. 1 OHIO

While nineteenth-century physicians certainly knew about heart failure, it is fascinating how often "dying of fright" is cited as a cause of death in news items. Whether or not it was true; it was *believed* to be true. It may simply have been a journalistic convention to describe an unexplained death, or a way to make a story more sensational.

DIED OF FRIGHT

Miner Sees an Apparition and the Scare Proves Fatal.

[Susquehanna (Penn.) Cor. *New York Press.*]

Robert Montgomery, a well-known resident of Wanamie, Penn., recently died from fright or a belief that he had been warned of his approaching death, and that he had a premonition that he could not live.

Montgomery, who was a brave soldier in the war, was employed in a coal mine near Wilkesbarre. Two weeks before he died he said that when working he heard a peculiar noise in the mine. He paid no attention to it.

Soon a strange feeling came over him as though there was a strong draught circulating through the mine, and he became chilly. He looked up from oiling the machinery at the repetition of the strange noise. He said he felt as though there was some one else there besides himself, but he could not see any one.

Then he beheld something white like a man's figure. It moved as though floating in the air and kept a certain distance from him. He spoke to the apparition, but it made no answer and soon disappeared.

Montgomery made search, but did not find anyone. He told his friends that he regarded the wraith as an omen of death. He at once gave up his position, and in two days took to his bed, although he had no specific sickness which the physicians could discover. He continued to talk of the wraith, and said it was of no avail to take medicine because he was doomed.

His friends tried to dispel his thoughts about death by saying that the "supposed" wraith was a man sent into the mine by the company to see if he performed his duty. But Montgomery would only believe that it was an omen of death, and gradually grew weaker until he died.

Cincinnati [OH] Enquirer 5 December 1896: p. 11 PENNSYLVANIA

COW'S MOO KILLS CHILD

Baby Frightened into Convulsions When Wandering Bovine Puts Head in Window

Investigation by Dr. H. Albert McMurray, coroner of Westmoreland County, into the death of James Henry Pershing, 3-year-old son of Mr. and Mrs. Lawrence Pershing of Grapeville revealed that the child literally was frightened to death.

Several days ago the boy was playing when a cow at pasture in a lot adjoining the house looked in at an open window of the room where the child was. As the little one glanced toward the window the cow mooed loudly.

With a scream the child collapsed and went into convulsions. A physician was unable to give the boy any relief, and death ensued twelve hours later. *Greensburg (Pa.) Dispatch Philadelphia Record.*

The Tulsa [OK] Star 18 December 1915: p. 7 PENNSYLVANIA

Then there was a little-known occupational hazard for bodysnatchers.

A Man Hung by a Corpse

The *Cincinnati (Ohio) Gazette* states that on Saturday night, a fellow was stealing a dead body from the graveyard at Cumminsville near that city, when in crossing the fence, he slipped and fell on the outside, and the rope which held the sack containing the corpse, sliding from his shoulders to his neck, at daylight his body was found hanging on the outside of the graveyard fence, while the corpse he had stolen, hung on the inside, both equally lifeless.

Weekly Vincennes [IN] Gazette 12 March 1859 OHIO

In this heart-rending story, a father's grief drove him to literally join his lost child in the tomb.

Extraordinary Suicide in New Orleans.

A MAN BURIES HIMSELF ALIVE

HE TAKES POISON IN A TOMB

The *New Orleans Crescent* of the 24th gives the following remarkable story of a suicide

Sylvester Rupert, 37 years of age, an Englishman by birth, and by trade a ship carpenter, lived with his wife and two children in a house on Perdido street. In October last the yellow fever, then prevailing, counted among its victims the youngest child of the Ruperts—their little girl Lizzie, about four years old, and the particular pet of the father. This was a blow from which the father never recovered. Not able to buy a tomb, he had the child buried in the ground in Greenwood Cemetery. The grief preyed heavily upon him. It was his only thought; and, being out of his regular employment, he found employment in his grief.

He bought a burial lot and some bricks and other material, and with his own hands, and all alone in the Cemetery, built him a brick tomb. He had not the means to make the tomb a stylish one; so in its mouth or entrance he fitted a wooden frame, and on this frame he fitted a piece of board and secured it with screws in its four corners. On this board, with which he enclosed the vault, (in lieu of the usual brick and mortar or marble slab) he had carved nicely with his knife the burial inscription of his child. The tomb finished, he disinterred the child's body and placed it there. He fastened the board with screws, in order that he might afterward have no trouble in removing it when he felt like gazing upon the decaying remains of his child.

This employment finished, it was his habit to visit the Cemetery, open the tomb, and look at the corpse of his pet. He always carried a screw-driver in his pocket with which to remove and replace the board and also to remove and replace the lid of the coffin. Neither the haggard aspect of the shrinking little corpse, nor the foul odor of its decay could repel him, and his morbid grief. His visits were frequent, and sometimes his wife went with him. He frequently complained to her that he could not get work; and this inability doubtless fostered the despondency which was drawing him to death. He frequently spoke of having no faith in the future, and of death as a desirable thing.

On Wednesday he went to the Cemetery with two shrubs which he had purchased and planted them in front of the tomb. On Thursday, when he left home, he told his wife that if he had no better luck in finding work she would never see him again. He also said something about having a place in which to rest.

That evening, or that night—for no one saw him in his gloomy proceedings—he visited the cemetery; taking with him his screw-driver, an iron trunk-handle, a small rod of iron, a piece of wire, some new screws, and a large vial of laudanum. Unscrewing the board of the tomb, he threw away the screws and filled the screw-holes in the board with clay.

With his new screws he then secured the trunk-handle to the inside of the board. This work, of course, had to be done outside the tomb. Pushing his child's coffin aside, he got in by its side, taking with him his poison and the other articles with which he had provided himself. His hat he placed upon the coffin; his coat which he had taken off, he wrapped around a brick for a pillow. He shut himself in with the board, by means of the handle he had screwed to it; the board fitting outside the wooden frame. The iron bar, which was of the proper length, he placed across the frame inside. The thickness of the frame would not allow the bar to pass through the trunk-handle on the inside of the board; so he secured the handle and the bar by means of his wire, coiling it through the one end around the other. He did not succeed in fitting the board squarely upon the frame. One corner of it caught upon the brickwork outside the frame; this he did not discover, probably owing to the darkness of the night; and but for this little circumstance his fate would probably have never been discovered, or not at least for many years. Having thus hid himself away, as he fancied, beyond mortal discovery, he drained off the contents of his laudanum bottle, composed himself on his back, placed the brick and coat beneath his head, and went to sleep, and on into the unknown region of the suicides.

As he did not return home on Thursday night, his wife feared the worst, remembering well the tendency of his late conduct and the tenor of his parting words. On Friday morning she rose early and went out to the cemetery. She looked all around, and failed to find her husband. She went and looked at their tomb, and was about to leave, when she happened to notice that the board did not fit snugly into the frame as usual. Looking closer, she discovered the mud in the screw-holes; and putting her hand on the board, found it was standing loosely. She pulled it out a little, and the first thing she saw was the dead face of her husband. She fainted away, and laid in the grass she could not tell how long. She recovered at last, got up and went and informed the sexton, Mr. Merritt, of her discovery. The latter went and looked at things, and sent word to the coroner; and the inquest was held, as we have stated, on Saturday.

The coroner's verdict was in accordance with the facts so plainly apparent—suicide by laudanum.

Albany [NY] Evening Journal 2 February 1859: p. 2 LOUISIANA

NOTE: This story was so detailed, yet so bizarre, that I thought it might have been a journalist's invention. Grave records show that Sylvester Rupert, who died 20 January 1859, is buried in Greenwood Cemetery.

A minor, macabre theme of the later nineteenth century was the self-decapitation suicide, complete with ingenious inventor. It is not easy to cut off one's own head without mechanical assistance, although there was much loose talk in the press about people "cutting their own heads off," when in reality, they had "merely" managed to cut their throats from ear to ear. If one really wanted to do the job properly, one needed a device like a guillotine. If no guillotine was to hand, trains were readily available. We need only look at reports of railway accidents and the folklore of headless conductors to acknowledge the train's peerless efficiency at taking off heads.

Workman Thrusts Head Under Moving Freight

Toledo, O., Feb. 25. Within view of a score or more employees of the Toledo Stove and Range Company, George Mould, 68 years old, committed suicide by allowing a New York Central freight to pass over his body here today.

Witnesses say he took off his glasses, placed them on a window sill of the stove company and then walked to the track, placing his neck over the rails in the path of a backing freight train.

His head was cut off before the spectators realized what was taking place.

Lexington [KY] Herald 26 February 1922: p. 4 OHIO

Even with the ease and convenience of trains, a surprising number of tinkerers built their own devices.

AN INGENIOUS SUICIDE
A Bostonian Builds a Self-acting Guillotine and Inhales Ether Till it Chops his Head Off

Boston, April. 19 A remarkable and ingenious suicide occurred in Chelsea yesterday. Stephen M. Pillsbury, Jr., was found by his father in a barn where he was last seen on Sunday. The head was nearly severed from the body, connected only by the skin front.

Pillsbury had committed suicide in a most methodical manner. He built a guillotine of joist and plank, and took for a knife a carpenter's broadax, set in a wooden slide, the latter being held in position above by resting on a weighted lever. The weight was a large watering pot full of small leak holes at the bottom. A large box filled with stones was placed on the knife slide to weight it. Pillsbury's plan being that, when the water had escaped enough, the lever would release the knife, which would instantly drop. At the foot of the posts Pillsbury made a collar for his neck, and made close by a hollow in the joist, holding about a quart. The collar was fastened by heavy boxes of stones to keep him quiet if he struggled.

From appearances he had filled the hollow with ether, placed himself in the guillotine, fastened himself with his nose and mouth over the ether, and probably became insensible. The knife fell, nearly severing his head from his body.

Pillsbury was about thirty years old, and probably insane, as insanity occurs in his family. He left a letter addressed: "Dear parents, brothers, and sisters," saying he believed the step he was about to take was right.

Cincinnati [OH] Daily Gazette 20 April 1880: p. 2 MASSACHUSETTS

Accounts of religious self-decapitations in Asia state that the victims almost always start at the back of the neck. Did this doctor, who had the right tool for the job, know exactly where to cut through the backbone?

Dr Harvey Smith, a wealthy physician, of Blanchester, Ohio, recently warned his family that he was losing his mind. While walking with his wife a few days later he drew an amputating-knife from his pocket and, like a flash, beheaded himself.

Sacramento [CA] Daily Record-Union 11 November 1882: p. 1 OHIO

Standing head and shoulders above the nation's auto-decapitants was Mr. James A. Moon, an Indiana inventor who captured the imagination of the country with his ingenious device. Moon's success may have inspired Pillsbury, the Bostonian's design for his own guillotine, complete with a place for the anesthetic.

Here is the story. This was written long after the fact. A few distortions have crept in, but the article offers the historical perspective from an eye-witness.

KILLED HIMSELF BY HIS OWN INVENTION
MADE A KARIKARI FOR WHICH HE APPLIED FOR A PATENT
HAD GENIUS FOR MECHANICS
Thought to Make His Name Immortal by Dying by Means of Invention.

"Sunday morning, June 11, 1876, I [an unnamed Indiana "state officer"] was stopping at the Lahr house in Lafayette, when one of the chambermaids rushed into the office, pale with fright, and said that the gentleman in room 41 had been murdered. A number of us went at once to the room, and there I witnessed a sight that will never fade from my memory. Strapped to the floor was the headless body of a man and the floor around was covered with clotted blood. His head had fallen into a box, which was partly filled with raw cotton, and a broad ax lay upon the edge of the box, upon which the head had evidently rested when the fatal blow was struck. Rigged up near the body was a strange mechanical device, and on one of the beams of this was printed in large letters, 'Karikari. Patent applied for.'

"The dead man was James A. Moon, and he had taken a room at the hotel on the preceding Friday evening. It was at first supposed that a murder had been committed, but a little investigation demonstrated the fact that Moon had deliberately planned his own death, and had determined that it should be brought about by an invention of his own. He was 35 years of age and was a crank on mechanical construction. From the time he was 15 he and his father had worked upon divers impossible problems, among them being that of perpetual motion. Moon always contended that he could make a machine that would eclipse anything ever invented for taking human life, and it is said that he once went to Europe to study the guillotine and improve upon it. His 'Karikari,' as he termed the machine, was the result of years of study, but he was the only one that ever died by it.

"Coupled with his fanatical mechanical genius, which he inherited from his father, it is said that he inherited a suicidal mania from his mother's side of the family. His mother committed suicide and so did two or three other members of her family. Moon himself had twice before attempted to take his own life. Once he crawled into a hay rick and was nearly smothered to death when found. Again, he made the attempt at another hotel in Lafayette with morphine, and by a curious coincidence the number of the room was 41, the same as that at Lahr house in which his body was found.

The inquiry set on foot developed these facts: On the Friday preceding the finding of his body he was at home and was apparently cheerful. During the day, however, he had his beard shaved off, and from the barber shop he went to a hardware store and purchased two heavy bars of iron. He had purchased a broad ax some days before, and this he had ground to a razor edge. He purchased three ounces of chloroform and then left home with a trunk containing the things he had purchased and a framework for his machine. He went to the Lahr house and was shown three rooms before he found one to please him. This was located on the third floor and was one of the most secluded in the house.

"'Karikari' was an ingenious device and was so well constructed that the expected end was perfectly accomplished. The two bars of iron had been fastened to the broad ax to insure a sufficient weight when it should fall upon its victim. This was mounted on a beam, the other end of which was fastened to the floor. A hook had been screwed into the wall and the suspended as was held in place by a cotton cord which was fastened to the hook. Immediately under the hook Moon had placed a small shelf, and on this he set a candle which extended up above the cord, but which burned the string in two when the candle shorted to it. When the string was severed the ax, weighted by the two bars of iron, came down upon the box on which Moon had placed his neck.

"Everything indicated the utmost deliberation and care, and the plan must have been studied out months before it was carried into execution. After placing the machine in position Moon lady down upon the floor, his head in such a position that it would fall into the box when severed from his body. Before doing this, however, he strapped his legs to the floor by means of staples on either side, when he lay down he drew another strap across his breast, fastening it with a buckle and thus preventing the possibility of moving in his sleep. The cotton in the box into which his head was to fall was saturated with the chloroform and he inhaled the fumes at once and was no doubt soon asleep. The candle burned down to the string, severed it and the ax fell and his head was severed from his body. The calculations were precise in every respect, and so completely was the head severed from the body that not a ligament was left to join it to the trunk. There can be no question but Moon wanted to demonstrate the utility of the machine, as well as to put an end to his own life, there is little doubt that he believed that someone would eventually patent 'karikari,' and, that his own memory, as the man who had demonstrated its perfection, would be perpetuated by the act."

Evansville [IN] Courier and Press 22 July 1901: p. 4 INDIANA

The New York Times, writing just after the death, was fascinated by the story, saying, "The appliances which had been used to produce death were most wonderful and will stand in the history of suicides without a parallel."

We must wonder just who was to benefit from that "patent applied for." The U.S. Patent Office says that "articles contrary to the public good are not patentable." Suicide was illegal at the time of Moon's death, so a machine dedicated to enabling it, could not have been patented.

The *Times* summed up Mr. Moon's career:

> Mr. Moon was well known in this city. He owned a fine farm near the Farmers' Institute, and leaves a wife and four children. He served with Capt. Haggard in the Sixteenth Indiana Battery during the war, and was a gallant soldier. Upon his farm he had a blacksmith, wagon, and carpenter shop, and was considered a mechanical genius, though he never learned any trade—a sort of "jack at all trades and good at none."

New York Times 15 June 1876: p. 3

That last sentence seems most unfair.

It is the small, human-interest details in various newspaper versions of Moon's story that hold the attention:

The hotel porters complained that his luggage was very heavy—the trunk contained the pieces of his machine. The device was marked "for sale or rent." The chloroform was purchased in a two-ounce bottle from R. Schwegler & Brother's drug store. Moon fastened brown paper over the transom so no gust of air would accidentally blow out the candle. He thought of everything.

Except, possibly, his wife and four children.

4.

The Trades of Woe:

Undertakers, Grave-diggers, and Dead-Men's Razors

Once the doctor had gone quietly away and the crape had been hung on the door, there began a solemn procession of mortuary professionals to support the journey of the corpse to its coffin and crypt.

Let us start with the undertaker. Undertakers were seen as grim gougers of the grief-stricken, but based on the pen-portraits found in the papers, undertakers were either "characters" or jolly old fellows, not the stereotypical lugubrious, pursed-mouth men in weepers. Undertaker interviews were a perennially popular subject, often with the "oldest" undertaker or hearse-driver or coffin-dealer commenting on changing funeral customs throughout the nineteenth century.

AN UNDERTAKER'S STORY

FIFTY THOUSAND BURIALS IN FIFTY YEARS

How He Learned His Business and Buried Zachary Taylor, Gen. Harrison, John Quincy Adams, and Other Prominent Men

Changes in Funeral Fashions

From *The Philadelphia Times*, Aug. 24.

"Yes," said William Hill Moore, settling himself back with his snowy-haired head against the cushion of an easy chair and crossing his legs, now somewhat attenuated with age, "yes," said he, "I believe I am the oldest living undertaker. I've been active in the business over 50 years. I began in an alley, but I was not above my business, and I gave my whole time to it, and, of course, the business grew, and I made lots of money. There are a hundred undertakers who have started since, but I was the first one to keep ready-made coffins on hand in Philadelphia and supply funerals as a regular business, and, so far as I know, it had not been done anywhere else at that time. That was in 1826. I learned the business during the cholera of 1819-20 with a man who buried the dead for the prisons and Coroners and that like, and there's no telling the many a one in those days that went in the ditch who'd never died at all."

"Why, William," said a little, thin, nervous lady in the room, "you don't mean they were buried alive? Ugh! It makes my flesh creep."

"Yes, Martha, that's it exactly. No telling how many. A good old Quaker friend of mine—I buried him afterward; he had everything very plain, I remember, and no handles on the coffin said to me once: "William, said he, "is thee sure that all thee buried with the cholera were dead when thee put them in the ground?" Said I: "I never thought whether they were dead or not; I just buried them as fast as I could."

"Well, I never forgot the remark. When I fixed up a place for myself on Fifth-street, I forget the builder's name now, but I buried all his family, and a large family it was, too. I had two rooms where I used to do embalming and keep bodies until some one would come to pay for them, but I made up my mind that I'd never bury any of these or anybody else until I was sure they weren't alive. But it's easy to tell. With such as die from apoplexy and sudden like that it actually seems" and here the jolly old undertaker laughed a broad, hearty laugh "it actually seems they'd decomposed before they died. Ha! Ha! Ha! It's remarkable how plain the signs of decomposition become to the practiced eye. Why, Sir, I can tell a dead body as quick as that," and he snapped his long fingers in front of his shrewd gray eyes "but we always put off moving the body as long as the relatives like, unless it gets very bad, and then we does our duty and moves them off. They always like, you know, to have their little cries, and we lets them have their way. John Swift, who was the Mayor, that time we buried him in a double coffin, I remember, didn't like the idea of my keeping the bodies a month at a time, but I didn't mind it the least, and I soon showed him there was no danger.

"Why, Sir, the dead are no more to us than the sheets of paper you write on. We never think any more what a person dies of than you do of asking the people you meet in the street what disease they have. I've been all through cholera, small-pox, and yellow fever, and never had so much as a sick stomach. Most contagious diseases are caught through fear, but a great deal depends on the way a man lives. No undertaker can touch liquor if he wants to keep free from disease. He has to be strictly temperate. He has to be very careful what he eats, too. It's my experience that if a man is careful what he eats and drinks and keeps his stomach in order he need not be afraid of any contagious disease.

I had a friend, buried him, too, by the way who lived to be 90 just by eating as little as possible."

The gaunt, strange-looking old man at this point let his eyes relax somewhat from their usual dim, vacant gaze, and in response to a motion, put the large speaking trumpet which he balanced on one finger to his ear. All he had said up to this point was suggested by a single question shouted into the ear trumpet, and it now became necessary to start him on another train of reminiscences.

"You buried Gen. Patterson, did you not?" he was asked.

"Yes, but I was scarcely able to get there," he replied. "I've been very sick, but I'm not quite ready for the undertakers yet. Up to a very little while ago we buried all the Judges and Commodores and Generals, and almost all the great people it seems to me, but Lincoln—we didn't get him."

The undertaker was unable to repress a heavy sigh at the thought of missing the melancholy pleasure of laying away this truly great man.

"There were the obsequies of Zachary Taylor," he resumed: "The hearse cost $8,000. There were eight gray horses, with black covers, trimmed with white, and the men who walked as leaders wore long white bands on their hats and white gloves. It was a grand sight. There was a single tassel that cost $45. Then I had the obsequies of Bushrod Washington, and Chief Justice Marshall, and General William Henry Harrison, and John Quincy Adams. You may be sure they were the best that could be had. When the body of Henry Clay passed through the city in 1852 there was a funeral procession, and I had that, too, but it was not so much of an affair. Dr. Kane, the Arctic explorer, I buried and Judge Kane and his wife, I buried them too…Ah, my memory is getting poor and I can't think of them all. Funerals are very different to what they used to be. Matters are simplified in the burial, but funerals are more numerously attended and more expensive. It costs about $400 to bury a man of any consequence now. The use of ice is comparatively new, and they never used to line coffins with satin.

"I think Dr. Bedell set the style. He was buried in his robes, and the casket was lined with satin. I don't know where they got the idea from, but after that every one who could afford it wanted satin. We get a great many orders in advance from people about the way they want to be buried. I have known persons to come in and look at the different styles of coffins and pick out the kind they wanted years before they died. We have had the full directions for the funeral on the books in their own handwriting. There is a very wealthy gentleman and his sister who have given us orders for their coffins and funerals. "I would like the casket lined with white flannel," the lady said in the last letter, "like that one you furnished Mrs.__, which was chaste and elegant; only I would like six handles and, besides the plate, a little silver cross on the lid. But be sure and let me lay in the room until you know I am decomposed, for I'm awfully afraid of being buried alive."

"Up to 20 or 30 years ago there were no carriages. The burial places were not far away, and people walked, the coffin being carried on the shoulders or on a bier. I have often carried little babies in coffins under my arm myself. The great cemeteries had not grown up then. Eli K. Price and myself are about the only ones remaining of the starters of Woodlands Cemetery. Judge Mallory, who was interested in it at first—I buried him afterward—persuaded me to go into it. There are some ten thousand buried in it now, and I think I have had something to do with its success. The number I have buried is something incredible. For many years it averaged 100 a month. Mr. Kellogg, my partner, who has kept track of it, says we have buried over 50,000 in the 50 years...

You know a great many commit suicide that nobody knows anything about but the doctor and the undertaker. Many a one I've buried no one knows but me to this day they had the rope around their necks. I always used to carry a crooked needle to sew up gashes in throats. I found it handy to have around. One day a lady very rich and elegant she was, and had an A-1 coffin when she died, showed me her husband who had just cut his throat and said: "Oh, what shall I do?" "Do," said I, as I commenced to sew up the cut and put a clean shirt on him, "don't tell a living mortal, for it's my experience that if you tell anybody a secret you might as well put it in the newspapers; don't tell a living mortal, and it'll be all right." And sure enough it was. His own brothers don't know to this day but that he died a natural death.

"Ghosts, did you say? Do undertakers believe in them? Fiddlesticks! But strange things happen. The most curious thing is the horses. It's very common for horses to refuse to pull a dead body. I remember one time one of our best teams had just started off when they stopped, trembled, stuck up their ears, and wouldn't budge one inch further. Coaxing was no use, they wouldn't go. We had to take a team out of a hack and put them in the hearse. It was a little child that time, but another time the same thing happened when we were burying a man and his wife together." With this the conversation closed. The old gentleman drew himself to his fullest height, listened to the words of parting shouted through the ear-trumpet, and bowed his visitor out. With age he has lost none of the urbanity peculiar to him in his sturdiest years. Constant intercourse with grief often assumed has shaken his faith in many things. Half a century of hand-to-hand familiar intercourse with the dead has given him a quaint pensiveness mixed with a strange, grim humor. Careful habits leave him in complete possession of all his faculties except that of hearing. One can still imagine what he was in his best days, when it was said that Billy Moore looked more truly mournful than all the other mourners put together. Among the many stories told about him is this one concerning the cemetery, the name of which was sometimes jocularly applied to him in the appellation of Laurel Hill Moore. After scores of years of constant funeral attendance, it is related, Mr. Moore was called upon to officiate at a wedding of a relative. In his long black coat and longer face, with his hands crossed before, as usual, one holding the melancholy beaver hat, he stood ready to nod for the carriages as soon as the minister finished. One by one the vehicles came up. With slow step and look of resignation Mr. Moore escorted the bride and groom down the steps, and as they sprang in and the driver cracked his whip, the old gentleman, the ruling habit overcoming him at the last moment, clapped the carriage door with a bang and shouted, "To Laurel Hill."

The New York Times 28 August 1881: p. 8 PENNSYLVANIA

NOTE: Moore was one of four young men who buried Philadelphia's yellow fever dead during the 1819–20 epidemic. They worked under very difficult conditions; victims could be buried only between 10 P.M. and sunrise. He felt that being exposed to the yellow fever made him unafraid to handle victims of any contagious disease. [Source: *The Biographical Encyclopaedia of Pennsylvania of the Nineteenth Century*, Philadelphia, PA: Galaxy Publishing Company, 1874]

General Robert Patterson served in the Civil War and was a wealthy businessman, influential in Philadelphia politics. Bushrod Washington was a nephew of George Washington and a U.S. Supreme Court associate justice. Chief Justice John Marshall was the fourth Chief Justice of the United States Supreme Court. Dr. Elisha Kent Kane, the Arctic explorer, was said to have been married to Margaret Fox, one of the

Spiritualist Fox sisters. Dr. Gregory Townsend Bedell was the Rector of St. Andrew's Church, Philadelphia. Eli K. Price, was a lawyer and Pennsylvania State Senator.

Laurel Hill was the second "garden cemetery" established in the United States.

Grand funeral pageant at New York July 23, 1850, in honor of the memory of Major General Zachary Taylor 12th president of the United States. Library of Congress Prints and Photographs Division Washington, D.C. 20540 USA

Many of the articles on undertakers comment on their professionally sober expression.

IN GHASTLY HUMOR

Country Undertaker: Do you make any difference in your manner and expression in conducting different funerals?

City Funeral Director: Certainly. I have three expressions. One for first-class funerals, one for medium and one for cheap funerals. First-class funerals, as I call them, are when the family have wealth and social position. These people are calm and undemonstrative in their sorrow and I use what I call my "dignified sorrow" expression—a calm, sad look, with a white tie. I charge $10 extra for this in my et ceteras. For the medium class I just sling in a sort of a "ministerial sadness" look that costs them $5 extra. If the family have lots of money and are pretty shoddy and bound to make a big show I use a "suppressed grief" expression that I pride myself on. It is really pathetic. That costs the mourners $25, but it's a dandy.

The Topeka [KS] Daily Capital 11 April 1888: p. 3

The female members of a bereaved family might have their own personal shopper, in the person of the sable-clad "professional widow."

REAL WIDOW USED TO BRING TRADE

Store Has a Professional Mourner Who Gives Advice to the Bereft.

'TIS A NEW IDEA

New York, Oct. 9. Rendering first aid to the bereft is the latest novelty in the department store's field of activity. One of the large centers of fashions for women has just opened a section where may be found everything required by the woman in mourning. To the smallest detail of her costume the outfitting displayed is complete and embodies the most approved ideas of the French dressmakers and milliners.

This new department is arranged to supply immediate sartorial assistance to a woman who finds herself suddenly plunged into the deepest grief by the death of someone near and dear. Instead of concerning herself at such a critical time with the purchase of dresses, hats, gloves and other feminine belongings, she can now leave it all to the professional widow who presides over this unique mourning department.

A letter or telephone message will bring the professional black-dressed woman to the residence of the grief-stricken family. She will arrive quietly in a perfectly appointed limousine, with two liveried men on the box. Accompanying her will be a smart little maid, also in deep black, who will carry into the presence of the widow, mother or sister a choice selection of dresses, hats, shoes, silk stockings, veils, gloves, handkerchief and wraps, to be examined and tried on. If the articles do not suit they can be exchanged at once for different styles or sizes, for the mourning department carries a large stock of all articles required in such cases.

It is the aim of the new department to give promptly and correctly that special assistance which has usually been delegated to a friend who may not know the first thing about mourning style vagaries. The expert understands these perfectly and will proffer advice, make suggestions and see that the conventions are observed to fashion's decree.

She will include in her outfit brought for trial even a box of black bordered engraved cards which the family will find useful in acknowledging notes of sympathy and condolence. Orders for mourning stationery will be filled in the shortest possible time.

The professional widow wears the latest Parisian creations. Her soft white hair is dressed according to the newest mode, in her ears are hoops of pearl and jet, at her black swathed throat is an inconspicuous brooch of accepted style, while on the third finger of her left hand is seen the latest novelty in mourning ornaments, a black and jewelled wedding ring. No truly fashionable widow now wears a hoop of yellow gold or even one of more modern platinum, for only black ornaments are considered suitable with heavy crepe and dull finished silk costumes.

There are a hundred and one little things which the average person does not know about correct mourning according to the widow who has a professional knowledge of them all, and of course the best way to learn them is to send for the expert in dress for the bereaved.

The Fort Wayne [IN] Sentinel 9 October 1912: p. 13 NEW YORK

NOTE: This service is a version of that offered by "Black Peter Robinson's," the London mourning emporium, which advertised that they would send out lady fitters at a moment's notice to fill orders quickly.

FAMILY BEREAVEMENTS Upon receipt of letter or telegram, PETER ROBINSON'S experienced dress-makers and milliners travel to all parts of the country (no matter the distance), free of any extra charge, with DRESSES, Mantles, Millinery, and a full assortment of made-up Articles of the best and most suitable description, also materials by the yard, and supplied at the same very reasonable prices as if purchased at the warehouse in Regent-street. Mourning for servants at exceptionally low rates, at a great saving to large or small families. Funerals conducted in town or country at stated charges. Address 246 to 252, Regent-street, London—Peter Robinson's.

The Times [London, England] 3 June 1886: p. 15 ENGLAND

Since it was considered improper for the bereaved to leave their house without wearing mourning, it was essential that mourning clothes be delivered quickly. Sometimes short-cuts were taken.

This morning I was asking a dressmaker how she contrives to put a family in black between a death and a funeral. "Oh," she said, "The dresses are run together, with basting threads mostly, and afterwards they are returned to me to be stitched properly."

"And how can a woman who has just suffered a bereavement stand to be fitted?"

"Indeed, I ask myself that question often, but it seems as if people were more particular at such times. They notice and find fault with every little thing."

The Courier-Journal [Louisville, KY] 6 July 1890: p. 15 NEW YORK

Like undertakers, grave-diggers were thought to be grim and superstitious men, albeit with a touch of gallows humor about them, like the bantering grave-diggers in *Hamlet*.

"Gravedigging is not a gay business," said a gravedigger, "but it is a very old one, and many curious superstitions surround it. One of these is never to buy a new spade. To dig a grave with a spade that is new is supposed to bring death in the family within a twelvemonth. Hence gravediggers buy their spades second hand as a rule. Another superstition with some is that a grave should never stand open overnight. It should not, they say, be dug till the day of the funeral. If it is made the day before, beware. There is a third superstition that if a cock crows once while a grave is being dug one friend of the digger will die; if it crows twice, two will die; if thrice, three."

Arizona Republican [Phoenix, AZ] 20 July 1906: p. 4

Spring Grove Cemetery, in Cincinnati, Ohio was very conscious of its position as the resting place of many eminent people such as Salmon P. Chase, Levi Coffin, Joseph Hooker, Dr. Daniel Drake, and a host of politicians and military men. Uncharacteristically for an interview with a grave-digger, there isn't the slightest hint of humor, just a bureaucrat's account of the services performed by the gravediggers and the public health benefits they provide. One suspects that this soberly informative article was crafted as a public relations exercise to uphold the dignity of the cemetery.

THE GRAVE-DIGGER
His Cheerful Life in the Cemetery.
An Occupation Which Few Men Care to Follow
The Manner in Which the Work of Interment is Performed.

The grave-digger has a thankless job. His position is not envied by any one, for he is always seeing the most painful side of life, mourning over beloved dead. One of Shakespeare's most amusing characters is the grave-digger in "Hamlet," and the terrible sadness of the scene is relieved by the cheerful jokes of the men engaged in preparing the fair "Ophelia's" grave.

There are seven grave-diggers in Spring Grove Cemetery who attend to the interment of all bodies sent there. John Trotter, the boss of the men, has been a professional grave-digger for eighteen years in that city of the dead. He is a man forty-seven years old and a funeral ordinarily has no more call on his feelings than on the marble monuments which mark the resting-places of the wealthy and illustrious dead. It's

A VERY BUSY TIME

Just now at Spring Grove.

The bodies which have accumulated in the public vault during the past four months must be buried before the 1st of April. Four weeks ago nearly one hundred coffins of various sizes filled the great stone vault.

On Wednesday the number had dropped to thirty, and on Thursday ten of the corpses were buried.

Trotter, who is designated as the Sexton, rather than by the hard title of Chief Grave-digger, doesn't like to talk about graves and burying people. Not that the matter is particularly disagreeable, but rather on account of his belief that the subject is distasteful to the friends who have sorrowfully laid their departed away, under the careful eye of John Trotter, who never permits any awkwardness on the part of his subordinates.

Mr. Trotter is an unmarried gentleman, entirely and enthusiastically devoted to his occupation. The Superintendent of the cemetery, Mr. Salway, who has done so much to improve and beautify the grounds, has great confidence in Trotter, and the interments are always properly attended to.

"GRAVES AND GRAVE-DIGGING

Is not a cheerful topic," remarked Mr. Salway, "but I am willing to impart any information desired."

"How many styles of graves are there in this cemetery?"

"Three. The plain grave, where no box is used and the coffin is covered up with earth, the box-grave, in which a pine box encloses the casket, and the brick grave. Of these, the box-grave is used in about 65 per cent of the burials, the plain in 15 per cent, and the brick in 20 per cent. It is very horrifying to most people to put their dead right in the earth, but that is only a foolish sentimentality. The sooner the body returns to dust the better. It is a popular error that bodies are eaten by worms after being buried. That is another error, for the worms that would feed on human flesh do not exist two feet below the surface. I can't see any use in preserving bodies, but the wishes of lot-holders are, of course, respected in every instance. The graves are all six feet deep, and there is considerable knack required in digging them. Some days we open as high as a dozen, and, again, there will only be two or three."

Many heaps of dirt dotted the cemetery at intervals and the information was given that

TEN BODIES WOULD BE BURIED

From the vault the next day without counting those which would be interred by regular funerals.

"I suppose you witness some very harrowing scenes sometimes?" was suggested to Mr. Salway.

"Yes, indeed, but we must attend to our business just the same. The grave-diggers are not callous to human grief. Trotter has told me that he often turns his head away on account of the dreadful agony of some daughter or wife. Occasionally a frantic relative of the dead attempts to jump in the grave, but that is a rare occurrence. Women frequently faint at the side of the grave."

Mr. Salway thinks that in mid-winter bodies ought to be buried at once. When spring opens there is a great deal to do in improving the grounds, and then there is a rush of friends to inter the dead. The public vault one month ago contained considerably more than a hundred corpses, with the caskets covered with floral offerings which have now all withered as did the life of the silent form within the sealed receptacle. In some of the cemeteries in Europe the caskets are piled up by the hundreds in vaults and allowed to remain....In Spring Grove the dead placed in private vaults must be hermetically sealed.

One reason that the Spring Grove authorities prefer to have corpses buried instead of being deposited in the vault is that there are often two funerals re-enacting the same pitiful scenes a second time.

The grave-diggers make a little more money than ordinary day-laborers. It takes them about an hour to dig a plain grave, but some time longer to prepare a brick grave. Twice a day a messenger is sent out from the office of the cemetery in this city with an order for graves. This order recites the name of the person to be buried, the lot and location of the grave, when the burial is to take place, and the cause of death. No one who has died of a contagious disease can be put in the public vault, and the consequence is that, no matter what time of the year or how disagreeable the weather,

THE SMALL-POX VICTIM

Is interred the instant the coffin reaches the cemetery. Any one who has many acquaintances can go into Spring Grove and he will be pained and surprised to see the number of people whom he formerly knew now reposing in eternal sleep. The grave-diggers' occupation is far from being unhealthy to him. He is constantly in the open air, and most of the diggers at the various burying-grounds around Cincinnati have been engaged in the work for years.

The *Cincinnati [OH] Enquirer* 27 March 1887: p. 12 OHIO

Ghouls prowled the cemeteries of the nineteenth century, seeking corpses to unearth, sack, and sell to the anatomist. While our Victorian ancestors were terrified that they might be buried alive, they had an equally deep fear that their dead bodies would be resurrected, not on the Day of Judgment, but in the dead of night by the body snatchers.

To prevent this, sometimes bodies were held in vaults until they were too decayed for dissection. Sometimes heavy weights or cages were placed over graves to discourage diggers. Family members took turns standing vigil over graves and many cemeteries had watchmen.

It was a thankless job. The ghouls at the head of their profession could open a grave, extract the corpse, and refill the soil in under an hour. A watchman had to be vigilant: walking the grounds of a cemetery in the dark, and in all weathers, for rain softened the ground and allowed for a quicker opening of a grave. Body snatchers might be armed and more than one watchman was murdered or exchanged gunfire among the tombstones. It was no wonder that, in the 1880s, a new occupational disease emerged.

TOMBSTONE MADNESS

A New Form of Mania that Affects People Who Guard Cemeteries.

[*Philadelphia Times*]

The men who patrol the cemeteries after the sun has gone down are armed with pistols and clubs, and are generally accompanied by trained and savage bloodhounds. In addition to these external and tangible means of defense they must be gifted with rare and peculiar mental organization. So many men have lost their reason through watching graves at night that persons in that position have come to believe that they risk lapsing into a state of melancholia perfectly distinct from any other form of insanity. Sextons and grave-diggers called this affliction "tombstone madness."

A startling realization of this fact was telegraphed throughout the country yesterday. It was announced that several of the soldiers who do sentry duty day and night at the tomb of Garfield, amid the dreary solitude of Lakeview Cemetery, near Cleveland, have become insane. Anything or any device is used by the men to get away from the ghostly muster of tombstones or the dark array of mounds.

An old watchman at Glenwood Cemetery explained this to a *Times* reporter yesterday by saying that in all probability the soldiers detailed at the grave were not picked.

"Take half a dozen men from any walk of life," he continued, "and place them at night to watch graveyards, and the chances are that in a short time five of the six will feel like retiring permanently to a lunatic asylum.

"If a man wants to enter this profession and be a success at it, he must be about as impressible as brick and mortar. If he has the least bit of imagination he had better abandon the business, for when the moon is obscured by clouds and he is walking about a cemetery, shivering from his heels upward, he will mistake tombstones for ghosts. He will think that the owls, as they whiz past his ears with their mournful hoots, are unquiet spirits come to haunt the receptacles of the bodies which they once permeated. When the noise of his footsteps makes the rats disappear with rustling sounds into little thickets of evergreens he will start and grasp his weapon. The very whine of his dog will make him feel nervous, and bit by bit his reason would become impaired."

"I could give you some sad reminiscences of people who watch grave-yards," said one of the oldest watchmen at Laurel Hill cemetery, in a strange, solemn tone. Then, half jestingly, he added: "But they're buried in the past, and it's my business to let what's buried remain so." He did not mind telling one story, however.

"I used to work in a Brooklyn cemetery before I came to this city," he began. "It was then that the terrible scene I shall speak of occurred. We wanted an assistant night watchman very badly, but none of the persons who presented themselves could endure staying up with the graves for more than two or three nights each. At last there came an unfortunate man whose health seemed shattered by overwork and privation. It was his last venture. He had tried to get employment everywhere without result and his wife and children were suffering. We took him on. I don't think I shall ever forget his face the morning after his first night in the graveyard. He said he had endured unheard of agony, but was hopeful of getting over it in time. The following night was dark and windy. Rain came down in torrents, and there were flashes of lightning every few minutes. At about one o'clock the head watchman heard a loud cry; there was a sound of running feet, followed by the report of a pistol. A search was made, and the unfortunate man found lying on his back across a grave, dead. There was a small hole in his temple, and his own revolver, one barrel of which was empty, lay three feet away where he had flung it, imbedded in the ground. It was certain that some fearful creation of the imagination had so terrified him that he took his life to escape from it."

When the old man had finished this narrative he was silent, with a vacant look, and allowed bright tears to chase each other down his cheek. Suddenly he made a brisk motion and forcibly forgot the subject of his narrative. "There are amusing things sometimes," he said, speaking at first with an effort. "A short time ago a man was put to work at night in a cemetery not far from here. He strolled around in an affected, indifferent way, whistling tunes dear to his countrymen. In the course of his rambling he tumbled bodily into a newly-made grave and a lot of loose earth fell on him when he reached the bottom. He struggled wildly, and in about an hour and three-quarters managed to get out, screaming lustily that the devil had dug a grave and tried to bury him in it. With a single bound he cleared a four-foot fence, rolled down a forty-foot hill, and that's the last of him, for no one about here ever set eyes on him again, dead or alive. He must have gone back to Ireland, for he wasn't hurt at all. Some practical jokers once tried to scare a watchman, a friend of mine. It was immense fun—for the watchman. They got into the cemetery disguised as body-snatchers, and pretended to be opening graves. There were three individuals. One got seven buckshot in him, the second received five in his leg, and I forget what happened to the third. The only thing that is more dangerous than watching graves is robbing them."

"What is it produces the dreadful melancholia?" asked the reporter.

The old man looked around him mysteriously and added, as he moved away: "I'm not a doctor nor a scholar, but I have my belief that it's the miasma from the graves that poisons the blood and warps the brain. Just see, cool as it is this evening, the vapour is rising—rising."

And the old watchman pointed toward the setting sun, against which blazing background a filmy mist could be seen ascending from the ground like the genie from the fisherman's box in the Arabian tale.

Texas Siftings [Austin, TX] 28 April 1883: p. 3 PENNSYLVANIA

NOTE: One could also perhaps point to exposure to the heavy metals used in embalming and in coffins or to overindulgence in the warming flask sometimes employed to ward off the cold. It may also have been a profession of last resort for those with few prospects, although several of the soldiers who were guarding the Cleveland grave of President Garfield, had breakdowns.

There was also a mysterious disease called "Corpse Quake," which affected grave-diggers with ague-like shaking.

Another guardian of the graveyard was the little-known Tombstone Censor.

THE TOMBSTONE CENSOR

He Sees That No Unseemly Inscription Mars the Cemetery

A tombstone censor is employed by most large cemeteries. It is the duty of this man to see that nothing unseemly in the way of a tombstone is put up.

A young engineer in a Norristown mill was killed by the explosion of a boiler, and the family of this young man, believing that the mill owners had known all along that the boiler was defective, actually had carved on the tombstone the sentence, "Murdered by his masters." The tombstone censor, of course, refused to sanction such an epitaph.

On the death of a certain noted prize fighter the surviving brother of the man wanted to put in a glass case beside the grave a championship belt, four medals, a pair of gloves and other trophies of the ring. But the censor's negative was firm.

A widow who believed that the physician was responsible for her husband's death wished to put on the tomb, "He employed a cheap doctor," but the tombstone censor showed her that such an inscription would lay her open to heavy damages for libel.

Atheists sometimes direct in their wills that shocking blasphemies be carved on their monuments. The censor, however, sees to it that these blasphemies do not disfigure the cemetery.

Patriot [Harrisburg, PA] 22 June 1905: p. 3 PENNSYLVANIA

A noteworthy funeral fad around the turn of the nineteenth century was the funeral stenographer, who took down the words of the eulogist.

OFFICIAL FUNERAL STENOGRAPHER.

The young woman in black looked at the clock and grabbed her notebook.

"Dear me! " she said, "it is almost 11 o'clock, and the funeral is set for quarter past. I'm afraid I'll be late."

Her hostess smiled wonderingly. "You seem to be attending a good many funerals here of late," she said. "I know of four that you have gone to in the past ten days. I didn't know that you were possessed of such a sombre streak. What is the cause of it, anyway?"

"Business," returned the young woman. "I am reporting funerals for the comfort of bereaved families. It is a fad just now to have the proceedings of a funeral taken down in black and white just like a political convention or a murder trial, and I am profiting by the fashion."

"Is there money in it?" asked the hostess.

"A little," returned the young woman, "or I wouldn't be doing it. If I got paid at space rates I would never break the mint, because, as a rule, funeral sermons don't amount to much, reckoning from the standpoint of quantity. Fortunately, my services are valued on the basis of quality, and I scoop in some nice little sums as a kind of side issue. Some funerals pay better than others. It all depends upon the circumstances and disposition of the mourners.

"Naturally, any family that can afford to indulge the fancy of securing a verbatim report of their relatives' funeral exercises can afford to bestow a goodly fee upon the official stenographer, but, unfortunately, many well-to-do people are cursed with an economic temperament and are not disposed to pay in proportion to their means. These prudent folk religiously screw me down to the very cheapest rates.

"The last funeral I did was managed by the brother of the deceased, and he cut me down to five dollars, which was the lowest figure I ever agreed to accept. To be sure, the services were short, and I didn't lose anything on the transaction. Still, as a matter of self-respect, I like to hold out for good terms now while the fashion is new and exclusive. Today I have contracted to do the work for $8, which is little enough, considering that the minister engaged is long winded and apt to speak from a half to three quarters of an hour."

"But what do you take down at a funeral?" asked the hostess, still somewhat bewildered. "What part of the service is supposed to be your prey?"

"The whole of it, although the sermon is naturally the pivotal point. It is easy enough to guess at the remarks sandwiched in between hymns, and the prayers are all about alike, but in his sermon the preacher is apt to say some pretty fine things, and it is the desire of many up-to-date families to keep a record of them. In no way other than by the employment of a stenographer can this record be secured, for, as a rule, funeral sermons are extemporaneous speeches. The average minister has not the time to write them out beforehand and commit them to memory, and as it is bad form to read an obituary discourse, obviously there is nothing for it but to call in the stenographer. Hence my novel occupation."—*New York Times.*

The Journal of Commercial Education, Volume 18, 1901 NEW YORK

Tuberculosis, known as consumption, was usually a death sentence before antibiotics. The dry air and sunshine of the western United States was said to be beneficial for sufferers. This express company found an ingenious and heartless way to exploit the deaths of consumption patients under the guise of reuniting loved ones.

AN INDUSTRY IN CORPSES
How an Express Company and an Undertaker Whack Up on Consumptives.
[*St. Louis Globe-Democrat.*]

The Wells-Fargo Company does some queer things in the way of business, but the strangest perhaps is a new line, worked up by one of the shrewdest agents of the country at Denver. Colorado is a sort of last chance of consumptives, and pretty generally they die there. Most of them are supplied with money from home in regular installments, so when they die not enough coin is found among their effects to pay an undertaker. Undoubtedly many of them would be buried by the county [as paupers], but right here's where the company gets in.

It has a contract with an undertaker who takes charge of the body, embalms it, and gets it all ready for shipment. Then the Fargo agent wires to the agents in the towns from which the deceased received letters. If any relatives can be found it is a sure thing, and nine times out of ten enough friends can be found to put up a check for the undertaker's charges and transportation. When this has been done the body is shipped to the friends or relatives by fast train, and turned over by the agent. The company makes a fat annual profit out of this melancholy business—"the corpse industry," they call it—it is a good snap for the undertaker, and this county is saved just so many dollars. Many a time there have been three to four corpses at once in the company's "cooling room" at Denver awaiting notice from friends in just this way. It is a cold day when W. F. & Co., can't discover a new way to turn an honest penny.

The Pittsburg [PA] Dispatch 19 July 1891: p. 18 COLORADO

These next four stories highlight a gruesome sideline of the mortuary profession, little mentioned in the standard histories.

THE DEAD MAN'S RAZOR

Odd Experiences of a Barber With His Deceased Customers

STYLE IN THE COFFIN

Dead Woman the Worst Subject of the Loquacious Shaver

"Don't be alarmed, sir. We never use that razor on the faces of living men. We call that the 'Dead Man's Razor.'"

Grim and hideous enough it looked, too; a long black handle, that insensibly reminds one of the hull of a rakish, piratical craft. Exactly in the middle was rudely scratched a skull and cross bones. The back of the blade gleamed over the ghastly symbol seeming to bring it out in bolder relief. The razor was in a rack in a west side barber shop.

"Just a little fancy of mine," said the barber, as he splashed the brush around in the lather cup. "Thought it would be better to put that death's head on the handle so I wouldn't be picking it up by mistake and using it on a customer who could turn his head without being helped. Dead men can't, you know. Most people have an objection to being shaved with the same razor used on the face of a corpse. Don't know why. Same feelin', I 'spose, that prevents a man who would tackle a burglar at midnight from walking through a graveyard at the same hour."

Rather more loquacious than his kind was this Sir Tonsor. A cadaverous man with deep set eyes and hair plastered close to his head. A mustache whose ends curled like the horns of a Southdown ram was the only hairy adornment on his face. His hands were long and his fingers were supple. Three of them on his left hand were up in the air when he worked, like the legs of a boy standing on his head. The barber, like all other barbers smelled of pomade and bay rum.

GIVING THE RAZOR A REST

"Haven't used that razor for nigh on to three weeks now," he went on, as he dipped up a brush full of lather; "only wish I had a job for it every day in the week. The pay runs from one dollar up. I've had as high as ten dollars, but that included a haircut.

DEAD MEN'S BEARDS GROWN.

"I guess you've often heard it said that it was nonsense to say that the beard doesn't grow after death. Well, it isn't nonsense, and I don't care who says so. I shaved a man named Farley, on the Bowery, about six years ago, and shaved him a second time before he was buried. Yes, sir, just as true as I'm telling you. He died on a Wednesday night. I did my work early on a Thursday morning, and I never did see such a stiff beard as that man did have. He was dark complected, and the skin on his chin looked almost blue, the beard was so close. He always wore a smooth face. I finished the job, as I said, on Thursday morning. The funeral was set for Sunday. On Saturday afternoon I was sent for again, and I found a very heavy growth of beard on the corpse just as heavy as you would see on a living man. His chin and the sides of his face were black with it. I shaved him again.

"That job made me feel all creepy like. It was like cutting hair off a block of marble. Then his eyes were half open, and I imagined that he was watching me to see if I was doing the thing right. I got $2 for the first shave, but they couldn't pay for the second. Said it was all one job. I didn't kick. If they was too mean to pay I wasn't mean enough to kick up a row, and a funeral going' on.

"I had one experience," continued this man of queer experiences, as his razor swept over the customer's chin, "that I'll bet knocks out any barber in New York. I shaved a dead woman once!"

The grimace of incredulity on the listener's face nearly turned the edge of the razor.

"That's a frozen fact," said the barber, solemnly, "and the family is living in New York city to-day. I know it sounds rather tart, but you ask any old barber and I'll guarantee that he will tell you he has shaved living women often enough. I have shaved a dead one. Women don't have beards? I know they don't, as a rule. Neither do cows have two heads, nor are calves born with six legs every day in the week, but you'll run across 'em once in awhile, you must admit. Same way with human beings. There are lots of women who have hair on their faces, and either shave twice a day or use some sort of a powder. The number is small and the number who intrust the secret to a barber is smaller still. If five hundred women have beards, not more than three out of that five hundred would trust another person with the knowledge. Certainly not half a dozen. Sit up a little higher, please. Because a thing seems out of the usual run that doesn't argue that it isn't so, and this experience of mine, while it mightn't be the experience of one barber in a thousand, is just as true as God made little apples.

SHAVING A DEAD WOMAN

"It was ten years ago last April. I was workin' in a shop on the east side then, having been driven out of my own shop by family troubles. An undertaker who used to give me a good many odd jobs shaving the dead came to me and said, 'Frank, I want you to come around to my place to-night and go out to Fifty-seventh street. I've got something for you to do.' That was every word he said. Well, I takes that very identical razor you see there with the death's head on it, and I reaches his undertaker's shop about eight o'clock. He puts the icebox in the wagon and off we starts.

"When we gets to the house an old gentleman comes to the door and asks the undertaker if that was the barber—meaning me, of course. 'I am the barber,' says I. 'Well,' says he, 'I suppose you've got good common sense and don't want to have the feelin's of a respectable family hurt. I never want you to tell what you did in this house, and I'm going to pay you $10 for doin' it.' 'All right,' says I. 'I think I know my business.' Then the undertaker fetches me upstairs and takes me into a small bedroom. 'Now it's nothin' to be scared about,' says he, 'but I want you to shave a woman.'

"Well, sir, you can depend—which side do you part on? You can depend I was surprised, but I said nothin' at all. The undertaker pulled down the sheet and there I saw the body of a rather stout woman who looked to be forty or forty-five. Her hands were shut tight and her face was all drawn up and twisted. It looked horrible. I gets up a little closer and see that she has hair on her upper lip and chin, and I could tell by the stiffness that she had been shaved before.

SHE HAD BEEN CRAZY.

"While I was latherin' up I asked the undertaker why the woman hadn't shaved herself before she died. It was a month's growth, I should judge, and I supposed—like most women with beards—she was her own barber. 'Well,' says the undertaker, 'she was crazy for three months—clean gone, a maniac—and never still for a minute. She had shaved herself for more than twenty years and not a living soul outside of her family knew the secret. When she went out of her mind she forgot all about her beard and no one dared to use a razor on her. For the last three weeks she was strapped down in bed, but her head kept wagging from morning till night and from night till morning. Her people don't want the world to know what has been so long concealed. Do you understand?'

"I just kept on latherin' and when I got her lathered I shaved her, and when I shaved her I puts up my razor and says to the undertaker, 'Excuse me, if you please. I don't want any more such jobs as this. That corpse looks ready to jump out of bed. I'll shave dead men, and all you want of 'em, but when it comes to this kind of work, why, just leave me out. I think I can say that I've seen some things out of the common, can't I? Of course, in a hundred dead men's jobs you see ninety-nine dead bodies with a week's beard on 'em and nothing more. The hundredth case might be something strange.

"Shaving a dead man is easy enough, easier, in fact than shaving a living one. Death makes the flesh firm and the razor slides over the face just as if going over ice. Then, if you happen to make a slip there is no blood to tell on you, and a dead man never kicks about not being shaved close enough. Good day, sir."

New York Herald 7 August 1888: p. 2 NEW YORK

NOTE: It is difficult to tell whether this story is a genuine human-interest interview with a real barber or something invented by the journalist. I have seen a practically identical interview, supposedly with a different barber, yet with nearly the same incidents, from the *New York World*. Did dueling papers send out reporters to discover the dead-man's barber with the most lurid stories? Or were reporters always on the lookout for a good yarn, even in the barber's chair?

THE DEAD MAN'S RAZOR

Peculiar Experiences of a Veteran Barber

[Philadelphia Cor. *New York Mercury*.]

In 1874 I lathered and shaved the faces of fifty-eight corpses, an average of more than one a week....On the afternoon of April 1, 1875, one of my old undertaker friends in West Philadelphia called at my shop and said he had a job for me. I jumped into his wagon, and we drove out to the receiving vault of the Malcom Church. A body had been taken from the vault, and as the relatives insisted that the coffin-lid should be removed for one last look, the undertaker got the foolish idea in his head that the face of the corpse should be shaved and the mold scraped off, so that those who wanted to look should not be shocked. The remains were exposed, and, as decomposition had set in, the sight was not a pleasant one. A greenish grave-mold covered the lower part of the face and the top of the head. This was removed, and then it was found that the beard had actually grown at least a sixteenth of an inch

AFTER A MONTH'S INTERMENT

I went to work and covered the face of the corpse with a thick lather and then attempted to use the razor. Owing to the condition of the body it was not taken from the coffin. The head was propped up on a board. The position was an awkward one, and I could not work freely. For this reason, and a little unusual nervousness, perhaps, the razor slipped. It was very sharp and went deep into the dead man's face. In attempting to remove it I made a horrible blunder. I unintentionally turned the edge sideways, and the whole lower part of the face of the corpse gave way and came off, and left the chin, jaw-bones and lower teeth almost bare. It was a hideous sight, and despite my long experience, I grew faint and sick. There was no help for it, however, and the coffin lid was screwed on again. I never learned whether the relatives saw the remains or not.

"In 1876 I made more money than I ever did before or have since. I remember a rather singular experience which took place that summer. My services were needed to shave a young man who had died after a lingering illness. He left a wife—a pretty girl—and one child. I went to the house with one of his friends, who had called me, as I learned afterward, without consulting the widow. I took two razors with me, which were contained in one case. I was conducted to the second-story front room, where the corpse lay on a cooling-board

COVERED WITH A SHEET

The widow sat on the floor moaning and going on at a terrible rate. Without saying anything I took one of the razors out and began whetting it on the palm of my hand. The wife happening to glance up saw the gleam of the instrument. With a loud scream she rushed towards me, shrieking, 'You can't cut him up! You shan't cut him up! He is mine—my poor, dead husband, and his body shall not be mutilated.' I tried to explain, and so did the young man. It was no use, however, and I went away without my usual fee, and got home to find that an apprentice had disappeared with $15 and several fine razors. So," concluded Swartz, "even if there are some unpleasant features connected with it, you will concede that the dead man's razor is a profitable instrument."

The *Cincinnati [OH] Enquirer* 6 September 1882: p. 6 PENNSYLVANIA

NOTE: The unfortunate widow thought that the barber was a medical student, ready to autopsy or dissect her husband.

During a trip through Ireland, a New Yorker one day found himself without his razors, which were in a hand-bag he had left behind at the hotel where he had stopped the day before. He accordingly told the landlord to send him a barber. The landlord was doubtful if there was a man in the village who could serve him, but presently sent up a man who expressed his willingness to undertake the job. The New Yorker decided to risk a gash or two.

"Well, sir," said the amateur barber, after a little hesitation, "will you please to lie down flat on your back, while I shave you, sir?" Thinking it was probably a custom of the country, the New Yorker stretched out comfortably on his back, and nearly went asleep while the fellow shaved him, so light was his touch. When he had finished, the New Yorker arose and said: "I am curious to know why you asked me to lie down to be shaved?" "Because, sir" was his ingenious reply, "I never before shaved a live man, sir."

The Argonaut [San Francisco, CA] 11 April 1898 IRELAND

For one unfortunate gentleman, it really *was* a dead-man's razor.

Death from Poisoned Razor.

Mr. Mazaraki, a member of one of the richest and best families in Austria, has just died of blood poisoning, brought about in a very extraordinary way. Several cases have already occurred of contagious diseases communicated by a cut from a razor that the barber had neglected to clean; but this is the first case of death. Mr. Mazaraki at first paid no attention to the cut, but swelling and fever compelled him to call in a surgeon, unfortunately too late. The poison had entered his system, and he died in a few hours after the operation. It is supposed that the razor had been used to shave a dead man before he was laid out in the coffin, and that it had not been cleaned afterward. It appears

that there is no law to punish a man who thus causes the death of a fellow-creature, and as there are no public inquests in Austria, there is no official information even as to the name of the barber. *Chicago News.*
Idaho Falls [ID] Times 17 January 1901: p. 5 AUSTRIA

The late nineteenth century marked a new era in embalming methods. Honey, salt, alcohol, and arsenic had all been used in the past, but when arterial injection embalming began to be practiced during the Civil War, chemists and medical men set out to discover new fluids and formulae to halt the ravages of death. Dr. Arnold Rosett of Atlanta claimed to be able to turn flesh to glistening silicon in 4 to 6 months. Mr. Levy McCoy of Memphis was said to be "one of the best embalmers of modern times." His methods of embalming "seem to transform the remains into stone." This series of articles tells of some of the chemicals and embalming innovators of the late nineteenth century.

GHASTLY SECRETS

Unconsciously Revealed by an Unsuspecting Undertaker
The Physician Whose Art Perished With Him

[*New York Mercury.*]

"Funerals are very troublesome affairs," said the head of a leading undertaking establishment to a *Mercury* reporter, "for the reason that the mourners are never on hand, and you are kept always an hour behind time. The only time we have things as we wish them is when we are first notified to come and take charge of the remains. Then we have all to say, and can proceed with our work without delay."

THE SECRETS OF EMBALMING

"How do you preserve or embalm the dead?"

"Well, I can frankly tell you that to-day there is no sure and per-fectly successful means of embalming remains known; of course, we can embalm remains so as they will keep for a week or perhaps a month, but not longer. I speak as an undertaker, not as an embalmer, and the sums of money I have paid in having embalming done, and its effects gives me good experience. I only know of one man who ever accomplished embalming successfully and that man is dead, and his *modus operandi* was a secret and has been buried with him. That man was a physician who once resided on Lexington avenue. From my own observations I can describe how he performed his work, but can not tell what ingredients he used. When I received an order for embalming a body I notified the Doctor, and on an appointed night or morning, taking care that none of the friends of the family should see us enter, we cautiously made our way into the room in which the body lay, then we of course made it known we were in the house. You see the Doctor carried some tools with him in a good-sized satchel. He did not want them to know how much luggage he took in because he would take out just twice as much and that would look suspicious. The first thing done was the cutting of the scalp at the back of the cranium. The scalp was then quickly slit around and all loosened from the skull to the forehead and here it was held or let fall over, so that the hair covered the face; then a small sharp saw was used in taking off the top of the skull; this with the brains and all in the head was placed in a rubber bag provided by the doctor, and after the inside of the head was cleaned thoroughly. He then deposited pieces of cotton saturated with some liquids and other ingredients into the head until it was completely filled and compactly set. The scalp was then drawn back and replaced over the cotton and fastened at the back of the neck, and to all appearance the scalp and hair looked as if they had not been disturbed. Then he next took his knife and opened the abdomen, and after taking out the contents turned up the skin nearly to the lower ribs, where it stayed until he had placed in the same cotton and ingredients to fill up. Next he drew back the skin, sewed it up and gave orders for the remains to be prepared for removal. This completed his work and he left with his rubber bag filled with remains. The body at once resumed a most remarkable appearance, and from that time forward the color was a glowing hue and the features like one calmly reposing in sleep. Of course the charges were high, but his work was decidedly successful and not pleasant to perform.

The Times-Picayune [New Orleans, LA] 16 December 1879: p. 2
NEW YORK

EMBALMING AND OTHER FUNERAL BODY PREPARERS

EMBALMING GENERAL GRANT

Why the Body Turns Black and Other Facts.

Interesting Chat on the Processes of Preserving the Dead With a Leading Undertaker.

"I notice by late dispatches that the embalming process that the undertakers are applying to General Grant's body is not likely to prove as successful as at first anticipated," said an *Enquirer* man to Mr. Estep, a leading Seventh-street undertaker, yesterday afternoon.

"Well, no, and yet if the undertaker has succeeded in getting the blood all out of the body, he has taken a great step, and I see no reason why the process should not be a success. The black discoloration that you speak of may come from the coagulated blood, which through the transparent skin assumes a dark hue, or it may come from using an impure quality of zinc for injection. If you recollect when President Lincoln died, his body was embalmed, and it was said that his face looked as if he had been injured by gun-powder. Now this I attribute to the fact that the zinc was impure and contained too much lead."

"Is embalming often resorted to nowadays?"

"Oh, yes. We frequently embalm bodies that are to be shipped a great distance, and they are opened for the inspection of friends and the features are found to be in a fine state of preservation."

"The weather may have something to do with the decomposition?"
"Oh, certainly. I embalmed the body of a lady once in the fall, and the body kept in a fine state of preservation all winter, and in the spring when the casket was opened the friends declared the corpse looked more beautiful in death than life. There was no sign of discoloration...."

MODERN EMBALMING

"How do you embalm now; what chemicals are used?"

"Oh, there are a number of processes. Dr. Chaussier had the body thoroughly emptied and washed in water and kept it saturated in corrosive sublimate. The salt gradually combines with the flesh, gives it firmness and prevents decay, and in process of time the flesh becomes as hard as wood.

GOUNAL'S PROCESS

"There is another method known as Gounal's. He injected the veins with a concentrated solution of sulphate of alumina and Dr. Ure used a solution of chloride of mercury and wood vinegar. M. Falconi recommended sulphate of zinc prepared with different degrees of strength. An injection of a gallon would preserve a body. Most undertakers today use what is known to the trade as Clarke's preparation, and zinc largely enters into this.

DURING THE WAR

There were several processes invented, some of which kept bodies tolerably well for quite a space of time. One consisted of injecting a strong solution of creosote or carbolic acid into the veins and arteries and sometimes removing the contents of the abdominal viscera. A strong solution of alum and sugar of lead was used, and sometimes chloride or sulphate of zinc. One of the latest plans I have seen is to inject with carbolic acid and camphor dissolved in petroleum and colored with vermilion.

"What is your method to inject the arteries?"

"Well, no. I inject the nasal parts, and should inject the veins, as I believe that when death ensures the arteries contain no blood except perhaps a little venous, while the veins are surcharged with dark blood. It is not necessary to remove the brain and viscera. I suppose in the case of General Grant it would have been better to have removed and cleaned the entrails, but possibly there were objections made [by the family.] However that is a matter I do not wish to criticise."...

"Embalming is then, by no means a lost art?"

"Not at all. There is hardly an undertaker in any of our large cities that has not at some time or other been called upon to perform the process, of course with a greater or less degree of success; but if the venous blood is drawn off, the viscera removed and the latent heat drawn off and pure injections used, there is no reason why success should not be complete. I recollect once in warm weather of embalming the body of a young lady who died of typhoid fever. The body was sent by rail and boat seven hundred miles, and, arriving at its destination, was in a fine state of preservation. So that the embalming process is a fixed fact, and then, I think, too, it's the coming plan, and will go into more general use than at present. It is a beautiful idea to preserve the lineaments and features of our friends, so that even in death, they still seem to be with us, though motionless and silent."

The Cincinnati [OH] Enquirer 3 August 1885: p. 8 OHIO

A GRUESOME INVENTION

One of the most interesting patents in the mortuary lines is the invention of a citizen of Canandaigua, N.Y. It is a process for preserving the ashes of the dead, and it is designed to do away with some of the prejudices against cremation. The ashes of the late lamented, as they come from the crematory, are to be mixed with silicate of soda and formed into a paste. This paste is molded into the shape of a bust or statuette of the defunct. If preferred, it may be made into a paper weight. However fashioned it serves to remind the bereaved of the dear departed. To an heir to a large estate such a memorial would be most interesting. The inventor makes the additional suggestion that the statuette or bust might be electro-plated with copper, silver or gold for the sake of decorative effect.

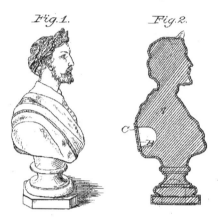

(No Model.)   E. C. TOWNSEND.
Urn for the Reception of the Ashes of the Dead.
No. 232,782.   Patented Sept. 28, 1880.

Fig.1.   Fig.2.

Patent drawing of Urn for the Reception of the Ashes of the Dead, 1880.

Another inventor has devised a method of preserving the bodies of the dead by plating them with silver or gold. His idea is to embalm the corpse in the customary manner, and then place it in a chemical bath, depositing the metal upon it by electricity in the ordinary fashion. Nickel, of course, would be good enough for persons of moderate means.

More practicable would seem to be a scheme for desiccating bodies by a process that is guaranteed to reduce them to absolute dryness and about one third of their original weight. The bodies thus mummified are to be placed in a mausoleum with compartments like those of a safety deposit vault. These compartments could be hired in sets of suites of sepulchers, each of them having an outer door of iron and an inner door of glass, so that the owner of a compartment could at any time obtain a view of his defunct relatives by the use of his private key. A system of electric alarms would give notice in case of any person prematurely desiccated should come to life.

The Cincinnati [OH] Enquirer 21 June 1896: p. 25

Of course the old ways died hard. There are a number of stories of persons dying at sea being brought home in a barrel of spirits, hence the phrase: "tapping the Admiral," referring to the tale that sailors drank dry the barrel of brandy in which Admiral Horatio Nelson was being transported back to England.

EMBALMED IN WHISKY

Kentucky Man to Be Buried in a Tank of Old Bourbon

Charles Bramlett, aged 80 years, died the other day. He owned several plantations in Harrison county and had been a very prosperous man all his life. At a low estimate he was worth $100,000. He was peculiar in nothing but his ideas of his own burial. He was a great reader, and perhaps drew his notions of his own interment from the histories of ancient Egypt.

About 15 years ago he hired a skillful stonemason to make him a sarcophagus of Kentucky blue limestone, which is much more durable than the hardest marble. At the same time he bought a barrel of the best old bourbon the state could produce and ordered that at his death the whisky should be poured upon his body after it was placed in the stone coffin. The sarcophagus was then to be hermetically sealed and placed in a grave near his residence.

All his directions have been followed to the letter. It took a number of strong horses to carry his body in its heavy receptacle to the grave already waiting for it. One cannot but think of the ages to come when this singular coffin shall be unearthed and the remains exposed to the gaze of wondering men. The tombs found recently in Egypt will not be more curious, even if they are more elaborately carved.

Bramlett was a constant imbiber of apple brandy and never left his house without a flask full in his pocket. His body was almost ready for spontaneous combustion before his death, and yet none ever saw him too much intoxicated to attend to business and to talk sensibly on any and all subjects.

Morning Star [Rockford, IL] 2 February 1897: p. 4 KENTUCKY

Conveying corpses in casks of spirits occasionally led to some embarrassing moments.

Pakenham Preserved in Rum

A strange story comes from Chester county, in this state. It is said that the body of Gen. [Edward] Pakenham, who commanded the British in the attack on New Orleans in the War of 1812, is buried in that county and his grave has been found. The general's body was said to have been placed in a cask of rum and sent to England. On its arrival there, it was through mistake, not even opened, but shipped again, this time to Charleston. Reaching this city it was sent to McMillen, who kept a general stock of groceries and liquors. There a spigot was placed in the barrel and the boys who had returned from the war would congregate around the store, take large potations of the good old Jamaica rum and tell their exploits in the war.

After the rum was exhausted the head of the cask was knocked out and the body of a man was found therein. The news spread like wildfire and the boys gathered to inspect the body. Several of them had been to New Orleans and had seen Gen. Pakenham, and at once identified it as being no less a corpse than that of the general. The body was enclosed in a coffin and buried near the store. Mr. Austin now owns the property. He lives a few miles from Rossville, Chester county. Until recently there were still living some of those who helped to drink the rum and who identified the body. Charleston Cor. *New York Tribune.*

The Topeka [KS] Daily Capital 31 January 1888: p. 7 PENNSYLVANIA

Even with advanced embalming techniques, there was still a call for cosmetic treatment of the dead.

PAINTING DEAD FACES.

The Strange Occupation of a Metropolitan Barber.

[*New York World.*]

"Painting the dead?" queried a *World* reporter, astonished at the remark of a down town barber, as the scribe settled himself in a chair for a shave.

"I mean touching up the faces of the dead with water-color paints to make them look natural. Never heard of it? Raise your chin a little. I do such jobs in the most artistic style. You ought to see some of the dead men that I have painted. Razor dull, eh! No?"

"Why is it done?" asked the reporter.

"To make the faces look nice by concealing the discoloration that sets in shortly after death. Oh, I tell you I can fix 'em up nice," and the barber smiled grimly as he took the flattering unction to his soul and stropped his razor.

"Have you had any subjects lately?"

"Not very lately. A while ago I was called by a friend of mine, an undertaker, to touch up the discolored face of a dead man who had been brought all the way from California to be buried in Greenwood. Close shave? No? I went to the house where the corpse lay, ready with my box of paints and fine brushes, and a bottle of collodion. The undertaker was there, and he told me the friends of the deceased were wealthy. He had also told them that I was an artist in such work. Bay rum? Yes? Sit up in the chair, please. The body had been on the railroad for seven or eight days, and the face had become badly discolored—almost black. I looked doubtfully at that corpse, I tell you, but I said I would fix it up nicely. Your hair's long; better have it cut. No? I struck a bargain." "How much money did you ask?"

"Thirty dollars. Dandruff in your head; better have a sea foam. No? I had to give the undertaker a 'tip out of it, and get him to find out just when the corpse would be planted, for I knew that my work would not last longer than two or three hours at most. Just as soon as the paint gets dry the discoloration shows nearly as much as before the operation begins. I had the corpse all to myself in a room, and I frittered around it so that I could put the colors on about two hours before the coffin lid would be closed. I had also previously found out what the complexion of deceased was in life so that I could paint his face accordingly. I first rubbed the face with a wet sponge, applied the collodion, and next used the brushes and paints. I put a sort of a cream color all over the face and finished off by touching up the cheeks with a pink tint. I combed and brushed the hair smoothly and then had the undertaker's assistant put the lid of the casket on. You could see the face through the glass cover and the undertaker's man said it was a daisy job and would please the folks who saw it mightily. I surprised myself at the naturalness I had given to the face of that corpse. When I got all through the undertaker came and called in the relatives of deceased to see how the corpse looked."

The *Cincinnati [OH] Enquirer* 27 December 1884: p. 10 NEW YORK

As we will see in stories later in the book, some spirits had an ongoing interest in the fate of their dead bodies or were active participants in their funeral preparations. These mysterious spirits ordered their own coffins.

Spirit Calls Upon an Undertaker

About twelve years ago I was in the undertaker's business in a certain city of Georgia. I am deaf, so that any one has to talk in a high tone of voice for me to understand. At 3 a.m., on the 13th of September some one called me and said: "I want a coffin." I awoke instantly, lighted a lamp and began to dress. My wife asked what was the matter, and I told her that some one had called for a coffin. She said that she had not heard any call. I went out into the street. The moon was shining brightly there was no one in sight. I then went around to the store, and still did not find any one, and went back to bed. Along toward noon, old man Joseph S. and four or five of his relatives, all young men, came to the store. Joe said he wanted a coffin for his little boy. I got it out and we agreed upon the price, and I then began to trim the coffin. Joe went out and I asked one of the young men at what time the boy had died. He said 3 o'clock this morning. Had he ever been in my store? No; but he saw a man buried in a coffin that came from here last week. "Well," I said, "he came and knocked on the door and waked me up at 3 this morning and said he wanted a coffin." Now my wife, who had good ears and was very easily waked, heard nothing.

On the 1st of October I was called again at 4 a.m. in the same way, my wife hearing nothing. I got up again and went to the store and found no one. At 8 o'clock Dr. Y. called and ordered a coffin for Mrs. E., saying that she had died at 4 o'clock. Thoughtlessly I spoke of these two calls and there was considerable talk and the spirits of those who died afterward stopped calling.

St Paul [MN] Daily Globe 12 August 1889: p. 3 GEORGIA

NOTE: The sounds of making a coffin: sawing, planing, and nailing were regarded as omens of death in the folklore of the British Isles and of Germany. According to folklore, speaking about something advantageous, such as the calls for coffins, causes it to be lost.

After the Civil War, the undertaking trade became more concerned with the elegance and expense of the funeral appointments, as these next two stories show. I wonder if any of the miniature tombstone models survive?

AN ARTISTIC UNDERTAKER

The Element of Uncanniness Eliminated in His Pretty Shop.

The most artistic undertaker's shop in New York is on Eighth avenue. Most undertakers are content with one fine casket under a glass case for their show window display, with perhaps an impressive velvet curtain as a background. But this Eighth avenue man has what might be called a "dressy" window. He has all the newest ideas for making undertaking and its trappings less uncanny in their aspects than formerly.

For this purpose he has filled his immense corner show windows with a quantity of palm trees—not the real, but the artificial sort—high and imposing, with drooping spiked leaves and all the melancholy of the willow, with a certain modern style of their own as well as a suggestion of tropical warmth. Beneath these palms he has carelessly scattered a number of caskets of different colors, sizes and finishes.

For the frivolous, there are shades of violet velvet from faint lilac to deepest purple and the very latest things in embossed cloths and fruity interior decorations. Then there are odd complicated arrangements opening with springs like folding beds and metal caskets with locks and keys of heavy and substantial make. Beneath the palms these are displayed with as much careful grace of arrangement as regards shade as though they were park benches.

But the daintiest touch is given by the tombstone models, miniature replicas of beautiful designs in monuments. Time was when one selected a tombstone from a book of cold black and white designs, but here you can see the styles, gay little arched effects and tiny angels showing the color and general effect of the tombstone when finished. They are small, for the tall, sky piercing shafts in the samples measure no more than two feet. Little girls wander in now and then to try and buy them for their dolls, but they are intended solely for undertaker's bric-a-brac. *New York Sun.*

Irish American Weekly [New York, NY] 15 June 1901: p. 6 NEW YORK

ART AND UPHOLSTERY IN COFFINS
IN AN UNDERTAKER'S SHOP

The establishment designed to supply the needs of those who are in need of nothing which the reporter visited is one of the largest in the city. The visitor passes through plate glass doors into a spacious and extended *salon*. From the ceiling depend at intervals six handsome gasolieres of silver and crystal; along the floor is a broad central aisle formed of inlaid woods, the rest of the space being handsomely carpeted. Near the entrances before the window stand one or two burial cases of superior finish....

To the left is seen a superb open casket, enshrined in a large plate glass case. It is covered with black velvet, and about the sides hang graceful festoons of velvet drapery held in place by chenille and gimp tassels, and edged by a chenille fringe in tufts as soft and rich as that which bedecks Mme. HautTon's brocade velvet wrap when she drives in splendor in the Park. The raised lid is stuffed and tufted in small diamond-shaped puffs, studded with tiny white satin buttons, like split peas in shape, and edged around with double rose quillings of white satin ribbon. A pillow cut in singular form, a deep notch being left for the head, is trimmed to match, and woos to a repose "silken, hushed and chaste."

ELABORATE BURIAL CASES

On either side of the *salon* are glass enclosed rows of less showy burial cases, grimly closed. Some are covered with heavy black cloth, relieved by huge twisted cable cords of silk; others have velvet moldings enclosing panels. Some have ornaments of acorns, chenille or gimp. These caskets vary in price as well as size—ranging from $50 to $200.

The old style coffin is nearly obsolete, and only used by eccentric persons under the domination of old school philosophy which rejects newfangled notions. The proprietor said that the most expensive casket ever ordered of him was for the body of a woman who before she died was in possession of a fortune of eleven millions. It cost $1,100 and the hearse containing it and her was drawn by six horses to the grave, followed by seventy-five carriages. To accord with such regal display there are stored in the burglar proof safe of the warehouse solid gold plates upon which inscriptions can be engraved for the modest consideration of $200. Solid silver costs only $20.

There are caskets for little children, of snow-white cloth, plush or velvet, of daintiest form and finish. They look as if they had been formed by nature to enclose the pure, unsullied clay, and had not been manufactured by the hands of men all defiled by the grime and dust of life's workshop. In the matter of children's caskets the fond fancy of parental love has demanded everything. Nothing can be too fair, too bright or too sumptuous to enclose the precious form, yet warm from the mother's clasp, hardly yet free from the detaining pressure of her sheltering arms.

Samples of exquisite materials and tints are shown—pale pearl, snow, cream and ivory white, baby blue, tender, pathetic grave heliotrope, lavender, pansy, violet, primrose and old gold—from which may be selected the covering for the last cradle love can supply.

In the rear of the store was seen a rest or support, upon which small caskets are placed during the funeral rites, a pedestal covered by fine heavy white cloth. Two columns rising from the lower support the upper slab. These columns are made in tufted white satin, the upholstery being most artistically managed. The moldings are in cloth; from the top falls snow white chenille fringe. Between the columns is hung a floating Parian angel. The whole arrangement constituted an ideal object to replace the old-time unsightly funeral rests or a commonplace table. No charge is made for the use of this artistic accessory to the funeral rites. It forms part of the furnishings which those who take pride in their calling deem requisite for successful effects.

Even the *salon* before described may be used for funeral services free of cost, the announcement of the place being considered sufficient recompense from a business point of view. The convenience to families, a member of which has died at a hotel, boarding house or flat, accessible only by elevators or narrow staircases, is one not to be overlooked....

The custom of private funerals is also on the increase—that is the burial service is performed at one time, the interment takes place at another. In some instances (for originality and individuality sometimes step over the funeral director's directions) the body is not placed in its burial case, but lies upon a couch, sometimes gracefully canopied. In one case, that of a young lady, the corpse, beautifully robed in lace and decked with roses was placed upon a lounge as if cosily reclining among its pillows. Everything was arranged to exclude the conventional symbols of death; it was like a reception given in honor of the "sleeping Princess" of an olden fairy tale. Music and memorial services of an unritualistic sort occupied the time, which was after gaslight. This has the advantage of a private leave-taking by the family, avoiding the exposure of sorrow's sacred anguish to a crowd often only curious if not callous. To quote the consoling words of the reporter's courteous cicerone among post-mortem mysteries: "Everything is done nowadays to make death pleasant." "To the survivors!" one may add, *sotto voce*.
The New York Herald 11 May 1884: p. 8 NEW YORK

The same accusations of overcharging, gouging and the encouragement of extravagance have bedeviled undertakers probably since the embalmers of ancient Egypt set up shop. When certain funeral professionals started offering all-inclusive, cut-rate funerals, undertaker wars broke out with each side hurling bitter charges of racketeering and price-fixing at the other.

BARGAIN COUNTER BURIALS IN BALTIMORE

Baltimore, Feb. 24. For the first time in the history of the world complete funerals have been put on the bargain counter.

An up-to-date Baltimore funeral can now be purchased, ready made, including five rubber-tired carriages, a massive hearse with black horses, a mahogany casket with silver handles, silver name-plate suitably engraved, a fine burial suit or slumber robe, grave dug to order according to plans and specifications, warranted embalming, correct public advertising, rugs, chairs, pedestals, candles, silver and gold crucifixes, necessary draperies and six pairs of white gloves, also the operations necessary to the deceased's final toilet such as washing, dressing and shaving, and one large bunch of crepe for the front door—all for the insignificant sum of $75.

The firm which advertises this particular bargain combination adds; "Let competition try to match it! They will either charge you more, or give you a funeral that is not complete!"

This unprecedented rivalry has also found expression in huge coffins, which serve as signs, grewsome appeals on hundreds of billboards and glaring placards all over the city, which read: "Try our funerals. You will never use any other."

The undertakers who refuse to adopt these modern methods are speechless with indignation. The up-to-daters are jubilant because they are getting the business.

The Spokane [WA] Press 24 February 1908: p. 2 MARYLAND

The tradition of post-burial feasts—funeral baked meats—is found in the remnants of food and drink found in graves thousands of years old. It may have begun with the idea of placating hungry ghosts, but by the nineteenth century it had evolved into a rite of drowning one's sorrows and reassuring the mourners that they were still alive. A cluster of saloons sprang up outside Bellefontaine and Calvary cemeteries near St. Louis, Missouri to serve mourners thirsty for life.

CEMETERY GATE INNS
Where St. Louis Funeral Parties Assemble to Feast After the Sad Journey.

Doctors, undertakers and florists are not the only persons who prosper on death. The more funerals the more business for half a dozen saloons about the very gates of Bellefontaine and Calvary cemeteries. After dark the saloons might as well close their doors, for the amount of custom they get, but while funeral attendants are being driven back along the dusty, wide road to the city the cemetery saloon keepers reap their harvest. There is keen competition among them, and all sort of signs are resorted to for attracting the attention of the thirsty or hungry mourners who have just buried their dead relatives or friends. Each saloon has carriage sheds and hitching posts for horses, and each has a more or less pretentious waiting-room, where refreshments, lunches and all sort of drinks are sold, just as in any wine-room downtown. Several of these rooms are large enough to accommodate a mass meeting, and they are so crowded with little square tables and chairs that locomotion at times is difficult when the chairs are occupied and the tables surrounded by hungry and thirsty people.

To many of these people time is not the only great assuager of grief. They find it in food and drink. The distance of the cemeteries from the city, which is itself a city of magnificent distances, and the presence of the saloons, with their commodious waiting-rooms, have led to the origin of a very peculiar custom—the giving of funeral feasts. In England there is an old custom of serving a funeral dinner to the mourners and attendants after the funeral, and just before the will of the deceased is to be read. These are sometimes very pretentious banquets, but the St. Louis funeral feeds are different. When the earth has closed on the casket and the new mound is spade-shaped in Bellefontaine or Calvary, the long strings of carriages begin to break and empty their occupants at some of the wayside saloons.

In some cases the entire procession of carriages at a funeral proceeds to one of the saloons, the occupants alight and are entertained at the expense of the chief mourner, the husband probably, who has just buried his wife or the son, who has consigned a parent or brother or sister to a last resting place. Lunch is ordered for the entire company, seated at the little tables, and drinks are served those who desire them. White-aproned waiters do the serving, and generally the eating and drinking is done in silence, out of respect to the feeling of the host, or to the memory of the dead.

The convenience of these saloons at the cemetery gates can be appreciated best by the people who have gone the greatest distance. A funeral from anywhere south of Chouteau avenue would probably be more than three hours in reaching Calvary or Bellefontaine, and, if started at noon, it would be considerably after dark before the people could be at their own homes again if they stuck to the carriages. These people were responsible for the start of the funeral lunch in St. Louis.

Competition between the cemetery saloon keepers is keen, consequently they are compelled to give good service at moderate prices, and several have resorted to the expedient of serving a free lunch at all hours of the day, patrons being charged only for their drinks, each being expected to spend a minimum of 15 cents in the place. Here, at 7000 North, five and one-half miles from the city's dividing line "Hot Lunch All Day" signs can be seen, and the lunch is as good as that put up in the average saloon downtown. Nearly opposite the gate of Calvary there is one man who is a florist, sells grass seeds, cares for lots in the cemetery, and conducts a coffee saloon, where hot coffee and sandwiches are dispensed. His coffee saloon has purple decorations, the chandeliers are hung in purple and the flower pots are covered with purple paper. Purple is considered a second mourning color.

In the saloon waiting-rooms, where the funeral lunches and drinks are served, the waiters appear to have been selected for their especial fitness for scenes of mourning. As a rule their faces are long and their appearance most solemn. They wear black coats and black cravats, not the white so much affected by their brothers downtown, and many have rubber heels to their shoes and move noiselessly as they take the orders and serve the patrons of the place. Remove the aprons and the wearers would make excellent mourners for a funeral, such is the force of habit and environment. Even the very bartenders seem imbued with the idea of death and mourning, and in these cemetery saloons there is probably less levity than in any similar resorts in the world. The air seems heavy, and there is seldom loud or boisterous talk, and generally no talk at all.

No matter what the patrons may be in the saloons downtown, they are quiet and reserved in those at the cemetery gates, even when not in funeral parties and simply chance or holiday visitors to the "city of the dead." In a district so small in area and so thickly studded with saloons, constant police surveillance would be needed in any other part of town, but a blue coat is seldom seen in that neighborhood, and is not needed, for barroom fights and brawls are unknown.

People eat or drink, pay for what they get and soon go about their ways, for the surroundings seem to oppress them, and they have no desire to make merry almost in the very presence of the dead. Whether it is the nearness to the dead or simply the solemn-visaged bartenders and waiters, the casual patrons generally find their wants assuaged with the first drink, and they spend no time in loitering about the places. *St. Louis Republic.*

Warren [MN] Sheaf 26 April 1900: p. 6 MISSOURI

Let us close this chapter with a muted interview with a New York undertaker who is a keen observer of human reactions to grief.

THE UNDERTAKERS
[New York Herald]

A *Herald* reporter called at the place of business of this gentleman who is so exceedingly popular with the ladies and so much in demand by the friends and relatives of the recently departed. It was about an hour before midnight. The lights were burning low, save one, which was blazing. Every now and then the burner gave out a shrill, queer sound. By the flaming light of the single jet the master of the store-room sat reading. Around him, in glass-cases, stood rows of coffins and caskets. They were all tufted, upholstered and embroidered.

"Is Mr. S__ in?" asked the reporter.

"I am Mr. S___," said the man, closing his book without noise."By chance I happened to be here tonight. Can I be of any assistance to you?" he continued, softly, after a pause. It was noticeable that Mr. S. spoke with a pause between every sentence. His face was placid, sad and sympathetic. No commercial smile betrayed pleasure upon seeing a customer, to whom it might be objectionable. Every line of his face was in keeping with the lines of grief, and his heavy black mustache suggested a sort of facial drapery rather than facial ornament. In answer to the question, the reporter said he should like to be shown the caskets.

"Certainly. This is something very choice in rosewood, nicely finished. This one the same, except the lining. Satin, you see. Die sudden, sir? 'Not sudden.' Oh. Well, there is comfort in that in a long illness. 'Not long illness,' did you say? Well, I was remarking that in a long illness the sufferings are very wearing on the afflicted family. This one? That's for a child of about sixteen. Didn't you say your wife? Excuse me. Have you sent for an undertaker? No? Then can I be of assistance? No one dead? Glad to hear it, glad to hear it. In the trade?'

"No. I am a reporter."

"Well, you looked so glum I thought you had lost somebody or something. Come over and sit down. It is very hard to tell what to think when people come in. They come so soon after death that they are not in black. Sometimes a man will come in sobbing, and tell me the whole story of his life, how he met his wife, her sickness and death; or it will be some young fellow, who will tell me what he wants quickly and be off. He will speak as promptly as though he was leaving an order for a pound of butter to be sent home.

QUEER PEOPLE

"No, there is no accounting for people," he continued, reflectively. "About five years ago a man came in weeping as though his heart was broken. His wife had just died. It was in the summertime, and the undertakers had to be quick. He told me the same old story. He had loved his wife as a girl, he had carried her books to school, he had gone hunting huckleberries, and all that sort of thing, and was completely broken-hearted—left alone in a big, strange world, with no one to love. You know the way them—excuse me, those—fellows will talk.

"Do you believe it," he continued, forgetting his pauses and betraying surprising animation for an undertaker, "that that fellow married within one year, and last month I buried his second child by his second wife? But some people are different. One day a man walked in here and said: 'I live at No. __ street. My wife died an hour ago. Can you attend to matters?' He looked at his watch in a most unconcerned way, shut it, lit a cigar, said something about good cigars at moderate prices being hard to get, and left. My partner—he is dead now—he said: 'That's the coolest I ever met.' I saw him at the house. His manner was just the same, except when he raised his dead wife's hand. I was surprised to see how tenderly and lovingly he did it. The servants told me that he had nursed her day and night through all her sickness. But that is not all; he died within two months; went mad with grief, the doctors said, and died in a fit. Just see. All the time I thought him so indifferent he was suffering intense anguish. A strange business, this! But what, after all, would people do without undertakers? When we come in the doctor has done his work and the trained nurse hers. What bad work we cover up! Often the family are either broken down with care and anxiety or hysterical with grief and excitement. Then they speak out. Dear me, we hear dreadful things—awful things; the doors to family closets are thrown wide open and we see the skeletons. But we are supposed to be blind, deaf and dumb. We must be quiet; move softly, as though the dead might hear us. If we made a noise it would distress the family. Yes, it is because we are so quiet people do not think we are about, and so it is we see and hear too much for their good and for our own."

San Francisco [CA] Chronicle 11 February 1886: p. 2 NEW YORK

5.

Crape:
Its Uses and Abuses

"There is crape on the door" is the opening line of many obituaries and stories of tragic deaths. Crape was the essential and unmistakable badge of the widow. Deep bands of crape on gown and veil marked the first and darkest stage of mourning. Many widows commented that the crape veil protected them from harsh public scrutiny. It hid their sorrow from an unfeeling world at a time when they were most vulnerable, and for that they were grateful.

Yet, the fabric seemed God's curse on widows. Crape, which might also be spelled "crepe," was rough, snagged easily, smelt bad, shed flakes of dye, stained hands and face, was saturated with poisonous chemicals, and the weight of the veil was substantial, putting pressure on the head and neck. Crape spotted easily with rain or tears and was constantly in need of refreshing. Its darkness depressed already despondent spirits and eyes dimmed with tears would be dimmed still further by the veil—an emblem of isolation, suggesting a walking quarantine.

Crape and mourning clothes had one other drawback: they were expensive.

CLARA BELLE ON MOURNING
New York, September 30, 1881.

No male mind can appreciate the great responsibility of being a widow in crape. None but widows wear crape lavishly, for even where mourning is assumed for a father or mother single bands of crape laid on other goods are sufficient, while some persons are satisfied with unobtrusive self-trimmings. Entire costumes of crape over silk used to be common for all degrees of bereavement, but the highest usage is now against it for all except widows. Crape is the easiest to rumple, the quickest to show dust, and altogether the hardest of all fabrics to wear neatly. When clad in it you never feel quite safe, and cannot hope at any time to experience the sweet consolation of knowing beyond a doubt that you are really and truly well-dressed. As to expense, mourning brings sorrow to the pocket-book, because common material in black betrays itself at a glance. Cotton can not by any art now known to the dyer be made to take on a perfect, lusterless black. Therefore satisfactory mourning goods must be fine linen or silk....

The Pittsburg [PA] Dispatch 31 August 1890: p. 10

In other words, cheap mourning will not do.

Crape, usually made of silk, wool, or a combination of both, had a crinkled appearance, created by coating the fabric with a liquid glaze called sizing and then pressing it with hot irons to give it a crimped pattern like the folds of the brain. The best crape came from the mills of Norwich, England. It was stiff, uncomfortable to wear, and, it is said, had a smell to it. In 1868 the Rev. Henry Ward Beecher wrote: "The smell of crape is to me like the smell of a charnel-house." Although folklore held that it was unlucky to keep crape in the house once mourning was ended (a belief fostered, one suspects, by an international crape syndicate) there is a good deal of information in the press on how to maintain crape and restore faded mourning textiles. Mourning costume was so expensive that it is unlikely that crape really was discarded.

While much was written about the veil protecting the widow from intrusive glances and how widows shrank from the public's gaze, there were concerns about the effects of breathing through chemically treated fabric, the lack of sunlight, the stuffiness, and the sensory deprivation. While some progressive doctors recognized the perils of crape, it is interesting to note that most of them did not advocate the abolition of the veil, merely the substitution of the less toxic nun's veiling or silk gauze for crape.

The thick crape veil was condemned by lay persons and physicians alike:

People with weak eyes or lungs must not wear a heavy crape veil over the face. It is loaded with arsenic and is most dangerous to sight and breath.

Manners and Social Usages, Mary Elizabeth Wilson Sherwood, (New York: Harper & Brothers, 1887)

A human being absolutely concealed from all recognition, breathing over and over her own breath—a hideous mass of shapeless black, feeling its way with difficulty along the familiar streets—that is the true and correct mourner.... She must shut out of her house the light of heaven, and make it a stuffy darkness, at once sickening and perilous...

Fortunately, however, the *physicians* are getting courage to take the matter in hand. Thick black crape veils are, as everybody might have guessed, exceedingly dangerous. [Un]fortunately, they sometimes produce *horrid blotches on the face;* pimples, purple stains, all sorts of abominations. They also produce intolerable headache. And, accordingly, some of our most sensible and courageous physicians are beginning absolutely to forbid them. The milliners and dressmakers must invent something equally expensive, but less unwholesome; and we shall be very much astonished if they prove unequal to the occasion.

We are not speaking of mourning, but of "mourning"—the mere technical thing, the milliner-and-dressmaker thing; and we rejoice in the prospect of a change of fashion...It is fashionable, indeed, to die; but not, thank heaven, to go the length of committing suicide, even by the poison of crape veils.

The Laws of Life, A Family Health Journal, Volume 28, 1894

Others found the wearing of mourning to be objectionable for the attention it drew.

The number of people who find the wearing of crape or of any outward badge of unhappiness repugnant to their feelings increases yearly. The widow's weeds call the attention of every casual observer at a time when least of all she wishes a stranger to read her story in her attire or peer for a sight of the pale face under her veil...The regalia of heavy mourning makes a uniform by which she becomes a marked figure. It is not long since I knew of a woman's laying aside her sable garb after wearing it for two or three months only, simply because she felt the sacred privacy of her grief intolerably invaded by the conspicuousness of her clothes. She preferred to go up and down about her business in quiet, sober-colored frocks, which did no violence to her feelings and yet drew no eyes.

The Courier-Journal [Louisville, KY] 6 July 1890: p. 15

This widow felt that the mourning veil was not long for this world and points out several other logistical problems with the garment.

Tiring of Their Weeds

[*Chicago News*]

"I predict the extinction of the mourning veil..." said a handsome widow in the hearing of a *Daily News* reporter, as she unfastened the flowing cumbersome badge of grief and hung it wearily on her arm.

"Physicians, you know, have always cried out against the wearing of crape. They declare it to be one of the worst things possible for a grief stricken mind. The very weight of a heavy crape veil is enough to depress one. And," she added, dropping her voice confidentially, "I don't mind telling you they are the very worst things to manage....The first time I ventured out into a street car with my long veil settled it. I caught it in the door when I entered, and as I seated myself nearly jerked my bonnet off my head. The conductor released the veil, and as I prepared to gather it about me a fat woman put her foot through it, and a horrid young man opposite grinned....

"By far the most complete mourning effect is produced by a costume composed entirely of veiling. Really, it just makes a woman look as if she never could smile again."

Kansas City [MO] Times 16 October 1885: p. 4

Crape was rarely color-fast and bled in rain and humidity. Stains on the skin were a constant problem. The methods for cleaning the skin seemed to be just as toxic as the fabric itself.

TO REMOVE THE BLACK DYE LEFT ON THE SKIN FROM WEARING MOURNING IN WARM WEATHER.—Ladies that wear mourning in summer are much incommoded by the blackness it leaves on the arms and neck, and which cannot easily be taken off by mere soap and water. To have a remedy always at hand, keep on your washing stand a box or gallicup with a cover, containing a mixture, in equal portions, of cream of tartar and oxalic acid. Get at a druggist's half an ounce of each of these articles, and have them mixed and pounded together in a mortar. Put some of this mixture into a gallicup and moisten it slightly with a little water, to prevent its after awhile becoming too dry and hard; and cover it closely. To use it—wet the black stains on your skin all over with water, and then with your finger rub on a little of the mixture. Then *immediately* wash it off with water, and afterwards with soap and water. The black will thus entirely disappear.

This mixture (applied as above) will also remove ink and all other stains from the fingers, or from *white* clothes. It is still more speedily efficacious if applied with warm water. No family should be without it.... Keep this powder out of the way of children. If swallowed, it is a poison.

Godey's Magazine, Volume 38, Louis Antoine Godey,
Sarah Josepha Buell Hale, 1849

The later Victorians were mesmerized by "correct mourning;" filled with a near-constant anxiety about doing the wrong thing, of getting some detail wrong. This led to an obsessive interest in the minutiae of handkerchief borders, the width of crape trimmings, and the depth of the black edge around an envelope. Following these protocols reassured mourners that they could not be censured by society for failing in their duty to the dead. Such a failure to honor the dead by correct mourning might render one suspect in the eyes of society, as a person deficient in all proper human feeling.

Just as modern wedding websites and magazines of the Wedding Industrial Complex take a simple social ceremony and burden it with carloads of expensive "traditions" and checklists of garments and things to do, so it was with late Victorian mourning. Articles appeared in newspapers every few months giving the length of time and proper costume for each type of loss. The constant repetition in newspapers, magazines, and etiquette books suggests a heightened level of disquiet about "correct mourning." As we will see in this book, mourning protocols were satirized, but they were also followed.

Many of the articles on women's mourning note with irritation how little men must do to indicate their status as mourners. Here is an inch-by-inch guide. It is interesting to see the Astor men cited as setting the social standard for gentlemen's mourning garb.

MOURNING WEAR AND CUSTOMS
THE MAN OF FASHION
Mourning Styles for Society Gentlemen

How the Bombazine Band Should be Worn on the High Hat and the Derby—How Long It is Fashionable to be in Mourning—Jack Astor in Mourning Attire—the Necktie and the Gloves for Men Who Have Lost Someone Near and Dear to Them.

With the death of William Astor one of the first families in the land has retired from social life for a year or more, and it may interest the man of fashion to know how John Jacob Astor, the heir, appears in gentleman's mourning garb and how the remainder of the family will follow the dictates of society in this regard.

THE MOURING STYLE FOR HATBAND.

The band of fine bombazine comes within half an inch of the top of Mr. Astor's high hat, and that, it may be said, is de rigueur. For a year the band will be worn at this height, then it may be worn lower or removed altogether and replaced by the staid black ribbon and bow.

"It is almost impossible in this country," says an authority, "where there are no hereditary customs, to lay down exact laws, either as to the length of the period during which mourning should be worn or as to the extent to which it should be assumed. There is, however, a certain etiquette of mourning, which, while not as arbitrary as the French code (which declares a widow must don weeds for one year and six weeks exactly), is usually followed in this country, where most of the customs are borrowed from the English. It would be interesting in this connection to know how the arbiter of English fashion, the Prince of Wales, attires himself for the Duke of Clarence. His mourning is, of course, much modified by the exigencies of his position, but it is safe to assert that it is distinguished by that perfection of detail, that faultlessness of selection that shows the perfect gentleman.

"The laws governing the depth of the band on the hat have become mathematically exact, and it is the first article of attire to consider in this connection. For deep mourning for the day of the funeral, for church, for all occasions except business and traveling, the high hat is in style.

"For the widower the band of fine bombazine comes to within one-quarter of an inch from the top. For the father or mother one half an inch from the top. For brother or sister or grown child, three and one-half inches up from the brim, and for an aunt, uncle or collateral relation, three and one-half inches up from the brim.

The same rule holds good for the band worn for brother or sister, one year being the proper duration of deep mourning. For aunts, uncles, cousins and collateral relations the period varies from three to six months, according to the degree of intimacy and affection existing between the dead and bereaved.

In "complimentary" mourning, a ghastly term used to denote that worn for parents-in-law, the rule is the same as for the closer and truer kinship. The mourning for parents-in-law is, however, purely arbitrary and depends principally upon how much they leave. The bigger the bank account the deeper the mourning, especially for mothers-in-law. Any man, however, who honors his wife will show her deceased parents the same respect he would his own, and nothing could possibly appear in worse taste than to see a woman in all the trappings of woe, while her husband disregards the custom entirely.

For round topped derbys the band for wife and all the closer kin-ships must be as high as the shape permits. For the other ties of kindred it can be about half way to the top. The square topped derbys are regulated exactly as the high hats.

In deep mourning the rough cheviots, and any and all black goods, but more particularly the rough woolens, are in good taste. There should be no deviation from the rule of all black for one year; after that the band may be lowered and fancy trouserings in gray and black and goods with a mixture of these colors may be adopted.

Beau Brummel was once asked what was the distinguishing char-acteristic of a gentleman's attire and he replied: "Good linen, plenty of it, and country washing;" and good linen, plenty of it, and pure white is essential in mourning. Nothing is so suggestive of a cake walk as a black and white shirt and don't be deluded into considering it mourning. Handkerchiefs should also be pure white; the black bordered affairs, permissible to women, are abominations when carried by men. They are extremes and extremes are always vulgar. The man of taste is a conservative being and oversteps the boundaries in nothing.

For the first year ties should be all black and nowadays the "man in black" has a range of choice both in material and shape. A few years ago only gros grain silk was admissible, and this after a few wearings looked shiny and greasy; now, the soft crepe de chine, china silks and armures [wool or silk with a cobble pattern] are made up in the ever popular four-in-hand and puff shapes, the former being preferable for deep mourning, requiring no pin.

Jewelry, except what is absolutely necessary, is tabooed. A black silk watch guard is better form than a chain, and it is debatable whether the usual plain gold studs and sleeve buttons are better taste than the black ones, whether of onyx or enamel. For a widower there is something incongruous in the glitter of gold, and the black studs and sleeve buttons seem more consistent; but for heaven's sake don't wear a black jet or onyx watch chain, they make the gods weep. And, by the way, a velvet collar on the overcoat is not mourning, nor this garment made of brown and blue chinchilla, however dark; neither are black satin ties, nor a brown derby with a band on it, which last eyesore is not infrequent. It would be impossible in the limits of this article to enumerate the various solecisms of fashion even well-informed men commit in wearing mourning. Only a few general rules can be given and you do the rest.

It is, however, in the matter of gloves that men err most frequently. Most men hate a black glove, buy a pair for the funeral, wear them till worn out and then buy their favorite color. They must, however, in wearing the deeper grades of mourning, wear only black gloves for one year, or go bare handed, a mechanic-like alternative, but far better than to don pumpkin-colored dogskins or even brown ones. As fashion, however, is great, so also is she merciful, and at the end of the year a very dark tan may be permitted, another instance of those unwritten laws which smooth the way of man....

In deep mourning, for three months at the very least, men should attend no theaters, banquets or festivities requiring a dress suit. After that time he may, if he cares to, and should, wear a black tie of dull silk. Satin is never mourning. His jewelry in full dress should be the white enamel so generally worn. There is something absolutely ghastly in seeing a man arrayed for a function with such grave-like suggestions as black jewelry about him.

The simple and beautifully pathetic mourning of the soldier and sailor, the black band on the coat sleeve, has something infinitely touching about it, and appeals to one's sense of the fitting more perhaps than the trailing weeds that women wear or the crow-like attire of men, but we have not as yet arrived at any such simple solution of the problem of black, and as the etiquette of mourning now stands it should be respected. It is, after all, a matter of sentiment, above all a matter of good feeling…. Above all, no man should be judged harshly for any deviation from the custom, even though he might show better taste by conforming to it. Many a sad heart throbs beneath a gay mantle and many a happy one has crape, so to speak, on its door bell; like the pathetic emblem waving at many a door, while the "wakers" make merry within.

Repository [Canton, OH] 30 July 1892: p. 12

Widows often felt judged on the depth of their mourning, fearing that they would be accused of not truly grieving for their husbands. This satirical piece suggests a similar fear for widowers.

Max Adler's Rivalry in Crape

I learn from a newspaper that "a Kansas widower was tarred and feathered the other day because he didn't wear deep enough mourning for his departed spouse." This reminds me of the contest that has been raging in our village between Brown and Jones. Both of them lost their wives on the same day, and after the funerals, Brown appeared again in public with three inches of crape on his high hat, while Jones only had two. Jones was so much afraid people would think he didn't mourn for his wife as deeply as Brown grieved for his that he added four inches of crape to his hat, whereupon Brown, apprehending that people would believe that he thought more lightly of his loss than Jones did of his, put eight inches of crape on his hat. Then Jones, determined not to be outdone as a mourner for the dear departed, put on so much more crape that it extended considerably above the top of his hat crown. Whereupon Brown became excited, and, cutting the crown from an old hat, he dovetailed it on his new one, and swathed it in crape to the summit. Jones was unwilling to display envy, but the memory of Mrs.

Jones was so sacred to him that he enveloped his hat in pasteboard four feet high and wrapped it in all the blackest crape he could buy. But Brown, feeling that his love for Mrs. Brown demanded energetic action, bought fifteen feet of stovepipe, jammed it down over his heat, bandaged it with 200 yards of crape, and once more appeared upon the street. Then Jones sent to the city and ordered a hat eighty feet high, craped six inches thick. It was sent home from the freight office on a dray, and the next morning Brown knocked off, married the widow Metcalf, and resumed business in a straw hat. Jones is having his mourning hat cut up into lengths and he hopes to be able to fill his bets with them if his side lost in the election

Reading [PA] Times 20 January 1875: p. 2

State mourning for Presidents Lincoln, Garfield, and McKinley was a crape-swathed affair, with whole buildings and city blocks shrouded in black fabric. President Polk's widow, despite her political differences, used some treasured crape to mourn. The article reinforces the idea that crape for a loved one was not necessarily discarded.

A Nashville correspondent writes as follows: "I learn that the widow of a former president, James K. Polk, who has been in sympathy with the Confederacy from the first, draped her house and gate on the day of the funeral obsequies of the lamented President Lincoln, with the crape that was used on the occasion of her husband's death, and has been treasured up by her as a sacred thing ever since. As she brought it out, with tears, she said, "she felt that it was due to the country, to herself, and to the memory of the president."

Daily State Sentinel [Indianapolis, IN] 29 April 1865: p. 2 TENNESSEE

Public mourning might be held for anyone from the President down to the local victim of an accident.

CRAPE ON TROLLEY CARS

"While reading of the numerous trolley accidents in Brooklyn," said Alderman Brandt, of Binghamton, "it occurred to me that Brooklyn lines would do well to adopt a unique custom, which, as far as I know, is peculiar to Binghamton car lines. In our city the trolleys occupy all the principal streets, but the motormen are very careful, and it is seldom that there is an accident. Last winter, however, a man was run down and killed...When that particular car appeared on the following day it was a sight to be seen. Long streamers of crape floated dismally out from the sides, black and white rosettes ornamented the space between the windows, and conductor and motorman wore badges of mourning. Not only that, but every car on that line was draped with black, and all the trolley cars in the city displayed in one way or another some sign of mourning..."

The Piqua [OH] Daily Call 7 August 1894: p. 3 NEW YORK

Physicians, social critics, and Spiritualists often railed against the gloom and expense of mourning. Some persons left instructions in their wills that their heirs should not don black.

> Mrs. Pretty: "Isn't it strange? Mrs. Beauti has not put on mourning for her husband?"
>
> Mr. P.: I understand that her last husband particularly requested that she should not."
>
> Mrs. P.: "The brute! I s'pose he knew how lovely she would look in black."

Evansville [IN] Courier and Press 3 October 1903: p. 6

Others, caught short by death, conveyed their wishes post-mortem, at a séance.

> After funeral services in the Episcopalian Church, in Eighty-second street, crowded with friends (among whom was the usual group of half a dozen ladies, who looked like pyramids of black crape...) we had rather a long journey to the grave-yard on the further end of Staten Island, called the Moravian Cemetery, where the remains of Mr. Newman were to be buried.
>
> [The narrator describes going to a séance after the funeral and seeing the ghost of Mr. Newman.]
>
> "Do you see me?" he asked in a whisper which all could hear. "Yes, William. It is indeed you. You now see that I was right in regard to this." "Do you see me well?" and he advanced so as to bring his face under stronger light. "Yes, in all my experience I have never seen a materialized face more distinctly." He held out his hand, and his warm, natural grasp pressed mine as I had pressed his in its icy coldness just about twelve hours before. "Have you any message for me to take?" I

asked. "Tell her I still live. Tell her I LIVE"—(the capitals representing the strength of the emphasis thrown on the word)....."Tell my wife not to wear those hideous black things. Tell her to wear this. [Shows white cloth.] And again: "Tell her not to look for me in the grave." And again: "Tell her not to weep for me—tell her not to weep for me."—the voice dying out as the form slowly disappeared.

That he was William H. Newman, not exactly as I was familiar with him in life, but as I had seen him beautiful in death six hours before, and through the preceding two days, with his parted white hair, his mustache and his white beard clipped to a rounded point, I positively affirm. Neither the medium nor any one present knew of my relations with him, nor my object in going to the séance...He shared my own opinions about the common practice of black crape mourning, and, as a spirit certainly gave emphatic practical expression to them.
The *Cincinnati [OH] Enquirer* 13 February 1887: p. 13 NEW YORK

When the late Mr. Newman advised his wife to wear white, he was in the vanguard of mourning reform. Several decades later, white mourning was still something of a novelty.

WHITE MOURNING GAINING FAVOR AS SYMBOL OF SORROW

Whether it be the weeds of woe dictated by the heart's agony over the loss of a beloved one, or the conventional mourning imposed by state or custom, the sartorial symbols of grief vary with times, places and people. Only in deepest, most lusterless black have we Americans of the nineteenth century been able to show to the world how great was the loss imposed upon us by the death of those dear to us.

Since the twentieth century came in there has been a noticeable tendency toward the lightening of the outward gloom, the sign of our inward grief. An increasing number of persons have protested against donning prescribed mourning, and a still larger number, while adhering in the main to the old order, have modified it so as to make their mourning less oppressive to the wearer and to all beholders...

Intrinsically, the hue of the garb has no significance other than convention gives. If one has courage one may refuse to accept the dictum of convention. When it was announced recently that Mrs. Madeline Force Astor, the youthful widow of John Jacob Astor [who went down with the *Titanic*], would wear white instead of black, a sigh of relief went up from many who shrink from the somber robes and suffer from their discomforts in warm weather. If one of such social standing could so break with conventions others would surely follow her example. The announcement did not mean that Mrs. Astor would not wear any black during her period of mourning. On ceremonial occasions she will doubtless conform to the prevailing custom and wear black to escape being conspicuous, but she will have a supply of white gowns, hats and accessories which will be easily distinguishable from white wear which is not mourning. All of the white garments worn by her will be guiltless of sheen or luster. Flowers and lace are taboo; white crepe and all kinds of dull, soft white materials are employed....

White in mourning millinery makes its appearance in the becoming "widow's cap..." and the all-white hat to be worn with white frocks, especially by the young girl. These white hats are trimmed sometimes with a band and bow of white crepe or with French crepe, which, of course, expresses a lesser degree of mourning than the regular English crepe.... White mourning veils are usually made of net with a white crepe border, the length of the veil and the width of the border indicating the period of mourning. Bands of white crepe on dull finished white gowns are correspondingly graduated....White mourning parasols are made of lusterless silk, plain or with tucks, and have dull finished white handles.

The San Francisco [CA] Call 7 July 1912: p. 32

Despite efforts to popularize white mourning, black for mourning remained the standard.

Tears of grief, as well as a rainy graveside service, could destroy expensive black crape. Much advice was given on how to renovate it.

TO REMOVE WATER STAINS FROM BLACK CRAPE.

When a drop of water falls on a black crape veil or collar, it leaves a conspicuous white mark. To obliterate this, spread the crape on a table (laying on it a large book or a paperweight to keep it steady), and place underneath the stain a piece of old black silk. With a large camel's-hair brush dipped in common ink go over the stain, and then wipe off the ink with a small piece of old soft silk. It will dry at once, and the white mark will be seen no more.

TO REMOVE STAINS FROM MOURNING DRESSES

Boil a handful of fig-leaves in two quarts of water until reduced to a pint. Bombazines, crape, cloth, &c., need only be rubbed with a sponge dipped in this liquor, and the stains will be instantly removed.

Enquire Within Upon Everything, (London, UK: Houlston and Sons,1903)

RENOVATING CRAPE

Information Obtained from a Successful Dyer and Cleaner.

To those who are in deep mourning it may be useful to know how to renovate crape...

Go into the kitchen, have the clothes boiler two-thirds full of boiling water, throw in five or ten cents' worth of gum Arabic, place a new sheet of heavy brown wrapping paper, doubled over the top, arrange your crape on this and await results. The fire in the range must be brisk so that the water will boil steadily while you are at work. Feel the crape and in a few minutes you will find it moist and sticky. Now with your two hands press out the creases, smoothing here and arranging there, so that all parts get an equal steaming and all turned-in and rumpled places are renewed. If your paper be too thick, try it single and take another piece when it becomes wet. I have succeeded best with it doubled, tripled and sometimes quadrupled. But it depends.

If it be trimming you are doing over, be particular about those creased and wrinkled places, the careful manipulation of your hands over the broad, smooth surface of the paper and the constant steam will make the material stiff, crisp and like new.

If it be a large piece of crape, as, for instance a veil, be careful to fold it so that the folds will not come immediately in the back or in any part of the headgear where they will look badly. I always do over my own crape, and as dampness takes all the stiffness out of it I find this process a great economy. Annie Milford Barton, in *Chicago Record.*

Perrysburg [OH] Journal 25 May 1895: p. 6

Renovate Crepe

Skimmed milk and water, with a bit of glue in it, made scalding hot, is excellent to restore old rusty black crepe; if well squeezed and pulled dry like muslin, it will look as well as, or better, than new.

Lexington [VA] Gazette 18 September 1912: p. 6

Mourning calicoes were dark-hued cotton prints for everyday wear. Some anonymous wit dubbed them "prints of darkness."

> Mourning calicoes may be washed repeatedly without losing color if they are first placed in boiling hot suds, left there until the water is lukewarm, and then washed in the usual way. Starch used in stiffening them should be mixed with an infusion of coffee rather than of clean water, and like other calicoes, they should be ironed on the wrong side.

San Francisco [CA] Bulletin 26 July 1873: p. 1

The expense of mourning clothing was a substantial one and was a frequent cause for complaint. One option was to rent a mourning outfit.

MOURNING GARB RENTED

Novel and Well Paying Business Built up By a Dealer in Old Clothes

Persons who are forced to undergo a sudden change of clothing because of the death of relatives and who haven't the ready money to buy outright an entire outfit of black for brief use have found a welcome assistance in their embarrassment in a man whose business is obscure, comparatively, and of recent origin, but who has an active trade, says the *New York Herald*.

The office of this man, in Eighth avenue, has a funereal aspect, filled as it is with heaps of sombre garments, but its proprietor is anything but grave. He was, until lately, a dealer in old clothes, and was dismayed at the amount of competition. Everybody seems to him to be dealing in that commodity.

A friend, short of cash, whose father died, borrowed a mourning outfit from him one day, paying a small sum for the loan. This transaction suggested to the dealer the idea of hiring out mourning dress as a business. He tried it and soon found his peculiar trade well patronized.

He began to read death notices in the newspapers and to send his agents to visit those whom he considered were not in extra good circumstances. Seven agents now act for him, being paid in commissions. Each has a regular circuit of streets marked out for his canvass.

Daily Journal and Journal and Tribune [Knoxville, TX] 16 August 1896: p. 6 NEW YORK

NOTE: Milliners also rented veils and bonnets and there was a thriving second-hand trade in mourning.

The hanging of crape on the door was a well-known and terrifying symbol for a death in the household. But there was also a practice—now lost—of hanging crape on the door either as a threat or as a "joke." Most recipients of such jokes were distinctly not amused.

Patent sketch showing method of attaching crape to a door, 1901.

STOLE CRAPE

From the Dead and Nailed It To the Door of the Bride Who Had Jilted Him.

Chicago, March 10. August Barth was fined $10 and costs for stealing crape from a house at Blackhawk and Mohawk streets, where a death had occurred. After stealing the crape, it is said, Barth nailed it to the door leading to the home of Mrs. Johanna Kleman, who was married recently.

Edward Muelhoeffer, an undertaker at 112 Claybourne avenue, found that some one had stolen the crape. By chance he passed the home of Mrs. Kleman, 85 Gardner street. Seeing his crape nailed on her door he investigated.

Barth had proposed marriage to Mrs. Kleman and was rejected.

The *Cincinnati [OH] Enquirer* 11 March 1905: p. 9 ILLINOIS

CRAPE ON THE DOOR

A Practical Joke on a Barber

How William Lawson Played It On Jake Rudolf and his Sweetheart.

An amusing sequel to the Barbers' Day celebration at the Centennial has just leaked out.

Jake Rudolf, a tonsorial artist whose place of business is opposite the St. Clair Hotel on Sixth street, was the victim of a rather ghastly practical joke. Jake is a jolly barber with lots of friends, and he told all his customers what a good time he intended to have on Barbers' Day. He was

ONE OF THE LEADING SPIRITS

Of the occasion and did the Exposition for all it was worth. William Lawson, son of F. H. Lawson, of West Sixth street, is one of Rudolf's customers. He knew all about the shop being closed, and he determined to have some fun at his barber's expense. When Jake and his men left the shop Lawson procured a liberal supply of black crape and just as the shades of night were falling he tied it on the knob of the shop-door. Pasted on the window in explanation of the crape were the mournful words, "Closed on account of the sudden death of the proprietor, Jake Rudolf." Hundreds of people on their way home from work stopped and read the inscription. Some of the barber's friends were

ASTOUNDED AT THE NEWS

Not realizing that the skillful hand of the practical joker had been at work. They went home and told their families and there were anxious inquiries as to the cause of the sudden taking off. Charley King, the druggist next door, was besieged with questions, but he knew no more about the real facts than any one else. Rudolf keeps bachelor's quarters over his shop, but the most vigorous pulling at the door-bell failed to elicit any response. One of the sorrowing friends took it for granted that Jake was really dead because there was crape on the door, and made no further investigation, although a second thought would have told him that it was Barbers' Day. He took upon himself to

INFORM A YOUNG LADY.

The prospective Mrs. Rudolf, of the sad event. She almost went into hysterics, and her family had a terrible time to calm her. The girl had not accompanied her intended to the Exposition, and the news of his sudden death gave her a shock which she did not get over for several days. Jake Rudolf was one of the liveliest men in town at that moment. He was smiling with the boys at the Centennial and acknowledges that he didn't get to his shop until the wee sma' hours of Tuesday morning. He saw the crape on the door and read the notice of his death, and for a few minutes thought he was somebody else, but the crape staid there till morning. The other barbers in town are having lots of fun with the late dead man, but Rudolf set 'em up to Lawson and his girl has been pacified.

The *Cincinnati [OH] Enquirer* 21 October 1888: p. 12 OHIO

A St. Louis husband, after a quarrel with his wife, took a singular revenge by putting crape on his door and announcing her death. This so enraged the lady that she immediately eloped with an affinity

Boston [MA] Traveler 29 August 1868: p. 4 MISSOURI

CREPE ON THE DOOR

Shocked Coppinger and He Died a Week After His Father's Demise

Alton, Ill., December 15. William H. Coppinger, the twenty-one-year-old son of the late Senator John W. Coppinger, died here to-day, one week after his father's death, from shock, caused by the sudden realization of his parent's demise.

Young Coppinger was studying for the Catholic priesthood at Niagara University, Buffalo, N.Y. While home on a visit he took a trip to St. Louis, and was summoned to Alton by telegraph. On arriving, and seeing crepe on the door, he

---

WHO TIED THAT CRAPE ON THE DOOR?

Mother, dear Mother, oh, don't look so sad,
Wipe the warm tears from your cheek,
Tell me, oh, tell me, can't I make you glad?
Why don't you look up and speak?
Why do you sigh like your poor heart would break?
Tell me, I beg and implore,
Look up and speak to your own darling boy,
Who tied that crape on the door?
Oh, who tied that crape on the door?

CHORUS—
Who tied that crape on the door?
Oh, who tied that crape on the door?
Look up, ask God, and the angels will say,
Death tied that crape on the door.

Come here, my boy, let me look in your face,
Then bow your dear little head,
Let me then fold you close in my embrace,
There lies your poor Papa, dead.
Look up and tell me you'll always love me,
Answer, I'll ask you no more,
Papa has left us, for God called him home.
Death tied that crape on the door!
Oh, Death tied that crape on the door!

Poems and Songs,
William Shakespeare Hays, 1895

fell into a swoon. The shock caused cerebral meningitis, from which he died....

The *Cincinnati [OH] Enquirer* 16 December 1900: p. 1 ILLINOIS

A little six-year-old maiden in Norwich last week was reprimanded by her father for something, and, being indignant thereat, went out and tied crape on the front door, remarking: "Now, every one will wonder, as they go by, who is dead in our house."

Commercial Advertiser [New York, NY] 27 November 1874: p. 1 CONNECTICUT

FATHER'S STRANGE ACT

His Daughter Married and He Put Crape on the Door

Long streamers of white crape hung from the door-knob of the little millinery store of Charles Simon of Milwaukee, lately, while below was a card bearing the inscription in German, which, translated, was an announcement of the death of Simon's daughter, Amanda.

It was intended as an expression of Simon's feeling toward his child, who was united in marriage to L. D. Goldberg, of Marion, Wis. Some months ago Goldberg's first wife died, and, while still in mourning for her, he met Miss Simon. It was a case of love at first sight on both sides, and a few weeks ago when the horseman made a proposal of marriage he was accepted. The betrothal was not to the liking of the girl's father, who strenuously opposed the match. But despite his objections, the couple were married.

When Simon heard of the wedding he was enraged beyond measure, and ordered his daughter to leave his door forever, and took her trunk from her room and placed it upon the sidewalk in front of the store. Later it was removed to the residence of neighbors, where Mr. and Mrs. Goldberg spent the afternoon, leaving last night for their future home in Marion. After putting the young woman's trunk in the street Simon visited an undertaking establishment and obtaining some crape pinned it upon the door.

This attracted a crowd, and when Simon saw that his actions were being watched by an interested knot of spectators, he delivered an address, in which he declared that his daughter was "dead to him." So violent were his demonstrations that his neighbors became alarmed at his actions and notified the police authorities, and two officers were detailed to watch him the remainder of the day.

Rock Island [IL] Daily Argus 29 June 1893: p. 8 WISCONSIN

Sometimes a thoughtful suicide would notify the world of his demise by crape.

TIED CRAPE

Outside His Window and Then Suicided

Cleveland, Ohio, February 15. Tired of life because his wife left him, Robert Russell, aged 70, shot himself this morning through the mouth, dying instantly. Before committing the deed he nailed a lath to his bedroom window and hung crape on it.

The *Cincinnati [OH] Enquirer* 16 February 1900: p. 1 OHIO

Before committing suicide Stephen Bowman, aged 72, of Vigo, O., hung crape on his door. On seeing it, his friends went to investigate and found the old man's body hanging by a rope.

Semi-weekly Interior Journal [Stanford, KY] 16 June 1896: p. 2 OHIO

Crape could also be used as a form of political protest.

HUNG CRAPE ON HIS DOOR

Threatened Riot in Kansas City Because of the Action of a Shoemaker Opposed to War

Kansas City, Mo., April 22. Thomas Collins, a shoemaker of Kansas City, objected to war between the United States and Spain, and when the announcement came that hostilities were to begin he closed his shop, hung crape on the door and posted this notice: "Closed in memory of a Christian nation that descends to the barbarity of war." In ten minutes a crowd gathered, the door was burst in, but just in time a platoon of police rushed in, rescued Collins and hurried him off to police headquarters.

Sun [Baltimore, MD] 23 April 1898: p. 6 MISSOURI

Today Brigadier General Gobin received a pathetic letter from the wife of a non-union workman who is employed in the Gilberton colliery of the Reading company, in which she tells of the treatment accorded her by strikers in that vicinity. Among other things, she said, rocks had been thrown through the windows at night, one of them nearly striking her sleeping child; the house damaged, and while she was outdoors one night a bullet was fired at her. She also said that crowds gathered around the house, hooted and jeered at her and the children and hung crape on the door.

The Scranton [PA] Tribune 9 August 1902: p. 1 PENNSYLVANIA

NOTE: This was the Anthracite Coal Strike of 1902, an action begun in May 1902 by the United Mine Workers of America, asking for higher wages, shorter workdays and recognition of the union. Non-union workers were seen as disloyal and sometimes threatened with violence. President Theodore Roosevelt appointed a commission to study the situation. Their intervention ended the strike in October 1902.

This last case of funeral symbols on the door is a genuine mystery.

FLOWERS

Are Left By a Stranger

At a Palatial Home Every Time There is a Death in Bellefontaine

A Mystery

Bellefontaine, Ohio, August 21. An affair extraordinary and unaccountable is furnishing an interesting topic for citizens of Bellefontaine. After the funeral of Mel Mitchell, son of Eugene Mitchell, who died after his return as a volunteer in the Second O.V.I., a black satin bow of crepe, yards in length, was found securely fastened to the door of his bedchamber, and over the crape a long, bony hand, cleverly sketched, in colored chalk, pointing upward

NO EXPLANATION

That some vandal or evil-disposed person might have planned this misapplied pleasantry was probable, and no attention was paid to the incident at that time. But one week later the death of a child was reported, and that evening a long, white satin bow was pinned to the front entrance of the beautiful Mitchell residence and above it 24 white roses bunched in clusters with blue satin ribbon hung suspended.

The family became worried and alarmed from the expensive floral displays and satin material, and it was plainly evident that no practical joke or child's play was meditated and all steps possible were taken to discover the originators of these unaccountable performances. But all to no avail.

PERSISTENT ATTENTIONS.

Every time a death is reported the most expensive satin folds and beautiful and rare flowers are to be found fastened to some entrance of the Mitchell palatial residence and interest in this city over the strange affairs is increasing daily.

Your correspondent called at the Mitchell residence this morning. Mrs. Mitchell said: "We are worried nearly to death over these unaccountable affairs. My mother, who is sick with anxiety and grief, is out of the city. We have no known enemies and are not superstitious.

A watch was instituted several weeks ago, but to no purpose. The gloomy and sad paraphernalia was on the door next morning in spite of two men watching the front entrance.

The *Cincinnati [OH] Enquirer* 22 August 1899: p. 1 OHIO

NOTE: Melville B. Mitchell [1871–1899], died of "consumption, after passing through a severe case of typhoid," contracted during his service during the Spanish-American War. He is buried in Bellefontaine City Cemetery. He left behind a five-year-old child, having divorced his wife several years previously. The house still stands, but it is scarcely "palatial," and looking at its size and location, it is difficult to see how the culprit was able to evade the watchers.

Even animals understood the symbolic value of crape, as these next two stories show.

A FUNEREAL ANIMAL

Force of Habit Makes a Horse Stop When He Sees Crape.

A Philadelphia resident claims to possess one of the best and most intelligent horses in the city. In speaking of the horse's good qualities, he said:

"I really believe that animal can reason and think, and I am sure that he possesses better sense and sounder judgment than some of his drivers. For years I sent him to all funerals in the neighborhood in a gratuitous way, his gentleness always placing him with the carriage in the head of the procession. His particular duty was to carry the officiating clergyman to the cemetery and return.

"If he attended one funeral in this way he has occupied the right in line in at least a score or two. He is getting old now, and I have refused to allow him for funeral service any longer, but, singular to relate, the force of habit has become second nature, for in driving about the city I find that he insists upon stopping in front of every house where he sees a piece of crape "fluttering from the doorpost."

Arkansas City [KS] Daily Traveler 5 December 1893: p. 3 PENNSYLVANIA

A GOAT ATE THE CRAPE

What Has Caused Hard Feeling Between the Walshes and the Travises.

[Philadelphia Press.]

John Walsh's billy-goat is making a great furor in his part of the Twenty-sixth Ward. Mr. Walsh lives at 111 Snyder avenue, and the goat has a home of his own in the back yard. The animal is at home at nights, but he wanders where he will in the day-time. His appetite is omnivorous, and he has even been known to devour a big piece of looking-glass with pleasure. The neighbors say that he gives them more trouble than their own children. He has just brought a series of bad actions to a climax by eating a big string of crape off Mrs. John Travis' bell-knob at 1105 Snyder avenue. Mrs. Travis, it is understood, is to enter suit against the owner of the billy-goat to obtain damages for the loss of the crape. Lawyers hold that Mr. Walsh is clearly liable in damages for the depredations of the goat, and that besides the value of the crape itself, Mrs. Travis may perhaps recover for the pain to her feelings caused by seeing the goat devour the crape under her own eyes.

AN AUDACIOUS GOAT.

The crape was hung out in memory of Mrs. Travis' son, a bright and good boy of nine years, who died on Friday. Neighbors who were looking at the billy-goat say that the sight of the crape gently swaying in the wind seemed to surprise the creature at first, then to attract him. The goat hopped over hesitatingly; then, apparently satisfied that there was no danger, he began gently to nibble the soft cloth. His appetite grew, as Shakespeare says, with what it fed on, and when he had eaten quite as far as he could reach with comfort he gave the remnant a tug and pulled it down from the bell-knob.

Mrs. Travis, attracted to the door by a gentle jingle of her bell, appeared sad and tearful, expecting to greet a sympathizing friend. It was only natural that after a shock of surprise her feelings should undergo a change as she saw Mr. Walsh's bill-goat calmly chewing the remnant of the crape on her doorstep.

She endeavored to chase the audacious goat away and save the rest of the crape. But though the goat hopped away gaily enough, he carried the crape with him and swallowed the last shreds just as a little girl shied out of a gateway and gave him a whack on the back with a broom-handle.

Mrs. Travis thinks that the crape was worth at least $5, and her lawyer in entering suit will feel justified in adding several hundred dollars more for the shock to Mrs. Travis' feelings. The defense of the claim will raise an interesting question. Mr. Walsh holds that the crape, having already fulfilled its purpose as a sign of mourning, has no appreciable value, except perhaps considered as food for the billy-goat. Besides, it will be contended the crape did not belong to Mrs. Travis at all, but was borrowed from a neighbor, and, therefore, Mrs. Travis has no claim on the billy-goat's owner.

DEFENDING THE GOAT

Mr. Walsh was not at home yesterday when the reporter called, but Mrs. Walsh said that she was sorry for what the billy-goat had done. "He is really a good goat," said she, "and wouldn't harm any body, although some people have taken a prejudice against him. But, then, it is hard for a goat to please everybody. I am very sorry for what has occurred and I have done all I could to alleviate Mrs. Travis' distress by attempting to buy her some new crape. I tried half a dozen stores, but could not get the material. Then my husband, who has been out of work for a long time, tried to square things by offering Mrs. Travis fifty cents. What more could we do? Besides, anyhow, Mrs. Schenk, 1103 Snyder avenue, owned the crape, and Mrs. Travis borrowed it from her."

Mrs. Schenk said that the crape did not belong to her either. She had borrowed it from a friend, whose name she could not recall, and had lent it to Mrs. Travis. Mrs. Travis herself did not have any thing more to say.

The goat which has made so much trouble was bought some two years ago by Mrs. Walsh's little boy Johnny from Farmer Isaac Brown, who has a truck farm down on Long Lane. It cost $2. It was a refractory creature from the beginning, and the only way that little Johnny could get it home was by carrying it. Mrs. Walsh does not intend to give up the billy-goat, and if a suit is brought she and her husband will fight it to the bitter end.

The Cincinnati [OH] Enquirer 17 July 1887: p. 12 PENNSYLVANIA

6.

Fashions for the Dead:
Life's Vanities Perpetuated in
the Costumes of the Grave

 The well-dressed corpse was above all, dressed. To be buried naked or naked under a winding sheet was at best indecorous and at worst heartless and unchristian.

BODY WAS BURIED WITHOUT COFFIN;
CITIZENS OBJECT

Fort Towson, Okla., Feb. 27. Local officers failed to establish the identity of the man who was killed here last Sunday afternoon by a Frisco railway train. After the inquest the body was wrapped in the overcoat worn by the man at the time he was killed, and the body was buried without a coffin. Citizens of Fort Towson objected to the manner in which the body was buried. A number of citizens went to the cemetery, exhumed the body, dressed it in good clothing and after placing it in a coffin reburied the body.

The only identifying mark found about the dead man's clothing were the initials "J.W.P." sewn into the overcoat.

The Daily Ardmoreite [Ardmore, OK] 28 February 1916: p. 6 OKLAHOMA

The British Parliament passed several "Burial In Woolen" Acts in the years 1666-1680, requiring that nearly all citizens be buried in a shroud of pure English wool. These shrouds were plain woolen sheets, wrapped around the corpse and tied in bunches at the head and foot, leaving a package that looked something like an ear of corn in the husk. This is probably the image we think of when we hear the word "shroud."

The term "shroud" had several different meanings in the United States. It could mean the old-fashioned wrapped cloth; it could refer to a special garment, rather like a night-gown, often sewn by the eventual corpse and kept until needed; or it might mean a specific burial suit—elegant or showy on the front, but backless for ease of putting onto a body with the edges tucked underneath. The dead were only rarely buried in their own clothing and even less often in someone else's clothing. There was a nineteenth-century superstition about interring the dead in the castoffs of the living—as they decayed, so would their former owner in a kind of sympathetic decomposition.

The scriptural "I was naked and you clothed me," could be applied to the dead as well as the living. There were religious committees where ladies gathered to sociably sew shrouds for the poor. For example, we find notices of the meetings of the "Ladies' Shroud Sewing Society" in Denver, Colorado in 1904–12, where the women of the synagogue made shrouds both to sell as a fund-raiser and for burying the poor.

I have heard it said that, because of high rates of death in childbirth, women made their own burial clothes as part of their wedding trousseaux. However, I have found no evidence of this practice in the popular press.

This undertaker explains about some of the funerary fancies requested by the dying. Extravagance in mortuary fashions extended, of course, to specially designed shrouds or burial robes.

QUEER SHROUDS

Chattanooga [TN] Times

"I have always maintained that every man ought to go to his own funeral dressed like a gentleman," said the undertaker with artistic tastes. "No matter how many hard knocks he has had to stand all through life; no matter if he has had to shift along with only one suit to his back, and that a hand-me-down; when the struggle is all over and done with, he ought, I say, to make his last appearance dressed in the fashion. The world owes every man at least one good suit of clothes, and if it doesn't pay its debt before his death it ought to see to it that the account is squared afterward.

"Women are more given to freak burial clothes than are men. Sentiment is largely responsible for their fantastic ideas. They have a special predilection for wedding gowns. I have known women who have been married thirty or forty years to cherish that one precious dress through all the ups and downs of life that they might wear it again on the last great occasion. These gowns look awfully old-fashioned and have a musty odor appropriately suggestive of the grave, after having been done up in lavender and tissue paper for so many years, but vanity no longer plays a part in the scheme of the old ladies' existence, and style to them is a small matter compared with the gratification of sentiment.

"'It brings good luck to be buried in wedding clothes,' one woman told me shortly before she died.

"'Good luck to whom?' I asked. 'How can that possibly benefit anybody? It certainly cannot be much of a mascot for the mourners, and the deceased is done with luck, both good and bad.'

"My answer puzzled her a good deal. 'I don't know for whom,' she said, 'but I do know that it brings good luck.'

"She evidently believed it, too, for when her time came she was laid away in a wedding outfit that was complete even to the slippers and bonnet. The incongruity of the headgear as an accessory to a burial toilet was enough to make an angel weep. It was an enormous, high crowned, white silk affair, fully fifty years old, and was fearfully unbecoming to her emaciated face, but her relatives had promised that she should wear it, and they were courageous enough to keep their word.

"I buried another woman not long ago dressed in a complete set of furs. Spite, not sentiment, was at the bottom of that exhibition of bad taste. The furs were very costly, and there had long been a bitter dispute among the female members of the old lady's family as to who should wear them after she was done with them. As the time of her departure drew near the quarrel over the prospective ownership waxed hotter. The old lady herself was sorely perplexed over the merits of the various claimants. Now she inclined toward this one, now toward that. Finally she concluded that since the coveted furs were bound to create discord so long as they were above ground, nobody should have them, but that she should settle the rivalry and spite the whole brood of scheming nieces and cousins by wearing the furs herself to the end of the chapter.

"One of the oddest whims I have ever been called upon to humor was that of the man who insisted on going to his grave wrapped in the traditional winding sheet. He sent for me several days before he died and explained his fancy. I misunderstood him at first. I thought he meant an ordinary white shroud. I could remember the time, away back in my childhood days, when it was the custom to clothe both men and women in those flowing white robes, and I took it that he was simply a little old-fashioned and wished a reversal to primitive customs. But he quickly corrected that impression.

"'I don't mean anything of the kind,' he said. 'I want to be buried in a sheet—a plain, everyday white sheet.'

"For once my curiosity got the better of my good manners.

"'I'll do as you ask, of course,' I said; 'but will you kindly tell me why you want to be dressed in that peculiar style?'

"The old fellow's answer fairly staggered me.

"'Because I'm going to do a good deal of haunting when I'm through with the flesh,' he said, 'and I'm going to take the sheet along with me, so there will be no delay about getting down to business. I'm going to leave lots of people behind who have been playing me mean tricks all their lives. I've never been able to get back at them in my present state, but just you wait till I get clear of these fetters, and if I don't haunt them good and hard and make them wish they'd done the square thing by me when they had a chance it won't be my fault.'

"I couldn't make out then, and I haven't been able to make out since, whether the old chap was downright crazy or just eccentric," concluded the undertaker. "Anyway, it was not my business to investigate his mental condition. My business was to bury him in a sheet so long as he asked me to and was willing to pay for it, and I performed my part of the transaction to the letter."

Current Literature, Volume 34, Edward Jewitt Wheeler, editor, 1903
TENNESSEE

There is a strange element of sexuality in articles about burial fashions. Women's burial robes, with their embellishments of lace and embroidery, are lovingly described in the same language used in the fashion magazines for wedding gowns or for tea gowns, informal robe-like garments designed for wearing with intimate friends, and as an aid to afternoon seductions. It was as if the dead were dressed to seduce Death Himself.

One of these, which the reporter saw, folded in its box, was of fine cream tinted cashmere, made like a matinee or tea gown, the front traversed by diagonal folds of satin the same shade and ruchings, quillings of the same extended from shoulders to knees, below which were plaited flounces. The sleeves were fully trimmed, and the robe was entirely ready for wear with fine full crepe lisse ruchings at throat and wrists. A carelessly knotted sash of ribbon confined the robe. This cost only $25.

The New York Herald 11 May 1884: p. 8 NEW YORK

The newspapers of the period often printed articles such as the following, about the prudent men and women who prepared their burial clothing in readiness for the Great Dissolution. One supposes that dusting around a shroud stored beneath the bed was a kind of domestic *memento mori*.

SHROUD

Kept Beneath Her Bed

By Woman Who Dies in New York at the Age of One Hundred and Seventeen Years.

New York, December 23. Cheerful to the last moment of consciousness, Mrs. Hannah Kosokopp, the oldest woman in New York and perhaps in the country, died to-day at the Home of the Daughters of Israel, 32 East One Hundred and Nineteenth street. She was said to be 117 years old.

Cheerfulness had been her secret of health and of long life. In the three and a half years she had been in the institution, Mrs. Kosokopp had not been ill, and had never made a complaint of any kind.

Mrs. Kosokopp was the most petted person in the house. Only a few days ago, on December 8, she celebrated her 117th birthday. She was born at Kovno, Russia, and remembered shaking hands with the Czar, grandfather of the present ruler of Russia. She also saw Napoleon, she said, when he invaded her country.

Sixty years ago she came to this country and made her home on the east side of this city.

"When I had been in New York a few years," she said not long ago, "I became sick. I thought I should die. While I was in bed I made with my own hands a shroud in which I said my body should be wrapped when prepared for burial. I still have the shroud, and keep it beneath my bed."

The shroud was still beneath her bed when she died, and she will be buried in it.

Cincinnati [OH] Enquirer 24 December 1914: p. 1 NEW YORK

THE SHROUD

Of Mrs. Mary Leonard Made By Her Own Hands Nearly Sixty Years Ago.

In the County of Roscommon, Ireland, nearly 60 years ago, Mrs. Mary Leonard knit and sewed with her own hands a shroud which was to envelope her form when her body was consigned to mother earth.

During this long period of years Mrs. Leonard has treasured the garment and her express wish, as old age steadily advanced, to those near and dear to her, was that she be buried in it.

The shroud was a simple pattern, made of brown goods and fashioned somewhat after sailor style. White braid nearly an inch wide securely covered the edges and on the bosom, with the same material, is inscribed the symbol of Christ, "I.H.S." Yesterday, at the age of 98 years, Mrs. Leonard died at St. Mary's Hospital, and the hope she had so long cherished was carried into execution....

Cincinnati [OH] Enquirer 18 February 1895: p. 8 OHIO

Like crape on the door, a shroud could be a threat.

T.S. Maguire, an undertaker of St. Paul, has been drafted and has taken with him to camp at Camp Wadsworth, S.C., a burial shroud he made for Kaiser Wilhelm. He confidently expects to take it along to the front and have it in his kit when he marches into Berlin.

The Bismarck [ND] Tribune 5 August 1918: p. 6 SOUTH CAROLINA

If a person did not make their own shroud, where did they purchase one? Undertakers kept them in stock. A dressmaker might make a shroud and a mourning dress at the same time.

FOR A SHROUD

A Modiste Sues Martin Link for Money Due Her for Making One.

Suit was brought before Squire Friend yesterday by Mrs. L. Miller of No. 13 Bank Street, against Martin Link , a section boss on the Big Four railroad, living on Nevada street, for $9. Mrs. Miller claims in her suit that when Link's wife died recently he employed her to make a shroud for the body and also a black dress for his little daughter. She further claims that she did as he requested and has asked him for her money on several occasions, but has been put off each time with a promise, until now she has concluded to bring suit for her money.

Cincinnati [OH] Enquirer 14 February 1892: p. 8 OHIO

This man seems to have purchased linen, which he would have given to a dressmaker to make up into a shroud.

From the *New Albany (Ind.) Ledger*

A Supposed Dead Woman Comes to Life.
Her Husband Purchases the Shroud and Returns to Find Her Alive in Bed.

This morning we were made acquainted with a few facts in relation to a singular affair which occurred in the West End a few days ago. It seems an elderly lady living in that part of the city has been sick for some months past, and a few days ago she fell into a stupor and was supposed to have died. Her husband, believing she had passed from this world, began to make the usual preparations for burial and with this end in view, came up to town and purchased the material to make the shroud. Upon his return home with his purchase he was astonished and horrified to find his wife, whom he had left for dead, not only alive, but sitting propped up in bed, looking better than she had for some months. As a matter of course he was agreeably surprised and lost no time in putting the linen he had brought for his wife's shroud in some secret hiding place to prevent her being painfully reminded of the fact that he had been in such haste to dispose of her body.

Cincinnati [OH] Enquirer 21 February 1868: p. 1 INDIANA

Shrouds were also made in factories, usually by young women seamstresses.

SEWING FOR THE DEAD

Girls Who make Good Wages and Are Contented in an Undertaker's Shop.

"Isn't it lovely?" asked a young sewing girl, holding up for inspection something of white satin and lace.

"We are crowded with work just now, so I brought this home to finish it to-night."

"You have a trousseau on hand, then? I suppose that fancy garment, whatever it may be, is for a bride."

The sewing girl opened wide her eyes. "We don't make no trousseau," said she. "Did you think I worked at a dressmaker's?"

"Yes? Aren't you with Mme. X.?"

"Not much! I left there a month ago. The madame gave me too much sass and too little pay. I'm in Y___'s undertaking establishment and am earning half as much again as I did at Mme. X___'s, who is the most awful crew in this city. The season is longer, too, though of course there ain't half the number of girls employed there I know that there were at madame's. When I worked there I was laid off reg'lar three months in the year, while four weeks is the longest that the girls at the undertaker's are idle. When there is a full supply of robes in stock they are put to making coffin linings, which most of 'em like because it isn't fussy work, though, for that matter, none of their work is half so fussy as what I had to bother with when I sewed for live people. Miss B___ (she is our forewoman) used to have the same place at a dressmaker's, and she says she has grown ten years younger since she went into the robe-making business, because she has so much less worry of mind. She sometimes used to have to keep her girls up till 12 o'clock Saturday night to finish a dress for some rich customer, and early Monday morning here would come the dress back again to be altered, and a sassy message along with it about its want of fit. Now, there ain't any particular fit about a burial robe as you can see by this; it is made only to go over the corpse. Miss B___ says it is a great comfort to her to know that them as wears 'em don't make no complaint, and in the main they are becoming, which can't be said of live dresses—I mean the dresses live people wear.

"To see them in their coffins you would think they were completely dressed, but really all their finery is on top. Even the men's solid looking black coats and smooth shirt fronts can go on and off without removing the corpse. What I am making is for a young girl who died yesterday, and will be buried to-morrow. She was to have been married next month, and her trousseau was begun at Mme. X___'s before I left there. She will look just as sweet in this robe I am making for her as she would have done in her wedding dress.

"Afraid of the coffins? Not after the first day. It would be a pity if we were, as our sewing room is at the end of the loft where piles upon piles of them are stowed away. We talk and laugh and sing, just as we did at Mme. X___'s, and Miss B___ is an awful lot nicer than the forewoman we had there, because, as I have already said, she isn't being constantly worried out of her life by fussy ladies; and, as it is piecework, she never has to scold the girls for loafing. She says that what she can't get used to is to have to go downstairs and take orders for robes for folks that still have breath in their bodies. Some people seem to be in an awful hurry to get their dead put underground.

When Miss B____ was downstairs today at noontime and the rest of us were eating lunch, one of the girls had her chair break down under her, and, as there was no other to be had, what did she do but go out and drag in a coffin to sit on! When we had finished our lunch we took and laid her out in it and covered her with a robe, and then we began to cry, and talk about the virtues of the deceased, and were having a real jolly wake, considering there was no candles, when in come the boss. We didn't know but we'd all be fired out for meddling with the coffins, but all he said was that it would be money in his pocket if we lazy loafers were all of us in our coffins, as our custom would pay him better than our work. The girl in the coffin—she's awfully cheeky— jumped up and told him it was playtime, as it was not yet half past 12, and then he said what was fun to us would be considered death by most folks and with that he went out. One of the girls said he was in a good humor because there was talk of the yellow fever coming here this summer, but that wasn't so. Undertakers ain't no more heartless than other men, and when it comes to paying their girls they ain't half such skins as some women." *New York Tribune.*

Huron Daily Huronite [Huron, SD] 16 January 1890: p. 3 NEW YORK

When I owned a vintage clothing store, I purchased a box lot which contained a pair of shiny brown lace-up shoes. Closer examination revealed that they were not made of leather, but of some brittle synthetic material and that, while they had normal laces, the backs of the shoes also laced. They were cardboard shoes for the dead—the heel laces made it easy to slip them onto a corpse's foot.

Shoes were an important part of a corpse's wardrobe. There were some ancient Christian beliefs relating to shoes being necessary to help the dead man walk the thorny path to Heaven or of shoes allowing the dead to face judgment on a sound footing. Some Native American tribes plaited special cornstalk slippers for corpses; Egyptian mummies were furnished with gilt papier-mache sandals; some Chinese women used to be buried in shoes with embroidered soles and a pearl on each toe to light the way to paradise. These dead men's shoes are not nearly so elegant.

SHOES FOR THE DEAD

A Novel Industry in Which Chicago Supplies the Whole World.

That there is nothing small about Chicago has been so frequently demonstrated as to need no reiteration, truthfully remarks the Chicago *Herald*. But that Chicago supplies an article in the production of which it has no rival in the world may be news to many readers. It is an article for which there will be a ceaseless demand so long as people die and are buried in the prevailing style. If cremation should become general, or if the Stanford idea of squeezing the remains of beloved relatives into symbolic figures should prevail, the article spoken of would, of course, become useless. To the present funeral, if it is carried out in the height of fashion, belongs a burial shoe. It is as necessary as any other part of the garments worn on the last journey by young or old of either sex.

The fact that the rigor mortis made the feet of dead persons so unwieldy as to necessitate a foot-gear several sizes too large for a long time painfully impressed a Joliet dressmaker, a Miss Loomis. She went to work and constructed a shoe which not only did away with clumsy leather encasements, but, in true feminine style, she brought her ingenuity to such a point that the corpse of a person may be buried in number 2s while the wearer in life required number 4s. Of course the invention was promptly patented, and in the course of time a company was incorporated which supplies two-thirds of all the manufacturers of and jobbers in funeral supplies throughout the United States, and sends the product of the Joliet dressmaker's inventive genius even across the ocean.

The invention is, like many others, so simple that the wonder is why burial shoes have not been made before there were patent offices. The shoe consists of knitted pieces of wool or silk, which are inserted at the heels and at the insteps, making it possible to cover the rigid "understanding" of dead persons not only with a snug fit but in becoming style. In a block on Dearborn street a dozen or fifteen girls are at work from morning till night of each working day to manufacture nothing but burial shoes of all sizes—from those for tiny babies to the ones for the oldest inhabitants. They are made in four colors—white, cream-colored, brown and black—and three grades—brocaded satin, quilted satin and felt. Of the latter, which is the cheapest grade, but three of the colors are being manufactured, the natural felt being a sort of cross between white and cream-color. The brown color is principally demanded for the funeral of Catholics, and white and cream-colored for babies and women. Material, as well as ornamentation, are of such a variety and style as—to use a business man's phrase—to suit the most fastidious. The firm turns out from fifty to a hundred pairs a day, and they are all taken rapidly, because burial shoes have, since the last year or two, become a necessary part of the outfit of the dead.

Patriot [Harrisburg, PA] 11 September 1888: p. 2 ILLINOIS

Jones: I say, Brown, do you known when a pair of boots are like a dead man?
Brown: Can't say that I do.
Jones: When they are mend-ed—men dead—see?
Brown: H'm very funny. Perhaps you know when a pair of shoes are like dead men?
Jones: I don't.
Brown: When their soles (souls) have departed, my boy.

The Day Book [Chicago, IL] 18 March 1912: p. 6

Not all aspects of the funerary business were profitable. Here a maker of shoes for the dead is "stiffed" by the living.

SHOES FOR THE DEAD

The Gruesome Trade Pursued by a Young Woman at Detroit.

Out in the eastern part of the city there is an establishment which announces the preservation of funeral flowers and immediately under it this sign is displayed:

SHOES FOR THE DEAD

A representative of the *Free Press*, mindful of the maxim "waiting for dead men's shoes," rapped at the door and was answered by an ancient woman smoking a pipe. She took this out of her shrunken jaws and saying she smoked for the toothache—though not a tooth was in sight—directed the way to the mortuary shoe dealer. It was up a winding stair. A pale young woman answered the rap.

"Yes, we make shoes for dead folks: here are some," and she took several pairs of black, shapeless-looking boots from a box on a chair which seemed to have more left in it.

They were crotchet shoes made to button up the back, and with the flimsiest of soles, and they had no shape and were made to fit any foot.

Seeing the representative of the *Free Press* examining them, the young woman said sharply:

"They're for comfort; they ain't for style. They're warm and snug if they don't look pretty. Mother and I wear them and we ain't dead, either."

The price was seventy-five cents a pair without ribbon bows. Cheap enough, and yet the young woman said trade was dull. The undertakers wouldn't patronize them, and a good many people buried their dead without shoes; others didn't pay for them.

"The very pair I have on," she said, "were returned for debt. The corpse's sister took them off at the last moment. The dead woman had worn them two days, and they knowing all the time they wouldn't pay for them." *Detroit Free Press.*

Jackson Sentinel [Maquoketa, IA] April 10, 1890: p. 3 MICHIGAN

The incomplete nature of burial dress is often mentioned in articles on funeral practices, as if it is some secret of the dismal trade. Let us finish the chapter with this tongue-in-cheek look at the practical reasons behind "sham burial suits."

SHAM BURIAL SUITS

Robbing the Grave of Valuable Raiment—Another Step Toward Economy in Funerals—How a Body May be Arrayed Without Waste of Wardrobe—A Real Masquerade of Death

Of late years the fashion in funeral wardrobes has materially changed. Where our ancestors used to be put to their last quiet bed in a plain shroud, their descendants make the same journey in full dress. In the case of a gentleman, a black coat and pantaloons, with a white vest, shirt and tie have been defined as the last tribute of decency he can pay to the social system from which he has departed. A lady is required to be attired in attire whose quality is generally decided by her dressers, but which is of a sober hue.

There are few men who would through choice wear a dickey over their breasts instead of a suit on their bodies. Yet the sham burial suits are nothing but dickeys. A *Sunday News* reporter saw one in an undertaker's window the other day, or rather he saw two. One was intended for a gentleman, and the other for a lady. They were enclosed in neat boxes with glass covers, and would have been quite pleasant to look at if it hadn't been for the coffins which formed a background to them, and the photograph alongside of an embalmer inspecting the corpse of a man who, if looks go for anything, must have been hanged for slaughtering three or four infant schools from a tub of chemicals through a garden hose. At first sight they seemed to be what they were evidently intended to represent. The reporter was examining them, when a rosy man, who had been telling a story to several cheerful gentlemen, who laughed heartily at it, called from his arm-chair in the doorway, "What do you think of them, eh?"

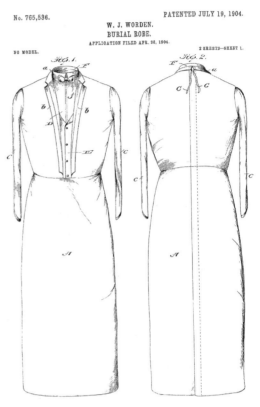

No. 765,536.

PATENTED JULY 19, 1904.

W. J. WORDEN.
BURIAL ROBE.
APPLICATION FILED APR. 28, 1904.

NO MODEL.

2 SHEETS—SHEET 1.

"They seem to be real nice," the reporter responded.

"Nice!" repeated the rosy man; "Why, they're just bang up. Look at 'em in here close to. How is that for high, eh? Only take that in."

And yanking what had seemed to be a black coat, vest, shirt, collar and tie complement from its case, he waved a fluttering rag over the reporter's head. The arrangement was simply a front, no longer than a waiter's jacket, and with tapes behind to tie it to the body. "Nobody ever sees the back of 'em," said the rosy man, "and half of the lid covers 'em up to the waist. So what's the use of

Patent sketch for a man's burial robe, 1904

buying a forty-dollar rig or so when you can get one of these for ten dollars, I want to know? Ain't the deceased loss enough without chucking his clothes in too, eh?"

The reporter admitted that, taking this view of the subject, the idea was certainly an admirable one. Encouraged by this endorsement, the rosy man sent a rosy boy, who was cracking peanuts and throwing the shells into an open casket, for a pint of beer and went into details. He had long noticed with pain that the poorest of people buried the best suits of clothes they could obtain with their dead. According to a computation he had made with great care, something over $3,000,000 was squandered annually in this way, literally thrown to the worms. This was very wrong. It was an outrage on the whole system of social economy. Somebody could wear those garments, and get more good out of them than the man or woman who had them on. Then why didn't they wear them?

They didn't wear them because they were "down on" shrouds, and couldn't bury the "diseased" with nothing at all on.

But the present improvement supplied a happy medium. It arrayed the body in a stylish garb wherever the body was seen. In the hidden recesses of the casket, where no eyes had access, it didn't matter in the least how it was dressed. One of these suits only cost from $5 to $15, according to its quality. Ladies' dresses, constructed on the same plan, rated according to the same schedule. The idea was a new one, but it had made a hit, and the sham suits were selling, to use the narrator's own picturesque figure of speech, "like hot cakes." The illusive garments were made in all styles to suit all tastes. One dress had lately been made for a young lady who desired to be buried in pink. Her family were going to sacrifice her best dress when this substitute was suggested to them.

"And her sister wore that dress to a ball last week," said the rosy man, triumphantly. "Simmy seen her in it, didn't you?"

Simmy set down the beer and responded in the affirmative. As the reporter prepared to depart he asked: "Are they patented?"

"You bet," replied the rosy man. "When you need one, let your folks give us a call, will you? Simmy, hand the young man a card."

Reading [PA] Eagle 6 November 1880: p. 7

7.

The Corpse Sat Up:
Wakes and Watches Gone Wrong

The dead must not be left alone. Evil spirits might reanimate the body; the Devil might try to claim his own; a cat leaping over the corpse would condemn it to a vampiric afterlife. A dead body might even rise in its shroud under the realistic and terrifying compulsion of rigor. No, a corpse could not be trusted.

While holding a wake, known as "waking the dead," was a token of respect and could be a religious practice, the custom may have also served to confirm that the person was actually lifeless. The literature is full of stories about persons declared dead who stubbornly refused to decay or who came back to life at a wake.

Some wakes involved prayers, or perhaps the recitation of the Rosary. Some traditions required that food or drink be consumed from or over the coffin. The corpse might be offered a drink. Stories were told, pipes smoked, or cards played.

The solitary vigil, as opposed to the riotous communal wake, could be a gruesome experience. Windows were often thrown open in the dead of winter to keep the corpse cool; embalming fluid was sometimes kept on hand to pour over or around the body. Despite the best precautions, decomposition might proceed rapidly, with its attendant vile liquids and insect infestations. And no matter how beloved the corpse had been in life, in the dark, in the quiet watches of the night, strange things could be imagined.

Many stories tell of life detected in a corpse at a wake and a happy ending. In others, there is a painful ambiguity.

THE CORPSE SAT UP

A Watcher's Grewsome Experience In the Room of a Dead Friend.

"I am not a believer in the supernatural," said a young man to a writer for *The Courier-Journal*, "but every time I see a copy of Wilkie

Collins' novel, 'The Woman in White,' I get the creeps, for it recalls one of the most awful experiences in my life. I boarded in the southern portion of the city, at the home of a widow, in whose family was an interesting youth about 16 years old. He and I were exceedingly fond of one another, perhaps from the fact that he was afflicted with epilepsy, and I was the only person about the house who understood how to relieve him and was able to handle him without his hurting himself while in convulsions. He did not live long after I knew him and died in my arms in one of his attacks. The incident I am speaking of occurred on one of the very coldest nights in January. The boy had died at noon, and the family sat up with the corpse until midnight, when I relieved them in the watch, requesting all to retire, as I loved the boy so well I felt it my duty to stay near him in death. An hour passed, and I picked up a copy of 'The Woman In White' to while away the somber watch. I drew near the fireplace and turned up the lamp a little higher, as the rest of the room was very dark, and a window was raised back of the corpse on the cooling board. After all had gone to bed the realization of the somber situation obtruded itself upon me, and as I perused the novel its contents were not calculated to reassure me. I thought about everything possible, and for the first time in my life I began to quake with fear.

"I was in such a condition of mind that the dropping of a pin would have been noted at once, and the creaking of a piece of furniture or the swaying of a shutter would have sent terror through my heart. In this overwrought state of mind I heard a light noise and turned toward the corpse, when, awful to relate, I saw my friend raise his hands, throw back the pall and sit stark upright. The eyes, which had never been closed, looked searchingly about the room until they rested on me, the open mouth contracted, and the countenance took a distorted expression. Without pausing I dashed from the room into the dark corridors.

"When I reached my bedroom, I fell in a swoon, which must have lasted several hours, for on awakening I saw the sun just tingeing the eastern horizon. Finding myself on the floor with the novel clinched in my hand recalled the dreadful scene, and pulling myself up from the floor I rang a call bell for a servant. The servant came, and we descended to the parlor after I had told him what had happened. Yes, I had actually experienced that dreadful scene, for the corpse was found lying across the bier. We went over to it. The muscles were all relaxed, and it appeared sleeping peacefully. It was laid back as it had been arranged by loving friends. As I could not explain the phenomenon I had witnessed, I went for a physician. He said the boy had been dead all the time, but that the muscles contracted during his fit had been relaxed in my presence. We agreed not to tell the circumstance to the family, but it is true in every particular, and when I think of the awful scene even in daytime I am filled with terror.

"I have never got into 'The Woman In White' farther than three chapters, and I do not think now that I shall ever finish the story that is so intimately associated with this awful ghost story in real life." *Louisville Courier-Journal.*

Sandusky [OH] Register 23 July 1894: p. 6 KENTUCKY

THE LAUGH OF THE DEAD
WEIRD INCIDENTS OF BOY'S DEATH

The final examination was made on April 12 of the body of Wallis Allsopp, a South Normanton boy, who, after lying in a coffin for four days, raised doubts in the minds of three doctors as to whether he was dead or not.

Drs. Harcourt and Le Grand determined that there was now no doubt as to the boy's death, whatever might have been the case before.

The funeral was proceeded with, and the scene at the graveside was extremely pathetic. The grief of the parents who adored their only child was painful to witness.

One of the doctors says that he believed the case was one of suspended animation. It was possible that the boy had lain in the coffin in a cold room for four days with just a spark of life in him, but the signs after he saw the body were not sufficient for him to make a definite statement. He certainly could not sanction burial at that time. All doubts had since been set at rest because decomposition had set in.

Stories which have a weird significance since the extraordinary developments are being told. While the body lay in the coffin in the front room four persons in an adjoining room heard a laugh.

"That is Wallis's laugh," one remarked, and all agreed on the remarkable resemblance, but they did not think of going to look at the boy.

Another person says that while alone in the house she heard the boy laugh, but said nothing, being afraid of ridicule.

The boy himself was an extraordinary character. Last Christmas he told his parents that he would be in heaven next Christmas, asking that the Christmas tree should not be untrimmed. He had for a long time been saving coppers that were given to him, saying the money was to buy a cross for his grave. During his illness he once observed, "Perhaps the Lord will raise me up as He did Jarius's daughter." When his uncle took him a bunch of daffodils he said, "How nice they will do to put in my coffin."

The Star [Christchurch, NZ] 3 June 1905: p. 4 ENGLAND

NOTE: Here is the original story of the deferred death of Wallis Allsopp.

LIFE IN THE COFFIN

An extraordinary instance of temporary revivification occurred last month in the mining district of South Normanton, near Nottingham. Wallis Allsopp, the 9-year-old son of a mining carpenter, was believed to have died on April 6. The funeral was fixed for the next Monday, and while the hearse was standing at the door the relatives went to take their last look at the little lad. As they gazed into the coffin the parents saw signs of life. A rosy tinge overspread the lips and ears and moisture was deposited on a mirror which was hastily brought and held before the lad's lips. Three doctors were summoned, who, after a cursory examination, countermanded the funeral, and sent word to the minister and the mourners, who were waiting at the churchyard. The child was lifted out of the coffin and placed in front of the fire, and a careful watch was kept throughout the night, but no further signs of vitality were seen, and the medical men believe that life finally departed on April 11, although it had lingered for four days after death was thought to have occurred.

The Advertiser [Adelaide, SA] 16 May 1905: p. 6 ENGLAND

Some earthbound spirits were solicitous about the care of their remains and made helpful suggestions in the séance room.

COL. J. M. ROBERTS,
Of *Mind and Matter*, Phila.

The fact I am to relate has reference to the possibility of departed spirits looking after the disposition of their own remains. It was in the year 1877, the exact date I do not remember, that I attended a séance given by Mrs. James A. Bliss, in Philadelphia. On going to the séance room I learned that Chauncey Barnes, a very peculiar, remarkable man had that day died, and was at the residence of a lady who, with

her two children, was living in the lower part of Philadelphia, the name
of the street being given, but no one being able to give the number of
the place where his body lay. During the evening, and soon after the
séance opened, the form of a fine, tall, portly man, of advanced years,
appeared in the cabinet and called me forward. I thought I recognized
the form, but to make sure I asked for the name, and, repeating the
alphabet, the initials "C.B." were given, making it evident that the
form was the materialized form of Chauncey Barnes, who but a few
hours before had passed out. All present were acquainted with him, and
were called up to the cabinet. He seemed to be rejoiced to be recognized.
At the close of the séance I started for my home, seventeen miles out
of Philadelphia. On my way down Chestnut Street to the steamer I
was wheeled around, as if somebody wanted me to go away from the
steamboat landing. I tried again to go, and again I was wheeled around.
Supposing there was some requirement for me to remain, I went to
the hotel. I got the impression that I must remain and see after the
body of this man, who had, by the bye, no claims upon me whatever.
I made up my mind, although I had a strong call to go home, that I
would remain and see what I could do. I went down in the morning
to find the place. To my great surprise I was taken to the very house
where his body lay. I went in and inquired as to what arrangements
had been made. The lady said that Dr. Rhodes had been down and
made all necessary arrangements, and that I would not be needed,
and that the body would be buried on the following Monday. This was
on Friday morning. Supposing that I had done all that was necessary,
I was about to leave when the lady said: "Mr. Roberts, would you not
like to look at the remains?" I am very much averse to looking at dead
bodies, and generally avoid it, so I was about to decline the invitation
when the impulse came over me: "You must see these remains." The
lady had not been up stairs; she slept on the lower floor. I went up, and
on opening the door was almost knocked down by the odor. I went down
and told her she could not keep the body till Monday morning. She said
Dr. Rhodes had gone off, and she could not alter the arrangements. I
asked: "Who has the body in charge?" She could not tell, and directed
me to the undertaker. I found him, and he said it was impossible that
the body could be in that condition. He said: "I put it in ice, and it
cannot be in a state of decomposition." I told him it was, and that he
must go and attend to it. He went with me and found that it was even
worse than I had represented. The result was I ordered the casket,

went to the receiving vault, purchased the right to lay the body there, got the undertaker to attend to it, and got the friends to have the funeral services on the following day. Afterwards Mrs. Cullen went into a trance and told me that Chauncey Barnes had appeared on the previous night, and told her to thank me for yielding to his influence.

I would add that his death was caused by rupture of the aorta. Whether this had any connection with his sudden decomposition or not, I do not know.

Facts, Volume 1, 1882 PENNSYLVANIA

NOTE: Chauncey Barnes was a Spiritualist medium in the 1870s. Col. J.M. Roberts, a lawyer and abolitionist, was editor of *Mind and Matter,* "the periodical of choice for free-thought, pro-phenomena, stridently-defensive American Spiritualism in the late 1870s and early 1880s. Based in Philadelphia, this was "the periodical of choice for free-thought, pro-phenomena, stridently-defensive American Spiritualism in the late 1870s and early 1880s. [Source: http://www.iapsop.com/archive/ materials/mind_and_matter/]

Possibly because cats, both feral and domesticated, were so common, they frequently figure in stories about funerals and wakes. Here we have a midnight vigil and a horror worthy of a Gothic novel at a Connecticut wake.

I was watching a corpse. In that part of the United States [Connecticut] the dead are never left alone till the earth is thrown upon them, and, as a friend of the family, I had been called upon for this melancholy service on the night preceding the interment. It was a death which had left a family of broken hearts; for, beneath the sheet which sank so appallingly to the outline of a human form, lay a wreck of beauty and sweetness whose loss seemed to the survivors to have darkened the face of the earth. The ethereal and touching loveliness of that dying girl, whom I had known only a hopeless victim of consumption, springs up in my memory even yet, and mingles with every conception of female beauty.

Two ladies, friends of the deceased, were to share my vigils. I knew them but slightly, and, having read them to sleep an hour after midnight, I performed my half-hourly duty of entering the room where the corpse lay, to look after the lights, and then strolled into the garden to enjoy the quiet of the summer night. The flowers were glittering in their pearl-drops, and the air was breathless.

The sight of the long, sheeted corpse, the sudden flare of lights as the long snuffs were removed from the candles, the stillness of the close-shuttered room, and my own predisposition to invest death with a supernatural interest, had raised my heart to my throat. I walked backwards and forwards in the garden-path; and the black shadows beneath the lilacs, and even the glittering of the glow-worms within them, seemed weird and fearful.

The clock struck, and I re-entered. My companions still slept, and I passed on to the inner chamber. I trimmed the lights, and stood and looked at the white heap lying so fearfully still within the shadow of the curtains; and my blood seemed to freeze. At the moment when I was turning away with a strong effort at a more composed feeling, a noise like a flutter of wings, followed by a rush and a sudden silence, struck on my startled ear. The street was as quiet as death, and the noise, which was far too audible to be a deception of the fancy, had come from the side toward an uninhabited wing of the house. My heart stood still. Another instant, and the fire-screen was dashed down, and a *white cat* rushed past me, and with the speed of light sprang like a hyena upon the corpse. The flight of a vampyre into the chamber would not have more curdled my veins. A convulsive shudder ran cold over me, but, recovering my self-command, I rushed to the animal (of whose horrible appetite for the flesh of the dead I had read incredulously), and attempted to tear her from the body. With her claws fixed in the breast, and a *yowl* like the wail of an infernal spirit, she crouched fearlessly upon it, and the stains already upon the sheet convinced me that it would be impossible to remove her without shockingly disfiguring the corpse. I seized her by the throat, in the hope of choking her, but, with the first pressure of my fingers, she flew into my face, and the infuriated animal seemed persuaded that it was a contest for life. Half-blinded by the fury of her attack, I loosed her for a moment, and she immediately leaped again upon the corpse, and had covered her feet and face with blood before I could recover my hold upon her. The body was no longer in a situation to be spared, and I seized her with a desperate grasp to draw her off; but to my horror, the half-covered and bloody corpse rose upright in her fangs, and, while I paused in fear, sat with drooping arms, and head fallen with ghastly helplessness over the shoulder. Years have not removed that fearful spectacle from my eyes.

The corpse sank back, and I succeeded in throttling the insane monster, and threw her at last lifeless from the window. I then composed the disturbed limbs, laid the hair away once more smoothly on the forehead, and, crossing the hands over the bosom, covered the violated remains, and left them again to their repose. My companions, strangely enough, slept on, and I paced the garden-walk alone, till the day, to my inexpressible relief, dawned over the mountains.

The New Monthly Magazine and Literary Journal Universal Register, 1834, 203–4 CONNECTICUT

NOTE: Readers might object to the notion of a corpse bleeding, apparently from the claws of a cat. However, issues of blood from the mouths and noses of the dead are commonplace. In the case of a young woman who died of tuberculosis, such a thing was very possible. The narrator might not have been able to tell the source of the blood.

An even more gruesome affray took place at an Irish wake in Indiana.

CATANKEROUS.

Cats Fighting for a Dead Man's Body in Indiana.

The following appears in the New Albany correspondence of the Indianapolis *Sentinel* of the 31st.

A remarkable scene occurred last night in that part of the city called "Hog Hollow." One Daniel Shehan, a former employee of the gas works, who lived in a small frame building in the locality referred to, died suddenly at 3 o'clock Wednesday morning. Last night some young people gathered to watch over the remains, but becoming, as the widow thought, a little too noisy, they were all sent away with the exception of Thomas Flinn and Wm. Lang, two young men aged about 21 or 22 years, and two young ladies.

About 12 o'clock Thomas Flinn went into the room to examine the corpse, and was horrified to see three cats on the body. He tried to drive them away by motioning with his hand, but they showed fight. He then seized a poker and commenced belaboring them with it, and they attacked him, and it was all he could do, with the assistance of the other watchers, whom his cries for aid summoned, to drive them from the room. The window was then closed, and cats of all sizes, colors, ages and of both sexes jumped on the glass with their eyes blazing and their fur all standing the wrong way. Finding they could not force an entrance there, they went to the roof and endeavored to tear off the shingles; got under the floor and sought for an entrance. Their screams, yells and groans in the meantime were frightful to listen to, and so scared the watchers that they were almost paralyzed with fear. The ghoulish beasts failed to effect an entrance and the watchers felt relieved. But it was soon discovered that they could not remain in the house with all the windows closed, as the odor from the corpse was too offensive, and the window was again raised, but not enough to admit a cat. Then the window was again assailed, and it seemed to the guardians of the remains that there were at least a hundred felines trying to force an entrance. Flinn stood at the window with the poker and beat them over the head, but they persisted in the effort to effect an entrance. Finally some of them got part of their bodies through and the window was closed down on them, two pokers heated red hot and the beasts burned in every possible way, the young people thinking it would drive the others away, but it did not, and the fight was kept up at intervals until after daylight. The watchers kept the window down as long as they could possibly bear the stench, and when they could do so no longer it would be raised and the war waged on both sides. It was a remarkable occurrence, the like of which was probably never known in this part of the country.

The watchers looked this morning like they had had a long spell of sickness, and say they would not pass through another such ordeal for the world. Some nine or ten dead cats were found around the premises this morning, and many of the neighbors will miss their grimalkins.

The Salt Lake [UT] Daily Tribune 6 February 1879: p. 3 INDIANA

NOTE: "It is reckoned so ominous for a dog or cat to pass over [the corpse] that the poor animal is killed without mercy...In one case, just as a funeral was about to leave the house, the cat jumped over the coffin, and no one would move till the cat was destroyed." *Folklore of the Northern Counties of England & the Borders*, William Henderson, (London: W. Satchell, Peyton and Co., 1879), 59

Rigor was a tricky thing to manage with cooling boards and ice and shocking when it went wrong.

CORPSE

Sat Up On Cooling Board

And One of the Watchers Fell Over Dead From the Terrible Fright.

Joplin, Mo., February 25. Word was received in this city to-day of the death of Miss Mary Garling from fright, at Garton, as the result of sitting up with the corpse of a friend. An undertaker, in order to get the body of Thomas Sharon, a cripple, of that place, straightened out sufficiently to get it into a casket, laid it out on a cooling board with ropes tied to nails driven into the floor. Sharon had died of rheumatism and was so stooped in life that when he walked his hands touched the ground.

Neighbors were sitting up with the corpse during the night, among them being Miss Garling, when one of the watchers stumbled over the rope that passed across the body of the corpse. The rope broke and the corpse sat up, facing Mary Garling.

The watchers fled from the room except the Garling woman, who uttered a shriek and fell to the floor in a dead swoon. When the watchers returned they found the corpse in a sitting position, its glassy eyes wide open, while Miss Garling lay upon the floor unconscious. She died in a short time.

Indianapolis [IN] Sun 28 February 1902: p. 8 MISSOURI

This next tale is troublingly vague as to whether the corpse had really come back to life before being reburied in such haste.

A young man died in Louglibrickland [County Down], who lived a very wicked life, disregarding the Sabbath, which he spent in drinking, and was also a notorious blasphemer. In the time of the wake, previous to burial, as the candles burned round him where he was stretched in a shroud, the looking-glass covered with a sheet, and others hung round the wall; midnight came, the wake was not attended as is too customary by drunkards and gossips, regaling with whiskey, snuff, pipes, and tobacco, while the young are taught to laugh away the terrors of death by obscene plays and ill-timed merriment; this corpse was attended by a single person to watch the candles, a most offensive smell rose from the body, and the attendant went out for a few minutes, on returning, it was perceived with horror and affright, that the dead man was up resting on his elbow; the family was called, and on their entering, the countenance of the corpse was ugly beyond human possibility, and with many violent gesticulations and distortions of features, began to utter a strain of unheard of oaths, with a fluency and originality not to be described.

The curate was sent for; the young gentleman soon came; but his prayers were drowned in the dreadful voice of the deceased. An old Presbyterian clergyman also came, he approached with his Bible, and never took his eyes off it, because he was told that the look of the corpse had disconcerted the curate. He abjured it by the three Holy Names of the Trinity, upon which the corpse immediately sunk down in its shroud; those in the room hurried to put it in the coffin, nailed down the lid, and buried it as soon as possible. Mr. S. was in the house, and witnessed the whole transaction, he said the voice from the corpse was most appalling.

The Supernatural Magazine, 1809 IRELAND

Naturally there were always mischievous boys to put the "fun" in "funeral." The Irish dialect sounds a bit like a typical Pat-and-Mike story, but the boys' hijinks ring true.

An Irish Wake after a sketch by M. Woolf. Library of Congress Prints and Photographs Division Washington, D.C. 20540 USA

FUN AT WAKES

How the Boys Used to Play Tricks

"No," said the graduate from the 7th ward, "There's no more fun to be had at wakes. That's why I moved up here above the bridge.

"When I was a boy a wake was an eagerly anticipated event in the 7th ward and an unexpected one was classed with windfalls. Where did we boys come in? Why, our fun lay in planning and executing divers tricks peculiar to the professional wake goer.

"For instance, a proud son of Tipperary would come in and sit down gingerly on one of the frail-looking camp stools furnished by the undertakers. Prior to his entrance one of the screws had been carefully removed. Of course he collapsed in a heap on the floor and his picturesque profanity was enough to make joy for one night.

"Again, some one of the boys would be selected to secure the supply of clay pipes. Some of these were carefully stopped up with cork.

"With a luxurious sigh, so loud that it shook the carefully shrouded pictures on the wall, the victim would stretch himself, stiffly across his knees, scratch a match along his trouser's leg, apply it to the pipe, and while he patiently waited for it to light, mumble from out the corner of his mouth, 'What wan av Murphy's girls was it that was married lasht Chewsday? Was it Cassie or Mary Ellen?'

"Then as the burnt match scorched his fingers he'd drop it and try another, until, seeing several neighbors engaged in a similar struggle, he'd catch on to the trick, and with a good-natured wish that the 'owld bhoy' would 'fly away wid them la-ads' he'd restore the pipe to active service.

"Another device that brought joy to the heart of wake-going youth was a judicious mixture of cayenne pepper with the Mrs. Miller's Best usually provided in those days. This was, however, attended with more risk to the joker than other forms of diversion, and when the pepper began to announce itself it was considered prudent for the gay spirits, who were responsible for its presence, to adjourn.

"But there was one joke that for delicacy and flavor far outstripped all others. It often happened that as the night wore on some of the mourners would adjourn to the neighboring saloon. There was the boys' chance.

"A keen-eyed sentry reported when the visiting contingent of mourners showed signs of returning to the wake house. Then was the crape removed from the door on which it belonged and hung on one further down the street.

The whole noisy party would thus be led to tramp up the stairs of a flat or tenement as they were then called, where every one was sleeping peacefully. Arrived at the second floor there would ensue the usual dialogue, while the boys downstairs hugged each other and rolled around in delight.

"'A-are you there, McManus?'

"'I am.'

"'On pwhat flure does the corpse live?'

"'Why, begob, I t'aut he lived on this flure.'

"'Faith, if he does then his family has all turned Protestan' an' gone to bed. Divil a candle is lit in there.'

"'Thry the flure above,' says McManus.

"Upon that the entire band would proceed all through the house, roundly denouncing the policy of a landlord whose meanness led him to put out the lights in the house where 'a corpse lived,' and incidentally frightening the tenants into the belief that the place was on fire.

"Of course the mistake would be finally discovered, but not until the lie had been given several times and stairs rolled down.

"What is that you say? I should have been ashamed of myself? Well, perhaps I should, but it was very funny, all the same." *New York Sun*

San Jose [CA] Mercury News 20 July 1902: p. 16 NEW YORK

Despite the sleeplessness of those waking the dead and the inherently gruesome situation, actual ghost-sightings at wakes are extremely rare. This one, from Yonkers, has many of the features of a classic apparition of the Virgin Mary.

GLORIFIED VISION OF DEAD GIRL APPEARS TO SEVEN AWED MOURNERS

Apparition of Julia Murray, of Yonkers, Visible to Her Friends and Relatives While They Were Watching Near Her Corpse in the Early Morning.

One of the most remarkable phenomena ever recorded happened in Yonkers about 4 o'clock Monday morning. To seven persons who were watching near the body of Julia Murray, a devout member of St. Joseph's Catholic Church, opposite her home, a glorified vision of the young girl appeared. It was seen at different times by these persons, who all agree in their testimony as to the appearance of the apparition. The witnesses are sober, industrious and devout persons.

Katie Kane, a cousin, who lives at No. 80 Orange Street, Brooklyn; William Murray, a brother, of No. 154 Ashburton Avenue, Yonkers; Nora Smith, a carpet weaver, of No. 99 Palisade Avenue; Mrs. Mary Corbalis, of No. 152 Ashburton Avenue; Rose and Tessie McGowan, of No. 154 Ashburton Avenue; Rose Kearns, of No. 58 St. Joseph's Avenue, and Mamie Regan, of No. 4 Mulford Street...

MRS. CORBALIS'S STORY.
"I Tell It in Fear of God and in Love of the Blessed Virgin."

I saw the vision of poor Julia Murray as surely as I see you now. I say it in the fear of God and in the love of the blessed Virgin.

I was sitting in the dining-room. We were all pretty tired, and the girls were falling asleep, but I was wide awake, and more, for I could not have slept then if my life depended on it.

There were five girls in the dining-room, and the young men were in the kitchen. Mrs. Murray, worn out with watching and tending her darling daughter, was sleeping in the next bedroom and two of the girls were lying on the bed with her.

Awed, Speechless.

Two others were in the parlor with the corpse and others were sitting in the bedroom where Julia died. Presently Miss Kearns came to the door of the dining-room, pale and frightened and weak. The two others stood beside her, but they could not speak. They stood with their heads bowed on their breasts and their hands crossed before them.

I heard a sound like someone falling and I went in through that room and into the room where Julia died to see what was the matter. Nora Smith had fallen in a dead faint.

There was a picture of the blessed Virgin hanging low over the bed, and when I entered there was a bright light on that side of the room and a vision was coming slowly from behind the picture.

It was the vision of Julia Murray dead in the next room. It rose slowly, slowly against and along the wall. The hands were crossed over the breast, the tips of the fingers resting on the shoulders.

Like Immaculate Conception.

She was all in a simple white dress or robe of linen just like in the Immaculate Conception, and was surrounded by white, filmy clouds.

It was Julia; I could see her soft, curly hair about her face floating like on the cloud.

She wore a beautiful wreath of roses and large leaves and her head was in a halo of bright red light. Kate Kane was beside me. She cried out to Julia's sister, Mamie, and their brother Willie:

"Come Willie! Come Mamie! Here is Julia!"

Willie came, Katie dropped down on her knees, sobbing, "Oh, Julia, pray for me!"

The vision seemed to understand, for the hands slowly changed to a position as of prayer, the palms together before her face, and then a rosary seemed to drop down and hang as if hung on the left hand.

I could see it plainly and the face took on a sadder look and the eyes closed, as if she was praying. The vision kept rising and moving along the wall and faded slowly out at the ceiling.

We all had dropped down on our knees for prayer. I said the rosary, fifty-nine prayers altogether, and the others made the answers. I was saying the 'Hail Mary' when Katie asked Julia to pray for her.

There were eighteen of us on our knees saying the rosary.

Julia's head seemed in a ball of fire. Her dress seemed like clouds. Her head slowly fell back, as the vision rose on the wall. When it passed away we all started for the dining-room.

Wonderful Moving Lights.

Rose Kearns and I were last. Rose looked back. Then she nodded to me to look back. The room seemed filled with light as if it was all afire.

I got a bottle of holy water from the kitchen and, returning to the room, sprinkled it in the sign of the cross. The light blazed up and was so strong it blinded me and made my eyes water.

Then it went before me like two torches, one of red and the other of blue and other colors. It passed into the parlor, paused a moment over the corpse and then passed out through the wall.

I asked the time and it was 4:30 in the morning. The vision must have lasted five minutes, the lights another five minutes or more.

It was the most beautiful thing I ever saw, and I shall not forget it as long as I live. It was not imaginary; it was real. There was no drink in the house, we were all awake, and I am a Catholic. I know that I should laugh if anyone had told this story to me, for I don't believe in ghosts or visions, but this one was real. I saw it.

I did not see it when its hands were crossed on the breast, before Katie Kane asked it to pray.

Its hands were clasped in prayer when I first saw it, and it faded out slowly with its head thrown back and a look of sorrow on the face. It all happened long before daybreak. It was a rainy morning, anyway, and there was no sunrise in Yonkers.

The heavy portieres between the two rooms prevented the candelabra by the corpse from making a shadow, and it was dark in the bedroom. That light was a supernatural light, and what we saw was a vision of Julia Murray...."

The Evening World [New York, NY] 27 March 1901: p. 3 NEW YORK

The other witnesses' affidavits were printed, but I have only included the most detailed. A further article in the next day's *Evening World* gave a few additional details: Julia's mother, brother and two sisters lived on the upper floor of 154 Ashburton Avenue, Yonkers.

"The flat is of five rooms—parlor, bedroom, where Julia died and the ghost was seen; another bedroom, dining room and kitchen in a row from the south front toward Ashburton Avenue.

"The body lay, completely covered, on a slab in the bay window in the parlor, with a candelabra at its head. On the west wall is a small mantel mirror, and this reflected the light of the candles upon the north half of the wall in the first bedroom."

The Evening World [New York, NY] 28 March 1901: p. 7 NEW YORK

NOTE: This case aroused much interest and was widely reported. Garrett P. Serviss, a famous scientific writer was called in to inspect the premises and he suggested three theories for the apparition: 1) a "Pepper's Ghost" apparition generated by a mirror; 2) a prankster projecting a magic lantern slide through the front window, and 3) the "excited imagination" of a sensitive little girl who fancied she saw something in the flickering candle light and communicated her vision to the adults. [Source: *The Bourbon News* (Paris, KY) 16 April 1901: p. 4]

8.

"A Ghastly Kind of Business:"
Photographing the Dead

A new technology that could miraculously capture the soul on a glass plate captivated the Victorian public. It was only a matter of time before the camera was used for one last look at the dear departed. An advertising slogan from an early daguerreotypist—"Secure the Shadow ere the Substance Fades," captured the essence of Victorian death photography: portraying a beloved face soon to be dust and ashes, all too often that of a child.

The popular interest in the art and science of photography warred with the emotional subject matter of dead infants. Parents wanted an image of their little one who had lived all too short a time; some reluctant photographers found it a lucrative, but gruesome business.

Earlier post-mortem photographs show less artifice: we see skeletal faces drained by dehydration, stark depictions of complexions discolored or as blanched as the frilled caps framing them. Later photographs are more artistic, carefully posed and retouched, as this photographer describes.

PHOTOGRAPHS

In New York Town

By Norman

New York, Jan. 20. There is a man who has a gallery on Fifth-av. and gets $60 a dozen for his ordinary pictures, who told a few evenings ago a little camera trick he once turned with pleasing financial results.

At that time he was not in New York, and he did not get $60 a dozen for his pictures. Nearer $6. He was on the lookout for any opportunity to increase his income. One afternoon he went to photograph the flowers which adorned the coffin of a little boy 3 years old, the child of rich parents. A nurse who was in the house stayed in the room with the photographer while he made the picture. She chanced to remark:

"What a pity that Robbie's parents haven't one picture of him!"

The photographer became interested at once. It appeared that never since the child was born had a picture of him been taken. This was, of course, back before the days of snapshot cameras in almost every household.

"If you will help me," said the photographer to the nurse, "we can give them a picture of Robbie."

TOOK A PHOTO OF THE DEAD BOY

"She was willing. So they closed the folding doors into the room where the body lay, took the flowers off the casket and opened it. The photographer lifted the little corpse out of the coffin and stood it up in a chair. The nurse held it in position and a flashlight picture was made. They put the body back and rearranged the flowers. The photographer asked the nurse not to mention the matter to anyone, and she agreed.

Just as the photographer was about to leave, the nurse happened to mention that Robbie had a brother a year older, who was very much like him, particularly his eyes.

"Bring him around to the gallery some day soon," said the photographer. The nurse did so. After studying the brother's eyes, the photographer went to work on his negative of the dead boy's face. He opened the eyes, filled out the hollow cheeks, touched up the curls. Many evenings he worked on the negative. At last, satisfied, he made an enlarged print and sent a letter to the father, asking him to call on him.

The father came, and without a word the photographer handed him the picture. The man burst into tears and it was some minutes before he could control himself. He was amazed.

"How did you do it?" was his first question. Having been told, he next asked. "How much will it cost?"

"That picture will cost you $100," was the answer. It was paid gladly and several duplicates at $10 each were ordered for other relatives.

Cincinnati [OH] Post 20 January 1910: p. 4 NEW YORK

While it was a lucrative business, not all photographers were enthusiastic about post-mortems.

POST MORTEM PHOTOGRAPHS

"How about photographing the dead?"

"We discourage it altogether. It is a ghastly process, and is suggested by minds insane with grief. It would be just as wise to keep the coffin plate or a bit of the shroud as a memento of those who are gone. A German family came up here once to get a baby photographed. They had a basket with them and we supposed it was the wardrobe, but the dead child was carried in it. The mother took it out and propped it up in a corner of the sofa and insisted on having it taken in that position. I could not see a basket for months after without a shudder.

The Boston [MA] Weekly Globe 26 June 1883: p. 6

PHOTOGRAPHING DEAD CHILDREN

The Queer Practice of Some Harrisburg Parents

"I want to tell you of a queer practice that prevails in Harrisburg," said an undertaker to a *Telegraph* reporter this morning. "Children who died of scarlet fever are placed in a sitting posture by their parents and then photographed. It is attended with great danger to all concerned, and I can't see why they should want a picture of a dead child, and especially of one who dies from scarlet fever, for in almost every case the face turns black after death."

Harrisburg [PA] Telegraph 13 July 1885: p. 4 PENNSYLVANIA

This photographer found in 1885 that photographs had become so inexpensive that most families had photos taken in life, hence there was no need for a post-mortem likeness.

Photographing the Dead.

[*Chicago Herald.*]

"Do we ever photograph dead people? Yes, indeed, though not so often as formerly. Photographs are so cheap now that nearly everybody gets them, and it is but rarely that death overtakes a man who has not left a negative behind him. Years ago this was quite an important feature of our business, especially in photographing dead children. All kinds of people order photographs of their dead relatives—from rich folks who spend hundreds of dollars for flowers to those too poor to pay for the cheap coffin. I've taken them in all sorts of positions too. People have so many fancies about such things, and we have to humor them all. Sometimes we'll take them as they are laid out in the coffins, sometimes on the bed. Children are often held in their parents' arms. Others are set up in their chairs.

"Some people insist on having the eyes opened. I photographed one old man, and they set him up in his big chair, dressed as usual, and with his eyes open. They took his old pipe, filled it with tobacco, lit it and stuck it in his mouth. I caught him that way, with the smoke rolling up. His folks said he wouldn't look natural any other way, and it was a great picture. You could hardly believe the subject was dead. I was once called to take a coachman on Michigan avenue. His widow was the cook where he had worked and she insisted that he be set upon the box. We tried to talk her out of it, but it was no use. So we carried him out to the stable, tied him on the box in full livery, with the lines and whip in his hands, and photographed him.

"The most odd, striking picture I ever made was of a little boy and a dog. The boy was dead and the dog loved him so he would not leave his side. When I pointed the camera at the boy the dog thought it meant harm to his young master, and he planted himself upon the boy's body as if to defend it, and would not stir. The family were about to tear the dog away, when I said to them: 'If you want the sweetest picture ever made, let him alone.' They took my advice, and the result was striking. It was a picture worth having, but the family would let me make but half a dozen copies of the negative and they took them all and made me destroy the plate."

The Topeka [KS] Daily Capital 18 July 1885: p. 3

The police and coroners were quick to see the advantages in photographing the unknown dead. Enthusiasts lent their talents to improvements in the art, creating special frames for holding the body and methods of making the dead look more life-like.

THE METHOD OF PHOTOGRAPHING THE DEAD FOR PURPOSES OF IDENTIFICATION.

(From the "*Lancet.*")

At two inquests held last week on the bodies of persons unknown the coroner commented at some length on the very unsatisfactory character of the photographs of the corpses prepared by the police authorities, and suggested that means ought to be taken to make such photographs more like the individuals when alive, and therefore more useful for purposes of identification.... One of the latest and most valuable contributions to [the] study [of the subject] is a paper by Dr. Minovici which appeared in the "*Archives d'Anthropologie Criminelle*" of November 15, 1904.

The writer, who is director of the Medico-Legal Institute of Bucharest, gives in this paper a detailed account of the apparatus which he employs for posing the body and of the methods to which he has recourse for restoring the appearance of vitality to the features, his observations on this latter point being of special interest. One of the most serious difficulties in post-mortem photography is due, as is well known, to the loss of the brilliancy of the eyes, which has a large part in determining the characteristic expression of the individual. It has been usual to deal with this difficulty by the method suggested by Dr. Gosse of applying compresses to the eyes, but Dr. Minovici has found that much better results may be obtained by the use of artificial eyes, dark or light, according to the colour of the individual's iris. A natural appearance can be given to the orbital opening by introducing beneath the lids an extemporised speculum of lead foil or by fixing the upper lid to the ball of the eye by means of a fine pin. The jaws can be drawn together with thread, and by appropriate arrangements of pins various emotional expressions can be given to the face. Even in cases where putrefactive changes have occurred, if there has been no actual loss of substance, the features can be in a large measure restored if the gases in the areolar tissues are evacuated through suitable incisions in the scalp and in the buccal mucous membrane. By the application of these methods in a case where the body had been immersed in water for six weeks Dr. Minovici succeeded in getting a photograph sufficiently life-like to establish the individual's identity. Photographs showing the successive stages in the preparation of the body in this case are reproduced in the paper, and give a striking illustration of the value of Dr. Minovici's ingenious artifices.

British Journal of Photography, Volume 53, William Blanchard Bolton, Editor, 1906

You can read about Dr. Minovici's artifices and see before and after photographs of some shockingly decayed and mutilated corpses at http://books.google.com/books?id=WzkoAQAAIAAJ&printsec=-frontcover&dq=intitle:Archives+intitle:d+intitle:Anthropolo-gie&hl=en&sa=X&ei=NfGZU9SuJsityATlyIKQBQ&ved=0CD-MQ6AEwAQ#v=snippet&q=Photographie%20des%20cadavres&f=false

It is not for the faint-hearted.

Despite a photographer's best efforts, sometimes the unknown dead remained a mystery.

A London photographer had

A QUEER EXPERIENCE

last year. He was one day waited on by a gentleman who gave him no name, but who, handing him four £5 notes, requested his services in the following case. A girl had been found dead in the Thames, and was then lying in one of the dead-houses. The photographer was to take steps to get a photo of her. If he succeeded, the gentleman, who appeared to be very wealthy, promised him another £20. As may be supposed, the photographer decided this was a matter worth exerting himself in. By the judicious laying out of a sovereign or two he obtained admission to the mortuary, took his snapshot of the dead girl, came away, and set to work to develop the photo for his mysterious customer. They were ready, 50 of them, when he called, were handed over, and the photographer received his promised £20.

"I often wondered what on earth he could want the photo for," my friend told me. "It seemed one of the saddest businesses I had ever undertaken. Photographing the dead is a gruesome job at any time, but the white face of that poor girl, quite a young thing with her wide, staring dark eyes and long, mud-stained hair, fairly haunted me. I had decided that I should hear no more of the matter, when suddenly the result came like a thunderclap upon me. A young gentleman at the West End committed suicide by shooting himself with a revolver one day. His reason for the deed no one could imagine. He was young, wealthy, an officer in a crack regiment, and was to be married in a day or two to a wealthy and handsome lady. He had sat down to breakfast, his valet said, and had proceeded to open his letters. The servant left the room for a few moments only, to return upon hearing a shot, followed by a deep groan. He found his master dying, and on the table beside him the photo of a girl, apparently dead, and lying on a slab in a mortuary. It was one of the photos I had taken. I learnt from the servant what did not come out at the inquest, that these photos had come by post each morning for some time past. Who sent them no one knew; and I held my tongue as to my customer. It was a queer case; and for the sake of all parties I kept silence."

Otago [NZ] Witness 23 September 1897: p. 47 ENGLAND

This very experienced photographer of the dead, who began his career on Civil War battlefields, reveals some of his technical strategies, the sensible rationale behind such apparently gruesome photographs, and a thrilling adventure in temporary body-snatching.

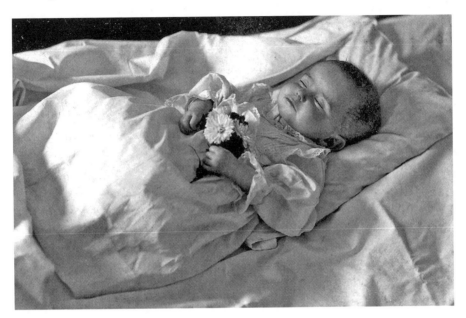

Private collection. Photographer: Teeple, Wooster, Ohio

GHASTLY PHOTOGRAPHIC EXPERIENCES.

[*Sunday Mercury*] I've been engaged in taking pictures of the dead for twenty years or more, was the remark of a photographer of Philadelphia, as he arranged his camera to photograph the first corpse ever brought to a Philadelphia gallery for that purpose. A little coffin or casket was under the sky-light in a slanting position, supported by two chairs, and in it was the body of a fair-haired child, whose peaceful, smiling expression, despite the ghastly pallor of death, made it appear to be in tranquil sleep. The head lay in a perfect bed of flowers, and the waxen hands, clasped, held a spray of mignonette and two delicate tea rosebuds. The sun, shaded as it was by curtains, threw a bright glare over one side of the little dead face, leaving the other half in shadow. The tube of the camera was brought to the proper focus on the silent subject, and in a few seconds the negative was ready to go into the "dark room" and be prepared for printing in its chemical bath. No one was in the place except the proprietor, a solemn-faced undertaker and your correspondent. This is the first time, said the photographer, as he critically examined the negative, that I have ever been called upon to picture the dead in my own place, but this case was such a peculiar one that I could not refuse, although it would undoubtedly draw away custom if it were known. People have a foolish horror of death, you know, and would actually be afraid to come if they thought I had dead bodies here. It only took a moment, and there was really nothing awful about it. The mother, poor soul, will have something to look at and cry over now, and the speaker stopped, as the undertaker had turned the last screw in the lid of the coffin and was preparing to carry it out to the hearse again....

[The author went onto the battlefields of the Civil War to photograph the dead and the living. After the war he tried to make a living as a regular photographer.]

A GHASTLY KIND OF BUSINESS.

Business grew dull, and I got poor. The war had just about ended, when one day, when pushed to my wits' end for money, I was struck with an idea which I have followed out successfully ever since. The death columns of the morning papers were carefully gone over, and when the funeral was advertised from a humble neighborhood I was usually sure of a five dollar bill. I visited the houses and offered to photograph their dead. Out of a dozen visits I would probably get one job. In a couple of years my reputation grew, and now I am almost as frequently sent for as the minister. Only last May a messenger came from a West Philadelphia family for me to photograph their dying father.

When I got there he was too far gone and I had to wait. Half an hour after the old gentleman had breathed his last, and before he became stiff, we had him sitting in a chair, with his eyes held open with stiff mucilage between the lids and brow, and his legs crossed. He made a very good picture. I once photographed two children—sisters—who had died the same day of diphtheria. They were posed with their arms about each other's necks. An Irish family, living in the southern part of the city, called on me about two years ago to take a picture of their dead son—a young man—with his high hat on. It was necessary to take the stiffened corpse out of the ice-box and prop him up against the wall. The effect was ghastly, but the family were delighted, and thought the hat lent a life-like effect. Sometimes, and at the suggestion of the family, I have filled out the emaciated cheeks of dead people with cotton to make them look plump. The eyes are nearly always propped open with pins or mucilage, but when people can afford to engage an artist it is an easy matter to paint the eyes afterward. Another time I took a picture of a dead man who had been scalded to death. It was a full-length photograph, and an artist was engaged to fill out the burns on the face and then make a copy in oil. For that piece of work I got $50, and I think he got no less than $500.

TAKING THE DEAD FROM THE TOMB.

I recall an instance, continued the photographer, which is probably the most remarkable thing ever related. Two young men came into my place in the winter of 1874 or 1875, I forget which, and said they wanted a photograph of their dead father, whose body was in the family receiving vault awaiting interment in the spring. They cautioned me that their step-mother was violently opposed to having her husband's body taken from the vault for such a purpose, and that she daily visited the place of sepulture to prevent any such attempt. It was agreed that I should engage a couple of men to assist in taking the body out, and another to keep watch for the widow. We went to the vault early in the morning to avoid the woman, who usually made her visit after twelve o'clock. It took some time to get the body properly posed against the side of the vault, and then it began to drizzle. We threw a horse blanket over the coffin and retreated to the shelter of a tree. About noon the sun came out, and I hurriedly prepared to secure the negative. The camera had just been placed in position when our sentinel came running breathlessly in, with word that the widow was nearly at the entrance to the cemetery gate, a quarter mile distant. It did not take a moment to restore the corpse to the coffin, screw on the lid, and carry all back to the vault. I packed up my kit, and with the two men got out of another gate. Four months after that one of the sons came to me with a most remarkable story. He said his step-mother had lost her reason. When the dead man's body was exhumed in the spring in the presence of the widow, she insisted on having the coffin opened. The corpse was found partly turned over and the lining of the coffin disarranged. The widow went into hysterics, under the impression that her husband had been buried alive. The stepsons tried to reassure her, and finally confessed that they had authorized the taking up of the body to have it photographed, but the explanation came too late. The woman's reason was affected, and she could not understand that in our haste to escape we had turned the corpse on its side.

Photographic Times and American Photographer, Volume 12, J. Traill Taylor, Editor, 1882 PENNSYLVANIA

Did the Dead Move?

A well-known photographer will vouch for the following facts: He was called in one day to take a photograph of a young girl of about twenty, who had died a few days before. The corpse was laid out upon a bed, with the hands clasped over the breast. Death had come very gently to her, and, except for the stillness, she lay there as if asleep. Some flowers had been strewn over the body and on the floor by the side of the bed and standing out in black relief against it was the coffin. The photographer silently adjusted his lens and took the photograph. During the ten minutes needed for the exposure, the photographer paced up and down in the long corridor outside the room where the dead girl lay. When he returned he saw that on the lid of the coffin was a flower, which was not so before. How did that flower come there? No one had entered the room; the windows were closed, and there was not a breath of air stirring. Why was the flower now lying on the coffin, when a few minutes before it was on the bed, between the hands of the corpse? The photographer listened, but he could hear no sound except the beating of his own heart. In a few minutes, however, he determined to dismiss the question from his mind, and busied himself with packing up his instrument. Then he paused—possibly the falling flower had left a trace on the negative, or, as the day was gloomy, the photograph might not be quite successful. He would try again. A second photograph was taken, and the artist returned home. That night, sitting up late in his studio, he developed the two negatives. The position of the corpse was not the same in the two negatives. The photographer strained his eyes, half disbelieving the evidence of his own senses, but there were the two negatives before him, telling in their silent, unmistakable truthfulness that between the taking of the two photographs the arm of the dead girl had distinctly moved. The mystery of the flower on the coffin was solved, but it was succeeded by a mystery more terrible still. *London Tablet.*

Themis [Sacramento, CA] 21 December 1889: p. 2 ENGLAND

NOTE: This article was widely syndicated and may have been a journalist's creative effort. There is another version in which the photographs lead to the discovery that the girl is actually alive.

9.

Fiends for a Funeral:

Amateur Mourners and Funerary Extravagance

Many Victorians had a feeling that the living owed the dead, if not a human sacrifice to accompany them, then at least a string of carriages filled with mourners behind the hearse, and, if not a granite sarcophagus and wrappings of linen, then a first-class burial robe and a solid mahogany casket.

The Civil War marked a shift in funerary practices from relative austerity to a fashionable parade of mortuary extravagance. While formerly a family might build a coffin and prepare a loved one's body for burial themselves, the Gilded Age was also an age of gold-plated coffin trimmings and funerals of an almost-Pharaonic splendor.

There was a fascination with the finer points of the mortuary trade: of suedes and bombazines and quantities of silver plate. Calculating the number of carriages and the floral tributes was a precise formula for a life well-lived and an object lesson in human vanity. There was a mortuary standard, often reinforced by the press, and it was news when someone flouted convention with a red-white-and-blue coffin, by wishing to be buried sitting, or laid away with a pipe or a favorite bottle of spirits.

Like weddings, Victorian funerals were often held at home rather than in church. It is a common belief that there were special doors used to remove the dead from the home parlor where funerals were held—later euphemistically called "the living room." This reflects folklore about removing the dead through an exit that is later sealed up so that the spirit cannot find its way back inside. While some Victorian homes had separate parlor entrances, I have seen no evidence in the popular record of the use of separate doors for the dead. As funerals became more ostentatious, they were often held in churches and at the new "funeral parlors"—beautifully appointed rooms made available at undertaking establishments.

Flowers are an appropriate symbol for the excesses of the Victorian funeral. Newspapers documenting large funerals would note the details of these sometimes bizarre floral arrangements and their donors as if keeping score and setting a societal standard for the next bereaved family. The florists claimed that excess was a result of customer demand; the public claimed that the pressure arose from florists. In addition, just as the dead were photographed post-mortem, floral offerings were also documented by the photographer.

Floral arrangements including a harp, a horseshoe, and a stuffed dove.

Although some families found funerary floral tributes touching, there were anti-flower groups working to eliminate them altogether on medical, aesthetic, and economic grounds.

The reformers suggest that the notice of the death which appears in the papers should end with the announcement: "No flowers." A novel argument against the sending of these tributes is that the petals of the flowers serve to keep the germs which are given off from the dead body, and in the case of people who died from infectious diseases they may become a positive source of danger, and... be absolutely death dealing. Then again the custom of preserving these wreaths is denounced by many medical men, who contend that they, containing as they do morbific bacteria, are a constant source of danger and a menace to the healthy life of those who afterward occupy the rooms.

Evening Star [Washington, DC] 14 February 1891: p. 12

FLORAL VULGARITY

Is it not time to cry a halt? Has not the attempted gilding of fine gold and painting the lily been carried far beyond the point of wasteful and ridiculous excess? These questions, surely, must strike any unprejudiced mind, any simple, natural, healthy, unperverted taste, in contemplation of the extreme lengths to which floral vulgarity and shoddyism have run. The writer verily believed that the end of the scale had been reached with such sacrilegious crudities as the "Gates Ajar," but what can be thought of a "funeral piece" consisting of a beer wagon, laden with barrels and drawn by horses, all made of roses and smilax, with straw for the horses' tails?

Going back a little, is not a flower a flower? What more can be made of it?... Is it artistic, to say the least, to torture what is already perfect of its kind into a shape altogether foreign to its character and which it was never intended to take?...

It is a beautiful custom—one most certainly founded upon the purest and holiest instincts of human nature, one to which even the most degraded of our species must surely respond—to deck our dead and adorn their last resting-place with flowers. But why seek to do what the old rhetoricians called "improving the sublime?" The result is caricature, if nothing worse. Imagine the steps leading to the "Gates Ajar" (what mortal has any adequate conception of the gates of Paradise?) lettered in purple chenille! Think of a silent harp with the back made of tin-foil, or a sickle whose edge will not cut, or a pillow upon which no tired head could rest, or a broken column with the break smoothly "plastered"! Still worse are funeral wreaths made of dyed immortelles and aniline-colored grasses, or of stiff, monstrous china roses, or death-like waxen ones mingled with tawdry, tinseled leaves.

If slaughtering birds for millinery purposes is sufficiently reprehensible to attract the notice of "Audubon Societies" and "Bird Defenders," what must be thought of our present custom of mixing the bodies of white doves among our floral atrocities? Are we much better than the old barbarians who sacrificed animals at the death of their relatives or of persons of distinction? What has become of the beautiful, heart-cherished superstition, if you choose to call it so, that it is a sin to hurt a dove because it is an emblem of the Holy Ghost? Even if the sense of the fitness of things in many minds were not outraged by such use of a lovely bird, common sense should teach any one that killing an inoffensive creature will not make the departed dear one any happier in the other world.

Talk to an intelligent florist and you will find that he agrees with you. "Floral emblems are in bad taste, I know," he admits. "Flowers cannot be made to look well in anything but the simplest designs, like a cross, a wreath or a basket. But what can we do? People want broken wheels and things like that; we must supply the demand for them or we'd starve. The worst of it is some people know that floral designs are generally signs of vulgar ostentation, but they feel that they cannot help themselves. They send a floral piece to a friend's funeral because they're afraid they'll be thought mean if they don't. Their hearts would prompt them to send simple clusters of cut flowers, but they fear that they'll be misunderstood. To my mind the floral pieces are more funereal, more suggestive of death than death itself.

"Some people order floral pieces because they feel that they are getting a bigger show for their money. In a piece, poor flowers can be worked up to look better than they are. Cut flowers must be good specimens or their case is hopeless. There is no way of disguising their imperfections.

"I heard about the beer-wagon. It was sent to the funeral of a brewer. It had to be made, because the brewer's employees wanted it. One might think that, in the presence of death, the brewer's friends would want to forget that he had ever had anything to do with beer. If talking shop is commonly regarded as vulgar, what must be thought of the intrusion of the man's business at his funeral?"

San Francisco [CA] Chronicle 22 November 1891: p. 10

In even worse taste was the practice of sending funeral arrangements to brighten up hospitals.

FUNERAL FLOWERS

Hospitals Do Not Like to Receive Elaborate Floral Pieces.

"What in the world inspires people to send elaborate and costly floral pieces directly from a funeral to a hospital?" said an official of Bellevue hospital the other day, when an undertaker unloaded a dozen anchors, harps, pillows, etc. on the hospital lawn, according to the *New York Sun*.

"This is only one case out of many in which people who think they are doing an act of kindness get no thanks whatever for their pains. What do you imagine would be the feelings of a score of patients, some of whom are dangerously ill, if they saw that big floral harp placed in a conspicuous position in the ward, knowing, as they certainly would, what purpose the flowers had recently served? Would the thought that their own friends might be contributing floral pieces before long hasten their recovery to any extent?"

"I won't allow such things in my ward," said a house physician. "The patients simply won't have them because they know immediately what use they have been put to."

As for these particular flowers, they were left on the lawn until nurses and hospital employees who didn't care what they had been used for carried them away and relieved the hospital authorities of the trouble of disposing of them.

Many undertakers separate the funeral flowers from the wire framework and turn them in to the hospital in the shape of bouquets, making them both useful and acceptable, and destroying the evidence of the purposes which they have served.

The Lexington [MO] Intelligencer 18 July 1903: p. 7 NEW YORK

Some very rich people took a stand against floral tributes, to the terror of the florists, who knew that the middle- and lower-classes would follow their lead.

NO FLOWERS AT FUNERAL
But You Can't Defeat an Enterprising Florist
[*Chicago Mail.*]

"Remember that that 'Gates Ajar' must go up to Brown's before 9 o'clock to-morrow morning," said a Wabash-avenue florist to one of his employees the other afternoon, "and don't forget that it is to be an n.f. affair and that you'll have to keep your eyes open."

"What is an n.f. funeral?" I ventured to ask, after the young man addressed had left us.

"No flowers," sententiously answered the proprietor.

"That means, then, that you are taking flowers to a funeral where they are prohibited?"

"Precisely."

"Do so frequently?"

"Every day."

"Then 'no flowers' really doesn't mean no flowers after all, does it?"

"It doesn't if we can help it—rest assured of that. We are here to sell flowers. The funeral trade forms an important part of our business, and we have to protect ourselves against the anti-floral cranks as best we can. The 'no flowers' order is a fashionable fad and nothing else. It originated in New York years ago at a funeral of one of the Vanderbilts, who requested that no flowers should be displayed during his obsequies. I was working for a New York florist at that time, and I well remember what a flutter this innovation caused among the tradesmen in our line of business. They did not care about losing the single Vanderbilt job, but they feared that such an example in the ultra-fashionable world would be followed by its general adoption. Thus a whim of fashion might deal a severe blow to the floral trade. The leading florists immediately held a conference and it was unanimously decided that the great funeral must not be permitted to set the fashion and inaugurate an anti-flowers era. Several very costly and elaborate floral pieces were prepared, but in spite of all we could do the orders of the deceased were obeyed to the letter and we were unable to get a solitary flower inside the Vanderbilt residence. An attempt to bribe the servants failed, as they had received ironclad instructions not to permit a floral offering of any kind whatsoever to be taken inside the house. This ultimatum fell like a wet blanket upon our hopes, but still we determined not to quit the field without making one last bold 'bluff.' A magnificent ivy cross was made—one of the finest that ever was seen in this country. It was about six feet high and was composed of a mass of English ivy leaves and tendrils. It represented a good round sum, let me tell you, and a good deal of work. But there was not a bud or a flower in it anywhere. Just before the time appointed for the exercises to begin we took the cross to the Vanderbilt residence, and, as we expected, were stopped at the door by a liveried lackey, who denied us admission.

"'But there must be no delay about this matter,' we insisted. 'It must go in and at once. Come now; we have no time to parley with you.'

"'You can not come in.'

"'We must.'

"'I have strict orders not to admit any flowers. I can not do it.'

"'But there are no flowers in this. Look at it for yourself. It was built entirely in accordance with the wishes of the family. You have no orders against admitting ivy, have you?'

"He hesitated. Just then something round and hard dropped into his hand. He was lost. A moment later that beautiful cross stood at the head of the casket. I shall always remember the remark of my companion as we left the house: 'Well, Jim. We've beaten the old man cold at his own game.'"

The *Cincinnati [OH] Enquirer* 8 August 1891: p. 11 ILLINOIS

In addition to floral tributes, sometimes touching personal mementos accompanied the funeral processions of deceased children.

DEAD CHILD'S DOLL CARRIED TO GRAVE

Schoolmates were pallbearers at the funeral Thursday of Edith Redman, 9, who was killed by a traction car near her Madisonville home. By request of her parents, the dead child's favorite doll was carried in the funeral procession.

Cincinnati [OH] Post 13 November 1903: p. 8 OHIO

CHILD'S DOLL BURIED WITH HER

Dying Wish of 7-Year-Old Girl Is Carried Out.

Wabash, Ind., April 15. A pathetic incident of the funeral of 7-year-old Dorothy Fountain yesterday was the burial of the little girl's doll with her body. The child was much attached to the doll, and just before her death, when it became evident that she would not get well, she requested that the doll be placed in the coffin with her. The little girl's dying wish was carried out.

The Inter Ocean [Chicago, IL] 16 April 1903: p. 7 INDIANA

A boy named Henry Turner, who had died of diphtheria, was buried at Orangeburg, Ind., recently. When the funeral procession left the house, a small pet pig the child had raised, and had been devotedly attached to, followed the hearse containing the remains of its friend, and in spite of the efforts to drive it back, followed the whole distance from the house to the burial-ground, seven miles distant, most of the way between the hind wheels under the hearse.

The Republican [Sycamore, IL] 17 October 1877: p. 1 INDIANA

As funerals became more elaborate affairs, some aficionados came to regard them as a species of entertainment. In the nineteenth-century press there was a slight, but revealing collection of stories about funeral fanciers. These were mourners without portfolio who attended funerals merely for the fun of the thing. As this fashionable undertaker reports, they do not seem to be ghouls, but are generally sympathetic souls.

FASCINATED BY FUNERALS

People Who Are Mourners Regularly, and Find Comfort in so Being.

[*New York Sun.*]

"Do you see that nice-looking little old lady over by the stained window?" asked a fashionable undertaker of the reporter. "I mean the quaint, respectable-looking little personage, with the black satin dress and the black crape shawl."

The reporter saw her.

"Well," continued the undertaker, with an appreciative smile, "she's as fine a regular attendant as any establishment in this city can produce. I send her an invitation to all my nice funerals, and I have sometimes sent a carriage for her when I knew mourners would be scarce. She is never really happy unless she is at a funeral. She won't touch weddings, as most women will; her sole amusement, so to speak, is a first-class funeral," and the undertaker looked over to the old lady with a tender professional interest.

"I have some other nice people on my list," he went on. "One of my most graceful mourners lives in Forty-eight street, and seldom gets down this way, but she hardly ever passes a day without a funeral, and I never saw her at one when she couldn't shed tears with the best of them. She's one of the heart-brokenest ladies I ever had for a 'regular.' Does she really feel badly? Well, I should say she did, most decidedly. She always has a word to say to the family, if she thinks they need comforting, and is very careful to learn all the particulars. Why, she can tell me all the details about some of my own funerals that I had forgotten years ago. She's as good as a set of books.

"Oh, no, there's nothing hysterical about these cases at all. I've got some men that do just the same thing. There is one now. He's a curious customer. I sometimes lose sight of him for six months, and then all of a sudden he'll turn up and not miss a funeral. Of course, I couldn't ask the women folks why they came, but I asked him one day. He said he couldn't describe exactly the kind of feeling it gave him, but he thought it sort of quieted his mind and soothed his feelings like. He made one remark about it that I never could quite get the hang of, though I dare say it had a certain sort of meaning for him. He said, 'I haven't got any friends at all myself, and so I like to go to funerals.' A lady volunteered almost the same kind of remark to me once after she had been to four or five of my best funerals. She said, 'It makes me feel kind of friendly, you know, and then they are kind to me, and, besides, I feel afraid and solemn, and it always does me good.'

"I think it would be unjust to call it mere curiosity that brings them here, though I have noticed that some of these people watch every detail with the most intense curiosity. They seem fascinated by the presence of death, and their sympathies are moved by the grief of the living. You might think they were very solemn people but the contrary is the case. Some of them are remarkably cheerful, in fact. That little old lady is always very pleasant and vivacious after the ceremony is over. She always comes up and shakes hands with me and is as agreeable a person as one would wish to meet.

"There's an unusually lively and pleasant gentleman living in the Ninth Ward who occasionally drops in at my funerals. He does not make it a point to go to them, but, as he says himself, he can never get past them. He told me he was obliged to go in; no matter how important business might be, he would forget all about it as soon as he saw the hearse and carriages. The first time I saw him at a funeral I thought he was certainly one of the nearest relatives. He is a very large, round-faced, benevolent-looking gentleman that would be observed in any crowd. On this occasion, after he had looked at the deceased person for a few moments, he became greatly overcome with emotion, and someone led him to a chair. Each one of the mourners supposed, of course, that he was known to the others. He wept throughout the discourse, and after it was over shook hands all around with the mourners, and showed a good deal of fervent, and, I have no doubt, genuine sympathy. I did not know until some time after that he was a dummy—that's the name we sometimes call them by. This man is really as jolly a fellow as you ever met, and they say he has been requested to leave theaters more than once, in case he would not subdue a particularly substantial laugh which he possessed. In fact, most of these people who love to go to funerals are good-hearted people. It is not true, as has sometime been said, that they are touched a little in the head. The fact seems to be that they are emotional and sympathetic, and are strongly affected by any awe-inspiring scene. Even young girls and boys have now and then a fancy for funerals, though none of them can say why. Most of them say it makes them feel better, but if you ask where or how, they cannot say. They all watch everything as though in a sort of a dream.

One of my best hearse drivers used, as a boy, to be a regular attendant at funerals. One day he came around to my stable and asked if he might help us. I let him do so, and after a while he used to take a hand regularly in keeping the hearse in order. When he got old enough to go to work his father had to bring him to me—he wouldn't work any-where else. If you ask him why he likes this business, he'll tell you he don't know."

A slim, middle-aged man here addressed the undertaker, and was received by that personage in a most friendly manner. The slim man suggested that there might be some way he could be of use before the services were done.

"Now, there's a man," said the undertaker, "who is interested only in the mechanical part of the business. He goes to almost all my funerals, but seems to feel no special sorrow or sympathy. His whole mind is taken up with the conduct of the funeral. To suit him, the business must be done with the most solemn exactitude. He said to me the other day that if he could only once have complete charge of a large funeral he would be happy for the rest of his life."

The Cincinnati [OH] Enquirer 25 August 1883: p. 11 NEW YORK

Moving beyond the *amateurs de deuil*, in some of the larger cities, and in Europe, professional mourners—some unionized—could be hired.

PROFESSIONAL MOURNERS' BUREAU
[By Telegraph to the *Tribune*]

Wilmington, Del., July 26. Wilmington will have a professional mourners' bureau. It was learned to-day that Richard Murphy is behind the innovation. His idea is to furnish substitutes for busy mourners, who will wail at funerals as loudly as may be required. Murphy says he can furnish substitutes to officials at weddings who will look correspondingly joyful.

New York Tribune 27 July 1906: p. 3 DELAWARE

In France, you could also hire a golden-tongued eulogist.

It is the custom in France for panegyrics to be pronounced at the graves of notable men, and even obscure persons have their praises sung in the cemetery. This has resulted in the appearance of a professional panegyrist, always to be found in a wine-shop hard by the cemetery. He is known as "Monsieur du Cimetiere." He has on hand an assortment of orations to suit customers of every description. All he needs are a few hints about the life and career of the defunct, and he evolves the rest from his imagination. The mourners never fail to be convinced that in the deceased the world lost one of its greatest men or women.

The Argonaut [San Francisco, CA] 2 January 1893 FRANCE

Unfortunately some mourners pushed their services too aggressively.

Professional Mourners Are Taken in Raid on Cemetery

Brooklyn, N.Y., Oct. 4. Because three professional mourners, two women and a man, were curtly informed their services to weep and wail at so much per grave were not desired, they loosed a torrent of abuse on a funeral party, and police of the Parkville station were called to arrest the trio. Complaints have been numerous recently that burlesquers of sorrow have been heaping vituperation upon the grief stricken who refuse to avail themselves of their services.

The Seattle [WA] Star 4 October 1910: p. 5 NEW YORK

PROFESSIONAL MOURNERS

Get No More Free Rides, Says an Akron Undertaker.

"The professional mourner will get no more free rides at funerals conducted by us," said an Akron undertaker, the other day, to a *Democrat* representative, with satisfaction beaming from every line of his countenance.

"Professional mourners! Free rides!" exclaimed the reporter in astonishment. "What do you mean? Tell us about it."

"Well, it's this way," said the undertaker. "At every funeral of which we have charge, we find three or four women, or maybe more, (professional mourners, we call them) who are in no way related to the family of the deceased, who had never perhaps even seen the person whose obsequies they are attending, and yet they are found occupying seats

The photograph above shows a poignant floral offering in memory of a young girl named Helen. The "language of flowers" was used to reinforce the sentiments of the bereaved. Forget-me-nots are an obvious example. Pansies/*pensees* for "thoughts," are another. Unravelling the puzzle of this floral symbolism would be rather like working a funereal-themed crossword or acrostic.

Carnations, lilies, forget-me-nots, and pansies as well as sprays of bleeding heart and several ivy leaves can be seen in the photograph. It is possible there are dahlias and anemones. The garland of white roses and leaves seems to be artificial. While photographs of floral arrangements in symbolic and sentimental shapes: hearts, anchors, and crosses, sometimes labeled with the name or title of the deceased spelled out in flowers, are common, this tribute is unusual in that the name is written in separate letters of foliage.

in the very front row, usually shedding tears copiously, and always dressed in black. When the time comes to go to the cemetery they are again found in the front rank and in spite of us, secure seats in the carriages provided by the relatives of the deceased for intimate friends, enjoy a free ride to the cemetery and back, and get all the choice morsels of news, which later is related to friends, all decked out with furbelows and embellishings with all the details of human grief and heartbreak which they have witnessed, worked in. To these people nothing is sacred, nothing too holy for them to gossip about.

"All this has been remedied, however, and the next time a professional mourner attempts to get a ride in one of our coaches a disagreeable surprise awaits her, for we have adopted a card system by which the names of the persons whom the bereaved relatives desire to have seats in the carriages is given to us. These persons are furnished with cards, and only those presenting cards to the driver will be allowed to ride."

Investigation proved the state of affairs to be general and there rarely are "professional mourners" in Akron. They are always women, and the attending of funerals is a mania with them. Never do they let one pass without their presence. It is their amusement, their one diversion and they make the most of it. They dress in black. They wear lugubrious expressions upon their faces and would be taken for the real mourners by the casual observer. They go to a funeral as other people go to a party or a theatre, for amusement, and any specially distressful case is a treat....

Akron [OH] Daily Democrat 15 March 1902: p. 1 OHIO

Sometimes the undertaking establishment's eagerness for new and novel technology provided a diversion for the mourners.

SERVICE BY PHONOGRAPH

This is new. The Deputy Coroner of Gravesend, being also an undertaker, has arranged a novel method for conducting funeral services. He had it all ready for a funeral today, but the clergyman was on hand and his part of the services was not needed. Nevertheless, there was a phonographic quartet appropriate to the ceremony. The device is a funeral service by phonograph. Its designer has purchased the instrument, and has had a funeral sermon preached upon it by a local clergyman, together with religious exercises, and several hymns by a good quartet. These are produced by the funnel-shaped annunciator, so that the assembled friends may hear, and, according to the genius who thought out the automatic service, the effect is serious and impressive. Scarcity of clergymen during vacation season is the excuse for this mechanical prayer and praise service. After a while mourning will be made easy, and there's lots of people ready to take advantage of anything in that line. *Pittsburg Dispatch.*

Boston [MA] Journal 29 August 1895: p. 7 NEW YORK

In some situations, improvements on the old ways were definitely needed. Funeral reformers often railed about fatalities when mourners were forced to stand in all weathers at lengthy graveside services. A portable chapel solved the problem.

A moveable funeral chapel is a novelty introduced by the managers of a Philadelphia cemetery, which is intended to be spread for each interment over the grave and its immediate vicinity. It covers an area sufficient to allow standing room for fifty to seventy-five persons, and here on dry ground they may remain sheltered from the inclemency of the weather, either sun, rain or wind, during the most protracted religious service.

St Albans [VT] Daily Messenger 27 April 1871: p. 2 PENNSYLVANIA

Any deviation from an orthodox funeral service was news, like the rites for this happy-go-lucky soul, who wanted to be the life of the party after he was dead.

NOVEL FUNERAL EXERCISES
Music and Dancing and Trees Decorated in the National Colors.

Petersburg, Ind., April 17. A most novel funeral exercise was held at White Oak twelve miles east of here yesterday afternoon. Two years ago Wm. Hayes died leaving a large estate. During his life he was very eccentric. For years he called himself 'Pike County Bill Hayes.' According to the provisions of his will his body was to be taken up and placed in a vault two years from his death which was Sunday. In accordance to this trees in the cemetery where the body was to be placed were to be decorated with red, white and blue ribbons and five dancing platforms were to be erected and two brass bands to furnish the music. Fifty kegs of beer were to be dispensed to the crowd and for failure to carry out the above provisions of the will Pierce Hayes, his only child, was to be disinherited. A crowd of 2,000 persons were in attendance and the terms of the will were fully complied with.

Wilkes-Barre [PA] Weekly Times 17 April 1899: p. 1 INDIANA

NOTE: A story in the *Salt Lake [UT] Herald* 28 March 1890: p. 2 tells of the "jolly" August T. Schweitzer, who had lager beer, Frankfurters, cheese, and pretzels served at his funeral. The undertaker then demanded payment of 30 cents per attendee and there was a frantic scramble for the cemetery gate by those unwilling to pay.

Just as the newspapers lovingly reported the details of fashionable weddings and balls, expensive funerals were a perennial theme.

A CONNOISSEUR IN COFFINS

Mrs. Hiller Spends Twenty Thousand Dollars For Her Own Burial Robe

[Boston Special to *New York World*.]

The eccentricities of the late Dr. Henry Hiller and wife, of Wilmington, Mass., whose fad was magnificently carved and luxuriously upholstered burial caskets, have been described in the *World* already. The doctor's funeral took place a year ago to-day and the corpse was carried to its last resting place in a silk-lined, gold-plated, elaborately carved casket of solid mahogany, enclosed by another casket no less extravagantly appointed. Six richly caparisoned coal-black Percherons in gold-mounted harness, each attended by a colored groom, carried the casket to the temporary vault. There the doctor's body has been guarded night and day by a grim old watchman. A $500 lamp standing in front has shed its bright rays in the path of possible body-snatchers or grave desecrators, and every morning the faithful widow has gone to see that everything about the place was all right.

Not satisfied with the ghostly magnificence of a year ago, the widow has been at work on the construction of new caskets, one for her husband, the other for herself, which easily surpass in magnificence and grotesqueness of ornamentation any thing of the kind the world has ever seen. Each casket is in two parts—the casket proper and the sarcophagus. The material in all four is solid mahogany, imported specially from South America. The upholstering inside is as elaborate as money could make it. Corded silk of the value of $10 a yard is the material used. The lids are made of separate panels, highly polished, richly carved and fastened by solid gold hinges with knobs of solid gold for opening them. The doctor's new casket is fastened by a heavy brass door of Gothic design, having a knob made of six pounds of solid gold. On the panels are solid gold tablets, inscribed with the doctor's favorite passages of Scripture, such as "I know that my Redeemer liveth." "Blessed are they that die in the Lord."

Standing at the head of the coffin is a figure of the doctor built out of solid mahogany and reduced to a height of eighteen inches. About him are the figures of four angels welcoming him to Paradise. Mrs. Hiller's coffin, on the other hand, has her figure recumbent on the lid, with three angels ministering to her and the doctor kneeling beside her with his right arm supporting her head. But the most remarkable feature of this remarkable burial casket is the carving on one of the side panels. The sculptor has drawn a sketch of a landscape, showing at intervals a meadow, a river, a hill, a forest, a valley, and, last of all, a mountain, at the apex of which is a white cross. Clinging to the cross is a naked cherub, and behind another cherub, and then another, until twenty-three are counted climbing toward the cross. During the twenty-four years of her married life, Mrs. Hiller says she bore her husband twenty-three children, none of whom lived. The procession up the mountain, she says, perpetuates the memory of her little ones.

Mrs. Hiller has also had made for herself a burial robe, of which it may be truly said that it beggars description. The dress-maker completed it after four months' labor and an outlay of $20,000. The robe is made of white ottoman silk, corded heavily. There is also a wilderness of white silk lace running in perpendicular panels and tucked and gathered and fluted until it stands out to a distance of five inches. There are other panels of white surah of the most expensive manufacture. Between the panels of silk and lace are intermediate panels constructed solely of daisies made in France of pure silk after a design bought in Boston for $40. It is estimated that 5,000 of these daisies are sewed into this gown. The robe opens in front and is fastened by upward of 200 solid silver hooks designed like a serpent's head.

The total outlay by Mrs. Hiller will be not far short of $500,000. The mausoleum will be of hammered granite. In the four walls will be gilt windows, through which it is planned to have rays of colored light enter, a different light to each window, which, blending, will fall upon the caskets resting side by side within. The caskets will stand each on four huge brass legs and chairs of magnificent design will be in the mausoleum for the accommodation of sight-seers. Mrs. Hiller will soon hold a reception for the exhibition of the caskets, the invitation to which is a picture of a coffin with "Admit one," written beneath.

Mrs. Hiller says Queen Victoria sent to her for all the American papers that contained notices of the doctor's funeral. When she had read them she said that Mrs. Hiller was the only woman who had surpassed Her Majesty in doing honor to a dead consort.

The *Cincinnati [OH] Enquirer* 21 December 1889: p. 11 MASSACHU-SETTS

NOTE: See this link for the full story: http://www.wilmlibrary.org/local-history/hiller

Dr. Hiller died in 1888 and was interred with much pomp. Mrs. Frances Hiller died in May of 1900. She had married her coachman, Peter Surrette, who, at her request, changed his name to Henry Hiller. He waived all rights to her estate, which was said to be worth $500,000. The funeral was a spectacle, with over 2,000 people turning out to stare at the much-vaunted casket, which rode on what looked like a crape-draped float from a morbid parade. The pageant quickly degenerated into a fantasist's farce. In truth, Mrs. Hiller had borne three children—one of whom survived. The $50,000 casket turned out to have cost $2,000 and the $500,000 mausoleum with solid-gold knockers was never actually built, leaving only the original stone receiving vault where Dr. Hiller slept to receive the remains. The cast couchant lion pedestals (the "brass legs" mentioned above) that were to have held the caskets, proved too tall for the small vault and were discarded in a corner. Mrs. Hiller's casket and the new one for her husband had been stored in an outbuilding and were not in the best of condition. But eventually Dr. and Mrs. Hiller were wrestled into their new sarcophagi, and the door, which had fallen into the tomb when the workmen uncovered it, was permanently bricked up. Several years later, cemetery authorities decided that the Hiller vault spoiled the entrance to the cemetery. They demolished the vault and had the mahogany caskets—still in good condition, reburied in the ground. *Sic transit gloria mundi...*

In stark contrast to the Hiller extravaganza is this account of a tenement funeral for an infant.

A FUNERAL IN A TENEMENT

The Unostentatious Service over the Death of a Baby.

[*New York World.*]

A little girl in a red-checked apron stood on tip-toe to tie two pieces of white ribbon to the front door-knob of the big tenement where she lived. It was in Rose street, just around the corner.

The ribbon was limp and old, and hung in a lifeless way against the worn panels of the door. She stepped back to note the effect and another girl about the same age came out from a door in the lower hallway and joined her. The two little ones were the only signs of life about the great building that looked black and forbidding with its range of grated fire-escapes giving it the air of a barred prison. The second comer stared at the first girl with bold eyes for a moment and said, pointing to the fluttering ribbons:

"What did you do that for?"

"Baby is dead."

"Do you live in this house?"

"Yes, on the fourth floor."

"Huh," with a sniff of contempt. "We live on the first floor and we've got a baby carriage." Then in a more conciliatory way: "May I come up and see it?"

"I guess so," and the two children, hand in hand, went up the dark steps to the little room fronting on the street where the mother and the woman of the next room were preparing the child for burial.

It was a bloodless little thing, the piece of clay the woman fondled in that lingering way they have with those they love. The mother seemed jealous of the attention her friend showed the child. She could not bear to have other hands touch the little thing. No other hands but hers should smooth the pillow for its last sleep. There was no wild outburst of weeping on her part, and, beyond a certain querulousness, no demonstration of affection. The mother did not even cry. She was too used to suffering for that. She talked reminiscently of the bundle of white on the bed. She told how she never expected to raise it; that it had always been thin and sickly; that it was the best child in spite of all that the world had ever seen; that she knew it could never stand the warm weather and a thousand little details that only a mother could remember and repeat. And every now and then she would begin again and go over its peculiarities, finding some new charm to tell of.

A SYMPATHETIC NEIGHBOR

The other woman was sympathetic and receptive, petting the mother and calling her "Dearie" and "My darling;" and flitting about the room putting things to rights with an air of proprietorship that would have been hotly resented at any other time. The two neighbors living so close together had been great enemies and had fought royally over the petty privileges of the fourth floor hallway. But all that was forgotten and laid aside now.

Pretty soon a young man with a week's growth of beard and furred silk hat came in softly without knocking at the door. He said he was the undertaker. Nobody knew how he had found out about the death. He had a book with pictures of coffins in it. He stepped on tiptoe across the room and asked in a subdued voice whether to-morrow morning would suit for the funeral. Then he said that for $14 one could get a beautiful casket. He always called his coffins caskets. The neighbor took him aside and conferred with him, finally getting the $14 casket for $11. Then he went away, after leaving a receipt for the $5 cash that had been paid on installment.

The mother took the cold form of her child in her arms and rocked it as she had done so often in life. It had a long white gown, with a bit of lace down the front. She took a wisp of pink ribbon and fastened it at the baby's throat. The neighbors protested that she must not do that; it would never do. But the mother persisted, and the bit of bright color remained.

The husband came home from work at the usual hour, and did not grumble at the cold supper that was spread for him. He kissed his wife in a way that he had not done since they were married. They were a loving couple, full of the truest affection for each other, but the affection did not often find outward expression. He sat with his wife for half an hour, and then feeling himself in the way went down and joined the group on the stoop. She did not care to leave the room.

He was working on a particularly urgent job and went off with his tools as usual the next morning. He kissed the mother of the little one again before he left. The woman across the hall came in early and put things to rights. Then she disappeared for a little space and returned, dressed in a newer gown of black. She brought a bunch of ox-eyed daisies with her and put them in the baby's hands. The little girl who had tied the white ribbon that served as crepe to the front door-knob, came up wondering and felt of the flowers. Then she took one for herself. The neighbor and the undertaker arranged the casket, the woman quietly slipping the bit of pink ribbon from the shroud. But the quick eyes of the mother saw it and would not have the child deprived of the bit of color. It had always loved the bright string she pleaded. So the pink knot rested there.

A young minister came—he was hardly more than a boy—and read a chapter from the Bible and said a few words of consolation in German. There were ten or twelve persons in the room. He prayed for the bit of clay in the coffin. Then the undertaker's man took the coffin in his arms and carried it down to the hack that stood waiting at the door. The mother cried softly to herself during the services, and her little girl stood by her and stared at the minister. There was no hearse and only one carriage. The man put the little coffin on the front seat of the hack, the mother and the little girl and the neighbor who had been so kind to her got in with it, one of the group waiting on the sidewalk slammed the door, and the carriage took its way over to Long Island to Cypress Hills Cemetery. Nothing was said at the grave by any one. They took the little box and put it in a great grave with half a hundred of the same kind of precious dust that had been already laid away to rest.

In the afternoon the three mourners came home. The mother went up to her room and the little girl again stood on tip-toe at the door to untie the fluttering white. She took the ribbons upstairs, folding them carefully and put them back in the box where they had been at first. They were the ribbons that her mother had worn the day she was married.

The Repository [Canton, OH] 22 August 1887: p. 5 NEW YORK

10.

Grave Errors:
Exploding Corpses, Flaming Formaldehyde, and Other Funeral Fatalities

Ideally, a deathbed, a wake, a funeral, and a burial would run as smoothly as a coffin on casters. The service would be something solemn and dignified, on the order of aristocratic English obsequies with grave-faced undertakers, feathermen, and mutes. Yet so many last rites went desperately wrong.

There are thousands of stories of coffin contretemps and fatal funerals including deaths from colds or paralysis "caught" at the graveside, diphtheria acquired from the corpse, fatal doses of funeral potations, runaway carriage horses, death from grief, shock, or graveside falls. Fights broke out in graveyards with mourners and grave-diggers attacking each other with wooden crosses, with shovels, or with stones and pistols. And this is not even counting the spirit-fueled brawls at wakes.

Deaths do not necessarily bring people together. Frayed family relationships were often rent in pieces by a death.

The Amenities of Undertaking

Alpheus Hickey, a well known resident of South Sodus, N.Y., died on a recent Sunday. At the request of the widow and her brother, Henry McMullen, an undertaker from Alton, George E. Burns, was summoned. Mr. Burns came and laid the remains out, embalming them, and hung crape on the door. Later in the evening a son, Charles, residing at Sodus, who was not very well liked by the deceased father because he had not visited him during his sickness, appeared, accompanied by James J. Wylie, an undertaker from Sodus. Wylie, at the son's request, re-embalmed the remains, tore down the crape and hung up his own. The son and rival undertaker then left. The next morning Undertaker Burns came to bring a coffin and the necessary chairs for the funeral.

Finding that Undertaker Wylie had been there, he again embalmed the remains, and gathering up the materials used by Mr. Wylie hustled them out to the barn on the premises, where they were thrown in a heap. The funeral services were held from the house Tuesday afternoon with Undertaker Burns officiating.

Little Falls [MN] Weekly Transcript 22 June 1894: p. 4 NEW YORK

CEMETERY FRACAS

A Lively Quarrel in an Ohio Graveyard Over an Inquest.

Cleveland, O., July 3. The coroner went to St. John's cemetery, yesterday afternoon, to hold an inquest as to the cause of death of Patrick Murtaugh, who died at a hospital, Murtaugh's widow having asked for the investigation and her dead husband's family opposing it. Twenty or more persons assembled in the cemetery and a quarrel arose, during which Mrs. Murtaugh was struck by one of the brothers of the dead man and fainted, and her father was knocked over a tombstone.

Hutchinson [KS] Gazette 4 July 1895: p. 1 OHIO

Human violence was not the only thing to fear at a funeral. Fire, from candle or corpse, was always a worry. In this mysterious case, which was possibly the result of some secret combination of chemicals, a corpse spontaneously combusts in a burst of purple fire.

HOW A CORPSE VANISHED

A Remarkable Case in Brooklyn Which Puzzles All the Doctors

A Lady Who Died From Hysteria Is Reduced to Ashes by Spontaneous Combustion

Her Embalmed Body First Throws Off a Rosy Glow

[New York Star]

"Spontaneous combustion" is a phrase very frequently used in jest, and many scientific men and most physicians are disinclined to consider the subject seriously. That it is a stern reality has recently been demonstrated in the vicinity of Brooklyn, but the case has been kept a profound secret, through ignorance or misapprehension of its nature. That a case of this character should not come to light is a public misfortune, as science seldom has an opportunity to set right a question of much importance to humanity. Spontaneous combustion, or more correctly, preternatural combustion, as it is designated by some scientists, is the term applied to that phenomenon by which, sometimes, the human body ignites without the application of external fire. The local case now under consideration is in many respects one of the most wonderful of its kind. The story was thus related by a very intelligent nurse a short time ago to an invalid lady on whom she was waiting in the City of Churches:

"I was attending a lady a few months ago," began Mrs. N___, "who had been a victim of melancholia and occasional hysteria for several years. Though she had the best physicians that money could provide—for she was wealthy—she always manifested a great aversion to medicine, and the doctors taxed their ingenuity to discover something that might be palatable to her. At length one of them succeeded in making a drink from a combination of three powders of different colors, which, when mixed in water, produced a liquid almost the hue of pale claret, and so agreeable to the palate that when once drunk of there was a peculiar desire to imbibe more."

"That is the case with all stimulants and poisons," said the invalid, whose medical education had not been totally neglected.

"This was not a stimulant," replied the nurse, "for it soon produced satiety without the indulgence of repeated draughts. It was more in the nature of a tonic, as I heard the doctor say, and it was productive of sound, but healthy sleep, though its effects in this respect were sometimes apparently remote, and the patient seemed to improve for several weeks after she began to use it."

"Did it cure her?" impatiently inquired the invalid, who was beginning to imagine some similarity in her own physical condition to that of the lady in question.

"No," said the nurse, heaving a deep sigh and averting her eyes toward the ceiling, at which she gazed steadfastly in silence for a minute, while the invalid eyed her with a feeling of intense curiosity and surprise.

"What happened then?" said the latter, attempting to arouse the nurse from her reverie.

"I don't like to tell you," she said, bursting into tears. "I was so deeply attached to the dear lady. It is so mysterious and nobody understands it. The doctors did not understand it themselves, but they were afraid it might be misrepresented, though they had done nothing wrong."

"What happened to the lady? Did she die?"

"Yes, she died and was embalmed; but you must never say that I told you."

"Why, is there anything wrong in embalming that it should be kept a secret?"

"No; but they didn't know which it was—the embalming or the draught. I never think of it but it makes me shudder."

"Don't be so mysterious, but let me know all about it."

"Well, she was embalmed, and she never looked more beautiful. She was so handsome and life-like, and the color came again, imparting a rosy tint to her cheeks, such as she used to have before she grew sick. It looked so natural, and yet it was not, for she had been dead several days. She seemed to be in a sweet slumber as she lay in that lovely casket."

"Well, gracious, what happened!"

"Oh, it is dreadful to think of. Her brother went forward to the casket and raised the veil to have a last look at his beloved sister, when instantly he was enveloped in a purple flame which rose from the casket and ascended to the ceiling. The heat was intense, but the flame did not catch the clothing of those standing beside the casket, though my own dress and that of the sister of the deceased lady were both very light. We thought this very strange, but we were all too much stunned to speak for a few moments, and could only look at the curious blaze. There had been no fire near that could have ignited anything in the casket. When the first shock of surprise had in a measure subsided, some one suggested water—I believe it was her husband—and a pitcher was immediately brought and dashed into the flame."

"Did this extinguish it?"

"No; to our consternation, it only acted as fuel, and the flame bulged out on all sides, forcing some of us to leave the room from its intense heat; and some of them were greatly frightened, not knowing what to make of it. The physician who had prepared the powder that seemed to cure her grew pale and was greatly agitated, but he was not to blame, for he did not give it to her until he had a consultation with the others, and we all tasted it. It was delicious, though not sweet. I do not think it could have been the powder."

"But you have not told me how the flame from the lady's body was extinguished. Finish that, will you?" said the invalid, with increasing irritation.

"Oh, it burned out; the doctors were at their wits' end, when the water made it worse."

"Burned out; what do you mean?"

"I mean that the body of the dear lady was reduced to ashes. Other doctors were called in, and they could only gaze hopelessly at the burning body. It did not take more than half an hour to consume it. It was alarming to see how quickly it was done. They only sprinkled a disinfectant on the floor to prevent the odor, which was very disagreeable at first."

"The body was reduced to ashes, you say?"

"Oh, the doctors were not so much surprised when it was over and they came to think of it. There have been other cases of the kind, but this lady never used stimulants. She was strictly temperate. Yes, all the soft parts of the body and most of the bones were left in ashes, but the head and hair, except a portion of the neck remained whole and almost as handsome as ever. It was a shocking sight, and her sister swooned."

"Was there no explanation about it? What did the doctors do? Who was the embalmer?"

"He was sent for—the embalmer—and examined by the physicians. They wrote down everything he said, but he had used nothing more in the material with which he embalmed than for other persons, except that he had put in a larger quantity of the ingredient, whatever it is that preserves the color and freshness of the skin and complexion, as she had to be sent a great distance out West...."

"What did the doctors think?"

"They did not know what to think, but they were very anxious, as was also the embalmer, that their names should not be mentioned in connection with the mysterious affair."

The *Cincinnati [OH] Enquirer* 9 October 1882: p. 2 NEW YORK

NOTE: The curious detail that water did not extinguish the Brooklyn corpse-blaze, but fueled it is a near-constant in stories of Spontaneous Human Combustion. The theme of intoxication is also a common one—the Temperance movement actually used the threat of SHC as one of their deterrents. The author seems oddly concerned over the legal aspects of SHC and the potential for accusations of murder and miscarriages of justice.

It was common in Catholic tradition to have candles around the corpse for the wake. There are all too many tragic stories of bier-burnings as candles fell over or burnt down to where they set the room—and the corpse—afire. Sometimes family members would risk their lives to retrieve the dead from a burning home.

5 MOURNERS RESCUED UNCONSCIOUS WHEN BIER OF CHILD CATCHES FIRE

Fireman Driven Back by Flames Finally Drag Out Adults' Bodies and Blazing Coffin.

New York, March 2. Five mourners around the bier of 4-year-old Angelina Zarcarese were seriously burned today when the draperies on the little coffin caught fire from lighted candles in the Zarcarese home in Brooklyn. The fire spread rapidly and soon the whole room was blazing. When the firemen arrived they tried to enter the blazing room, but were driven back by the intense heat and thick smoke. They had been able to see, however, the five bodies of the mourners lying on the floor where they had been overcome and at once a second attempt was made to enter the room.

Playing their hoses in front of them and stumbling through the smoke the firemen were able to reach and drag to safety the five adults and rescue the charred body of the little girl from the blazing coffin.

Philadelphia [PA] Inquirer 3 March 1922: p. 1 NEW YORK

At most burials, the coffin was carried by pallbearers and lowered on straps into the grave, leaving plenty of scope for things to go awry. Just getting the body safely interred in one piece could be a challenge.

SPILLED THE CORPSE

Erie, February 16, 1885

A remarkable burial scene is reported as having occurred in Wesleyville, four miles east of this city. Today, a large gathering assembled at the Methodist church to attend the funeral services of the daughter of Mr. John Wells, and as the coffin was being carried into the church by four young ladies, who according to the wish of the deceased, had been selected as bearers, two of them slipped on the ice-coated ground and fell, the shock bursting open the casket and exposing the corpse, which rolled upon one of the girls and held her to the earth. The contact with the dead body frightened her so that she relapsed into insensibility before the body was placed in the coffin again, and many of the ladies who witnessed the distressing scene returned home, so shaken were their nerves. The service over the remains ended, a second accident horrified the mourners. At the entrance of the cemetery, which adjoins the church, the handles of the casket became detached and the jar resulted in another exposure. The covering being partially turned, both arms and feet were thrust out, and in the excitement which followed three women fell fainting on the snow.

The body having been forced back and the lid nailed down, the procession resumed its way to the grave. All stood with uncovered heads around the excavation, in a blinding snowstorm, as the coffin was lowered. The cords were not properly adjusted, and, slipping off, the casket was dashed to pieces on the bottom of the pit. Losing his balance, the gravedigger was precipitated upon the body and was drawn out palsied with fright. After much labor, the debris of the coffin and its occupant were removed, and preparations for interment went on. It was found that the head had been crushed in and the shroud was in shreds, necessitating new habiliments, as well as a new coffin. Later in the day the remains were committed to earth without a recurrence of the painful scenes of the morning.

Indiana Weekly Messenger [Indiana, PA] 16 February 1885 PENNSYLVANIA

Sometimes it was a challenge just to get the corpse to the burial ground at all.

FORGOT THE CORPSE

Absent-Minded Hearse Driver Departs With Principal at a Funeral.

Elgin, Ill. April 22. An unintentional blunder by Chas. Heideman, a hearse driver at Dundee, Il., delayed the funeral of Mrs. Geo. M. Hayes of Chicago.

The mourners had gathered about the open grave when Heideman, mistaking the orders of the undertaker, drove rapidly away. He did not halt until he had reached the livery stable, when to his astonishment he found that the coffin had not been removed from the hearse. Frightened, Heideman hid himself for the remainder of the day. The mourners looking for the corpse did not arrive at the barn until the team had been unhitched from the hearse. It was necessary for the mourners to hitch up the team and convey the corpse back to the cemetery.

The Spokane [WA] Press 22 April 1910: p. 13 ILLINOIS

ENTOMBED IN AN INGOT

One of the strangest coffins ever told of is that for which the British War Department is said to be responsible. The story is that a workman engaged in casting metal for the manufacture of ordnance at the Woolwich Arsenal, lost his balance and fell into a caldron containing twelve tons of molten steel. The metal was at white heat and the man was utterly consumed in less time that it takes to tell of it.

The War Department authorities held a conference and decided not to profane the dead by using the metal in the manufacture of ordnance and the mass of metal was actually buried and a Church of England clergyman read the services for the dead over it.

American Architect and Architecture, Volume 48, 25 May 1895, 82
ENGLAND

The poor had few resources when it came to embalming or icing their dead and in finding a place to lay out a body properly. This magazine noted the dreadful effects of keeping corpses in the houses of the poor.

"Nearly the whole of the labouring population in my district," says Mr. John Liddle, Medical officer of the Whitechapel Union, "have only one room; the corpse is therefore necessarily kept in that one room, where the inmates sleep and have their meals; the corpse being sometimes stretched on the bed, the bed and bed-clothes being taken off, and the wife and family lying on the floor; at other times the corpse is stretched on a board, which is placed on chairs: when children die, they are frequently laid out on a table. Other deaths often follow the first death in the same family, especially in an epidemic season....

"In respect to decomposition, there is sometimes much liquid, and the coffin is tapped to let it out; has known them keep the corpse after the coffin has been tapped twice.—This liquid generates animal life very rapidly; and within six hours after a coffin has been tapped, if the liquid escapes, maggots, or a sort of animalcules, are seen crawling about: I have frequently seen them crawling about the floor of a room inhabited by the labouring classes, and about the tressels on which the tapped coffin is sustained. In such rooms the children are frequently left whilst the widow is out making arrangements connected with the funeral, and the widow herself lives there with her children. I frequently find them all together in a small room with a large fire...."

Dr. Milroy states: "That among the poorer classes, the corpses are often kept far too long before burial. If a person dies on Thursday or Friday, the body is seldom buried before the second Sunday following. He has been repeatedly obliged to forbid the coffin being taken into the church, to the great offence and grief of the mourners, in consequence of the horrible effluvia often perceptible many yards off. He has on such occasions seen the sleeves of the bearers quite dripping with the sanies that leaked from the coffin. How the men can stand the disgusting employment, walking as they often have to do, for a mile or more under a pall all the while, and this too generally in warm weather, (for the occurrence is most frequent then,) is indeed surprising. No wonder that they usually drink to excess after such work.

"He has repeatedly seen the putrid discharge from the coffin dripping down along the clothes of the undertaker's men who carried it, so that the whole line of the funeral procession from the gate to the grave might be traced by the drippings on the ground. This is a monstrous evil that cannot be too quickly put a stop to."

The Ecclesiologist, Volume 10, 1850 ENGLAND

As if decomposition was not bad enough, the final insult was the exploding corpse. The history of exploding corpses is a long and distinguished one. The corpulent corpse of Roderigo Borgia, known as Pope Alexander VI, who may have died of poison, swelled so much that the workmen had to kick and push the body until they could nail down the coffin lid.

There are stories that Henry VIII's lead coffin burst open at the Monastery of Sion. A contemporary wrote: "All the pavement of the church was with the fat and the corrupt and putrefied blood foully imbued." It was said that the workmen sent to fix the coffin found a dog licking up the King's blood from the floor.

Other famous bursting corpses were Queen Elizabeth I, William the Conquerer and "La Grande Mademoiselle," a cousin of King Louis XIV. When she died in 1693, her bowels were placed in a separate urn, as was the custom for royals. The urn exploded, leaving a dreadful stench, and the funeral party had to flee.

Victorian sextons knew to keep an eye on air-tight lead coffins. If they detected a swelling, the coffin was tapped and the gases lit to burn off. That was not an option when the body was not yet entombed.

THE COFFIN BLEW UP

Many Difficulties Attending the Burial of Mrs. John Peterson.

A most singular burial took place at Springfork, 15 miles distant from Sedalia, Mo., the other day. Among the early settlers of this county were a young German named John Peterson and his wife. Mrs. Peterson died of dropsy. At the time of her death she was a remarkably large woman, weighing nearly 300 pounds, says a dispatch to the New York *Herald.*

Immediately after Mrs. Peterson died arrangements were made for the funeral. The largest casket to be procured in the city was the exact measurement required at the time of death, but as it was not delivered until Friday morning the body had swollen so much that it was crowded into the casket with much difficulty. The lid was then screwed down and the body left in that condition for burial. Ice could not be procured. The funeral services were set for Sunday afternoon and, as is customary, a number of neighbors acted as watchers Friday night. At midnight the watchers were startled by a loud report in the room where the coffin had been placed. It was found that the gases of the body had accumulated within the casket until their force burst the glass over the face of Mrs. Peterson. So great was the force of the explosion that the body was shot forward and upward, the head protruding from the coffin.

A consultation was held and it was decided that owing to the condition of the body the burial should take place at once. The grave having been prepared, the coffin was carried to the burial place, and strong ropes were placed under the casket. Just as the coffin was being lowered, one of the assistants let go of his end of the rope. This threw the weight to the head of the coffin, and the ropes were jerked from the hands of the man stationed there. The coffin fell with great force, head down, and burst to pieces. Another consultation was held and it was decided to fill up the grave at once without waiting for another casket.

The Anaconda [MT] Standard 3 August 1890: p. 12 MISSOURI

A Coffin Explodes

On Friday last there was an occurrence in the cemetery at this place, the like of which, perhaps, was never known before. In 1875 Mr. James A. Watson, of Clover, whose family then resided in Yorkville, lost a child, aged three or four years, by death. At that time Mr. Watson was living in Baltimore, a teacher in the Bryant-Sadler Commercial College, and he could not conveniently leave his business to attend the funeral, and in his absence only temporary burial was given the body, awaiting his return home to secure a permanent burial lot in the cemetery. This was not practicable until recently, on the extension of the cemetery grounds, since which time he has bought a lot and on last Friday in company with Mr. J. Ed. Jeffreys and Dr. J. B. Allison he went into the cemetery to remove the body to his lot. The burial case—a Fisk metallic—was raised from the grave, and a natural desire to look upon the face of the child which died and was buried in the father's absence, prompted Mr. Watson to ask Mr. Jeffreys to remove the lid covering the glass panel over the face. The lid was unscrewed and removed, all three standing near, but observing a film on the surface of the glass, Mr. Watson requested Dr. Allison to procure some material for cleaning it off. The Doctor went to a residence near by for some cloth for this purpose, and while he was in the house an explosion of gas ensued, shattering the glass, which was ¼ inch thick, into numberless fragments, several striking Mr. Watson in the face, cutting it severely. One piece struck the bridge of the nose, cutting entirely through it. A few pieces of the glass also struck Mr. Jeffreys, but he was not seriously hurt. The casket had been out of the ground several minutes when the explosion occurred, which was the result of the expansion by the warmth of the sun of the gas formed in it. The report of the explosion was equal to that of a dynamite cartridge, and was noticed by persons on Main street, more than a quarter of a mile distant. The face of the child was in excellent preservation, as were also its burial clothes, and a wreath of flowers on the breast seemed to be nearly as fresh as when buried twelve and a half years ago.

The Anderson Intelligencer [Anderson Court House, SC]
7 January 1886: p. 1 SOUTH CAROLINA

There are also joke stories about frozen corpses, who had either drunk nitro-glycerine or had dynamite in their pockets, exploding when thawed. And there are tall tales of fighters and warriors who ate gunpowder as a strengthening tonic, exploding holes in crematoria walls.

The bereft sometimes chose to follow their loved ones to the grave at the cemetery—in a literal and very public sense.

DRANK POISON AT GRAVE OF HIS SUICIDE BRIDE

Surgeon Dentist Kneeling in Woodlawn Cemetery Takes His Own Life

New York, Dec. 1. Despondent over the death of his young wife who had committed suicide about two weeks ago, Dr. Rudolph Haas, a surgeon dentist, ended his own life today by drinking a quantity of carbolic acid, while kneeling beside the grave of Mrs. Haas in Woodlawn Cemetery.

A special watchman in the cemetery, who had seen the physician drinking the acid, ran to him, but arrived too late, and when an ambulance from the Fordham Hospital got to the place Dr. Haas was dead.

Mrs. Lillian Haas, the wife of Dr. Haas, was 27 years old and a bride of only a few months when she committed suicide by shooting herself at her home, 439 Manhattan avenue.

For some time Mrs. Haas had been a sufferer from nervousness and melancholia and been under the care of a physician.

Philadelphia [PA] Inquirer 2 December 1908: p. 1 NEW YORK

NOTE: Mrs. Haas was said to have shot herself on November 13. "Dr. Haas had been away from his home for three days just before his wife killed herself. She took him to task for remaining away without sending any word and when he could not give her a satisfactory account of his absence she told him she intended to kill herself, and that he would be responsible. Haas believed the threat an idle one and started for his office...He had barely left the room when he heard a revolver shot and rushed back to find his wife dead." *Evening News* [San Jose, CA] 9 December 1908: p. 3

DRANK POISON; FELL INTO HER BABY'S GRAVE; DIED

Philadelphia, Feb. 27. In the most dramatic manner conceivable, a grief-stricken mother yesterday, ended her life at the funeral of her beloved child, just after she had met her estranged husband for the first time in more than a year.

As the body of her seventeen-month-old son, Nathan, was being lowered into a grave in Har Nebo Cemetery, Frankford, Mrs. Fannie

Pollock, of 144 Laurel Street, raised a bottle of carbolic acid to her lips, and drained the contents, pitching headlong into the grave on top of the casket. She died in a few minutes.

The child had been the victim of an equally tragic fire horror.

Trenton [NJ] Evening Times 27 February 1913: p. 3 PENNSYLVANIA

NOTE: Mrs. Pollock had lost her first child to illness. Then her husband left her and their young son Nathan. Mrs. Pollock went to work at a shirtwaist factory while relatives watched the child. Nathan's 3-year old cousin Ethel was playing with matches when his clothing caught fire. He was badly burned and died in the hospital a short time later. Mrs. Pollock openly carried the carbolic acid to the graveside; everyone thought it was smelling salts.

Mrs. V. Woodward also met her estranged husband at their child's graveside.

A DEVIL, LOOSE FROM HELL

A Human Being Who Flirted at His Dead Child's Funeral.

New York *Dispatch*, 27th

A statement alleged to have been made on her death-bed by Mrs. V. Woodward was to-day read to Justice Bartlett, in the Brooklyn Supreme Court. In it she declared that her husband, George S. Woodward, carried his amours so far that while going to the cemetery to bury his dead child, he tore off the apple blossoms that the mother had put on the coffin and tossed them to flirtatious young women whom they met on the way. The dying declaration was read to convince Justice Bartlett that Mr. Woodward, who is a theatrical man, is not entitled to the custody of his little girl Lillian, aged 3. A number of affidavits were read, in which Woodward is accused by various persons of such crimes as larceny, embezzlement, bigamy, seduction, criminal malpractice, conspiracy, cruelty and extortion. The case was not concluded.

Charlotte [NC] Observer 30 June 1893: p. 3 NEW YORK

NOTE: Mrs. Woodward told her own mother, who had temporary custody, to "kill my baby," rather than let it fall into the hands of the father or his family. I have not found a ruling in the case.

Animals frequently left a wake or funeral in shambles, as we have seen in the previous catastrophic tales of cats at wakes.

Bees at a Funeral

A Swarm of Them Attacks and Drives Away Mourners From the Grave.

West Chester, Pa., Aug 15.

A swarm of bees created great consternation among a funeral party on Tuesday in Union Hill Cemetery, near Kennett Square, this county, during the burial of Joseph Frey.

At least 400 persons gathered around the grave in which the body was to be interred. Just as the coffin was lowered a multiplied cry went up from the center of the crowd and the whole ceremony was thrown into confusion.

A swarm of bees that had settled on a grave nearby had been disturbed by some of the mourners, and they proceeded to wreak vengeance on the entire party. Dozens of persons were badly stung, and the greater part of the procession immediately dispersed and ran off for shelter. The services were cut short and the mourners retreated hastily.

Pittsburg [PA] Dispatch 16 August 1891: p. 8 PENNSYLVANIA

NOTE: It is an old custom to "tell the bees" of a death in the family so that they will not fly away. There are a surprising number of stories of bees, especially bumble bees, breaking up funerals by invading the church, swarming out of the pulpit, stinging the hearse horses, or attacking the pallbearers.

Articles about the acquisition of hearse horses often stressed the animals' training, yet there were hundreds of accounts in the newspapers of hearse horses running away or colliding with trees, trains, or telegraph poles, often with tragic consequences.

FUNERAL HORROR FRIGHTENED HORSES

The Corpse of a Man Pulled After the Demolished Hearse in a Runaway

Rochester, N.Y., Feb. 24. A ghastly accident occurred at the double funeral of Mr. and Mrs. John Hackett, held near Lyons yesterday afternoon that has deeply shocked that community.

While the first hearse, drawn by a spirited team of blacks, was passing through a deep snow drift the horses became frightened, and, unseating the driver, ran away. The hearse containing the coffin and the remains of Mr. Hackett tipped over and the casket was demolished, throwing out the corpse, which, becoming entangled in the wrecked hearse, was dragged a considerable distance over the bare road and through deep snow drifts. When the terrified team finally broke loose from the wrecked vehicle and its ghastly occupant, the corpse was so badly mangled as to be almost unrecognizable. A driver was sent to look up another casket, which was procured several hours later, after which the funeral procession proceeded to the cemetery, where both bodies were interred in one grave.

Tucson [AZ] Daily Citizen 24 February 1902: p. 4 NEW YORK

KILLED BY LIGHTNING

A Hearse Driver Meets Death at the Side of a Grave

A scene of unprecedented horror was enacted at Baltimore, Md., during the electric storm a few days since, when a funeral cortege had drawn up to the entrance of the Sharp Street Cemetery at Mount Winans. It was the misfortune of the party to arrive at the cemetery entrance just as the worst storm of the season broke.

When the funeral procession arrived at the cemetery and had almost stopped at the side of the grave bearing the dead body of Mary Brown, a colored woman, a lightning bolt, which stunned all the members of the party, instantly killed William Alsup, who was driving the hearse, and started the horses drawing the hearse on a dead run. The deadly bolt at first stunned one of the hearse horses, bringing him to his knees. He was but shocked, however, and being, like his mate, a fiery steed, the regaining of his feet was but the signal for a runaway.

Meantime, the driver, already dead, sat bolt upright, the reins in his clenched hands, and there was presented to the horrified on-lookers the ghastly sight of the maddened chargers, dashing over the narrow abodes of the silent dead, controlled only by the reins in the convulsed hands of a dead driver, and bearing within the somber vehicle a burden attesting the mortality of human flesh. The frightened horses, in their mad career, were thrown upon their haunches by a collision with one of the trees of the cemetery, and then the lifeless driver was hurled from his seat to the ground. The horses struggled to extricate themselves, but before they could continue their mad career they were restrained by horror-stricken members of the funeral party.

The Coffeyville [KS] Daily Journal 21 April 1896: p. 2 MARYLAND

The poet, Dante Gabriel Rossetti is notorious for having had the body of his wife, Elizabeth Siddal, exhumed in 1869 to reclaim a volume of poems he had buried with her in a spasm of guilt-edged sorrow. Was this New York man inspired by his example?

There is a man named Hicks living at Brady's Bend, Chautauqua county, who buried his wife nine years ago. Like many another man he married again. About two weeks ago he got into a dispute with his present wife and during the controversy he cast up to his other half that the dead wife had been the best looking woman of the two. The new wife denied it; he insisted, and finally said his dead wife had a miniature of herself on her person, and he would dig up her body and get it, so as to satisfy the doubter as to the truth of what he said. Accordingly he got a pick and spade and proceeded to the graveyard, and in a short time disinterred the body, found the locket and brought it forth.

Plain Dealer [Cleveland, OH] 2 December 1872: p. 4 NEW YORK

Police often warn about thieves targeting a bereaved house, looting it during the visitation or funeral. Death and mourning provided an excellent cover for crime, ranging from the pathetic to the coldly calculated.

STEALS MOURNING DRESS

Young Woman Taken for Shoplifting Says She Needed Black for Funeral

By *Plain Dealer's* Leased Wire

Cincinnati, Nov. 2. "I took the black silk in order to get goods to go into mourning. My father lies dead at home. I had no black clothing and came to this side of the river and took the black silk to get a black dress."

This was the explanation of a young woman arrested in a large department store this morning by detectives on the charge of shoplifting. She gave the name of Mamie Schmidz of Covington. She was caught by a clerk after, it is alleged, she had tried to go away with two pieces of silk.

The Covington police found that a man of the same name as the girl's was dead at the address given by her. The funeral is to be held tomorrow.

Plain Dealer [Cleveland, OH] 3 November 1909: p. 11 KENTUCKY

BOUQUET RIBBONS STOLEN FROM GRAVES

Ghost-Like Woman Who Haunts Cemeteries Taken to Police Station

Chester, Pa., April 19. An unknown and mysterious woman is detained at the police station charged with an unusual offense—stealing ribbons from bouquets laid on the graves of the dead. Talk of ghosts in broad daylight in several neighboring cemeteries led Superintendent Gove Burton of the Chester Rural cemetery to keep a lookout for the intruder.

Late one evening a phantom-like apparition entered the cemetery and was crouching near a grave. He was not a believer in fleshless spirits that are said to frequent graveyards, and stealing upon the figure, he leaped on it. It was his.

The figure was a woman dressed in white. Burton dragged her to the house and summoned the police to City Hall. A search of her person revealed hundreds of yards of ribbon which she had stolen from bouquets placed on the graves.

She refused to divulge her name. She is young and pretty.

The Salt Lake [UT] Tribune 20 April 1904: p. 9 PENNSYLVANIA

A CALCULATING CORPSE

He is Caught in the Act of Counting the Money Contributed to Give Him a Christian Burial.

Baltimore, Md., Feb. 23. Several days ago a pretty little woman went to one of the largest Methodist churches in Baltimore and asked for money to bury her dead husband. She gave her name as Hester Green and said she was ashamed to ask the city to bury him. Two worthy women were sent out to investigate the case. They went to a house in Perkin street. There was crape on the door, all the blinds were closed, and the stillness of death brooded over the place. They entered the house. In one corner of a darkened room lay the corpse, and near it was the wife bowed with grief. The visitors looked at the body, and then comforted the bereaved woman. The pathetic story so touched the hearts of the brethren that $17 was raised to give him a Christian burial.

Next day one of the women who had investigated the case went to the house and found the wife a little more "resigned to the will of heaven," as she expressed it, and the corpse still there. The money was left and the visitor departed with the consciousness of having done a good deed. She found after walking a few squares that she had left her umbrella. She returned to get it, opened the door, and there sat the corpse counting the money, clinking one half dollar against the other to see if it was not counterfeit. The woman was thunderstruck, and although she was "sold," was determined not to be beaten out of $17. So she compelled the corpse to return the money that had been contributed for the purpose of burying him like a Christian.

Jackson [MI] Citizen 2 March 1886: p. 7 MARYLAND

We read earlier of the amateur mourners who attended funerals for the fun of it. Some of them were con-men and con-women, who followed the coffin to exploit the vulnerable bereaved.

AT MANY FUNERALS

When Arrested She Wails Some More and Borrows From Judge.

LIVED OFF HER TEARS

Wore Reversible Coat With Gray Inside to Turn When Work Was Done.

It will be some time before Clara Howell, professional mourner and weeper at funerals, will be back at her vocation again. She has been arrested by Policeman Burdette and was released by Justice Gavin on her promise to go to Littleton, where she has relatives, and remain there. Incidentally she "touched" the justice for 25 cents to pay her fare out of the city.

Clara Howell continually wears a black scarf, which extends over her head and under her chin. She never has been seen on the street or at funerals without it.

She was arrested at Miller's undertaking establishment, Seventeenth and Curtis streets, by Burdette, who had been watching her.

She has been in the habit of begging, says the policeman, and never overlooks a chance to ask for money. But it is in the role of professional mourner that she shines.

Slipping quietly into an undertaking chapel or even a private home where funeral services are being conducted she would take a seat and begin to weep. Naturally some of the relatives of the deceased person would be anxious to learn the identity of the mourner and in many cases would address her, whereupon the disconsolate one invariably would say that she was acquainted with the departed one and incidentally call attention to her own poverty.

On such occasions it was easy to beg or borrow and, in this manner, Clara Howell succeeded in "getting the coin."

The woman wears a reversible coat, one side being black, for mourning purposes, and the other gray, for street wear.

Policeman Burdette received many complaints concerning the woman from undertakers and finally decided to arrest her on a charge of vagrancy.

The Denver [CO] Post 8 March 1910: p. 6 COLORADO

This next story tells of a man whose "whole time is devoted to attending funerals." He tells the reporter, after consulting his pocket-book, that he has attended 10,375 services. This individual does it for pleasure but he knows those who attend funerals for profit:

THE FUNERAL FIEND

"I follow the profession solely from the love of it. I would rather any day see a dead man than a live one, but in my travels around the country I have met those who make it a sordid trade, and derive a large income from it."

"How do they do that?"

"Well, to show you, there was a woman in the business whom I knew ten years ago. She went by the name of 'The Widow.' A long black veil was part of her stock in trade. She never attended the funerals of any but the rich. She used to appear on the scene with this long black veil drawn over her face, and made good use of her handkerchief while the service was in progress. When the time came for the friends to take their last look at the departed she contrived to be among the last.

"When she came opposite the head of the coffin she would begin to sob passionately, and fairly fling herself on the bier so that her veil covered it. In the moment that she remained in this posture she had time to search the corpse for rings or other jewels, and you may be sure that if there had been any trinkets of the sort on the body at first, when 'the widow' had ceased mourning and passed on they were not there. Then in the after confusion no one thought of them. She told me that the biggest haul she ever made was in Sacramento, Cal., where she bagged $300 worth in one week. It was a poor week with her when she could not make $100. She kept her eyes open, and if people's suspicions were ever aroused she got out of town.

"Then I've known men who make a business of stealing coffin-handles. Early in the day of the funeral the thief comes to the house, and, announcing himself as the undertaker's assistant, gains admission to the room where the coffin stands and quickly screws off the handles and other silver trimmings. But, of course, that is risky work...."

Lawrence [KS] Daily Journal 15 December 1887: p. 2

This next story highlights a custom where a new bride might assume mourning for a dead relative of her husband's, in this case, his mother. But here, the seemingly reasonable request took a sinister turn into psychological abuse and domestic violence.

MOTHER-IN-LAW WAS DEAD

Professor MacArthur Wanted His Bride to Dye Her Trousseau Black and She Objected.

The mourning of sable and crape is not the only mourning in the life of Mrs. MacArthur, of 59 Hull street, Brooklyn.

Mrs. MacArthur appeared yesterday morning in the Gates Avenue Police Court fairly framed in grief. Her father stood by her side.

Three months married, she wanted a warrant for the arrest of her husband, Professor Daniel MacArthur, who gives music lessons. The charge is assault. Having listened to her tale of sables, as it might be called, Police Justice Connelly gave her the warrant, and Mrs. MacArthur returned to her mother, Mrs. Lundt, of No. 2287 Pacific street, Brooklyn.

Although this sad story is a case of mother-in-law, it is the funniest case any one ever heard of, inasmuch as mother-in-law is not only dead but has been dead for twenty years.

Little troubles Mrs. MacArthur put up with, and, like a Mrs. Bre'r Rabbit, said nothing. On their wedding night, the Professor, she says, set the pace for their future happiness by giving his little eighteen-year-old wife a deliberate, faithfully administered spanking. It was a sad disappointment to Mrs. MacArthur, who had looked forward to the same tender treatment from her husband that she had received from her fond parents.

But she accepted it, not only then, but often, she says. It was only when the Professor invented a new torture that she rebelled against it. When it came down to the point where he not only insisted that she must go into mourning for his long dead mother [who died when he was five], but the blackest kind of mourning trappings at that, then she was angered all the way through.

She saw first one and then another of her fine new wedding gowns dipped in the dye pot. Not figuratively, mind you, but literally, those delicate pinks and blues became the grizzliest of blacks. Probably, too, they shrank fearfully, although she did not mention that in her complaint. They always do. But dyed they were and dyed she had to wear them until a few days ago, when she not only resisted, but resisted like a woman and a tactician with the aid of a broomstick. She had threatened to leave the Professor and return to her mother. This threat, she says, the Professor resented forcibly, and then she protected herself.

Of the result of that encounter Mrs. MacArthur is evidently not ashamed. Having a disagreeable role to play as the worm that turned she played it with enthusiasm. Then she went to the home of her girlhood, leaving the Professor in charge of their apartments. Court Policeman James Moore is looking for him now for the purpose of serving the warrant.

New York Herald 29 November 1893: p. 5 NEW YORK

NOTE: Professor Daniel McKinley MacArthur fled to New Jersey. Mrs. Louisa MacArthur's neighbors told how she would be sent to bed without supper, like a child, for some trivial thing that didn't suit her husband or for chatting with the neighbors. He would lock her in their apartment and paste sheets of paper across the doors, so he would know if she had left the building. Mrs. MacArthur obviously had grounds for an annulment, but I have found no record of one.

We have to admire the breathtaking nerve of this plausible young man who impersonated both the bereaved lover *and* the undertaker's son, come on an unpleasant errand.

GRAVESIDE SWINDLING

The Ingenious Way in Which a Plausible Young Man Collected an Undertaker's Bill.

Precisely who is swindled in a recent transaction of a very novel nature is what a bereaved family and a bewildered undertaker are now endeavoring to discover. Both parties are, however, certain that a few hundred dollars which belonged to one of them passed into the hands of an astute young man they would both like to meet. The story of the clever and decidedly new method of swindling was related during a conversation which followed the annual meeting of the lot owners in Greenwood Cemetery at No. 30 Broadway yesterday afternoon. Stealing plants and flowers in cemeteries had been a prominent topic during the meeting, and the conversation which followed drifted naturally into stories of thefts in and around such institutions, the following instance being the most remarkable that was related:

A wealthy family some few weeks ago buried an only daughter. She was an estimable young lady, was idolized by her parents, and they spared no expense in arranging for her funeral. Two or three days after the interment a very genteel, well-dressed young man called on the undertaker. He announced himself as the betrothed lover of the deceased young lady, and said that the object of his visit was to give some token of the extent of his affection for her. "I wish," said he, "to pay her funeral expenses. A few days more and she would have been my wife; now she is dead and I have given no evidence of the value I placed on her love."

In vain the undertaker told him that it was not customary for families to allow such bills to be so paid. The young man was so evidently affected by the loss of his loved one and so anxious to pay the expenses that he at least persuaded the man of coffins to make out the bill, which his mourning visitor took with him "Just down to his father's office, who would make out the check and send it back at once." No check, however, came, but a day or two ago the father of the young lady, meeting the undertaker, said: "I was as sorry as surprised at hearing of your embarrassment and hope the money was sufficient to fully relieve you."

The undertaker, aghast, stammered: "Money! Embarrassed! Relieve me! Why, I haven't asked you for any money, and did not intend to for some weeks yet."

It was next the gentleman's turn to express himself, and somewhat nettled he tartly replied, "And yet you dunned me for the expenses of my daughter's funeral within three days and I paid the bill." A comparison of notes followed and then they ascertained that the plausible young man had within one hour of getting the bill from the undertaker called on the father of the lady, representing himself as the son of the undertaker. He told a story of his father's embarrassments which moved his hearer to that extent that he paid the amount of the bill in currency, and the question now is, Who is swindled, he or the undertaker? The trail of the money and the young man is cold, and the police think he will be more difficult to find than the young man who is striking false alarms of fire.

New York Herald 16 March 1882: p. 5 NEW YORK

NOTE: The false alarms plagued the New York Fire Department for some three years. They were sent from all over the city, sometimes half a dozen times in a single night. One William McCabe was the "False Alarm Fiend," leader of a gang of burglars who sent in the false alarms "for fun," or, more plausibly, as a diversion.

We cannot leave the subject of grave errors without touching briefly on premature burial, a topic that fairly seethes with maggots of horror. It is an immense subject and, in fact, there are several books listed in the bibliography that cover the subject definitively. I will simply offer an overview, since a book on Victorian death would be incomplete without it. But how much of a problem was burial alive—really? Let us hear from a notable member of the British Medical Association, Dr. J. Stenson Hooker:

> "Even if one is unwilling," he added, "to go as far as the English investigator who estimates that 2,700 people at least in England and Wales are yearly consigned to the tomb while alive and to accept the conclusion of Le Guern who calculated the premature burials in France at two per thousand, it is nevertheless beyond question that the peril of living sepulture is an actual and terrifying menace."
>
> *Aberdeen [SD] American* 22 July 1922: p. 6

Strong words, yet even allowing for exaggeration, the thousands of lurid newspaper articles about the prematurely buried and the nearly-buried bear testimony to the extent of the fear.

I have just heard of one of the most horrible, heart-rending, and yet, perhaps, unavoidable affairs which it has ever been my lot, as a newspaper correspondent, to record. It is nothing more nor less than the frightful reality of being buried alive. A most estimable lady, named Mrs. Crane, whose husband is a book-keeper in Flemming & Co.'s drug store, on Magazine Street, in this city [New Orleans, LA], died very suddenly last July, of what was pronounced sun-stroke. She was a school teacher in one of our most popular public schools, and resided, if I am not mistaken, on Dryades Street. It was in the afternoon, after school was out, that she went to visit a neighbor on Felicity Street and just as she entered her friend's house, she fell insensible to the floor and expired, to all appearance, in about two minutes, a doctor pronouncing it sun-stroke. Her body was interred the next day, at ten o'clock, and her mother, an old lady about fifty years of age, and her husband and one little son, went home almost broken-hearted and have since been nearly distracted, being at times unable to sleep, and, in fact, leading a most miserable and disconsolate life; and well they might, as the sequel will show, had they known what they had done. Well, one night last week the mother, after passing a most distressing day, fell asleep late at night and dreamed that her daughter had been buried alive. She jumped up in a frantic state and rushed to her son-in-law's chamber crying, "My daughter is buried alive! Oh, my daughter is buried alive! What shall I do!" To sleep any more that night was out of the question; she still crying that her daughter was buried alive, whenever her son-in-law would try to quiet her. At length the proposition was made to have the body disinterred just to satisfy her. So, early the next morning the grave was opened and the coffin raised. Oh, what a horrible sight met their view. Pen is powerless to portray the scene which followed. The body, which had been placed in a metallic coffin, was turned over, the glass covering the face was broken to atoms, the ends of her fingers being beaten and battered all to pieces; her hair torn out in handfuls and her shroud torn in many places—all presenting the appearance of one of the most desperate struggles to free herself from her terrible misfortune.

If any of your readers could have seen the relatives of this unfortunate lady, when the condition of what they supposed was the perpetually silent tomb had been brought to light, it would have forced a tear from the most stolid and adamantine heart. It was one of the most distressing affairs ever recorded in this State and I sincerely hope it will be the last I am ever called upon to record.

I have not seen this affair mentioned in any of our city papers, but as far as the truth of the matter is concerned, I can vouch for it having occurred, as I have it from parties intimately connected with the unfortunate family and whose veracity I cannot doubt. The husband and mother, it is now said, are almost entirely bereft of their reason, and it is feared they will go permanently deranged; and, indeed, they have sufficient reason.

This should be another warning to all who read this of the uncertainty of death until the body begins to decay. It is generally conceded by physicians that as long as there is a possibility of returning life the body will not show any signs of decomposition. Therefore, in warm weather, when a body does not commence to decompose immediately it is a sure sign that the life has not left it, and the body should not be buried.

Cincinnati [OH] Enquirer 3 December 1868: p. 2 LOUISIANA

This sound advice on decomposition is a common warning in the literature of premature burial. While today the boundaries of death are a shifting ethical minefield, without the benefit of modern medical technology Victorian physicians relied on the misted mirror and tell-tale heartbeat to confirm that life still lingered. In cases of coma, catalepsy, or cholera, more drastic measures had to be taken: electric shock, red-hot pokers on the soles of the feet, "irritating" powders, needles run beneath fingernails, whipping with wet towels, burning the skin to see if it blistered, placing a "necrometer" under the arm to measure body temperature, and holding the hand up to the light to see if it was red with circulating blood.

Cholera was a particularly insidious dissembler of death, as those who were infected seemed to die very quickly, but might actually be in a coma. Attendants were disposed to bury first and ask questions later. Victims were sometimes thrown into mass graves while still alive and more than one cholera cemetery is reputed to be haunted by those tortured ghosts.

To counteract all these distressing possibilities, an Association for the Prevention of Premature Interment was founded in 1895 by Colonel Edward P. Vollum, a US Army surgeon, and Sir Benjamin Ward Richardson, eminent sanitary reformer and anesthetic researcher. One of the suggestions made was to leave a flask of lightly stoppered chloroform in each coffin so that the person buried alive could drift painlessly off into a real death. When Dr. Richardson died in 1896, he was cremated.

Nonsensically this was another method advocated for avoiding premature interment. One must question the logic that promotes being burned alive as a more desirable outcome than being trapped in an airless casket.

The questions of life or death, of burial—or premature burial, left the dying in limbo, balanced on a knife's edge. Some left horrific orders to make certain nothing went wrong.

FEAR PREMATURE BURIAL

GHASTLY DIRECTIONS FOR THE DISPOSAL OF A PHYSICIAN'S REMAINS.

Dr. Charles F. Heuser Left a Will in Which He Requested His Heart be Taken from His Body to Make Sure He was Dead and That His Body be Cremated

On the Death of His Wife He Drove a Knife Into Her Heart to Protect Her from Being Buried Alive.

Baltimore, January 24. The body of Dr. Charles F. Heuser was cremated at Loudon Park yesterday afternoon. He was a well-known physician and apothecary. The circumstances connected with his ghastly directions for the disposal of his remains makes his story and that of his family a very remarkable one.

Dr. Heuser left a will in which he requested that his heart be taken from his body in the presence of witnesses on the day of his death, and that his remains be afterward cremated, the ashes to be distributed among his friends.

The strange clause concerning the heart of the dead physician caused somewhat of a sensation, but his friends resolved to carry out his wishes as nearly as possible. A number of physicians and surgeons declined to mutilate the corpse of their dead friend, but yesterday Dr. Bernard T. Meyer, in the presence of a few friends,

REMOVED THE HEART FROM THE BODY,

Then replacing it the remains were made ready for cremation. The ashes will be disposed of as directed in the will.

The strange request of the physician is accounted for by one who knew him well, from the fact that he had entertained a horror of being buried alive. He often talked on the subject, and his

FEAR OF PREMATURE BURIAL

Was increased after a talk he had some time ago with a Virginia physician, who said that in a number of cases he had seen corpses disinterred which showed that the persons had come to life after burial. Some of the bodies were drawn up in the coffins or lay on their sides dreadfully contorted.

Resolved upon escaping premature burial by having his body cremated, he determined to avoid the possibility of being burned alive by the singular expedient mentioned.

A circumstance that adds additional interest to the singular ceremony is the fact that Dr. Heuser, after his wife's death, some years ago,

DROVE A KNIFE INTO HER HEART

to protect her from the possibility of being immured alive. He had frequently told the story of this affair himself, and said it was the most terrible duty he ever had to perform, to thrust the cold steel into the bosom of the woman he loved as she lay on the bier before him; yet he could not think of letting her run the awful risk of coming back to life in her grave.

Another similar circumstance is that many members of Dr. Heuser's family have had their hearts pierced or their veins and arteries cut after death. The fear of premature burial seems to have pervaded the whole family and led to the utmost precautions being taken to insure escape from such a fate. None of them, however, except the doctor, have been cremated.

Tyrone [PA] Daily Herald 24 January 1891: p. 1 MARYLAND

NOTE: I have not located Dr. Heuser in the census or grave records, although Dr. Bernard Meyer of Baltimore appears in a 1902 testimonial about the efficacy of Wright's Rheumatic Remedy. The remedies to prevent premature burial, stabbing through the heart and removal of that organ, seem the directives of a madman, but there are many other examples of people leaving instructions for arteries to be cut, heads to be amputated, and needles driven into hearts—such was the fear of being buried alive.

There are a shocking number of first-person narratives from persons buried alive, only to be saved by a dropped coffin, by thieves or Resurrectionists.

Even grave-robbers may once in a while be the unconscious means by which a human life is saved. Mr. Hayward, who lives in Missouri, is the man who went through this strange experience. The *Kansas City*

Journal, which I quote, contained the following: "To be buried alive while sorrowing friends stand about the open grave, and then come to life in a dissecting room, is the actual experience of George Hayward, an Independence jeweler...Mr. Hayward is a man of sixty-nine years of age. For years he has been in the jewelry business at Independence, and at present conducts a shop on South Main street. He has the belief that many people are buried alive, and his own experience has a tendency to confirm this belief. To a *Journal* representative Mr. Hayward related this burial and resurrection experience with the unconcern of a man who does not fear death. 'It was in Marshville, England, County Gloucestershire, where I was buried,' said Mr. Hayward very grimly. 'My father had a large family of boys, and he raised us all on the farm near the village. I was quite young, and it was my chief delight to go to the fields with my older brothers...It was a bright morning when we started for the fields, and I ran ahead of the horses. The horses in England are not driven with reins, but they follow the command of the voice. After reaching the field the pitching of the straw commenced. The men used hop picks, which are fashioned somewhat after a heavy pitchfork. While standing near one of the hands, by accident I was struck on the head with one of the picks. It penetrated my scull [sic], and at the time made me feel faint and dizzy. My injury was not considered serious. After returning to the house I was sent into the cellar, and, much to my surprise, I could see in the dark as well as in the light. After coming from the cellar my strength failed me, and I was soon bedfast. Two doctors were called. One of them insisted that my condition was due to the blow on the head, the other that I had pleurisy. At any rate two weeks elapsed, and my eyes closed in supposed death. It was death as far as my relatives were concerned, yet I was painfully conscious of every movement going on around me. My eyes were half closed, and as I was laid out I heard my elder brother, John, walk into the house. I saw him approach the cot with tears in his eyes, and sympathizing friends consoled him by asking him to dry his tears. "He is gone," they said, and other similar expressions were used around the bier. Well-known faces would peer down at me as I lay with my eyes half closed. Tears rained on my face as the burial shroud was wrapped around my body. As soon as the undertaker arrived I knew I was to be buried alive. Try as I would, nothing could break the spell which bound me. Every action and every word spoken are as distinct to my mind now as then. Well, the time for the funeral arrived, and the service was preached over my living but rigid body. The undertaker approached and the lid of my little prison-house was fastened down. Life seemed all but gone when this took place; but, as I stated, no effort of mine could break the spell. The coffin was shoved into the wagon, and the trundling of the vehicle sounded in my ears. I was painfully conscious of the fact that I was soon to be lowered into my grave. Strange as it may seem, at times I did not feel fear at my impending fate. The coffin was taken out of the wagon and lowered into the grave. In those days boxes were not used as a receptacle for the coffin. The clods of earth fell heavy on the lid of the casket. There I was being entombed alive, unable to speak or stay the hands of my friends. My effort to move proved futile, and the close air of the coffin seemed stifling to me. Suddenly the shoveling ceased and the silence of the tomb was complete. I did not seem to have the fear then that a person would naturally expect under such circumstances. All I remember is that the grave is a lonely place, and the silence of the tomb was horribly oppressive. A dreamy sensation came over me, and a sense of suffocation became apparent. My whole system was paralyzed; were it otherwise my struggles would have been desperate. How long I remained in this condition I do not know. The first sense of returning life came over me when I heard the scraping of a spade on my coffin lid. I felt myself raised and borne away. I was taken out of my coffin, not to my home, but to a dissecting room. I beheld the doctors who had waited on me at my home, dressed in long white aprons. In their hands they had knives. Through my half-closed eyes I saw them engaged in a dispute. They were trying to decide how to cut me up. One argued one way, while the other doctor took another view of the matter. All this I witnessed through my half-open eyes. My sense of hearing was remarkably acute. Both approached the table and opened my mouth to take out my tongue, when, by superhuman effort, my eyelids were slightly raised. The next thing I heard was: "Look out, you fool, he is alive!" "He is dead," rejoined the other doctor. "See, he opens his eyes!" continued the first doctor. The other physician let his knife drop, and a short time after that I commenced to recover rapidly. Instead of cutting me up they took me home. There was great rejoicing among my relatives. I owed my life to the doctors' dispute as to what ailed me during my illness. I suppose I was kept alive for some purpose,' continued Mr. Hayward, as he finished his grewsome tale, 'for I am the father of ten children.'

The Encyclopaedia of Death and Life in the Spirit-world, Vol. 3, John Reynolds Francis. (Chicago: The Progressive Thinker Publishing House, 1900) ENGLAND

NOTE: George Hayward died in 1903 and is buried in Woodlawn Cemetery, Independence, Missouri.

Before we look upon the face of this terrifying subject for the last time, let us note that burial alive, if properly executed, could be the ideal method for the perfect murder.

Supposed to be Buried Alive.

The Cincinnati Gazette of September 21, says, "There has been a rumor, current in Brooklyn, Ohio, for two weeks past, that a resident of that place named Powell had been buried alive. The deceased was quite advanced in years, and was buried the third day after he was taken sick. A minister, a friend of the family, who saw the body after it was laid out for the grave, said that if it was a friend of his he should not be buried. He said this because the body was still warm, and by pressing a finger upon the skin the color would come and go, as it will upon the skin of a person alive. Several persons witnessed this and others declared they saw a twitching of the muscles of the face. One of his sons was married within a week after the funeral, and the deceased, it is said, was not on the best of terms with his children.

Boston [MA] Herald 25 September 1860: p. 4 OHIO

A Fiendish Act

The driver of a pauper cart has just been arrested in New Orleans under singular circumstances. On the 25th ult, a young colored man died, or is said to have died, in the small-pox hospital of that city. The body was put into a rough coffin and started in the hospital wagon for the Potter's Field. Another coffin, containing a child was in the same wagon. In passing through the streets a number of persons were attracted to the wagon by seeing the lid of the coffin containing the body of the man removed and a hand appear from the aperture. The wagon stopped and the driver proceeded to replace the lid, when the following scene occurred, the facts being substantiated by a half-dozen persons who witnessed it. A Mrs. Smith says: "The wagon stopped and I thought it had broken down. A friend called me out into the street to see. I went close up to the wagon, and then I saw two coffins—one for a baby, the other for a grown person. The coffin for the grown person was open, the lid being partly off. I saw distinctly the man in the coffin moving his hand, trying to push off the lid. The driver took the cushion off the seat and put it on the man's face, and sat down on his head. In this position he sat for a square, when he stopped again and took a hammer and tried to nail down the lid. He then took the baby's coffin and put it on top of the man's feet and sat on him again. The driver said to me, in an angry tone: 'What do you want here?' I said I wanted to see, and he answered: 'Get away before I slap you in the mouth.' I said: 'You are carrying a live man to the grave-yard.' He drove on and I followed the wagon, but was not allowed to enter the cemetery.

Another woman, Mrs. Thompson, states that she saw the man raise his arms, put out his hands, and try to get up out of the coffin; that the driver pushed him back with great force, and then sat on his head while he drove on. A crowd of witnesses state that the man was alive while being conveyed to the cemetery, though the sexton says he was certainly dead when he arrived on the grounds. It seems almost beyond belief that such inhumanity should exist; but if any reliance can be placed in the word of witnesses this worse than savage barbarity was certainly exhibited as related. The hanging of a monster guilty of such fiendishness would be mild punishment for the crime. *Chicago Inter Ocean*

Perrsyburg [OH] Journal 18 June 1875: p. 1 LOUISIANA

An equally horrific story came from the time of the Spanish Influenza Pandemic. The disease, a drowning pneumonia, could kill a victim in a few hours. Two men driving a death cart in Cape Town, South Africa heard shouting coming from a coffin they had loaded that morning.

"He had seemed very dead when they found him in the tenement, twenty minutes back, but of course there had been no doctor to consult with.

"The two men looked at one another. He was the worst man in all that neighbourhood—a loafer, a drunkard, a wife-beater, a man for whom no one in their…community had anything but deep contempt. 'I reckon,' said Brown slowly, 'ain't no one going to miss him.'

"His mate nodded solemn agreement. They climbed back into the truck. It ground away down McKinley Road, the long trailing cries fading into silence as it went."

The Plague of the Spanish Lady: The Influenza Pandemic of 1918–1919, Richard Collier, (New York: Atheneum, 1974), 253 SOUTH AFRICA

Further Reading: "Taking the 'Fun' Out of 'Funeral.'" http://strange-co.blogspot.com/2014/07/newspaper-clippings-of-day-taking-fun.html#comment-form

"Buried Alive: 19th-century Safety Coffins." http://thechirurgeonsapprentice.com/2013/06/26/buried-alive-19th-century-safety-coffins/

"Premature Burial and Helpful Hints on How Not to Get Buried Alive." http://hauntedpalaceblog.wordpress.com/2013/10/05/premature-burial-and-helpful-hints-on-how-not-to-get-buried-alive/

"9 Weird and Unreliable Ways to Avoid Burying Someone Alive." http://io9.com/9-weird-and-unreliable-ways-to-avoid-burying-someone-al-1448575444

11.

The Picture on the Coffin Lid:
Haunted Cemeteries and Other
Venues of Death

The traditional city churchyard was a horror and a public health menace. Physicians railed against these gloomy havens of moss and morbidity, where human bones crunched underfoot and noisome liquids seeped from too-shallow burials. In the 1840s there was a movement to bury the dead in the country, outside city centers, in what were termed "Garden Cemeteries." These tranquil landscapes were to be filled with trees, flowers, beautiful vistas, and picnicking families. They were designed to elevate the populace, morally and aesthetically. And there was no place in the garden cemetery for ghosts.

The newspapers did their best to debunk and ridicule cemetery spooks in a jocular class of articles in which all the ghosts turn out to be white cows scratching themselves on tombstones or drunkards trapped in open graves. The wavering white mist rising from new-made tombs was gravely explained by eminent scientists as "phosphoretted hydrogen." Yet science could do little to stamp out cemetery superstitions. The credulous still feared, not mist, but the white-clad ghosts of the newly departed.

Cremation was a relatively new concept in the 1880s. It is fascinating to see one of the earliest crematories becoming haunted so quickly.

KEEPS ITS WORD

How Mr. Kilgore's Spirit Haunts the Philadelphia Cemetery.

Philadelphia dispatch to the *Globe-Democrat:*

The departed spirit of the late Damon Y. Kilgore, the well-known lawyer...is said to be ill at ease in his new abode. Mr. Kilgore was cremated as per his last wish, the crematory in Germantown, near

Washington lane, being the place of his incineration. Ever since the date of this occurrence the place has been gaining the reputation of being haunted. Strange and ghostly sounds have been heard from twilight until dawn, and a number of the employees about the place have resigned positions on account of the omens. Groans are heard, they say, in the dimly lighted corridors. Shadows have flitted about the sombre rotunda where the ashes of the dead repose, and one might imagine he could see hobgoblins going through some wild and fearful dance if he sat in the gloom of the basement and gazed at the weird band of light thrown on the cemented floor by the crackling furnace fire.

But it was not until recently that these manifestations were traced to the spirit of Mr. Kilgore. On Wednesday night Superintendent Beamsderfer says he was sitting before the furnace calmly smoking his pipe, when there came a sharp, resounding knock from the vicinity of the burial vault. It broke the intense melancholy of the place with startling force. The superintendent, a man who never feared the dead, looked about him with frightened eyes. His pipe fell from his lips, and, as he himself now says, he realized by instinct that his visitor was no human being. The raps seemed to come from the aperture in the floor where the catafalque slides downward. Gradually they increased in volume until Mr. Beamsderfer, unable longer to bear the suspense, grabbed his lantern with a trembling hand and started in that direction. Then he seemed to hear the sounds on every hand, growing louder every minute. As he neared the spot he saw, in the mingled dimness of the gloom and the rays of his lantern, what seemed to be a prostrate form, which slowly assumed material shape until he recognized the features of the departed lawyer. While he looked at it the form assumed an upright position, then struck several times upon the resounding walls and glided noiselessly away. Beamsderfer darted after it with his lantern held above his head, but the spectre vanished in the darkness.

The next night the rappings were repeated for several hours, but no phantom appeared.

Mr. Kilgore was a confirmed Spiritualist in faith, and believed in the communion with the dead. Before his death he is reported to have said that he would return to the scenes of his life, a fact which added to the terror of the superintendent. Although not a Spiritualist himself, Mr. Beamsderfer is convinced that Mr. Kilgore's ghost is keeping the pledge made in life, and he does not care to keep a solitary watch in the dimly lighted crematory.

Omaha [NE] Daily Herald 30 September 1888: p. 12 PENNSYLVANIA

NOTE: Kilgore died on 25 April, 1888; an obituary was published in the *Philadelphia [PA] Inquirer* 27 April 1888: p. 2. He was a Spiritualist and advocate for women's suffrage and had a reputation for eccentricity.

Morgues, also known as "dead-houses," were an obvious venue for hauntings.

GHOST LAYS OUT THE DEAD

Snapshot to Be Used on Morgue Wraith Keeper Saw

Cleveland, Oct. 8. The county morgue here has a tame ghost. This particular spook is a useful, handy wraith, and the morgue officers are tickled that it should take up its lodgings in their quarters.

When Keeper Cassidy stepped into the operating room to put the finishing touches to a corpse there yesterday, he saw a filmy white object gradually disappear in the corner of the room, and, to his great astonishment, discovered that the work he had expected to perform on the corpse had already been done. "It's an undertaker's ghost, that's all," said Deputy Coroner Houck, when Cassidy, streaming with perspiration told what he had seen. Cassidy maintains it was the spirit of the dead man in the operating room.

To ascertain just what it is, another corpse will be placed in the room tomorrow, and a photographer will be hidden there. A snapshot of the ghost will be taken if it does any more undertaker's work.

Winston-Salem [NC] Journal 9 October 1907: p. 3 OHIO

A HAUNTED MORGUE

Mysterious Rappings in the Omaha Dead-House

Omaha World

Coroner Drexel and his partner, Mike Maul, sleep in the rear of their undertaking rooms at Fifteenth and Farnam streets. Elias Gish and Will Baker also sleep in the same building. About 2 o'clock this morning the quartet were awakened by a terrible thumping and creaking among the coffins. They listened again and the sound grew weaker and weaker until finally all fell asleep. A half-hour later the thumping became so vigorous and loud that the men got up and dressed. Two carried lamps, while the other two examined the large cases which contained the coffins. As soon as the men entered the room with a lamp the light was blown out. Drexel did not stop running until he had reached the Merchants' Hotel, while Maul headed for the Paxton.

Baker and Gish remained in the room, and after lighting the gas several times just to see it go out, they got their pipes and sat up the rest of the night.

In a conversation with a reporter for the *World* about the matter, Elias said "It's no new thing for us to hear the creaking and thumping among the coffins at night, but it was never so bad before. Some persons believe that it is the spirit of the dead person who will occupy the coffin, and this may be true, for the following two or three days after these noises are the worst, we always sell a great many coffins. I believe that some person dies in this city every time the pounding takes place in a different coffin. The common theory is that the sudden change in the weather caused the noises, but it is hair-raising at midnight, let it come from whatever source it may."

San Francisco [CA] Chronicle 13 March 1887: p. 2 NEBRASKA

No roster of cemetery spirits would be complete without the blanched horror of a Woman in White. Of course, some graveyards contained statues of angels carved in snowy marble, their arms raised in benediction, and easily mistaken for ghosts in the dark. Could that be the explanation for this man's vision?

Saw His Wife's Spirit

[*New Moon.*]

In a city in the western part of Massachusetts lived a gentleman who had frequently boasted of his great personal courage—not obtrusively, but candidly—declaring that he had never yet known what personal fear was. He had an honorable record of three years' service in the war, and those who fought with him expressed their confidence in his great personal courage. He scouted all idea of ghosts or supernatural appearances, asserting that he would lie as peacefully in a grave-yard all night as in his own house, so far as ghosts were concerned. Nobody doubted his courage; nobody doubted his statements. In the course of time his wife died, and was buried in the village grave-yard. It was his habit to pass the grave-yard where his wife was buried, on his way home at night, at all hours of the evening. One night, when he happened by later than usual, just as he was passing the road skirting the grave-yard, the clock in the village tolled out the midnight hour. The gentleman himself told us that an involuntary shudder came over him; his whole frame shook; he felt an unearthly presence. Instantly his eyes turned toward the spot where his wife lay buried, when inside the fence he saw a female figure dressed in white, yet so strange was its formation that the whole form was transparent, at the same time as real as the grave-yard fence, over which he immediately sprang, to ascertain for himself whether or not the object before him was living or dead. It moved gradually away from him; he could come no nearer; when he advanced, she retreated; when he retreated, she advanced; and he found it impossible to close the gap between them. He shouted, but got no response, except that the object made a most distressing appeal to him with her arms, as if beckoning him away. Great drops of sweat poured down his face, and the man who had for three long years faced musketry and cannon now quailed before this unearthly visitor. He afterward brought friends with him to see the object; but it never made its appearance except when he was alone, and always at the same hour of the night. It will not do to say that the gentleman was drinking, for he was strictly temperate in his habits, and usually cool and collected; but this strange circumstance so worked upon him that he was found dead shortly after, and he was buried alongside his wife, whom he had loved dearly in his life, and who, he believed was beckoning him to come to her.

The Cincinnati [OH] Enquirer 20 November 1887: p. 16 MASSACHU-SETTS

Just as nineteenth-century journalists were mystified by petrified corpses, they were fascinated by images that appeared mysteriously on tombstones or coffin lids.

EXPLAIN THIS

Her Picture Appears in Her Gravestone

[Mendota (Ill.) Special to *Chicago Tribune*.]

Mrs. Ralph Shaffer died last Spring. She had been married but a short time, and was one of the city belles. Mr. Shaffer erected a fine monument to the memory of his dead wife, who was interred in her mother's burial plot. The young woman's mother dislikes Shaffer exceedingly and refused to allow him to have his wife's name engraved on the stone. Not wishing to have trouble with her, Shaffer has not insisted upon doing so.

Recently a distinct shadow of the late Mrs. Shaffer appeared on the tombstone. It grew until the shadow became life size. The mother was wroth, and had the monument-makers rub the stone down with pumice, but they could not efface the shadow. At first sight the shape has as much resemblance to a man's form as a woman's, but by a continued gaze one seems to see a woman's semi-profile with bangs and with the hair done up at the back of the head. The neck and chin show plainly, as do also the shoulders, and there is a scarf about the neck. The features are distinct, and bear a remarkable resemblance to the dead wife. The shadow is eight inches wide and fourteen inches high and is in the middle of the stone.

Los Angeles [CA] Herald 13 October 1891: p. 7 ILLINOIS

A GRAVE-DIGGER'S STORY.

THE PICTURE OF A WOMAN, BURIED THIRTY-FIVE YEARS AGO, ON THE LID OF HER COFFIN.

James Clareback, about 45 years of age, was yesterday engaged at Herrington's Corners, ten miles from this city, in resurrecting the remains of Mrs. M. C. Herrington in order to bury them in another place. The body had been under ground for thirty-five years, and in digging for it Clareback struck a great deal of water. He reached the remnants of the outer box surrounding the coffin, and when he pulled them out of the way he was greatly astonished to see what appeared to be Mrs. Herrington's body, apparently undisturbed and so lifelike as to convey to his mind the belief that a living, breathing woman was before him.

"I tell you I was scared," said Clareback to-day, "and I nearly fell over in a faint in the grave. When I made an examination, however, I discovered that it was not the body I saw before me, but an exact photograph of it on the top of the coffin lid. I then raised the coffin and opened it. With the exception of the head it contained only a few crumbling bones. The head, however, was perfectly preserved. The bones were covered with flesh which was petrified, the whole being as hard as a stone, while the hair had grown to an unusual length and was very abundant."

The coffin lid was exhibited to a number of people. It was made of cedar, and contained an exact and perfectly clear representation of the deceased woman as she appeared when she died thirty-five years ago. Just how to account for this no one knows, but, in lieu of any better explanation, that made by the grave digger is accepted. It is to the effect that the water flowing through the grave must have raised the body so that it was pressed against the coffin lid, and the action of the gases arising from the body, in conjunction with the nature of the wood, forced the picture to appear as it did on the outer side of the coffin lid.

Mr. Clareback will open a number of other graves in the same vicinity before long, and there is much curiosity to see if he will find any more "ghost photographs," as the residents insist upon calling them.

The Sun [New York, NY] 14 December 1892: p. 7 NEW YORK

Phantom hearses, like phantom funerals, were common in the British Isles, but rare in the United States. And, as is hinted, this one might have been a hoax.

GHOSTLY HEARSE

With Four White Horses Seen By New York Villagers

Here's a ghost story from Long Island City. It is based on the testimony of numerous sober, self-respecting, hard-working and altogether worthy persons living within the precincts of Blissville and Laurel Hill, and also on the experiences of several policemen detailed for special duty along the south side of Calvary Cemetery. Up to a late hour last night the Society for Psychic Research has not been heard in relation to it. This is the way they tell it in the neighborhood of the graveyard, adapting their language as nearly as possible to the weird and solemn nature of the subject:

"Just as the hollow tones of the midnight bells cease sounding the hour, the great gates of the cemetery swing open, and without sound of hoof beats or rumble of wheels, the apparition sweeps along. Four white horses with flowing manes, long tails and hollow eyes, prance on without the jingle of harness chains, silent as the dead. Perched high on his box, the spectre driver clutches the gossamer reins, while the hearse, which is also entirely white, seems to float over the uneven road. It is a small hearse, such as is used in children's funerals and is empty save for what appears to be a wreath of tangled flowers and a winding sheet. Ghostly hands close the cemetery gates as the spectre drives out and winds down Bradley Avenue. In the darkest night it glows luminously and casts a sickly light along its way. Two policemen the other night sought to hold it up. But they were driven back by the vapors of the tomb that seemed to surround it. Efforts have been made to follow it, but it passes lightly across Penny Bridge and disappears in the mists arising from Newtown Creek.

Night watchmen in the cemetery have often witnessed uncanny sights not intended for mortal eyes, but while many of them can in a measure account in their own way for the spirits of the dead haunting the spot where their own bodies or the bodies of loved ones or enemies repose beneath the sod, they are at a loss to solve the mystery of the empty hearse and its ghostly attendants. It betokens neither unrequited love, blasted hope nor unpunished crime, and it is surmised by those deep in the lore of departed spirits that it is a messenger of death to some distant family.

There is another theory, when, iconoclastic and materialistic as it is, may as well be set down for the sake of having the record complete. Some time ago the New York and Queens County Electric Railway laid tracks in Bradley Avenue, which skirts the south side of the cemetery. The cemetery authorities objected and a resolution was passed by the Municipal Council directing the company to remove the rails. The company has shown no disposition to comply with the Council's order and to prevent it from continuing the work policemen have been posted along the cemetery night and day. It was while doing this duty that the coppers saw the spectre. Now there are those who do not hesitate to suggest that the railroad people, who also do the electric lighting in that district, have gone into the spook-making business for the purpose of frightening away the bluecoats and getting an opportunity to go on with their track laying unmolested.

Cincinnati [OH] Enquirer 27 January 1900: p. 11 NEW YORK

Bodysnatching has been so thoroughly covered in multiple books, publications, and websites that there is little for me to add to the canon. Except, perhaps, this bizarre case.

STRANGE HALLUCINATION

A Widow Believes Her Husband's Dead Body Has Been Beheaded

And That a Noted Drunkard's Head Has Been Substituted for It.

Her Daughter and Others Make the Same Declaration – She Seeks a Legal Investigation.

New Albany, Dec. 18. Mrs. Eng is the widow of the late Martin Eng, who resided on the Cannon farm, one mile northwest of this city. Martin Eng was a good citizen, and his widow is a respectable lady, of fair intelligence. He died but a few weeks ago, and at the time of his death—the family not owning a lot in the Northern Burying Ground, the place of sepulchre for the city's dead—the body was temporarily placed in the city vault in that cemetery, where it remained for something over a week, when a lot was procured by the widow and the body taken from the vault and interred. It was at the interment of the remains that a supposed most remarkable discovery was made. Before the coffin containing Mr. Eng's body was removed from the vault, the widow requested that the lid might be opened, that the family and friends might take a final look and last farewell of the loved husband and father. The daughter and several of the friends of Mrs. Eng, owing to the rapid wastage and decomposition of the body tried hard to persuade her not to look upon it. But she insisted upon doing so, and claims that she at once discovered that while the coffin was the same in which her husband had been laid at his home, and the body was dressed in the clothes placed upon it for burial, and was probably the same body,

THE HEAD WAS THAT OF ANOTHER.

This, she says, was her immediate conclusion upon looking at the remains. Nevertheless the body was placed in the grave, covered up, and the mourners and friends returned to their homes.

That face and head haunted the widow, and she spoke of it to her daughter, and the latter, strange to say, had made the same startling discovery; and stranger still, they agreed in recognizing it as that of a notorious drunkard found dead at Jeffersonville last summer and buried in a pauper's grave near that city. From this time forward for several days there was no peace of mind left to Mrs. Eng, and finally she determined to have the body of her husband disinterred for further and more particular investigation. She hired a well-known negro of this city, Nathan Williams, to perform the work of opening the grave, and took with her as witnesses and experts, her grown daughter, Mrs. Whiteman, a neighbor, and other friends. When the body was again brought forth, it was discovered that the head was partially bald, the only hair remaining upon it being on the back part, and that thin and gray, and the whiskers on the face were also gray, whereas Mrs. Eng's husband had a very heavy suit of coarse and black hair, and a full and very black beard. After making these discoveries the body was again returned to the grave and covered with earth, and the widow, her daughter, and others present returned to their homes, all firmly convinced in their minds that the head and face were those of another person than the dead husband.

SEEKING A LEGAL INVESTIGATION

Yesterday Mrs. Eng came into the city, and going to the law office of Prosecuting Attorney Thomas L. Smith, of the Circuit Court, related to him in the presence of Col. D.C. Anthony, a lawyer of prominence at the New Albany bar the particulars detailed above, and demanded a legal investigation of the remarkable case. Of course Prosecutor Smith was puzzled at the startling narrative, and cross questioned all the parties with searching particularity, believing them the victims of a strange hallucination, if not really insane. But they all adhered most tenaciously to their statements.

SAMUEL B. BOROFF'S HEAD

Col. Anthony was called into the inquiry by Prosecutor Smith, but was not able to shake the statements of Mrs. Eng and her daughter, the latter being a lady of intelligence and respectability, as well as her mother. Nathan Williams, the grave digger, was then questioned by Col. Anthony and Prosecutor Smith. His statement was even more startling than that of the ladies. He said: "I knew Mr. Eng well. His hair was thick, coarse, and very black, and so were his whiskers. The head in that coffin is not Mr. Eng's head. But I know whose head it is. It is the head of Mr. Sam. Boroff. I knew Mr. Boroff as well as I ever knew any man. The hair on the head in the coffin is only a small patch on the back of the head and it is gray and the whiskers are also gray. I tell you, Colonel, that is Mr. Sam. Boroff's head. There's no mistake about it, as you'll find if they dig up the body again." "But," replied Col. Anthony, "Mr. Boroff was buried at Jeffersonville fully six months ago. It cannot be his head." "I can't help that," replied Williams, "and I know it's true: but that head in the coffin is not Martin Eng's. It is Samuel Boroff's. I'll swear to that."

FURTHER DEVELOPMENTS

In this, which promises to be a celebrated case, will doubtless be made, as Mrs. Eng has determined to have the body disinterred by those who were well acquainted with her deceased husband, and also by medical experts. It would be natural enough to arrive at the conclusion that Widow Eng, greatly troubled and morbidly sensitive over the death of her husband, to whom she was devotedly attached, had become partially insane and possessed by this hallucination; but it would be carrying such a hypothesis pretty far to conclude that her daughter and Williams, the negro gravedigger, were also similarly affected. Their statements that the head is that of Boroff, while the body is, to all appearances, and the grave clothes with perfect certainly, those of Martin Eng, are even more positive than that of Mrs. Eng.

THE SEXTON OF THE CEMETERY

Capt. Wm. Jones is one among the oldest and most reputable citizens of New Albany, and he states to the *Gazette* correspondent that he is positive the vault was not entered, nor the body of Eng interfered with. The locks on the vault are heavy, of a peculiar pattern, and are now, and always have been, intact; and if the vault has been entered, it was by some one having a key to fit the lock. Such an entry could only be made at a later hour of the night as the cemetery is carefully guarded. He is satisfied the parties in the supposed discovery are the victims of a strange and most remarkable hallucination. The *Gazette* correspondent agrees in the opinion with Capt. Jones. There could be no possible object in making such a change in the head of the dead Eng. He was a poor and somewhat obscure but good citizen without enemies; while Boroff who has relatives at Cincinnati, was an unfortunate drunkard, who had fallen from high respectability to the lowest depth of intemperance, and died alone in an old shed at Jeffersonville, and was buried in a pauper's grave in the Potter's Field of that city. But as Mrs. Eng seems determined to have the matter legally and thoroughly investigated, it will soon be known whether she is the victim of a crime committed that is without parallel in the history of grave robbery.

Cincinnati [OH] Daily Gazette 19 December 1879: p. 7 INDIANA

NOTE: It seems as if it would have so easy to have verified that the head was not attached. The Northern Cemetery is now Fairview Cemetery, New Albany, Indiana. Here is a note about the melancholy decline and end of Samuel Boroff.

New Albany, July 1. Samuel Boroff, of this city, was found dead on the platform of the O. & M. Railroad at Jeffersonville yesterday. It was not until some time after his dead body was discovered that he was recognized. He died from whisky and exposure. He was formerly a well-to-do book and stationery merchant of this city, for many years a popular conductor on the L.N. A. & C. Railroad, was a man of superior intelligence and excellent business qualifications. But he abandoned himself utterly to drink and died miserably; it is even thought starvation aiding in his taking off. He leaves a wife and son who reside at Cincinnati.

Cincinnati [OH] Daily Gazette 2 July 1879: p. 2

One wonders if this curious incident, which occurred just before Mr. Eng's death, could have figured in the bizarre accusation of Mrs. Eng.

A gang of desperadoes went to the farm of Martin Eng, six miles from the city, a day or two ago, for the purpose of stealing chestnuts. Mr. Eng arose from a sick bed, and armed himself with a shotgun to drive off the thieves, who had made a very indecent assault upon Mrs. Eng, but fainted and fell in the yard when the scoundrels came upon him with revolvers, threatening his life. Some of the parties are known and will be arrested.

Indianapolis [IN] Sentinel 4 October 1879: p. 1 INDIANA

There is a horrific tale called "The Croglin Grange Vampire" told by Augustus Hare in *The Story of My Life*. The hideous Thing in this story from Van Wert is strongly reminiscent of Hare's unearthly creature found in a churchyard vault.

HORRIFYING EXPERIENCE OF A MINISTER WITH A VAN WERT GHOST

We clip the following from Sunday's [Cincinnati] *Enquirer* and as it relates the experience of the narrator in Van Wert, it will doubtless be interesting reading. The gentleman alluded to is quite well known to us but we are not at liberty to use his name:

Washington C. H., July 9. A Methodist minister, lately a resident of Hamilton County, Ohio, who has been visiting friends in our city, relates the following thrilling episode in his life, which occurred while he was stopping at Van Wert, Ohio.

'It was on a beautiful moonlight evening in June, and the atmosphere was just about as sultry as it has been at any time during the present summer. I was enjoying myself in the company of some relatives who lived about three miles from Van Wert, on the old Willshire road. At a late hour I arose to go, but my friends insisted that I should remain for the night, as my way would be very lonesome. It was suggested that some ghost might appear to me at the cemetery or some individual might rob me. This was a beautiful burying ground, and was situated about midway on my route. I was quite amused at their artful method of persuasion and laughed vociferously. It was very ridiculous to me, indeed, that there should be a rattling of dry bones, or the apparition of a spirit in a modern cemetery. The people of to-day had made too much advancement, as I thought, for such idle fancies as that.

Thus I proceeded on my way with no thought of danger—indifferent to the warnings that had just been given me. As I drew near to the cemetery, however, and began to see the tall, white shafts of marble looming up among the evergreens my imagination was tensioned to its utmost capacity, and, I confess, I was a fit subject for terror. It seemed as if all the spook stories to which I had listened in my childhood chased each other in quick, succession through my brain, and the very chirrup of the crickets or the incessant song of the whippoorwill intensified the loneliness of this little nook of earth. The long line of dark trees that threw such strange shadows across the field and the mellow light that fell from the moon upon every grotesque stump or stately monument only served to intensify my loneliness.

I arrived at last at the corner of the cemetery, and, oh horrors! right in the very center of this field of dead men's bones, and from the shadow of a broad new tombstone, I saw a tall black creature rise and stand erect. The apparition seemed in the distance like a huge cadaver clothed in a robe of sack-cloth. The dreary eyes were sunken deep in their sockets, and the few irregular snags that served for teeth were pressed like fangs against the thin and wrinkled lips. The monster gazed a moment in all directions, then with a steady measured movement it made directly for me. I stopped and gazed upon the creature, and started back bewildered, but, at once regaining my senses, I concluded to proceed, and, if possible, to put on the appearance of unconcern. As I proceeded the spectre proceeded also, and, as certainly as I live in the present moment, it seemed as if we would both meet at the same point in the road. After going a short distance I slackened my pace, in order to let the mysterious something have all the room in front of me it might desire, and in a few moments I congratulated myself on being about twenty feet in the rear.

Contrary to my anticipations, there was no conversation opened between us but in a strange, ghost-like manner, the long withered form moved ahead of me until it reached a little, old, abandoned burying ground at the right of the road. This spot was far more desolate than the new cemetery, for it had become entirely neglected, and at that late hour of the night appeared as an interminable thicket, so completely were the weeds, bushes, briers and trees tangled and matted together. Into this uncanny place my ghostly terrifier passed and disappeared. I have never understood the nature of this apparition up to the present time, and I am perfectly willing to give my name to anyone who would be inclined to doubt the occurrence.'

The Van Wert [OH] Republican 14 July 1887: p. 5 OHIO

NOTE: The road called Willshire Road is now Shannon Street or State Route 118. The "new cemetery" is Woodland Cemetery of Van Wert. The older cemetery was on West Main Street. Its inhabitants were moved to Woodland. You can find the Croglin Grange story at http://augustus-hare.tripod.com/croglin.html

12.

The Habiliments of Woe:
Products for Correct Mourning

The Gilded Age was pure gold for the dark merchants of woe. The newspapers reported on fashionable mourners and funerals, giving delectable details of gowns and flowers, just as they did for cotillions and fancy dress balls, stimulating demand for the latest novelties in crape. Mourning products and services abounded for all tastes and purses. While a great debate raged about the morality of spending large sums on the dead, some of the bereaved were shamed or bullied into conspicuous consumption.

A superior servant, a mere girl, married a house-painter. Within a year of the event the husband fell from a ladder and was killed. The poor little widow bought a cheap black dress and a very simple black straw hat to wear at the funeral. Her former employer, who had much commended this modest outlay, met the girl a few days later swathed in crape, her poor little face only half visible under the hideous widow's bonnet complete with streamers and a veil... She explained that her neighbours and relations had made her life unbearable because she did not want to wear widow's weeds and at last she had to give in. "They said that if I would not wear a bonnet, it proved we were never married," she sobbed.

Funeral Customs, their Origin and Development, Bertram S. Puckle, (London: T. Warner Laurie, 1926) ENGLAND

The scene of the following incident was a house in one of the "best parts" of a well-known London suburb.

A death had taken place in the family, and it had fallen to the lot of the eldest daughter to make the arrangements for the funeral.
She asked for a plain elm coffin without any ornaments.

"Elm," said the horrified undertaker, "but you can't have anything but polished oak in a road like this."

Funeral Customs, their Origin and Development, Bertram S. Puckle, (London: T. Warner Laurie, 1926) ENGLAND

Yet extravagance did have its uses, according to the author of this article, who seems to have been an early proponent of trickle-down economics.

Some of the newspapers are using a great deal of ink and space in arguments in favor of cremation, because funerals within the last few years have grown into such extravagant affairs. But these writers do not seem to reflect that very little of the extravagance displayed on funeral occasions, goes underground. The corpse is buried, and with it, if the family is rich, and these are the only kind which can enjoy ostentatious funerals, a handsome burial suit and expensive coffin. The rest of the display, the plumes, the crepe, and all the other auxiliaries of a fashionable funeral, stay above ground and help to keep up the activity of the commercial world as much as the laces, the satins, the feathers and the furbelows which a fashionable marriage brings into requisition. And how would A. T. Stewart and other merchant princes make their colossal fortunes, if love and pride were to find expression, at weddings, in calico and jeans, and grief at funerals in plain muslin and the absence of somber satin and velvet pile? In the commercial as well as in the material world, nothing is wasted, and if people choose to have expensive funerals, the cost flows into the channels of trade somewhere and keeps things moving.

The Cairo [IL] Bulletin 28 April 1874: p. 2

NOTE: The "merchant prince" Alexander Turney Stewart made a fortune in dry goods and was one of the first mail-order entrepreneurs. A few weeks after his death in 1876 his body was stolen from his grave and held for ransom.

The funeral pre-planner in this joke took a bare-bones approach.

A rich miser was visited on his death bed by a fellow miser, who for want of a better subject, began to talk about his funeral. "It will cost a great deal," said he; "There will be the monument...."
"Oh! Don't have any monument."
"And the plumes..."

"Oh! Don't have any plumes."

"And the flowers, and the rose-wood coffin, and carriages..."

"Don't have any carriages; I had rather go on foot."

The Christian Recorder [Philadelphia, PA] 20 February 1869

The inventors of the nineteenth century seemed obsessed by mortuary innovation. From 1840 to 1924, hundreds of patent applications for coffins in all kinds of materials were filed with the U.S. Patent Office. The persistent inventor in the following story was a Man of Vision, picturing, not just glass coffins, but the design of the vaults to hold them, and a filing system for corpses. He even suggests a pleasant way to spend time with the dead.

COFFINS MADE OF GLASS

"It's almost worthwhile dying to be buried in one of them," said the inventor of a glass coffin yesterday to a *Times* reporter. Henry H. Barry, the speaker, who lives on Fifth street, just below Spruce has for many years interested himself in transparent systems of burial. After conceiving the glass casket he kept it a secret for a long while, until, on October 24th of last year, it was patented. He is searching for a capitalist and the reporter became one for the time being.

"Yes," continued the inventor, "I believe the success of this thing is going to be immense. There is one San Francisco firm that will take thousands of the coffins to sell to Chinamen." [to ship bodies back to China for burial.]

"What is the advantage of glass for domiciles of the dead?"

"In the first place, one has perfect preservation. Before being placed in the vial the patient is embalmed. I may say that the coffin is devised on the walnut shell principle, in two halves. After my customers are once securely packed in coffins I apply an exhaust pump, take out all the air and hermetically seal up the aperture. Then the thing is accomplished. I believe, sincerely, that the whole business will last through several generations. There is the advantage that no infectious disease can come through the glass. The flesh of the subject will preserve its natural tints and relatives and friends will be able to view the deceased for years to come.

"As a sanitary reform it is unparalleled," he went on; "tenanted coffins can be piled up like any other merchandise anywhere and stay there for years. Some people might prefer to keep relatives in their own houses, nicely put away in the coffins. There is nothing objectionable about the idea. When buried in cemeteries there will be no exhalations whatever, and in case of the removal of graveyards, the coffins can be taken up and carted away with no more offense than would be given by so many kegs of nails."

"What are [sic] the dimension and shape of the coffin?" asked the reporter.

"They can be made of all sizes. The glass is three-eighths of an inch thick, and the coffin is oval with a concave top. It would not do to have it flat as with a vacuum inside it the glass would collapse."

"Wouldn't they get smashed in cemeteries?" queried the incipient investor.

"On the contrary. We have a system of toughening the glass that makes it like iron. A spade struck against the coffin with a good deal of force will not break it. Body-snatchers would get their fingers cut, but that's all right. I don't legislate for ghouls. There is no end to the variations which can be made on these coffins. The glass can be clouded so that only the face is visible. It can be colored, or butterflies and weeping willows can be placed at intervals all over the surface. There are a thousand ways of ornamenting the exterior."

"What will they cost?" was the next question.

"From seven up. Seven dollars, I mean, of course. They could possibly be manufactured of such choice material and so beautifully etched as to cost as much as a thousand dollars each. I have often wished that at the time of President Garfield's death I had had a glass coffin. I am sure it would have been used. I propose to form a company, with a capital of some half a million of dollars. No, sir, I will not sell you the patent outright, so it's no use pressing me to do so. I have too much faith in its future for that. Another reason is that I am determined it shall not get into the hands of monopolists who will run up the price of coffins to a fancy figure. This casket was invented as much with the idea of benefitting the poor as anything else. Of course there will be money in it for me, and I suppose I shall have to accept whatever comes."

Mr. Barry then proceeded to unfold the particulars of a remarkable scheme. He said that he had often heard a proposition discussed for excavating and constructing huge catacombs in this city for the reception of the dead. In that case, he thought, his invention would be invaluable. He called the scheme a "trust and safe deposit idea."

"We should have a vast system of vaults," he explained, "in which coffins would be placed. Spaces could be reserved for families. Here, in a stall, would be a father; by his side his wife; on the upper shelf the grandmother and grandfather, and above that the other ancestors. Each coffin would have a number at its foot, and catalogues would be issued giving the names of the occupants, for instance, 'Henry Jones, 241.' Above the vaults would be a suit of elegant reception rooms into which visitors would be invited. They could sit down and call for, say, 'No. 241.' An attendant would go down stairs, slide the casket indicated up on to a little barrow, come back again and leave it with them as long as they liked. They could look at it, have it taken to its shelf when they were through, and return home. A certain amount of rent would, of course, have to be exacted. What do you say of going into the enterprise? It will 'take' assuredly. There are a lot of other millionaires thinking the matter over, so you had better decide at once. Good afternoon. Let me hear from you in a few days." *Philadelphia Times*

Jersey Journal [Jersey City, NJ] 29 March 1883: p. 2 PENNSYLVANIA

One of the oldest mourning products was the mourning ring, a melancholy accessory that had been in and out of fashion since the fifteenth century, but was especially popular in the seventeenth and eighteenth centuries. Here are two articles showing different philosophies about mourning rings.

Told by a Ring

"Did you ever see a mourning ring?" asked a Maiden Lane jeweler of a *Mall and Express* reporter yesterday. "Well, here is one." It is a heavy gold band, perfectly plain and with a seal in the shape of a coffin. It has a glass face, through which can be seen a skeleton in gold. On the inside is the inscription in black enamel giving the initials of the deceased and the date of death.

"These designs were used over a century ago and now they are to be revived as the latest fad. Some young widows who find it difficult to indicate their bereavement when indoors, with hat and flowing veil removed, take advantage of the ring to announce to susceptible young men that they have returned to the matrimonial market. They need not look melancholy. A turn of the finger and the sad news is told.

"Do men use them?"

"Most assuredly. Widowers have no way of announcing their loss except by the band on their hats. With a mourning ring all embarrassing inquiries regarding the deceased wife may be avoided and knowledge of the widower's restored eligibility quickly and neatly imparted."

Watertown [NY] Daily Times 11 February 1888: p. 2

The terrible casualties of the First World War brought a revival of the mourning ring in America.

Chicago Sets Style In Mourning Rings;
Like Wedding Bands

Chicago, Aug. 30. Mourning rings have begun to make their appearance here and there. They are a revival of an old custom in vogue in this country in the early days of the republic and of much earlier date in Europe.

The rings are intended to perpetuate the memory of some relative or friend who had died. They are especially appropriate now when many families are mourning the loss of a soldier son in the war.

The rings bear the name or initials of the dead and the date of death or the battle in which the "supreme sacrifice" was paid. They are usually made of black enamel with the inscription around the circlet in letters of gold. Some are of gold with the inscription in black enamel. Some are set with an amethyst which is considered a mourning gem.

The rings are not made to supply a general market demand. This is impossible because of the names and dates. Each one must be made to individual order. In view of the fact that so many persons are seeking some sort of permanent expression of their sorrow of heroic sons, sweethearts or relatives lost in the war, it is believed this antique custom of mourning may have a rather wide revival.

Tulsa [OK] World 31 August 1919: p. 2 ILLINOIS

During the First World War, deep mourning was discouraged as being bad for morale. This article makes a suggestion for an alternate symbol of sorrow.

Old-Fashioned Jet Brooch Replaces Crepe.
American Women Join in Move to Discard
Mourning Garments.

Now that almost all American women are joining in the movement to help win the war by banishing from the streets the depressing sight of crepe and deep mourning garments, the need is felt for some expressive symbol that shall be the privilege of those bereft by death, whether through the war or through other causes....Every woman who feels it a sacrifice to give up her mourning apparel would appreciate some distinguishing symbol the wearing of which would satisfy her own heart.

When the question was being discussed the other day in a room full of women, knitting for the Red Cross, one sweet-faced little woman pointed to a beautiful old-fashioned jet brooch at her throat. "This," said she, "is my mourning. It is a treasured family heirloom full of dear associations. The members of our family do not believe in mourning apparel, but this brooch represents to me, mourning. It is never worn except at such periods, and is then worn constantly—with all costumes. When I wear this brooch, I am in mourning as truly as though clothed in deepest black..."

Oregonian [Portland, OR] 23 June 1918: p. 73

Further Reading: For further information on mourning jewelry see:
http://artofmourning.com/
http://www.culturalinquiry.org/blog/recent-acquisitions/mourning-pins
http://www.historicnewengland.org/collections-archives-exhibitions/
    online-exhibitions/JewelryHistory/themes/Mourning.htm
In Death Lamented: The Tradition of Anglo-American Mourning Jewelry, Sarah Nehama, (Boston, MA: Massachusetts Historical Society, 2012).

Mourning rings were not the only custom products made by jewelers. This unique and probably short-lived concept for an umbrella handle, like all of the most fashionable mourning novelties, came from Paris.

BUST OF HUSBAND ON UMBRELLA WIDOW'S FAD
Miniature Model of Departed Mate on 'Rainstick' Grief Indicator

New York, Dec. 25. Wearing widow's weeds, a woman, seemingly about 45 years old, rode uptown in a Fifth avenue omnibus the other afternoon, watching the panorama through her lorgnette, while with the other hand she unconsciously twirled an umbrella that attracted the attention of those sitting opposite.

At the top of the handle was a design in silver which could not be distinguished at first, but when she held it in one position for a moment the ornamentation was discovered to be the bust in miniature of a man who, perhaps, was 50 years old.

The design was striking, for the silver had been variously treated in different parts, dark oxidation marking the hair and the cheeks in spots, while the mustache, cut off sharply at a level with the upper lip, was a dead gray. The remainder of the features was of slightly burnished metal. The eyes were bored out conically, as in bronze figures, to give expression.

Two men sitting across the aisle observed the strange ornament and began to discuss it in an undertone. After considerable discussion they decided that the miniature was not the bust of any celebrity they had ever seen or heard of. It was not that of any man who at any time had been prominent in music, literature, painting or any of the other high arts and they finally abandoned speculation.

Later in the day a reporter asked a prominent Fifth avenue silversmith if he could throw any light on the subject. His reply was that he could illuminate it thoroughly, for he knew from the description not only who the miniature represented, but the woman who carried it.

"It is an absolutely new idea in giving outward expression of devotion to a dead husband," he said, "and, of course, like most other novelties, it comes from Paris, where it has been in vogue for about six months. We did not make the one that was seen this afternoon, but another firm in New York made it.

"We are not anxious to have it become a fad here, because it is a world of trouble to make them, for the reason that they are made from photographs, and not from casts. Usually a full face photograph and a profile photograph are given to the modeler and he does the best he can from these, the tints in the metal being applied according to descriptions furnished by the mourner.

"There are only two of those miniatures ornamenting umbrella handles in this city, so far as I know. We have orders for one now, and we cannot refuse to take the contract because it is for one of our best customers. In her opinion her husband was the handsomest man that ever lived, and we are going to have our own troubles pleasing her with a design."

Los Angeles [CA] Herald 26 December 1910: p. 5 NEW YORK

Other essential mourning accessories were black-bordered stationery, funeral cards, and mourning cards, which were visiting cards with black borders. Upon hearing of a death, condoling friends would leave visiting cards without seeing the bereaved. She, in turn, would send mourning cards to those who had sent cards of condolence to indicate her retirement from society. No message was necessary. As a 1909 etiquette book says, "A black-bordered card or mourning cards tell their sad tale without words." Mourning cards were also used later in the mourning period to indicate that the bereaved was ready to accept callers.

This young mourner wanted a unique sort of mourning card.

Boston Mourning Cards.

The other day a very dainty young woman in black, with mourning veil so draped as to set off her shapely head and neck to advantage, entered a large stationery store on Washington Street, and said sweetly to a clerk behind the counter:

"Do you have all kinds of mourning cards?" "Yes'm; we have the cards, and can get them engraved for you." "Oh, I don't want the kind they get engraved—I want playing cards, you know."

"Mourning playing cards!"

"Why, yes; don't you think they would be real nice and tasty?"

The clerk was obliged to confess that the trade hadn't yet reached the point of supplying playing cards with mourning borders for bereaved lovers of whist and poker, and the lady left the store disappointed.

Boston Record

Fresno [CA] Republican Weekly 11 March, 1887: p. 2 MASSACHUSETTS

NOTE: "Tasty" in this context means "tasteful."

Funeral cards were usually black with white or gilt printing, giving the name and dates of the deceased. They were given to friends as a remembrance and were often kept in photograph albums. They are similar to Catholic funeral cards, which are printed with a religious picture and a prayer, as well as the dead person's details.

Like crape on the doorknob, a black-bordered envelope—the recognized harbinger of death—was enough to send a shockwave of horror through the recipient. The phrase "black-bordered letter" was shorthand for bereavement and while they were a vital product for the mourner, some recipients of such letters felt that they were overused.

Black Bordered Envelopes

Why, in the name of all the nerves that trouble us, do people who wear mourning insist upon clothing the envelopes of their letters in black, after the first announcement of death, notices of the funeral, and letters actually *on the subject,* have been dispatched? Considering the effect usually produced by such missives the fact that fashion sanctions the absurdity is no excuse.

To those who put a great stress upon mourning, the idea of abandoning it, even upon their pocket handkerchiefs, may seem sacrilege; but why, because a lady has been wearing the latest styles of black for three years or so, for a distant relative who has left her a legacy, should she give her stout friends apoplexy, and her thin ones spasms, whenever she invites them to a lunch with her or has a pleasant word or two to say?

The arrival of a black envelope usually frightens most people, or perhaps I should say, most *women*, into a condition which renders it impossible for them to examine the postmark or the handwriting. They tear the terrible thing away, look at the enclosed writing upside down, stagger to a seat, and reverse the paper to find the letters dancing beyond a red blur which blots out their sense and meaning; finally announce to the household that "somebody is dead," and beg to have the letter read to them.

Some calm elderly person—say, a maiden aunt, whose heart is untroubled by fears of bad news from any absent lover—undertakes the task; and while the wretched victim's heart out-trots Dexter [a famous champion race horse], fumbles for her glasses, selects a good seat by the window, and finally reads the following:

"Dear ___: I could not find that dress-maker who fitted your pink silk so charmingly. Please send me her number, and oblige, Yours, ___."

Now is there any sense or reason in clothing such a note in weeds

---

The Letter Edged In Black
Hattie Nevada, 1897

I was standin' by my window yesterday morning
Without a thought of worry or of care
When I saw the postman comin' up the pathway
With such a happy face and jolly air.

He rang the bell and whistled as he waited
Then he said; "Good morning to you, Jack"
But he little knew the sorrow he had brought me
When he handed me a letter edged in black.

With trembling hand I took this letter from him
I broke the seal and this is what it said:
"Come home my boy, your dear old father wants you
Come home my boy, your dear old mother's dead."

I bowed my head in sorrow and in sadness
The sunshine of my life, it all had fled
When the post man brought that letter yesterday
  morning
"Saying come home my boy, your dear old mother's
  dead."

"The last words your mother ever uttered
Tell my boy I want him to come back
My eyes are blurred, my poor old heart is breaking
So, I'm writing you this letter edged in black."

"Forget those angry words that we had spoken
You know I didn't mean them, don't you, Jack?
May the angels bear as witness, I am asking
Your forgiveness in this letter edged in black."

of woe?

And however fashionable black borders may be, should not a good Christian refrain from adopting them, at the risk of frightening to death the recipient of some lively little note? I have refrained from writing on this subject for a long while, because of the extreme sensitiveness of many persons on the subject of mourning, but when a fascinating widower invites me to attend a concert, upon paper with a weeping willow and a tombstone in the corner, wrapped in an envelope surrounded by broad black stripes and further ornamented by a black seal with "Niobe all tears" upon it, the thought suggests itself, that, under the circumstances, the wraith of the most exacting wife who ever left husband to his own devices, might have excused a plain white envelope. Mary Kyle Dallas, in *N.Y. Ledger*

Lowell [Ma] Daily Citizen and News 11 July 1870: p. 1

NOTE: Despite her light-hearted tone, Mary Kyle Dallas, poet and authoress [d. 1897] knew about mourning. She married at age 20, but her husband survived only a year and a half and her child only six months.

White ink is now sold for writing on black cards. It is the latest mourning fad. It is better not to mourn at all than to mourn out of fashion.

Bay City [MI] Times 18 June 1894: p. 5

A Parisian genius has got out a list of plays which may be properly attended by those who are in mourning. A half-mourning list will soon follow from the same authority.

It may interest fastidious letter writers to know that the very swellest mourning paper used by the elite of France measures eight by five inches and has a black border half an inch wide.

Kansas City [MO] Times 27 March 1888: p. 4 FRANCE

NOTE: The width of the black border was carefully graduated by one's relationship to the deceased. "The preferred widths of black-bordered paper have regular numbers, and that used by a daughter is the one known by stationers as number one, by a mother that known as number three, and by a widow that known as number four." [Source: *Ladies' Home Journal*, June, 1895] I have not been able to locate any more information on the proper mourning plays and this notice may have been a joke.

Fastidious, letter-writing mourners were dismayed to find that they had no choice of sombre-colored postage and demanded a mourning stamp.

MOURNING STAMPS

The Latest Fad to Have Sombre Postage

Receiving the Attention of the Post-office Department.

It is probable the post office department will take up the matter of providing a stamp of somber hue for use by persons in mourning, owing to the numerous demands that are made for these stamps at the various post offices over the country. Requests for such stamps are quite frequent and when informed that there are no such stamps issued, the would-be purchaser invariably suggests that the government ought to provide such stamps so that they would be in consonance with the stationery used on such occasions.

The post office department is constantly in receipt of requests for the issue of a mourning stamp for use on black edge stationery. Persons in all grades of life assert that there is no harmony or appropriateness in an envelope with a black edge and a red stamp. The department has given much consideration to the subject, but has been unable to comply with the request on account of the rules of the Universal Postal Union which prescribes that our lowest value of stamp shall be green; that the stamp used for domestic use shall be red, and the stamp carrying foreign mail—five cent—shall be blue. In view of all these restrictions, it has not appeared possible to meet the requirements for a mourning stamp, as the department does not deem it advisable to print a stamp in red and also in black. However, the suggestion has been made that the three cent stamp now printed in purple might be issued in black, so that persons desiring to use a black stamp upon their mourning envelope might do so by paying an additional cent.

The department may take up this suggestion and act on it later.

The Paducah [KY] Sun 21 October 1903: p. 2

Postage stamps were not the only stamps of interest to the mourner.

A PROGRESSIVE AGE

"I'm a practical and experienced widow," said the woman in black, "and I want to look at some coffins without any foolishness."

The undertaker looked up with the unhappy smile of his craft.

"We have them all styles and prices," he replied softly and hopefully.

"And how about trading stamps? Give 'em, I suppose."

"No-o," admitted the proprietor, almost losing his professional poise. "The truth is that at these solemn moments our customers do not, as a rule, indicate any desire for stamps."

"I guess I know a solemn moment all right," rejoined the widow; "but there's no use in making it solemner. I've just lost my third and don't intend to lose a chance at a cuckoo clock into the bargain."

She was gone. The undertaker realized that in the race for business he was being left behind.

The Mahoning Dispatch [Canfield, OH] 27 November 1908: p. 7

Trading Stamps With Funerals
CHICAGO UNDERTAKER VICTIM OF CRAZE
Bereaved Widow Cancels Burial Order Because Friends Got Stamps While She Didn't.

Chicago, March 25. "Trading stamps with every funeral" is the placard that one may expect to see soon in the windows of up-to-date Chicago undertakers.

That two or three funeral directors on the northwest side of the city have adopted the trading stamp system to increase business was revealed yesterday when a bereaved widow cancelled an order at a downtown undertaker's because he would not give her some stamps.

Friends of hers, she said, who recently had deaths in their families were given trading stamps by the undertaker and she insisted on getting the coupons or she would go elsewhere. The matter of trading stamps will be brought before the Chicago Undertakers' Association at its next meeting.

Harrisburg [PA] Telegraph 25 March 1908: p. 1 ILLINOIS

Widows were warned that it was in extremely bad taste to go directly from deepest black to colored clothing. Half-mourning was that time when the bereaved, like a butterfly emerging from a cocoon of darkness, would begin to add a white collar and cuffs or don clothing in shades of dark grey, then lighter grey, or pearl, with perhaps a dash of heliotrope, violet, or lavender. For some reason half-mourning perplexed many people and it was the butt of many jokes.

Not a Dandy

The Bucolic Customer: Young man, I wants a dark gray tie.

The Shop Assistant: Yessir. For half mourning?

The Bucolic Customer: 'Arf mornin' be blowed! W'en I puts on a tie I puts it on for the day! *London Sketch.*

Gulfport [MS] Daily Herald 9 May 1912: p. 3

A little girl happening to hear her mother speak of going into *half mourning* said "Why are we going into half mourning, Mama, are any of our relations *half dead?"*

Weekly Visitor [New York, NY] 15 March 1823: p. 12

"That's Mrs. Giltedge-Bonds, the prominent society leader," said the man in the crowd who knew.

"What's she in half mourning for?" inquired several voices.

"Three of her six former husbands are dead," said the man, whereupon the crowd expressed great admiration for her delicacy of feeling. *Philadelphia Record*

St. Albans [VT] Daily Messenger 4 September 1902: p. 4

Some widows made their coming out of mourning tantamount to a debut, complete with a new wardrobe.

AN AMERICAN'S FAD

A Fanciful Widow Who Celebrated Her Abandonment of Mourning

Illustrated America.

English newspapers and magazine paragraphers who delight to select and repeat for their innocent auditors all the curious fads and caprices of fashionable American women will doubtless remark with grave wonder on one of the last and most absurd arrangements in dinners lately given by a New York woman who is a lover of harmonies. Two years ago she suffered the loss of her husband.

After many months of travel abroad she returned home this autumn with boxes of exquisite creations of silver grays, violet, lavender and heliotrope, fresh from the hands of French modistes. After receiving many attentions from home friends, she decided to give what she chose to call "a going out of mourning dinner." Her idea was carried out to the last detail, and the whole filled her guests with amusement and surprise. Her gown was a superb combination of silk, velvet and chiffon, running through every tint of violet, lavender and heliotrope, and lavishly ornamented with jet and black lace. Her ornaments were black pearls and enamelled violets.

The dining table was laid with a white cloth overspread with a scarf and central square of white silk, and lines embroidered heavily in the delicate gray stems and lavender flowers of wisteria. Violets, heliotrope, and lilies-of-the-valley were the flowers used in decorating the table and for the men's *boutonnieres*. The candles, in silver candelabra, were of violet-tinted wax, with violet silk shades. The opalescent glass glowed with tints of violet and lavender, sugared violets were the only bonbons on the table, and great bunches of violets tied with violet satin streamers were attached to the right-hand side of the back of every woman's chair.

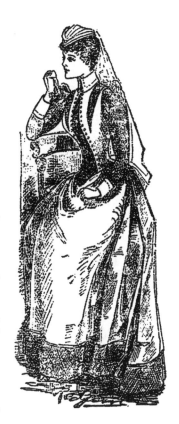

Wheeling [WV] Register 25 December 1891: p. 4 NEW YORK

Rather than coming out of mourning, this widow each year hosted a dinner to remember her lost husband.

DINED IN MOURNING

Novel Method of a Woman for Commemorating her Husband's Death

Although the culinary art has in the last twenty years made rapid strides, still there is a certain sameness about dinner parties which, in the habitual diner-out, comes but little short of dull monotony.

Now and again, however, one comes across a hostess whose imagination, or eccentricity, is the means of providing a meal for her guests upon lines other than those upon which the ordinary dinner is given.

Such a one was a lady who lived in the neighborhood of Kensington, and who every year gave what she termed a memorial dinner on the anniversary of her husband's death.

The room in which the dinner was given was draped for the occasion in mauve and black, no other colors being visible. The tablecloth was likewise of mauve silk, while the only floral decorations in use were violets. The lady guests were arrayed in either black or mauve dresses, the footmen were dressed in black plush breeches, mauve silk stockings and black coats.

On dinner being announced, the hostess took the head of the table, but on either side of her, seated upon two stools, sat two black poodle dogs, excellently clipped after the approved French fashion, and with mauve colored ribbon bows on their heads. These two dogs had been great pets of the lady's husband during his lifetime, and it was for this reason that they were allowed a seat among the guests at the dinner table.

The menu was remarkable for the absence of any color in the viands, save mauve, the rest being either black or white. Thus the soup was white, likewise the fish and entrees, as regards game, the lady got over the difficulty, or at least met it half way by providing blackcock [pheasant]. The sweets were either mauve colored or white, while at the end of the dinner black coffee was served.

Wheeling [WV] Register 28 October 1894: p. 9 ENGLAND

Then there was this widow, who entered into the letter, but not the spirit of deep mourning.

A somewhat eccentric dinner was given in New York last winter by a lady who was wearing very deep mourning for her husband. The table was decorated in black, purple, and white, the napery, of course, was white, but embroidered with the darkest purple pansies—with the monogram in black. Silver vases, filled with the same dark flower, were at the corners of the table, and the ices and small confectionery were all in violet and white. To make the whole thing consistent, the hostess requested all her friends to wear black, and a guest who presided at the foot of the table—and afterward, by the way, married the hostess—appeared with a broad band of crape around his left arm.

The Argonaut [San Francisco CA] 10 July 1893 NEW YORK

The "wheel" as the bicycle was called, whether adorned with nickel or not, caused controversy for women bicyclists. Bicycling was often associated with Suffragettes and unflattering bloomer costumes. Bishops condemned lady riders who rode astride as immodest, while beauty editors warned young ladies that they would be afflicted with "Bicycle Face." Yet bicycling was seen as healthy for widows and a special wheel was designed for the bereaved.

WIDOWS MAY RIDE

The "Mourning Wheel" Is the Latest Fad for Her Diversion

New York World

Widows who have given away their bicycles and who shrink from wheeling as an impropriety will delight to know that a wheel has been patterned for their special use. The "mourning wheel" is now thoroughly approved by mourning etiquette, and the widow can take her morning spin with the comforting assurance that she is doing quite the proper thing. The mourning wheel is an appropriately somber affair of solid ebony blackness, unrelieved by any gleaming steel or nickel. It is not nearly as conspicuous as the yellow and blue ones which are affected this year by some women, and surprise is no longer awakened by the sight of an occasional black wheel.

The widow who rides does not make any radical change in her costume. She still clings to her crepe bonnet and veil, unsuited as the latter is for combat with a stiff breeze. Her suit is of some soft black material, similar to that in her other gowns, and is made with a closely fitting belted waist and short skirt. Very often a little crepe is seen upon the gown, while the wheelwoman who avoids long and dusty rides, may venture to add a narrow white collar and cuffs to her plain gown. The mourning wheel marks a decided reaction from conventionality and has proved itself an admirable method of assuaging grief and getting wholesome exercise.

State [Columbia, SC] 30 May 1896: p. 5

Overheard on the Road

That the "mourning bicycle" is the latest craze, and has already been seen in the streets of New York. The machine is black throughout, unrelieved by nickel or colour.

That a fashionable widow recently appeared on one of these machines wearing a black sailor hat with a black crape band instead of a ribbon, and large black rosette in front. Her black tailor-made suit was relieved only by the shirt front, which was striped black, as also was her high linen collar. A black poodle was her escort.

The Wheelwoman 24 July 1897: p. 19 NEW YORK

While I have not been able to find an extant example of a mourning wheel, there was one category of mourning goods that was so popular that numerous examples survive. It was the hair wreath. The hair, collected during life or just after death, was often worked into flowers and leaves on wires, making the finished creation, which was usually displayed in a deep frame behind glass, quiver like a giant tarantula. They may not be to our modern taste, but they were a powerfully sentimental artifact.

Hair is at once the most delicate and lasting of our materials, and survives us like love. It is so light, so gentle, so escaping from the idea of death, that, with a lock of hair belonging to a child or friend, we may almost look up to heaven and compare notes with the angelic nature—may almost say: "I have a piece of thee here, not unworthy of thy being now."

Godey's Lady's Book [Philadelphia, PA] August 1861

Hair Wreath of Ten Thousand Locks.

Miss Hattie Chipps, of Budds Lake, N.J., once made a wreath (which she still has in her possession) wholly of human hair. It comprises 10,000 locks from as many different heads, and is arranged in curious and beautiful designs, principally leaves, flowers, etc. She spent over a year in collecting the hair, which is of every shade and color, before the wreath itself was begun. It is a unique ornament as well as a triumph of patience and ingenuity. *St. Louis Republic*

Trenton [NJ] Evening Times 13 August 1892: p. 2 NEW JERSEY

A WREATH

Made from the Hair of Members of a Murdered Family.

Lawrenceburg, Ind., April 13. A relative of the Wratten family, who were murdered by Stone in Davis County, this state, went to Cincinnati to-day to get a memento of the murdered family, which consists of a hair wreath made in the shape of a maple leaf from locks of hair taken from the heads of each member of the family that perished at the hands of the cruel wretch, who spared neither age nor sex in his savage thirst for human blood. The different shades of hair from the different heads of the victims give the memento the variegated hues of the maple leaf in fall time, and is regarded as a most valuable keepsake. Photographs of the hair wreath have been taken for the purpose of distributing among the kinsmen of the family who desire to possess such a keepsake.

The Cincinnati [OH] Enquirer 14 April 1895: p. 17 INDIANA

NOTE: James Stone, a neighbor, hacked Mrs Wratten to pieces during a robbery. He also murdered Mr. Wratten and three children. The sole survivor, Ethel, was taken to her uncle's home. Stone lived next door and Ethel fell into hysteria when she saw him. She was put to bed, but Stone offered to sit with the child while the family was at dinner. There was a strange sound and Stone came down shortly afterwards and said that Ethel was dead. Stone claimed that he had been set up by six other men, but later admitted he acted alone in murdering the Wrattens. [Source: *The Weekly Register* (Point Pleasant, WV) 25 October 1893: p. 2]

In the 1870s, hair wreaths were exhibited and judged at county fairs and expositions. By the 1880s the hair wreath was usually mentioned only in the context of a description of "the Old Parlor" or some other old-fashioned room. A newer and more up-to-date way of memorializing the dead through their clothing was invented by a Philadelphia artist.

FLOWERS OF FLANNEL

An Up-Town Artist Who Makes Gorgeous Posies of People's Old Clothes.

ART THAT OUTSTRIPS NATURE

Gaudy Wreaths Evolved From the Depths of the Family Rag-Bag.

"Remember the Loved Ones! Memorial Flowers Made of Your Deceased Friends' Clothing." This is the simple inscription on a tin sign, nailed against the front of a private residence on Columbia avenue, near Twenty-second street. A passing reporter saw the sign and sought an interview with the person who puts sentiment into old clothes. The bell was answered by an artistic-looking lass, who ushered the scribe into the studio to await the advent of the master, who happened to be the mistress of the establishment. Around the apartment there were distributed glass shades covering specimens of unnaturally luscious-looking fruit and supernaturally bright-colored flowers, all wax. On the walls hung several frames containing what looked like somber tinted prints of mournful weeping willows, monuments, crosses, wreaths, and other mortuary emblems, which proved, on inspection, to be human hair wrought into these various cheerful shapes. While the reporter was still inspecting these works of art and remembrance the lady of the house entered.

A LEADING FEATURE.

"Good morning. You're looking at some of my relics, I see. Pretty, aren't they?" was her greeting. Without ascertaining her visitor's wishes she began to explain the various designs and to tell how many premiums she had taken at country fairs.

"Do you really make flowers of old clothes?" asked the curious newspaper man.

"Yes, indeed; that is a part of my business. In fact, it is the feature that I want to make the leading one. It is a new departure, and there is no limit to its possibilities." Before the reporter had left he was fain to believe there was not.

"A great many people don't like hair work, and some say preserved flowers have too much of the waxy look of a corpse. The prettiest natural flowers are only emblems, after all; but bouquets made from clothes worn by those we wish to keep in remembrance are almost a part of our friends themselves...."

The process is much like that of making artificial flowers for ladies' bonnets, the difference being that instead of selecting the colors to suit the design to be wrought the design must be made to suit the materials at hand. Right there is where the skill of the manipulator to adapt means to end of ribbons and scraps of cloth comes into play.

DAISIES FROM WHITE DRESSES.

Two wreaths, in which the artist takes especial pride, were shown the reporter to illustrate this point. One was made from the clothing once worn by a dead grandchild. It contained, besides a number of roses fashioned of the white muslin of tiny skirts, a number of odd-shaped leaves made by cutting out the pattern of the embroidery upon the edge of the same. A daisy's blossom had the white stuff of a baby stocking cut in strips for petals and a yellow-covered button for a center. There were queer-shaped botanical specimens evolved from striped and plaid percale, and unnamable blossoms in navy blue and cardinal wool that only the brain of a grower of flannel flowers might conceive. The second wreath, the admiring newspaper man was told, contained flowers made of the clothing worn by the artist's own first infant. In this white blossoms predominated, as was explained by the proud mother, because "there is not so much variety in an infant's dress as in an older person's. But white flowers are so much more appropriate for a little babe that is all innocence and purity, and besides, they never will fade, you know." The skeptical scribe didn't pretend to know. With pride the mother proceeded to point out a pale buff pansy made of the kid of a tiny shoe, and a few little snowdrops of cotton that had been stuffed into the toe of the shoe to make it short enough for baby's foot. The gem of the whole collection and the one which was shown with most gratification was a cream-colored lily on the inner circumference of the wreath, which the loving parent triumphantly explained was a part of the crape scarf that hung on the door-knob when the little one lay cold in its casket....

"But only feminine apparel can be utilized for bouquets," objected the reporter.

"That's just where you are wrong!" the artist exclaimed. "Why, think of the colored shirts, flannel drawers, neck ties and stockings. They furnish an unlimited supply for as bright bouquets and rosettes as you could wish. I made a beautiful bunch of pansies not long ago of bits of a gentleman's kid gloves. Many of the pieces were the right shade, but a few had to be colored to suit. I am about to make a large bouquet for a downtown woman whose husband belonged to the old Moya Hose Company and was afterwards a soldier. The centre will be a large hollyhock. His red fireman's shirt will come into play here, don't you see? I can surround this by blue flowers of some kind..."

The many advantages of the faille and linen flowers are causing the trade in them to grow and the florist who now does the chief business in growing them has confidence that as soon as their virtues become more widely known some of the florists will be compelled to shut up shop for lack of something to do. When it is considered that they don't fade or wilt under the hottest rays of the sun or freeze though attacked by the coldest blasts of winter, the small sum of $20 asked for making a medium-sized wreath sinks into insignificance and it will be admitted that the genius that originated the idea of remembering dead friends by their old clothes is a benefactor of the race.

The Times [Philadelphia, PA] 24 June 1883: p. 3 PENNSYLVANIA

A Vermont widow found solace in a mixed-media memorial to her husband made from all manner of sentimental scraps.

A Widow's Fad.

Near Vergennes, Vt., lives an old widow, Mrs. Parthena Barton, who has just completed a novel memorial to her dead husband. This memento takes the shape of a wreath and the articles in it would start a junk shop. There are many different kinds of flowers composing the wreath, each one made of a bit of the neckties or trousers, or suspenders, which the deceased Barton had worn in life; the centers of the flowers are tender souvenirs in the shape of collar or coat buttons. The spoon with which Mr. Barton took his medicine, the cough drops and boxes of pills are all enshrined in the memorial wreath, as are a motley collection of watch keys, and samples of all the kinds of garden seed he last saved. There's a bit of the cushion of the church pew in which he sat Sunday after Sunday, a section of the saw he used in providing stove wood, and the awl and bristles he used in mending his boots. Indeed to make the memorial as complete as possible, the good widow included in the collection a souvenir of his first wife in the shape of a smelling bottle, and a match box some one had given Mrs. Barton No. 2, while for herself she only put in a lock of her hair. This huge wreath is enclosed in a frame and hangs on the wall. Both wreath and frame were made by the old lady herself, who views her work with much pride and says: "Taint natural to build monuments and put flowers on the graves of friends. What you want is something to remind you of them. That's why I made that wreath. Everything's got a history."

The Times-Picayune [New Orleans, LA] 7 November 1888: p. 4 VERMONT

Even toys could be pressed into service for mourning. It is said that black teddy bears were used in mourning for the victims of the sinking of the *Titanic*. They may have been, but black teddy bears are advertised as ordinary toys well before 1911. Mourning dolls, however, were a recognized novelty. They are mentioned in an 1877 *Godey's Lady's Book* as an "odd caprice," and in newspapers from about 1880 to 1892. In 1890, one type of "mourning doll" sold so well in Ohio that stocks were exhausted.

A private carriage the other day drove up to the main entrance of the Volks-garten in Vienna. Both the driver and the footman were clad in deep mourning and the horses were covered with black harness and trappings. There stepped out of the carriage a governess and three little girls, who were dressed in deep black from head to foot. Their appearance created a certain sensation among the bystanders which was heightened by the fact that each of the three little girls carried in her arms a large doll, which was attired in deep mourning. The

"Mourning Doll" is the latest freak of fashion as an outward and visible token of bereavement. *Allgemeine Zeitung*

Wirarapa [Masterton NZ] Daily Times 18 September 1889: p. 2 AUSTRIA

AN UNDERTAKER'S IDEA OF HEAVEN

A Second-ave. undertaker displays in his window a miniature hearse, drawn by four prancing horses, and a little coffin with a doll inside, surrounded by a group of mourning dolls. The whole thing is well adapted to bring a smile even to the faces of the recently bereaved.

New-York Tribune 29 December 1880: p. 8 NEW YORK

Even a widow's visit to the seaside was regulated by mourning. This widow seems to have started the vogue of black bathing suits for women; a decade later they were commonplace.

It is rigidly exacted of fashionable widows that they shall bathe [at the seaside] in mourning. If the dear departed is a recent loss they must mourn from head to foot and have not a touch of any color, not even white, about them; if time has somewhat assuaged the anguish of widowhood, the bathing dress may be embroidered in white or have collar and revers of the same, and if a year and a half has elapsed since her husband became an angel, even the most rigid consider her justified in having her bathing dress made either of gray, white or violet serge.

This fashion was started by the pretty widow of O'Donnell of Baltimore, who was called upon to mourn a rich young husband, who died after a brief union. This occurred in the spring, and when summer came the doctors insisted that sea bathing was necessary as a cure for her nervous relaxation brought on by mental suffering, and she appeared, shrouded in crape, at a fashionable watering-place. Then the question arose concerning the bathing dress. No one ever wore black bathing dresses, and the afflicted relict utterly refused to appear anywhere, even in the sea, except in garments of the deepest sable. There was a visible sensation when she came down to the beach one morning, all in black from top to toe, with her very white arms and shoulders bare, and a little blue silk handkerchief tied coquettishly over her golden hair. Before a week was over every man in the place was occupied in securing an introduction to that pathetic little black figure, and the cheerful women in their light-colored gowns were nowhere at all. Since that time widows all over the country have adopted the fashion and regulated it by fixed laws.

San Francisco [CA] Chronicle 14 July 1889: p. 6

Incredibly, a special product was created so that the fashionable widow could also enjoy a cigarette without displaying an incorrect flash of white.

Deep Mourning With Cigarettes

A New York manufacturer has placed on the market the last word in mourning novelties, in the shape of a slick, black-tipped cigarette wrapped in black crepe paper.

This, he says, is the very latest rage as a new article of mourning is used by all the best dressed women in town. He even mentions that the black crepe cigarette goes especially well with a dark or black velvet gown.

There is such a thing as too much mourning and this appears to be a splendid example of how not to mourn. We hear it said that American businessmen are the smartest in the world and this would lead us to believe that they are also the most versatile.

If this manufacturer can start a fad he will have to enlarge his factory. Perhaps he is beginning to cater to his feminine trade with something more distinctive than the violet scented fags! *Greensboro Record.*

The Danbury [NC] Reporter 16 January 1924: p. 3 NEW YORK

NOTE: "Fag" as slang for cigarette was more commonly used in the British Isles, but is sometimes found in the early 20th-century press.

If mourning cigarettes weren't lamentable enough, some women reverted to a Renaissance-era model, and draped their living apartments in black.

A MOURNING BOUDOIR

The Latest Alleged Absurdity in Grief for Lamenting Widows

"Come upstairs until I show you my room. It has all been done over in the neatest fashion, and is too sweet for anything," said a fashionable widow to our sweet girl reporter.

The handsome leader of fashion, who had been widowed for a year or so, led the way to a large room on the second floor.

The door was thrown open and the reporter took one glimpse and then started back. The place at first sight looked like the inside of a hearse.

"It's the latest English [style] don't you know, and so in keeping with my crape gown. I did not like it at first, but I do not believe I could sleep in colors again."

The room was furnished with a handsome suite of white enamel and the bedspread and the pillow shams were of black satin merveilleux, embroidered in black velvet applique with silver thread, the monogram of the widow being worked in silver on the centre of both spread and shams. The toilet table and little escritoire were draped in the same manner, and at the windows were thin curtains of black liberty silk against white lace.

"Look here," said the pretty widow, and she threw back the bed covers, displaying sheets of black silk hemstitched in white, and black silk slips on the pillows.

"I dress in black from top to toe," she continued. "I wear black silk underclothes, black satin corsets, and a black silk petticoat, and I even have my gowns lined with black. My friends tell me they would sleep as comfortable in a coffin as in my bed, but I find it a delightful resting place.

"And do you know" she continued, "a friend, who has just been made a widow, is having a room fitted like mine, only with black jet monograms. A great many English women who are not in mourning have black rooms, and that is where I got my idea."

Then she led the way into the boudoir all furnished in vivid yellow, even to the two canaries that piped in their golden cages.

"Yellow is the next color to black you know," she explained. "And then my husband was a Baltimorean, and I have the oriole colors, black and yellow, too, you see." *The Upholsterer*

St Paul [MN] Daily Globe 14 May 1889: p. 6

NOTE: It was an old French custom that a widowed Queen must be isolated for 40 days in a black-draped *chambre de deuil*. This was to ensure the paternity of any heirs-to-be, a notion which was laughably optimistic considering the notoriously lax morals of the French court. The lady in the account above—whose emphasis seems to lie on the "departed" portion of "Dearly Departed."—seems to be thinking more of how the black silk sheets enhanced her milky complexion than of her loss.

This tongue-in-cheek piece satirizes how the many categories of mourning might be parsed ever finer.

Widow's Weeds.

A friend tells us, that some dozen or fifteen years ago, when he had the "melancholy duty" to stand behind the counter in a country shop, dealing out the best selected stock west of the Alleghenies, he was once brought very suddenly to a state of unutterable wonderment. A youthful and pretty woman, robed in "deep black," approached him and asked to look at his "Gleam of Comfort."

"At what, madam?" said he, puzzled, confounded, and confused, at what appeared to him a singular request.

"Gleam of Comfort, young man; haven't you any, or don't you know what it is?" replied the lady.

"Yes, madam, most likely we have it; what is it like—is it dry goods or groceries?"

"Dry goods or groceries!" echoed the lady, looking at our friend in a way that made him feel decidedly uncomfortable. "Sir, it is a mourning calico of the second grade for widows of three weeks. It is well known, sir, with us in the city. I'm astonished at your ignorance."

The frightened young man could only stammer out—"they hadn't any of that particular kind of calico."

By John Bellenden Ker

Racine [WI] Daily Journal 14 February 1861: p. 1 WISCONSIN

We finish this chapter with a satirical piece which is uncomfortably close to the bone about the mourning industry. This is written about a *maison de dueil* [house of mourning] in London, England, and makes the point that it was difficult to purchase "correct" mourning outside of big cities. Mourners in the United States had the same problem.

FASHIONABLE MOURNING. THE HABILIMENTS OF GRIEF,

FROM A COMMERCIAL POINT OF VIEW.

On the occasion of a recent visit to London, whilst I was debating with myself over the breakfast things as to how I should spend the day,

I received by the post a letter deeply bordered with black, evidently a messenger of affliction. I tore the white weeping willow upon a black background which formed the device upon the seal, and read the contents. It proved to be an intimation from a relative of the sudden death of her brother-in-law, and a request that, under the circumstances of the sudden bereavement of the widow, I should undertake certain sad commissions relative to the articles of mourning required by the family. I at once set out upon my sad errand.

I had no difficulty in finding the *maison de dueil* to which I had been referred. It met me in the sad habiliments of woe; no vulgar colors glared from the shop windows, no gilding amazed with its festive brightness. The name of the firm scarce presumed to make itself seen in letters of the saddest gray upon a black ground. Here and there beads of white set off the general gloom of the house-front, like the crape piping of a widow's cap. The very metal window frames and plates had gone into a decorous mourning—zinc having taken the place of what we feel, under the circumstances, would have been quite out of the character: brass.

On my pushing the plate glass door, it gave way with a hushed and muffled sound, and I was met by a gentlemen of sad expression, who, in the most sympathetic voice, inquired the nature of my want, and, on my explaining myself, directed me to the Inconsolable Grief Department. The interior of the establishment answered exactly to the appearance without. The long passage I had to traverse was paneled in white and black borderings, like so many mourning cards placed on end; and I was rapidly becoming impressed with the deep solemnity of the place, when I caught sight of a neat little figure rolling up some ribbon, who on my inquiring if I had arrived at the Inconsolable Grief Department, replied almost in a tone of gaiety, that that was the half-mourning counter, and that I must proceed further on until I had passed the repository for widow's silk.

Following her directions, I at last reached my destination—a large room draped in black with a hushed atmosphere about it as though somebody was lying invisibly there in state. An attendant in sable habiliments, picked out with the inevitable white tie, and with an undertakerish eye and manner, awaited my commands, I produced my written directions. Scanning it critically, he said: "Permit me to inquire, sir, if it is a deceased partner?" I nodded assent. "We take the liberty of asking this distressing question," he continued, "as we are extremely anxious to keep up the character of our establishment by matching, as it were, the exact shade of affliction. Our paramatta and crapes give satisfaction to the deepest woe. Permit me to show you a new texture of surprising beauty and elegance manufactured specially for this house, and which we call the *inconsolable*. Quite a novelty in the trade, I do assure you, sir."

With this he placed a pasteboard box before me full of mourning fabrics.

"Is this it?" I inquired, lifting a lugubrious piece of drapery.

"Oh, no!" he replied, "the one you have in your hand was manufactured for last year's affliction, and was termed, 'The Stunning Blow Shade.' It makes up well, however, with our *sudden bereavement* silk—a leading article–and our *distraction* trimmings."

"I fear," said I, "my commission says nothing about these novelties."

"Ladies in the country," he blandly replied, "don't know of the perfection to which the art of mourning genteelly has been brought! But I will see that your commission is attended to, to the letter."

Giving another glance over the list, he observed; "Oh! I perceive a widow's cap is mentioned here, I must trouble you, sir, to proceed to the Weeds Department for that article–the first turning to the left."

Proceeding, as directed, I came to a recess fitted up with a solid phalanx of widow's caps. I perceived at a glance that they exhausted the whole gamut of grief, from the deepest shade to that tone which is expressive of a pleasing melancholy. The foremost row confronted me with the sad liveries of crapen folds, whilst those behind gradually faded off into light, ethereal tarlatan, and one or two of the outsiders were even breaking out into worldly features and flaunting weepers. Forgetting the proprieties of the moment, I inquired of the grave attendant if one of the latter would be suitable.

"Oh! no, sir," she replied with a slight shade of severity in the tone of her voice; "You may gradually work up to that in a year or two. But any of these," pointing to the first row of widows' weeds—are suitable for the first burst of grief."

Acquiescing in the propriety of this sliding scale of sorrow, I selected some weeds expressive of the deepest dejection I could find, and having completed my commission, inquired where I could procure for myself some lavender gloves.

"Oh! for those things, sir," she said, in the voice of Tragedy speaking to Comedy, "you must turn to your right, and you will come to the Complimentary Mourning counter."

Turning to the right, accordingly, I was surprised, and not a little shocked, to find myself amongst worldly colors. Tender lavender, I had expected; but violet, mauve, and even absolute red, stared me in the face. Thinking I had made a mistake, I was about to retire, when a young lady, in a cheerful tone of voice, inquired if I wanted anything in her department.

"I was looking for the Complimentary Mourning counter," I replied, "for some gloves; but I fear I am wrong."

"You are quite right, sir," she observed. "This is it."

She saw my eye glance at the cheerful colored silks, and with the instinctive tact of a woman guessed my thoughts in a moment. "Mauve, sir, is very appropriate for the lighter sorrows."

"But absolute red!" I retorted, pointing to some velvet of that color.

"Is quite admissible when you mourn the departure of a distant relative. But allow me to show you some gloves?" and, suiting the action to the word, she lifted the cover from a tasteful glove box, and displayed a perfect picture of delicate half-tones, indicative of a struggle between the cheerful and the sad. "There is a pleasing melancholy in this shade of gray," she remarked, indenting slightly each outer knuckle with the soft elastic kid as she measured my hand.

"Can you find lavender?"

"Oh, yes! but the sorrow tint is very slight in that; however, it wears admirably."

Thus, by degrees, the grief of the establishment died out in tenderest lavender, and I took my departure deeply impressed with the charming improvements which Parisian taste has effected in the plain, old-fashioned style of English mourning.

The Christian Recorder [Philadelphia, PA] 19 September 1863 ENGLAND

MOURNING STATIONERY.

SPECIMENS OF WIDTHS OF BORDERS.

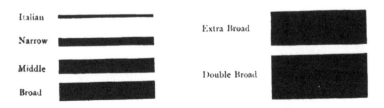

Mourning stationery borders, 1902

13.

The Inconsolable Grief Department:
Fashionable Widows and Their Whims

The widow occupied an ambiguous position in society. On one hand there were exhortations to be kind to the heart-broken widow and we find many stories in women's magazines about widows struggling with dire poverty. In these stories the widow either sinks under her privations and dies, leaving a child to battle on and triumph, or, when the family fortunes are redeemed by a clever child, she is restored to honor and comfort in her old age. In this fictional world, a widow remarried only rarely. Yet there were endless jokes in the newspapers about merry widows and their desire to bag another husband. These anecdotes and jokes capture a pervasive stereotype. Just as all mothers-in-law were meddlesome, all servants saucy, all wives spendthrifts, and all new brides comically inept cooks, all widows wanted a man.

The widow walked a dark and delicate line: she not only had to survive and look after her children and her late husband's business interests, she had to do it while seeming to be nothing more than a frail and "womanly" woman, rather than some mannish female, all business and bloomers. Often she found herself in an intolerable sexual limbo between virgin and temptress, regarded by men and their wives alike as altogether too fascinating.

It should be noted that while the modern age associates widowhood with old age, many Victorian women were widowed quite young, often by occupational accident or war. There was little in the way of a social safety net and upper- and middle-class women were not encouraged or trained to work. Remarriage might be the only economic option to maintain respectability.

The supposed frivolity and whims of widows have been a stereotype for as long as husbands have been dying. The "Merry Widow," that flirtatious figure of legend, has been the subject of jokes, editorials, and operetta for centuries. In 1734, it is said that the maidens of North Carolina petitioned Governor Robert Johnson to require young men to marry maids before widows, who, with their "foreward Carriages do snap up the young Men." [Source: *The Pennsylvania Gazette* (Philadelphia, PA) 28 March 1734.] Widows had the advantage of being "experienced," and were often described with adjectives such as "handsome," "pretty little," and (perhaps most popular) "buxom," all highlighting their sexual allure.

It was assumed that the widow's only goal was to replace her mourning veil with a wedding veil.

It's a poor variety of widow's weeds that won't bear orange blossoms. *Chicago News*

Evening News [San Jose, CA] 27 May 1904: p. 3

A wag in "what he knows about farming," gives a very good plan to remove widows' weeds. He says a good-looking man has only to say, "Wilt thou?" and they wilt.

New Hampshire Patriot and State Gazette [Concord, NH] 9 June 1875: p. 4

This young widow felt that memorializing her sorrow in a photograph would prove an inducement to new suitors.

A SPECTACULAR WIDOW

Wanted Her Photograph Taken While Weeping Over a Tombstone.

A young widow in London engaged a presumably also young photographer to take her picture while she leaned weeping over the tombstone of her "dear departed." On the day appointed the sentimental beauty in weeds went to the graveyard and at once opened the sluices of her great sorrow. She wept and wept for hours, but he came not. Finally she went dry and home, and straightway sued the photographer for the return of the money which she had paid in advance.

The artist claimed that the appointment had been vague; that he went to the cemetery and waited three hours for her at the grave, also in vain. No, they didn't compromise by marrying each other. The judge rendered a decision against the photographer, because "the photograph showing the undying fidelity of the pretty widow, might, if finished at the time agreed upon, have been instrumental in procuring her a second husband." At least, so says a Belgian paper.

Jackson [MI] Citizen 14 April 1896: p. 3 ENGLAND

Clearing the Field

"Widows' weeds are a good deal like other weeds, after all."

"What is the resemblance?"

"They get dragged off and burned in the spring." *Chicago Record*

New Mexican [Santa Fe, NM] 23 June 1898

NOTE: This joke refers to the superstition that keeping crape after the end of mourning was unlucky.

The cliché of the eager-to-wed widow was echoed in jokes, gossip about society ladies, and by etiquette experts like this one:

It is in questionable taste for a young and pretty widow to wear her mourning after she has become reconciled to the death of her first husband and is quite willing to marry a second. A widow still wearing her weeds, and at the same time carrying on an animated flirtation with some new admirer, is a sight to make the gods weep...To angle for a second husband with the weeds worn for the first, because they are becoming, is a thing that should be forbidden by law.

Social Customs, Florence Howe Hall, (Boston: Dana Estes & Co., 1911)

DUTIFUL WIDOW

The clerk of a large parish not five miles from Bridgenorth, Salop, perceiving a female crossing a church yard in a widow's garb, with a watering can and bundle, had the curiosity to follow her, and he discovered her to be Mrs. __, whose husband had not been long interred. The following conversation took place: "Ah! Mrs. __, what are you going to do with your watering can?" "Why, Mr. P__, I have begged a few hay seeds, which I have in my bundle, and am going to sow them upon my poor husband's grave, and have brought a little water with me to make them spring." The clerk replied: "You have no occasion to do that, as the grass will soon grow upon it." "Ah! Mr. P__, that may be; but do you know my poor husband, who now lies here, made me promise him, on his death bed, I would never marry again till the grass had grown over his grave; and having a good offer made me, I dunna wish to break my word or be kept as I am."— *Liverpool Courier*.

The Liberator [Boston, MA] 8 March 1834 ENGLAND

Not all Victorian marriages were love matches. Some were contracted for money, some for social prestige, or perhaps to please one's family. This may have made the loss of the spouse easier to bear. Some widows devoted themselves to fashionable and superficial details. The dead husband almost seems an afterthought.

The Widow's Weeds

"They say that Mrs. Jelliffe has given up that pet white poodle of hers," said Mrs. Jobson.

"Yes," said Mrs. Whilliger. "She's in deep mourning for Mr. Jelliffe, you know, so she has exchanged Toby for a black and tan." *Harper's Weekly.*

Albuquerque [NM] Journal 30 June 1912: p.3

Miss Gushington (to young widow whose husband has left her a large fortune): "That is the fourteenth mourning costume I have seen you wear in three days and each lovelier and more becoming than the other. Young Widow: "Oh! My dear, I have forty—but such a bother as they were to have made! At one time I almost wished that poor, dear George hadn't died!"

Arkansas Gazette [Little Rock, AR] 30 August 1883: p. 3

A Fifth avenue widow informed a friend at the funeral that she couldn't tell whether she would wear mourning or not until her husband's will was read.

Cleveland [OH] Leader 12 January 1876: p. 3

A classic newspaper feature story was the tale of a man declared dead and buried, but who then returns, either to the joy or chagrin of the widow. This one has a particular sexual frisson.

SAW HIS OWN SHADOW

And What is More He Took Her Photograph

A Queer Misunderstanding.

You may smile when I tell you so, says a New York letter, but there is a man living in a fashionable apartment uptown who has actually gazed upon his widow. I don't mean someone else's widow whom people call his, but actually his own widow. This favored mortal has not only seen his widow, but has photographed her. Nay, still more astonishing, on the back of the photograph you may read four obituary notices cut from New York papers and pasted there by the man himself. Mr. Carl H., a prominent art dealer and importer of paintings, finds it necessary to make several trips west every year to visit his rich customers in Chicago, Cincinnati, and St. Louis. While on such a journey last spring a train which Mr. H. had come very near taking playfully skipped the track and rolled down a hundred foot embankment. Several were killed, and Mrs. Carl H., the young wife, was terribly shocked to read her husband's name in the list. She telegraphed to the company to cause the body to be embalmed and shipped to her, she being physically unable to withstand the fatigue of the journey.

Now Mrs. H. is a charming blonde, with hair of rich gold and a skin like mother of pearl. To be sure she would look lovely in widow's weeds, and forthwith betook herself to Mme. M.'s and ordered a complete mourning costume to be ready in two days. Scarcely had the dress, bonnet, etc., reached the house when a telegram arrived from her lord and master, detained at Chicago, announcing that he would start on the limited that morning.

Great heavens! Carl had not been smashed up at all. It was some wrong man that had been embalmed and she now had the corpse on her hands, to say nothing of the widow's outfit. Fortunately just as the railroad people were about to ship the smashed up Carl to her, his own people appeared and proved property [claimed the body.] But the widow's outfit? It had cost $200. She hadn't the money.

What was to be done? At any rate Carl must not know of it; so, posting down to Mme. M.'s she gave strict orders to send no bill to the house and promised to call with the cash in the course of a few weeks. This was entirely satisfactory, but Mme. M. forgot to warn her bookkeeper, and that machine-like person not only sent a statement on the 1st of the month, but as was her custom, directed it to Mr. Carl H.

"In heaven's name, Blanche, what does this mean?" he asked.

"Why, dearie, you know when they telegraphed that you had been smashed up, and the newspapers all said that you were dead. I went and—and—"

"Where is it?" stammered the surprised Carl.

"Hidden away in one of my trunks, dearie."

Did Carl fly into a passion and accuse the poor girl of being a cold-hearted and calculating woman? Not he. He merely said, "Get it out, darling, and put it on. I want to try a new lens, and you'll make a delightful subject in a widow's rig."

"Bless your heart, dear, may you live a thousand years."

(Kiss-kiss-kiss-buss-smack-smack.)

The McCook [NE] Tribune 26 December 1890: p. 4 NEW YORK

Frank Nelson says his wife had bought so many fetching widow's weeds that she cried when he returned from hospital alive after doctors said he must die. She left him.

The Day Book [Chicago, IL] 26 August 1915: p. 32

Another cliché of widowhood was that women had no head for business and would be helpless without a husband. Wives often were kept ignorant of their husband's monetary affairs.

When a Widow Misses Her Husband.

"You will have to sign the document," said the insurance adjuster, addressing the widow of the policy holder.

"Where?" asked the woman in black.

"Right there," replied the adjuster, pointing to the spot where her signature was desired, "and you will have to have your family physician and friend of your husband sign these affidavits of his death."

"Do I have to go to all that trouble?" queried she, "I don't see why my poor dead husband could not have arranged these details before he died. In just such affairs a widow misses her husband terribly."

The Topeka [KS] Daily Capital 7 December 1886: p. 6

Willy: Pa, what kind of plants are "widow's weeds?"

Papa: "Oh! A sort of mourning glory, in most cases. *Puck*

Indiana State Journal [Indianapolis, IN] 15 December 1897: p. 6

Consistent Grief

Chicago Record

"Do you think Julia will always keep on mourning for her husband?"

"Yes, she is going to marry a man named Black."

Indiana State Journal [Indianapolis, IN] 15 December 1897: p. 6

Much was said about the expense of mourning, yet it could also be used as an aide to domestic economy.

A curious *ruse de guerre*, which is said to have been actually perpetrated in the fashionable world not long since, is recorded by a writer in the *Tribune*.

It seems that a certain business man found it suddenly necessary to curtail his very large family expenses, and, at the same time, he was particularly anxious, for financial reasons, that there should be no appearance of retrenchment. Unfortunately, it so happened that his wife had just issued invitations for a large and expensive ball, to be followed by a series of dinners; moreover, she had a younger daughter to bring out. The head of the house groaned in spirit as he mentally calculated the cost of a winter's round of gaiety for his womankind. His wife, however, was a woman of resource; on being made acquainted with his dilemma, she promptly rose to the occasion.

"I tell you what we will do," she exclaimed; "we will go into mourning."

"Into what?" gasped her astonished husband.

"Mourning, I said," continued his spouse, complacently; "I think it is the only thing we can do; as my people are Western, we can easily manage it, and no one will be the wiser. I will send out cards and countermand my invitations. I will buy a black gown, and the girls shall wear black and white all winter and go only to the smallest entertainments, and, I daresay, they will have a much better time than when struggling for partners at the big balls. As for me, I shall enjoy it beyond everything.

"Now, after all, it is only a fib that harms nobody and does us a lot of good," concluded this *fin-de-siècle* dame, who successfully carried her point, put her family into mourning, and withdrew gracefully from society and its requirements for the time being.

The Argonaut [San Francisco, CA] 23 January 1893

A DANGER OF CREMATION

Medium: Did you wish to inquire of the spirits, Madame?

Widow: Well, you see, I have always suspected that they mixed the urns at the crematory, and I want to know if I have been weeping over the right urn for the last three years.

Cincinnati [OH] Enquirer 13 March 1887: p. 15

It was taken for granted that widowers would remarry. If a man had children, he would almost have to wed again, unless some relative could join the household to care for the little ones. The division of domestic labor in the nineteenth century made it very difficult for a man to bring up children while working.

> In what period of his sorrow does a widower recover the loss of his dear departed?
> When he re-wives!

Puniana, Hugh Rowley 1867

NOT TWO OF A KIND

A Festive Widower Who Was Deceived in His Traveling Companion.

He passed down the aisle of the car to a seat occupied only by a man wearing a weed on his hat, and there he halted and sat down, and every passenger thought it a funny thing that two men, each a

widower, should thus be brought together says the *New York Sun*. At least one of the widowers also thought it funny, for after a bit he turned and queried:

"Your wife dead?"

"Yes."

"So's mine. Yours die of fever?"

"Yes."

"So did mine. Loving, faithful and economical?"

"Yes."

"So was mine. Broke you up, didn't it?"

"Yes."

"So it did me. Couldn't eat nothing for half a day. Have a big funeral procession?"

"Yes."

"So did I. Counted thirty-one buggies and wagons. Got a grave-stone up yit?"

"No."

"Neither have I. Death is an awful sad thing, ain't it?"

"Yes."

A Mourning Fad

"But we must make the best of it. We cannot help the dead by mourning. Got your eye on a second wife?"

"No, sir," was the indignant reply.

"How long's your wife bin dead?'

"A year."

The other picked up his valise from the floor, vacated his seat, and as he started for the car ahead he said:

"Stranger, I thought we was two of a kind, but I diskiver that I'm wrong in my figgers. One of us tells the truth and the other is a gaul__ liar, if I died for it! Good day!"

The Morning Call [San Francisco, CA] 4 May 1891: p. 8

NOTE: A "weed" was the crape mourning band worn on the hat. It was also sometimes known as "weepers."

The swiftness of a widower's mourning was axiomatic.

SECOND, BUT NOT SO VERY SOBER A THOUGHT.

A certain gentleman of a certain village lost his wife by death: he mourned much at her demise, as all good husbands are in duty bound to. Not having any relative near, one of his neighbors—a jolly good fellow—walked with the widower to the grave. After the ceremonies were gone through with, and the procession was returning homeward, the kind neighbor sympathized with the bereaved husband, and told him he must not give way too much to grief, for it would break him down, and he hoped to see him cheer up and be happy again, as tears would not regain his loss, and were of no avail!

"Alas!" sobbed out the mourner, "earth has no longer any happiness for poor me. What is life? What is this whole world to a man who has lost such a wife?"

"You have ever done your whole duty towards her," said the other, "treated her kindly and indulgently. Your wife can never come back to you, mourn you never so much; so all you have to do is to seek out another to cheer your way along the rough paths of life. There is the kind, amiable and pretty little buxom widow Cosey, she would make your home happy, I know you would like her, and I am quite sure she would be willing."

"My dear friend," replied the wifeless man, his eyes full of tears, "do not, I beseech you, speak of such a thing. My loss is irreparable."

The mourner invited all his friends who attended the funeral to sup with him that night, according to the usual custom of the place on such occasions. As the party was retiring, the widower urged his neighbor to stay with him till bed-time, as he felt so very lonely.

A bottle of choice wine was brought out, which the two friends discussed, then another was broached and finished. Finally, the neighbor arose and took his departure. He had not proceeded many yards when the man of grief and bereavement hailed him to come back, as he had a word to say to him. Then, placing his lips to his friend's ear, he whispered, "Neighbor, I think now that I could bear to hear that lady's name mentioned!"

Cambridge [MA] Chronicle 2 January 1864: p. 2

This whimsical dialogue between the paper and envelope of mourning stationery provides a surprisingly severe commentary on fashionable widows.

MOURNING STATIONERY.

"Dear me," said the Paper, "I feel awfully queer—so stiff round the edges. What is this black band for?"

"Hush!" said the Envelope; "don't you know? Her husband is dead."

"Well?" said the Paper.

"Well," said the Envelope, "how stupid you are. The black is mourning for him, that's all."

"Good gracious!" said the Paper; "does she do it like this? Do you suppose it comforts her to see a black edge on her stationery? How very funny!"

"It's the proper thing to do, at any rate," said the Envelope, sharply. "You haven't seen the world, evidently."

"But it is not my idea of *grief,*" persisted the Paper. "If I were sad I would go away from everybody and keep quiet."

"You are very simple-minded," said the Envelope. "Who would *see* you if you mourned like that? I knew a widow once who was very angry because she found a card with a wider black edge than her own. She said she had told Tiffany to send the widest that was made, and here was one wider. She almost cried, and measured the edges to make sure. That *was* grief, now."

"Was it, indeed?" said the Paper. "Well, times have changed, I suppose. Once when a woman lost her husband her eyes were so full of tears that she could not see how to measure black edges. This is the age of reason, I am told. All feeling is treated as weakness and soothed away by ignatia." [a homeopathic remedy for grief.]

"Oh, people feel, I suppose," said the Envelope, a little ashamed; "but, really, there are so many things expected of one now when one's friends pass away, that there isn't as much *time* for grief. Just look at our poor lady to-day. At nine the undertaker came upon a matter most painful. It was—well, the mountings on the casket. She was going to have hysterics, but couldn't, because he was waiting for her decision. Then the florist came to know about the decorations for the house. Then Madam Lameau with boxes upon boxes of dresses, wraps, bonnets, etc., and although our lady did sigh when she saw the deep black—tears spoil crepe, you know, and madam quickly diverted her mind by showing Lizette how to drape the long veil becomingly. Then came the jeweler with the latest design in jet, and her diamonds have to be reset now, you know, in black claws. After this the mourning stationery was sent with the crest in black, and all sorts of cards and letters had to be written. Then the servants' new mourning liveries and carriage-hangings were selected. When dinner was served, our lady was so exhausted by all this that she felt faint, and ate a really good dinner to sustain life. Now I should like to know what time she has had for grief, poor thing!"

"Don't say no *time* for grief!" said the Paper, rustling with indignation; "say no *soul* for it, and you will be nearer the truth. When a woman can choose bonnets and jewelry, her husband lying dead in the house, there is not much sadness in her heart. I see that she needs the black-edged paper to express herself. She might as well give up all this miserable farce and enjoy herself at once. Let her give a ball instead of a funeral, and show her diamonds in their new claws."

"Oh, dear me, do hush!" said the Envelope. "A ball in crepe and jet jewelry; you are not even decent; you don't seem to understand things at all."

"I don't, that's true," said the Paper, "and I hope I never *will;* when women have got to mourning by sending out black edges and wearing the latest thing in jet, I give them up. I never *shall* understand."

"Emotional people always make difficulties for themselves," said the Envelope, coldly. "I accept things as they are, and adapt myself—Hush! she is coming, and crying, too, I declare, after all."

"Well, really, Lizette," said a voice broken with sobs, "you are very thoughtless. How should I remember, in my distracted state, to say twelve-buttoned gloves? and here they are only six-buttoned; it is too bad. But every one takes advantage of me now. I am alone—forlorn—desolate," and the sobs redoubled.

"Poor thing," said the Envelope.

"What *hopeless grief*" said the Paper. "I *pity* her."

Arthur's Home Magazine, Volume 48, 1880

And finally, mourning—it's murder:

MOURNING COSTUME IS MURDER EVIDENCE
Detectives Think Widow Made Full Plans
Prisoner Still Maintains Husband Was Shot by Burglars While She Slept.

(By *Chicago Tribune* Leased Wire.)

Lakehurst, N.J., Aug. 18. The insistence of the detectives investigating the murder of William Giberson taxicab operator at Lakehurst, who was found shot to death in his bed at his home there Monday morning, that they had a complete case against Mrs. Ivy Giberson, the victim's widow, who is in Toms River jail charged with his murder, was explained somewhat to-day when some of the evidence to which they attach so much importance was disclosed.

In a closet in Mrs. Giberson's bedroom, it was learned, the detectives searching the house after the murder discovered a bundle of clothing. Taking off the wrappers, they found inside an entire mourning outfit, all apparently new and quite recently purchased.

Two black dresses, two mourning veils, a black hat and two pairs of black shoes, with several pairs of black stockings were included in the bundle.

It is apparently their theory that Mrs. Giberson, having planned to kill her husband, provided herself with a mourning outfit.

Mrs. Giberson's counsel scoffed at this strange piece of evidence and intimated that the presence of the outfit in Mrs Giberson's room would be explained at the proper time. The woman insists burglars killed her husband while she slept.

It was recalled that Mrs. Giberson on Tuesday made an urgent but futile request that she be allowed to attend the funeral of her husband Thursday. It is also known that she has sent several times to her home for changes of clothing.

Oregonian [Portland, OR] 19 August 1922: p. 1 NEW JERSEY

14.

The Restless Dead:
Ghosts With a Purpose

The dead are a demanding lot. They want to right a wrong or reveal their murderer or tell where they hid the will. They want their body found so that it can be buried. They want revenge. They want to be interred with their possessions or in a certain dress. They want to take someone with them. Or they simply *want*, which can be the most terrifying thing of all.

Some ghosts demanded the ultimate gift of a life. While there are many touching stories of relatives returning to escort a loved one to the Other Side, this apparition, though a child, proved deadly.

HIS CHILD'S GHOST

PETER GESSNER CRIES OUT THAT HE SEES AN APPARITION

AND CUTS HIS THROAT WITH A PEN-KNIFE

HE DIES BEFORE HELP CAN REACH HIM

AN AFFLICTED FAMILY

"There's the wraith of my child—she's winking at me—I shall, shall go."

Such were the words, uttered in a loud, strong tone, which attracted Mrs. Peter Gessner from bending over the bedside at her home, on the second floor of a building at Market and McLean Streets, shortly after 3 o'clock Tuesday morning. The woman, who was up and dressed to attend the wants of her two sick children and her husband, turned quickly toward the lounge on which the latter had been sleeping on the ground floor and saw him sitting up and staring fixedly before him. Gessner rose as he spoke and started for the staircase. Conceiving that her husband who had been extremely melancholy of late over the death of one of their children, had become crazed, the woman endeavored to calm him. He pushed by her without recognition and continued up the stairs. Mrs. Gessner hurriedly summoned the bartender who slept in another part of the house and a neighbor to aid her in preventing Gessner doing himself an injury. The three followed Gessner to the upper floor where they found him stretched in a pool of blood which flowed from a jagged cut in his throat. Still clutched in his hand was a small penknife with a blade scarcely an inch in length, but with which he had contrived to sever his windpipe and jugular vein. The cut extended from ear to ear. Efforts were made by the man's wife and friends to staunch the flow of blood while a messenger ran to Dr. McTaggart's home. The physician arrived within a few minutes but at once perceived that it would be impossible to save the man's life. He took a few stitches in the wound and did the little possible, but Gessner expired while he was at work. The dead man's wife, herself worn out with watching and sorrow, was prostrated by this additional blow.

Gessner was 37 years old and had been proprietor of the saloon for many years. The death of one of his children occurred a few weeks ago and Gessner, who was naturally superstitious and was also extremely fond of the deceased, brooded almost continually over it. He said often upon awaking from a fitful sleep that the dead child would come and stand by his couch at night and beg him to come to her. His wife sought to soothe his fantastic notions and watched him almost constantly. His death is mourned by a large number of his German friends...

Plain Dealer [Cleveland, OH] 17 September 1890: p. 4 OHIO

NOTE: The child was 4-year-old Lizzie. She is buried at the Monroe Street Cemetery in Cleveland, Ohio.

While cremation was regarded by burial reformers as a hygienic alternative to over-filled churchyards, it was still seen by many as the choice of the crank or the infidel. While we may wonder why the "spook" was so adamant, this is not the only story I have seen of a ghost returning when its wish for cremation was ignored.

SPOOK INSISTS ON CREMATION

Ghost of Ernest Heinig Upbraids His Sister for Burying his Body

Fort Wayne, Ind.; March 7. The body of Ernest Heinig was cremated Saturday evening at the Lindenwood crematory, under peculiar circumstances. Heinig committed suicide on Jan. 30, because of despondency, owing to having been thrown out of employment. Two weeks before he died he expressed to his sister, Mrs. Leuchner, the wish that in the event of his demise his remains might be cremated. Mrs. Leuchner, however, had a horror of cremation, and had his body buried. One night last week, Mrs. Leuchner says, her brother appeared to her in a dream and demanded why her promise had not been fulfilled, and insisted that she, even then, should cause the body to be exhumed and burned. So impressed was Mrs. Leuchner by the dream that she ordered the corpse taken up and cremated.

Jackson [MI] Citizen Patriot 7 March 1899: p. 1 INDIANA

NOTE: Heinig [1863-1899] killed himself at his sister's house. "Heinig purchased a new half-inch rope, took a revolver and a looking glass and repaired to the cellar. He placed the glass in front of him, tied the rope to a rafter and making a slip noose, tied it tightly around his neck. He then blew out his brains with a 32-calibre revolver and in falling tightened the noose. The shot however, was enough..." His sister, thinking that he had left the house, lit a candle and went to the cellar. To her horror she found the body of her brother hanging there, his face disfigured and distorted. [Source: *Fort Wayne (IN) Daily News* 31 January 1899: p. 4.]

The dreaded deathbed promise not to remarry haunted many a hapless widow or widower. Such promises had no legal force, but were seen by some as a binding vow, a sacred obligation.

A WARNING TO WIDOWERS

The Toronto *National* says: The Hamilton *Spectator* chronicles the appearance of a specter in Grimsby. The haunted man was a widower known as Old Kitchen, whose deceased wife had, before her death, a year ago, threatened to haunt him if he ever had anything to do with another woman. He promised to comply with her wishes, and kept his word until a short time since, when, in company with a man named Taylor, he drove to Smithville to visit a couple of young ladies. On his return home, late at night, Kitchen became visibly uneasy, his agitation increasing as they approached an old church, in a graveyard attached to which his wife was buried. When opposite the spot, "the white-robed form of a woman was seen to rise from the graveyard and float through the air toward them." Kitchen screamed out in an agony of terror, the horse gave vent to a wild snort of fear, and ran down the mountain at breakneck speed, and the apparition continued to follow them, floating through the atmosphere in terrible proximity to the faithless widowers. The other man states that it "looked like the corpse of a woman with the dead clothes on. The face was quite dead and expressionless, and the eyes were closed; one hand was extended toward Kitchen, almost touching his head, and the other pointing toward Smithville." Finally the buggy was smashed against a tree and the occupants thrown out, and when they recovered from the fall the ghost was gone.

Daily Inter Ocean [Chicago, IL] 31 August 1875: p. 2 CANADA

NOTE: See "The Death-bed Promise" in *The Face in the Window* for a detailed story of a marriage haunted by such a promise.

While there were dozens of accounts of the dead returning to deliver messages or sermons via entranced mediums at their funerals, it was rare for the dead to actually appear at their own obsequies.

Seen at His Funeral.—Dr. John E. Purdon, now of Valley Head, Ala., is authority for the following narrative, which records the appearance of a soldier soon after his death, and may be taken as evidence of the sensitiveness on one side, and of the reality of the existence of the appearance on the other:

"In the year 1872, while in charge of the convalescent hospital, Sandown, Isle of Wight, I returned from a short visit to London, bringing with me for change and rest Miss Florence Cook, who afterwards became so celebrated a medium. On the evening of my return home, I took a walk with Miss Cook along the cliffs towards Shanklin. During the walk she drew my attention to a soldier who seemed to her to be behaving in a curious way, turning round and staring at me, and omitting the usual military salute which she had noticed the other men give as they passed by. As I could see no one at the time my curiosity was excited, and when she said the man had passed a stile just in front of us, I crossed over and looked carefully about. No soldier was in sight; on one side was an open field; on the other, perpendicular cliffs. I asked a country man at work in the field if he had seen a soldier pass just before I appeared, but he had not.

"On my return from town I found that a certain chronic patient who had been a long time in the hospital, and on whom I had performed a minor surgical operation some time before, had died of pulmonary consumption.

"Miss Cook and another young lady on a visit to my wife, never having seen a military funeral, persuaded her to take them to a cross-road, where they would see the troops pass without being seen themselves. As we marched past, the coffin being carried on a gun-carriage, Miss Cook said to my wife, 'Why is the little man in front dressed differently from the other soldiers?' My wife answered that she could not see any one in front, nor could the other girl either. Miss Cook then said, 'Why does he not wear a big hat like the others? He has on a small cap and is holding his head down.' They then returned home, and the funeral party passed on to the graveyard which was two miles from the hospital. Just after the firing party had fallen in to march home, Hospital Sergeant Malandine came up to me in the graveyard and said: 'Private Edwards reports sick, sir, and asks permission to return by train.' I asked what was the matter, and the sergeant answered that Edwards had had a great fright from seeing the man we were burying looking down into his own grave at the coffin before it was covered by the clay!"

Studies in the Out-lying Fields of Psychic Science, Hudson Tuttle, (New York: M.L. Holbrook & Co., 1889) ENGLAND

NOTE: Miss Florence Cook was the medium who materialized "Katie King" for Sir William Crookes and others. In 1872 she had already begun her mediumistic career. She may well have had some psychic ability, but she also had youthful charms and a real gift for fooling distinguished scientists.

As recorded in the newspapers, some post-mortem obsessions of the dead seem very mundane: the corpse just wants a bent arm straightened or a move to a dry grave site or the burial robe was not what she had ordered—the list was petty and endless.

Clothing seemed to be an ongoing concern to the dead. One of the oldest ghost stories in the world features a ghostly wife who returns to complain that one of her sandals fell from the funeral pyre and she was forced to walk around the afterlife with only one shoe. Some dissatisfied decedents expressed their wrath at the wake.

A GREEN RIVER GHOST

A Tenacious Old Lady Rises in Her Coffin to Enforce Orders About Her Funeral.

[*Bowling Green (Ky.) Democrat*, 25th.]

The idea that mankind do not carry their grudges beyond the grave seems to have received a severe shock by a recent occurrence near Rumsey, a neighboring village of ours, located on Green river, in the junction of Butler and McLean Counties.

The story, as told by a credible resident of the neighborhood, is to the effect that some years ago an old gentleman died in that neighborhood and willed certain of his property to his relatives. He gave his wife a life interest in his real estate, which was to go after her death to his nephew, who was also to have the rest of his personal property not especially devised to others. Unexpectedly to his wife this amounted to more than was evidently intended, for he chose to claim and get possession of even that property, which she had considered and treated as her own. The avarice of the nephew so irritated her that she declared he should never enjoy the property after her death, and that she should live so long that his expectations and his hopes should be long unrealized.

Her tenacity of her own way was such that many of them declared they believed she would either live forever or haunt the nephew after death. For years there were bickerings and bitterness between the aunt and nephew and no opportunity was lost by either to annoy the other, and when the nephew was an old man the aunt died, apparently of natural decay; went out like an exhausted taper. Just before she died she gave directions to her attendants about the manner in which her remains should be prepared for the grave, and among other things she strictly enjoined on them to put no flowers about her corpse, to use no shroud, but to clothe her corpse in a black dress and have no useless paraphernalia or pomp in connection with her funeral. Her orders were strictly observed, except that after she was placed in her coffin a young lady, who had not heard of her antipathy to flowers, placed a small bunch on her breast. She had hardly laid the floral testimonial of her respect out of her hand when the corpse began to move, and in a few seconds the old woman sat up in her coffin and threw the flowers at the young lady, who, frightened half out of her senses, ran screaming from the room, while all those who beheld the spectacle were shocked beyond measure, but the old lady being apparently satisfied when the offensive ornaments were got rid of, quietly lay down again and was buried in due time. As soon as the funeral was over, the nephew entered and took possession of his inheritance, moving his family into the old house, which was a much better building than the one he had occupied. He was congratulating himself on his good fortune, while setting things to rights, but on the first night of his arrival he found that the old lady intended to keep her threat of haunting him.

He was not made of the metal that fears ghosts, and he allowed no trifle to disturb him; but about midnight he was awakened by the screaming of his children, who had been awakened by the well-known step of his aunt, as if walking about the room, and one of them declared she saw the ghost of her aunt and heard her footsteps clattering up the stairs. The father, although anxious to comfort his children, had to acknowledge he too had heard the steps, but scouted the idea of a ghost, and went to bed. The next night the step was heard by all, and a strange whitish light floated through the house, and was recognized by some of the members of the family as having the form of a woman, clad not in white, as ghosts are generally seen, but in the black dress in which the relentless aunt had been buried.

The same blood-curdling sights and sounds were endured for several nights, when the heir was entirely unable to longer endure the annoyance, and moved out of the house which has ever since remained untenanted. As the lonely traveler passes the house in the night, the strange light which so annoyed the family of the heir is sometimes seen passing and repassing before the uncurtained windows, and such is the reputation of the house that the owner cannot get a tenant to enter it, and even a greater portion of the surrounding grounds have been allowed to go to waste—so great is the dislike to approach the premises.

Daily Albany [NY] Argus 1 November 1873: p. 3 KENTUCKY

NOTE: A similar story is found in *The Ghost Wore Black* about a Baltimore "old maid," who haunted her old boarding house when she was not buried in the shroud she had chosen.

Other ghosts waited until they were buried to carp about their attire.

WRAITH

Of Woman Haunts Her Relatives Who Buried Her in a White Veil, Instead of Black.

New York, January 3. Declaring that since the death of Mrs. Gerardo Tramutola, on November 27, 1908, the apparition of the woman has appeared to them and protested that her life in the spirit world has been made unhappy because the woman was buried in a white veil instead of a black veil, members of Mrs. Tramutola's family have obtained permission from City Clerk Connelly, of Newark, to open her grave.

The relatives said they had been visited many nights by the wraith of their relative, who had declared to them that the white veil in which she was buried was choking her and that she has not been able to sleep in peace.

They said that as Mrs. Tramutola was dying she asked that she be buried in a black veil and that they had intended to carry out this request, which was the last she made. For some reason the woman's relatives used a white veil.

The apparition, which they say has appeared to them many times, has always reminded them that they had neglected to carry out the dying woman's wishes. The grave will be opened to-morrow.

Cincinnati [OH] Enquirer 4 January 1909: p. 1 NEW YORK

NOTE: Other articles add that her husband, Gerardo, feared that his wife had been buried alive. The cemetery superintendent refused permission to disinter the woman.

There was a pervasive belief that the dead should never be buried in the clothes of the living, who would waste away as the clothing decayed.

Robbed Corpse of Shirt

Easton, Md., Sept. 1. John Bell, Joseph Banton and Alberta Eaton, all colored, were arrested this evening by Constable Garev, at Ridgely and lodged in Denton jail for robbing the grave of Emma Gibbs, colored, who died in Ridgely a month ago and was buried near Denton.

The woman was buried in an undershirt belonging to Alberta Eaton, and she, being superstitious, feared that if she did not get it back she would die. She complained to her neighbors and John Bell and Joseph Banton are said to have volunteered their services to return the shirt. A few nights ago, in company with Alberta Eaton, they went to the graveyard, took up the corpse and replaced the undershirt with another.

The Concord [NC] Daily Tribune 3 September 1904: p. 1 MARYLAND

This corpse requested a change of venue when her husband put her in the wrong burial plot.

A HAUNTED SHOE

How a Husband Has to Suffer For Disobeying His Wife's Directions.

(*Boston Herald*)

Mr. Anthony Shoe is a clerk in a coal-oil factory at Allentown, Pa. Some little time ago he was so unfortunate as to lose the amiable Mrs. Shoe, who, before she died, laid especial emphasis upon certain ante-mortem instructions to the effect that she was not to be buried, under any circumstances in the family lot. Mrs. Shoe's prejudice against this particular burying-ground was based upon the fact that the lot aforesaid was uncomfortably wet, being frequently flooded with water when the river happened to be unusually high. So strongly was Mrs. Shoe disposed to insist upon obedience to her wishes in this matter that she solemnly declared before she took her departure to another and presumably a better world that if the damp cemetery did receive her remains she would "spook" her husband and children. Nevertheless she was buried in the objectionable graveyard, and, in fulfilment of her promise she has been engaged ever since in making existence as wretched as possible for her unhappy spouse. She makes nightly appearances at his bedside, and hovers over the cribs of the children in the shape of a spook, nearly frightening them out of their wits. The annoyance became at last so serious that Mr. Shoe appealed the other day to the police, and he says that if they can not do anything for him he will have to dig the old woman up again and plant her in a drier spot where she can rest peacefully in her grave.

The Daily Gazette [Fort Wayne, IN] 19 June 1886: p. 4 PENNSYLVANIA

Like the spirit of Chauncey Barnes, who alerted an acquaintance to the state of his corpse, these two ghosts had a message to deliver: the first thoughtfully provided his own obituary—when no one knew he was dead.

The second not only gave detailed directions on where to find his body, but broke the sad news of his death to his own family.

A GHOST AT THE KEYS

The Spectre of Sam Wall Wrote His Own Death Notice.

HAD COMMITTED SUICIDE

The Foreman of a Boston Newspaper Office Declares He Saw the Shadowy Figure of a Dead Man at a Type-Setting Machine.

The Foreman of a Boston Newspaper emphatically states that the spirit of Sam Wall, an operator, stood by one of the machines and with "long, bony fingers wrote out his own death notice, which was published the next day on no other authority than that his ghost had been there."

Special to *The Inquirer*.

Boston, May 17. Sam Wall, a Philadelphia man, who was a type-setter in a local newspaper office, was discharged some months ago. The foreman of the office says; "I had been running Sam's machine, and shortly before midnight had started for a fresh 'take' of copy. I lingered a little at the other end of the room chatting with a fellow-workman and was proceeding leisurely to the machine, when from the rear I beheld it in motion. This surprised me and I increased my speed, wondering who could be the intruder.

Rounding the corner suddenly I stopped, almost paralyzed with fright. For the operator was Sam, not the Sam of old, but an unrecognizable mass, from which peered the face of Sam, with glassy eyes, disheveled hair and death-like cheeks.

LONG, BONY FINGERS

Slowly and carefully the long, bony fingers covered the key-board and letter after letter was brought down, until, apparently satisfied, the head turned in my direction. Then with a sickening feeling I beheld a ghastly wound in the left temple, to which a few clots of blood still adhered.

Then I understood. And even as I looked the figure grew less and less distinct, seeming to disappear as a mist. Finally recovering my composure I managed to reach my seat. My thoughts were confused and my brain was in a whirl. I knew that Sam was dead. I knew that he had left a message. What was it? My curiosity was aroused. I would see. Slowly, still feeling those glassy eyes upon me I reached for the lines. They were very simple. They read as follows;

HIS DEATH NOTICE

"Died—In this city, March 9, 1895, Samuel J. Wall, aged 39 years, 4 months, 3 days. Philadelphia papers please copy.

"This notice was published in the paper in the morning on no other evidence of his death than my word. On that day his body was found in his room with a pistol shot wound in the temple. We found that for years he had been quite a figure in Philadelphia sporting circles.

Philadelphia [PA] Inquirer 18 May 1896: p. 4 MASSACHUSETTS

A SPIRIT TELLS WHERE HIS FROZEN BODY IS.

The great storm of 1873 was the most violent known in the Northwest for fifty years, as the records kept at Fort Snelling showed. ...The number of human lives lost in Minnesota was about seventy. But the one case, among the three fatal ones in Nobles County, which has been the subject of the greatest interest, because of the ghost story connected with it, was that of John Weston, of Seward township. Mr. Weston had been to Graham Lakes, and was returning with a load of wood when the storm caught him. He drove across his own farm and missed the house; turned and went in a circle, making the same circle twice, as shown by the tracks of the sled. He then turned north to the vicinity of the place now owned by H. D. Winters, in Graham Lakes township. He abandoned his team, and the oxen, after wandering awhile, turned the yoke and choked to death. Mr. Weston, from this point, evidently concluded to walk with the storm, and made a bee line for Hersey. He walked about twelve miles, and fell forward on his face, clutching the grass as he fell, and the blood gushing from his nose. His body was found the following spring, with the hands full of grass, and the blood on his face.

The story of John Weston's ghost was first published in the *Advance*, and widely copied, so that it became known throughout the country. Weston appeared to Mr. Cosper, who is still a resident of Seward township, and was an intimate friend to Weston. A few days ago we caught

Mr. Cosper in town, and had the story from his own lips. He is a practical, unimaginative man, and gives the story in a circumstantial way.

The day after the storm Mr. Cosper had been out with some neighbors searching for Weston's body. He had returned to his home, and was at the stable feeding his stock just before sundown. He came out of the stable, and passing around to the east end saw John Weston coming up the path from the creek. Weston had on the blue soldier overcoat which he usually wore. His hands were tucked up under the cape, and he approached Cosper with his usual smile and usual salutation, saying: "How goes it?" Cosper said: "Why, Weston, I thought you were frozen to death!" Weston replied: "I am, and you will find my body a mile and a half northwest of Hersey!" Saying this he vanished. Mr. Cosper says that even after Weston was gone, it took him some time to realize that he had seen a ghost and to 'feel queer.'

Before this, Weston had evidently announced his death to his wife. Mrs. Weston related the incident, and it was confirmed by her son. The second night of the storm she was awakened by a knock at the door. She dozed off again, and was aroused by a second rap, when she asked: "What is wanted?" A voice answered: "Did you know that John was frozen to death?" The voice sounded like that of her brother, Mr. Linderman, who lived in the vicinity. The boy heard the voice, and, rising up in bed, said: "Mother, did uncle say pa was frozen to death?" Mrs. Weston went to the door, but there was no one there, and no tracks could be found in the snow. Mr. Linderman had not been there, and it seems that Weston, wishing to announce his death, and at the same time not to frighten his wife too much, assumed the voice of his brother-in-law.

Now for the confirmation of Cosper's story. He told it at once, and it was published throughout the country before the winter was over. Search was made for Weston's body, but in vain. When spring came, however, and the snow began to melt off, Weston's body was found near a slough where the snow had been deep, a mile and a half northwest of Hersey.

The Worthington [MN] Advance 13 January 1881: p. 2 MINNESOTA

Occasionally we find stories of persons wishing to be buried standing, perhaps hoping to be found on their feet when the Last Trump sounded.

But this gentleman (in what is probably a folktale, since stories of petri-fied corpses were commonplace) had a motive of a more domestic nature.

STRANGE PHENOMENA CONNECTED WITH A GRAVE.

It appears from a dispatch from Galveston, Texas, to the Philadelphia *Times,* that twenty-five years ago there died in the neighborhood of what is now W. H. Master's ranch, in Montague county, a very peculiar individual named Bill Sterrit. Sterrit had one little girl and a wife, with whom he lived very unhappily—a woman with a violent temper and more than ordinary will power.

A few days before his death, Sterrit, who was able to hold his own against his termagant wife, called her to his bedside and requested that his coffin should be placed in the grave in such a way that he might be in a standing posture. He was afflicted with heart disease, and suffered from difficulty of breathing while in a reclining position. When Sterrit died, his wife, remaining obdurate in spite of the entreaties of his friends, had him laid in his grave in the usual way, flat on his back at full length. She "would get even with Bill Sterrit for once," she said.

Twenty-five years passed, meanwhile Sterrit had been almost for-gotten. His wife, leaving naught but the little wooden headboard to mark his grave, sold the ranch and moved to town. A few weeks since some new settlers, in excavating for a well on what had been the old Sterrit place, unearthed the petrified remains of a man in a standing posture. Old inhabitants identified the remains as those of Sterrit. Depositions made by them established the fact beyond a doubt; but no one could account for his being in a standing position, when they had the evidence of their own eyes to prove that he had not been thus buried.

Herein appears the strange part of the affair, which must, of course, forever remain a mystery. Mr. Masters said that while the figure, even the features, of Sterrit, are preserved almost in a state of perfection, the hands are mutilated, the knees very much scarred, and there is a considerable abrasure upon the forehead, running back into the hair. Persons who knew him have concluded that Sterrit must have been buried in a trance, and that when he regained consciousness and found himself buried, he first drew his knees up to their utmost extent, pressing upon the coffin-lid with all his strength. This would account for the disfigurement of his knees. Further, he must have beat his head against the top, finally clawing and tearing the lid with his hands. He managed to stand upright, and then died and was slowly petrified, to remain a perpetual defiance to his termagant wife, who lost her wits when she learned that Sterrit had thwarted her even in his grave, and is now in the asylum.

The Encyclopaedia of Death and Life in the Spirit-world: Volume 2, John Reynolds Francis. (Chicago: The Progressive Thinker Publishing House, 1906) TEXAS

Then we find this misanthropic gentleman who died in the glorious hope of, well, *not* resurrection.

Unusual Burial

In 1907, a brick, composed of five parts of cement and one part of ashes of the cremated body of a suicide, was buried in Hand-in-Hand Cemetery, West Roxbury. Pressed into the face of the brick is the epitaph:

Died May 30, 1907
HERMAN UNGER
Leave me in peace

Unger was a traveling salesman who believed that the human body after death would be revived in the form of a flowering growth which would spring from his mortal flesh. This thought being repulsive to him, and desiring to preclude any such resurrection, he left a will in which he directed that his corpse be cremated, and that the ashes be mixed with sufficient cement to form solid rock. This request was carried out, the brick being molded in a small square box.

American Clay Magazine, Volumes 2-7, 1907 MASSACHUSETTS

Of course, revenge was the classic reason that the restless dead returned.

HAUNTED

By Dead Wife's Spirit,

Thirsting For Revenge Murderer Thomas Geagan Met a Violent Death.

Toledo, Ohio, April. 21. Thomas Geagan, aged 60 years, was struck and killed almost instantly by an electric car early this morning on Adams street.

A peculiar feature of the old man's death was that a cruel fate pursued him for 24 hours prior to his untimely death. No matter where he went an evil spirit dogged his footsteps. After being pursued 10 or 12 hours by what Geagan declared to be the "Evil One," he cried out in despair, "I am doomed to be killed this very day. I can do nothing right to-day. Everything I do is wrong and I can't put my hand to a thing without breaking it and having an accident."

Before saying this Geagan, who was driving a coal wagon, had been struck twice by street cars, and had barely escaped with his life in each instance. Besides this he had slipped and fallen down a twenty-foot embankment, had fallen off a chair in the coal office and hurt himself and in other ways had encountered misfortunes during the entire day, until he quit work in despair. He was a strictly temperate man and liquor had nothing to do with the strange misfortunes that pursued him for hours before his death.

Geagan slept in the rear of the coal office and was on his way to retire when a car struck him in front of the office, killing him almost instantly.

To some friends Geagan made the remark during the afternoon after his misfortunes had begun to pour in on him thick and fast. "Well I'm doomed. She is after me and I can't get away from her. I can see her this very moment and she is demanding her revenge and I cannot escape. Something tells me she will serve me as I served her years ago."

It was learned at the police station that several years ago Geagan killed his wife during a quarrel and served eight years in the penitentiary for it, and the belief is that the "she" he alluded to in his premonitions of an approaching violent death was the spirit of the wife. The circumstances are the strongest ever related here, and Geagan, himself, fully realized he was a doomed man some hours before he was killed, and was convinced there was no way of escaping the fate which seemed to hang over him. He quit work deliberately under the belief that if he continued he would be killed in some manner before the day was over. He hastened to put himself out of harm's way and remained indoors until all traffic had ceased and he thought the danger period past, when he ventured forth to cross the street to go to bed in the office. A car that had never been known to run at that hour consummated the doom which Geagan felt was in store for him.

The *Cincinnati [OH] Enquirer* 22 April 1901: p. 2 OHIO

The corpse of the period did not always lie quietly in its grave. What with body-snatching and miraculous revivals from catalepsy, it was a wonder any bodies ever rested in peace. While burrowing through the literature of the resurrection of the entranced or cataleptic, I ran across several similar cases involving mysterious letters from the supposedly dead.

A Man Who Claims to Have Been Receiving Letters from His Dead Wife.

[*Nebraska City Press.*]

William S. Aimison, a farm-hand working for a man by the name of Bills, near Rock Bluffs, in Cass County, was in the city Friday, and told one of the strangest stories that the *Press* has ever been called to relate. Aimison says that he was married in Illinois about six years ago, and that three years later his wife died of consumption. He attended the funeral, of course, looked on the face of the woman he loved for the last time, and saw the coffin closed and lowered into the grave. Soon after he went to Kansas, and for six months has been in Nebraska. His story is that shortly after he reached Kansas he received a letter, dated and postmarked at his old home, in his wife's handwriting, in which he could not be deceived, and signed with her name, "Lulu." The letter told how she missed him and wanted him to come back, and how she needed his help. There was a sentence something like this:

"You all thought I died, but I did not, and am better than when I saw you last." That was the only thing in the letter that would have been thought singular or out of the way by one not knowing the facts. Since then at irregular intervals, several months apart, he has received other letters, all affectionate, but none attempting to explain the mystery, assuming that there is one other than some one is playing a ghastly practical joke. These letters came, the most of them, from Illinois, but one came in June last from Concordia, Kan., near which place he was located up to March, bitterly bewailing the fact that he had left there before the writer got to him.

Aimison has investigated the matter to some extent, sending one of the first letters received back to his wife's parents in Illinois and asking what it meant. They made nothing of the mystery, but agreed with Aimison that the handwriting was that of their daughter. He answered one of the letters addressing it "Mrs. W. S. Aimison" and it came back to him from the dead letter office.

On Thursday he received a letter from Table Rock saying that the writer, "Lulu" was there sick and without money. His visit to the city was on his way to Table Rock, the man stating that he was determined to get to the bottom of the matter, and if he discovered nothing by this trip he would work his way back to his old home and disinter his wife's remains or the coffin, to see if they were really in it. The story is a strangely fanciful one. Aimison is said to be a man incapable of its invention, but it is given for just what it is worth.

The *Cincinnati [OH] Enquirer* 30 October 1887: p. 16 KANSAS

NOTE: See the similar story below. Are these just variants of a nineteenth-century urban legend—the epistolary zombie, the Scribbling Dead? If they really happened, were they merely elaborate hoaxes designed to extract money from people like Mr. Aimison by claiming to be sick and broke? Or did such unlikely resurrections ever actually happen?

NEWS FROM THE GRAVE

An Ohio Man Comes to Life After Being Buried Thirteen Years

Toledo, O., Sept. 19. The *Commercial-Telegram* this morning publishes a singular story, which in substance is that thirteen years ago Thomas Hubbell, a farmer residing in Monrovia township, in this county, was supposed to have died and was buried. A few years ago his friends received a letter signed in the dead man's name, saying he was alive and would soon visit them. Recently a second letter of the same character was received. This caused an examination of the grave to be made and the casket was found to be empty. The explanation of the mystery is said to be that the grave was robbed and the body sent to a medical college in Michigan; that it was discovered that the man was not dead, but his mind being affected by disease, he could give no information concerning his friends and was placed in an asylum where he subsequently recovered. A brother of the resurrected party has gone to Michigan to investigate the matter. The widow of Hubbell married again seven years ago. The case has excited great interest in the locality of his former home.

Toledo, Sept. 19. The *Blade* this afternoon gives the details of an interview with some of the relatives of Thomas Hubbell. They place no credence in the story that letters have been received from him and that he is alive. They state that Mr. Hubbell died of pneumonia and four days elapsed before burial took place. The grave has been opened and the remains have not been found, but with this exception the story is pronounced without foundation in fact.

Arkansas Gazette [Little Rock, AR] 20 September 1885: p. 4 OHIO

NOTE: Unsettlingly, a Thomas Hubbell of the correct date did exist and his tombstone still stands in Swan Creek Cemetery, Monclova.

A tradition that may have come with the enslaved from Africa was that of placing grave-goods on the graves of the departed. The dead wanted their possessions and would haunt the living if they did not get them.

African-American burial practices are often absent from nineteenth-century papers or treated in a disrespectful way. The article, although it is written in dialect, seems to try to take a slightly more balanced view.

OBSERVE A CURIOUS CUSTOM

Colored Persons Who Litter the Graves of Their Departed Friends With Articles Used in Life

Old Mount Zion Graveyard and Its White-Haired Sexton.

A curious custom is still observed in an old negro burying ground in Washington—that of placing upon the graves of departed friends and relatives the articles that were most enjoyed or used by them while living and the bottles containing the residuum of the medicines that were administered during the last illness.

The Mount Zion graveyard, as it is called, lies in the shadow of the beautiful Oak Hill cemetery, on Georgetown heights. Both are charmingly situated on rising ground overlooking Rock creek at its most picturesque point. Separated only by a short stretch of land

and a high board fence, the two "silent cities" present the most vivid contrast imaginable.

On one side are soft green lawns, flowering shrubs, graveled walks and magnificent monuments, on the other, a rank growth of grass and weeds, worm eaten and discolored wooden headboards, and instead of flowers a miscellaneous jumble of toys, ornaments, tools, etc. But Mount Zion has its own peculiar charm, and its patrons are unique in the belief that the things used by the departed during life are needed by them in the land of shadows.

The old, white haired sexton, in his quaint dialect, gives many amusing obituaries and explains the significance of certain articles that litter the mounds.

The idea of the negroes in placing them in the cemetery is that they may be within easy reach of the spirits, whom they confidently believe revisit the scenes of their earthly sufferings. If they find familiar objects on their graves, they confine their manifestations to the cemetery; if not, they haunt the families who have neglected to provide them.

One grave has instead of a monument a large wooden hobby horse, buried to its haunches in the ground. It marked, so the sexton said to a reporter, the last resting place of one Mr. Johnsing, who while living was the driver of an express wagon. He was extremely fond of his horse, and his widow, who was obliged to sell it, used some of the proceeds to purchase a wooden one. A complete set of harness was provided also, and, to quote the old negro: "Ebery night he hitches and onhitches dat hoss, and den goes back and lies down again quiet. Ef he didn't have dat to ockerpy 'im, he'd hant de ole woman."

Often one grave is made to serve for an entire family. One of the most pretentious monuments in the cemetery—a plain marble slab—has carved upon its surface the names of Andrew Jordan and his four children—Erastus, Sophia, Andrew and Washington. "Ob course," said the sexton, commenting on the practice, "I has to dig de first grabe deeper, but it's eckernomical an sosherble in de end." Most of the inscriptions are real curiosities. With few exceptions they are painted roughly in black on white wooden tablets. Few of them bear any date whatever, and in the majority of cases names are not given in full. Nearly all of them are composed and printed by the sexton himself, who modestly deplored the fact that he was not as handy at it as he might be but the look of pride with which he regarded his handiwork belied the sincerity of his words.

On the grave of a little boy—Grover Hancock Van Clief—a high chair and a toy wheelbarrow stood guard. He had been a special pet of the old sexton, and the grass waving over him showed evidences of cultivation in striking contrast to the tangled, neglected growth on either side. The sexton admitted that these objects often disappeared from the graveyard, but, scorning the idea that there was any one mean enough to steal from "dead folks," asserted that it was a sign that the spirits were never coming back again and so had taken them to "glory." The medicine bottles, accompanied in most instances by a glass and spoon, were, he said, placed upon the graves that they might be "finished up."

The old man called attention to the grave of "Aunt Chloe Brown," whom he apostrophized as a "reg'lar terror." On its surface is a large palm leaf fan. It seems that "Aunt Clo" "Use ter git up in meetin' an talk an pray louder 'en anybody else an den go home an cut up lively." The chief bone of contention with her was that the rest of the family would insist on eating twice a day. She usually terminated the family repasts, when in her opinion they lasted long enough, by routing the feasters with a broomstick.

One day while chasing her husband, "who was the patientest [man] alive," she caught her foot in her dress and fell, striking her temple on a sharp stone. When they picked her up, she was dead.

"I put de fan on her grave," said the old sexton, finishing his recital, "'cause ef eber any one went to de hot place she did, certain shore, an she'll find it refreshin when she comes back in de night."

A grave in which he evidently took much pride has arranged around the mound a toy fence. Inside of the enclosure so formed a wooden soldier stands like a sentinel at either end. In front of each soldier is a row of smaller ones, and in the center of the mound three bottles are pressed into the earth.

"Lize Lundy" sleeps peacefully in an obscure corner under a pasteboard bandbox. "Lize was a good woman," said the sexton, "an earned a nice livin an enuff to die comfor'ble on a-makin dresses."

She liked to dress well herself also and had a regular passion for bonnets. Nearly every week she went to church with a new one and as often bestowed her discarded one upon a less fortunate friend in order to make room in her hatbox for the latest.

When she died, her sister put the last bonnet Lize bought in the cherished bandbox, together with a small hand glass with which she used to view herself, and placed it on the grave. All but the box disappeared long ago, which fact serves only to strengthen the belief of the sexton that they were just the things most desired by the spirit of Lize Lundy.

One grave, marked only with the single word "Cecelier," was kept in perpetual bloom by means of two immense rose-bushes, all made of waxed paper. *New York World.*

Patriot [Harrisburg, PA] 13 August 1894: p. 7 WASHINGTON D.C.

NOTE: John Michael Vlach, in a chapter called "Graveyard Decoration" in *The Afro-American Tradition in Decorative Arts*, notes that the objects found on graves included not only pottery, but also "cups, saucers, bowls, clocks, salt and pepper shakers, medicine bottles, spoons, pitchers, oyster shells, conch shells, white pebbles, toys, dolls' heads, bric-a-brac statues, light bulbs, tureens, flashlights, soap dishes, false teeth, syrup jugs, spectacles, cigar boxes, piggy banks, gun locks, razors, knives, tomato cans, flower pots, marbles, bits of plaster, [and] toilet tanks." *The Afro-American Tradition in Decorative Arts*, John Michael Vlach, (Cleveland: Cleveland Museum of Art, 1978), 139

These articles are "intended to placate the potential fury of the deceased." Vlach quotes Sarah Washington of Eulonia, Georgia as saying: "I don't guess you be bother much by the spirits if you give 'em a good funeral and put the things what belong to 'em on top of the grave." Her husband, Ben, added, "You puts all the things what they use last like the dishes and the medicine bottle. The spirits need these same as the man. Then the spirit rest and don't wander about." Vlach quotes others with similar traditions from around the south—sentiments which echo those in the article above.

Further Reading: Besides the "Graveyard Decoration" chapter in *The Afro-American Tradition in Decorative Arts*, which I highly recommend, see *The Death Care Industry: African American Cemeteries and Funeral Homes,* Roberta Hughes Wright, *et al* (Hughes-Wright Enterprises, 2007). [This is an updated edition of *Lay Down Body: Living History in African American Cemeteries*, Also *Gone To a Better Land: A Biohistory of a Rural Black Cemetery in the Post-Reconstruction South*, Jerome C. Rose, Editor, Arkansas Archaeological Survey Research Series No. 25, 1985.

15.

Bone of My Bone:

Collecting Corpses, Relics, and Remains

Nineteenth-century corpses were not confined to the dissecting room or the churchyard. The dead who lay upon the battlefield were captured by the photographer. Some families washed, shrouded, and coffined their own dead. Public executions made corpses a horrifying object lesson. In the larger cities, the dead were on display at the morgue. Yet there was always an endless morbid curiosity about the dead, which explains the corpus of stories about those who could not let go of their loved ones' remains, about exhumed bodies either incorrupt or turned to stone, and about ghouls, scientific relic collectors, and bodies reanimated by electricity.

We begin with poignant tales of a mother and son reunited in the tomb after thirty years of waiting and a poor, sadly deranged mother who would not let the grave take her child away.

THIRTY YEARS UNBURIED.

A Mother and Her Mummified Son Laid in the Same Grave.

Louisville, Ky., Feb. 8. A remarkable funeral took place at Rock Island, Tenn., yesterday, that was the talk of the whole county. The dead were a mother and her son, and the most remarkable feature of the event was that the son had been dead and unburied for thirty years. The truth of this is vouched for by responsible parties, who have seen the body at various times.

During the civil war the woman's son, then a mere lad, enlisted in the Confederate service and was killed at the battle of Murfreesborough. He was an only son—his mother's idol—and the shock completely prostrated her. She passionately declared that she would never part with her son while she lived, and that when death claimed her also both should be buried in one grave. She had an air-tight cedar casket made with a glass top, in which the body was laid. This was placed in a room assigned for the purpose, where the mother often repaired to commune with the dead. The body did not putrefy, but gradually became mummified. Thirty years it lay there. At last it was removed, and the devoted mother and her son were buried side by side in one grave.

An immense procession followed the bodies to their resting place.

New York Times 9 February 1893: p.1 TENNESSEE

SHE DUG UP HER BOY'S BODY

An Insane Mother's Ghoulish Feat at Her Child's Grave

Special Cable to the *Inquirer* [By Dunlap Cable Company.]

Vienna, Sept. 25. A horrible deed of a grief-demented mother was made public to-day. Helene Mueller, the wife of a master painter in Moedling, near this city, lost her only child, a boy 2 years old, by diphtheria, in February last, after an illness of only one day. The suddenness of the death appeared to paralyze the mother's brain and make it entirely impossible for her to realize that the child was dead. She has therefore devoted almost every daily hour to sitting on the baby's grave holding imaginary conversations with the dead one. One morning a week ago the sexton discovered that the grave had been opened, the coffin lid taken off and the body stolen. He at once went to the house of the mother, and after considerable trouble, found that the woman had dug the body up a few nights before, taken it to her home wrapped in a shawl, and placed it in her trunk. During the day she had taken it out and caressed it, and at night, after her husband slept, she had taken the baby to bed with her and endeavored to infuse warmth into it.

Philadelphia [PA] Inquirer 26 September 1890: p. 1 AUSTRIA

The Victorian press was fascinated by petrified corpses. There are hundreds of reports of these bodies, often described as white as marble, and always requiring many men to drag them from the grave. I don't know if such things still happen today with modern embalming and better cemetery drainage. Damp soil increases the odds of "petrification" or of what scientists call adipocere, or "grave wax," the result of saponification, a chemical reaction of body fat to bacteria in a cold and wet environment. Whether caused by natural conditions or chemical embalming, stories of corpses that did not decay were an eternally popular topic of interest to the Victorian public.

TWO WIVES BUT NO QUARRELS.

One of the Women is Petrified and Kept in a Box.

J.N. Rickles, the proprietor of a carriage establishment at Chanute, Kan., enjoys the unique distinction of having two wives who do not quarrel, although they are frequently in contact. He was visited recently by Mr. Broadhead of St. Louis. While the two men were talking in Mr. Rickles' office Mrs. Rickles came in and was introduced.

"This is my wife—that is, one of my wives," said Mr. Rickles. "She is wife No. 2. My first wife is over there in the corner."

Mr. Broadhead considered the remark a most unusual one. Noticing his perplexity Mr. Rickles volunteered to explain. He led the salesman to a pine box in one corner of his establishment. Lifting a lid off the box he displayed to the astonished salesman the form of a petrified woman. The form was perfect and the features almost as natural as one could expect to see in life. Mr. Broadhead says that Rickles explained to him that his first wife had died nearly a quarter of a century ago, while he was living in what is known as the "bad lands" in North Dakota. Several years later he had the body exhumed for removal and found that it had turned to stone. He then concluded to keep it in his possession and since then has taken the body with him wherever he went. In this instance Mrs. Rickles No. 2 is not the least bit jealous of having Mrs. Rickles No. 1 in the house.

Marshall [MI] Statesman 4 May 1894: p. 6 KANSAS

Strange Preservation of a Corpse.

In the town of Elizaville, Fleming County, Ky., is an old private burial place, where the dead of several private families are deposited. About twenty years ago Daniel Ficklin—whose name bears with it pleasant memories of the past—was buried at this place, and just after him his daughter Lizzie, aged about 4 years, died and was buried by his side. Several years after, Mrs. Lucy P. Rogers, daughter of Mr. Ficklin and wife of Elder John L. Rogers, died, and her dust was deposited with that of her husband. Her infant child died about three weeks after its mother, and was buried in a metallic coffin in the same grave last Saturday, at the instance of Charles L. Ficklin, of Memphis, son of Daniel Ficklin, the remains of the above-mentioned persons were disinterred, with a view to their removal to the cemetery at Flemingsburg. Each corpse has resolved into its native dust, with the exception of the infant, buried seventeen years ago. That was in a state of perfect preservation. Even the color of the eyes could be distinguished; the hair black and long; the face did not have the pallor of death, but had a bright fleshy color. A small gold pin fastened its burial shroud around the neck. The clothes in which the infant was dressed resembled white wax work, and the whole appearance of the corpse was so natural as scarcely to bear the features of death, while of its mother nothing remained but the decaying bones.

The Inter Ocean [Chicago, IL] 2 January 1875: p. 3 KENTUCKY

The nineteenth-century anthropologist had little compunction about collecting body parts from peoples they considered "inferior." Our museums struggle today with this legacy of indigenous bodies and artifacts: scalps, shrunken heads, and religious symbols blithely brought back from expeditions by scientists of past generations. Curtis obviously thought no more of these human remains than if they had been rock specimens.

PETRIFIED HUMAN EYES

Strange Sickness of Men Who Are Mounting Them.

[*New York Herald.*]

Mr. William E. Curtis, Secretary of the South American Commission at Washington, brought to this city some ago, a various collection of petrified human eyes, which he obtained in Peru. He took the eyes to Tiffany & Co.'s and left them there to be polished and mounted in gold in the form of a necklace. Three of the most competent workmen of the establishment were assigned to the remarkable order. The complete eyeball, which is soft as an onion and resembles iridescent glass, was cut into four or five layers, which were subjected to a powerful friction to obtain the desired finish.

On the first few eyes all went well, and the samples of the work were declared quite satisfactory. Some days later, however, one of the men complained of a bitter metallic taste in his mouth, accompanied by a burning fever. His illness was so severe that he was confined to his house for a week. Both the other men were also attacked with the same symptoms, although the disease was much less severe. The work was immediately stopped and Mr. Curtis was communicated with. There are about two hundred eyes in the collection, and much waste is said to ensue from the slicing process. A reporter was informed by one of the employees of Tiffany & Co. that the disease was thought to be caused by the acids and poisons used in embalming the bodies of the Incas, from whom the curious collection is supposed to have come. *N.Y. Herald*

Decature [IL] Daily Republican 2 January 1886: p. 4 NEW YORK

NOTE: At first I thought this must be a fantastic invention, but in one of his books, Curtis writes:

> The most curious things in Peru are the mummies' eyes — petrified eyeballs — which are usually to be found in the graves, if one is careful in digging. The Incas had a way of preserving the eyes of the dead from decay, some process which modern science cannot comprehend, and the eyeballs make very pretty settings for pins. They are yellow, and hold light like an opal. It is an accepted theory among scientists, however, that before the burial of their mummies the Incas replaced the natural eye with that of the squid, or cuttle-fish, and that these beautiful things are shams.

The Capitals of Spanish America, William Eleroy Curtis, (New York: Harpers Brothers, 1888)

But were they actually human eyes? Lieut. Rising of the Royal Navy had some specimens analyzed. They were found to be cuttlefish eyes. "On the Artificial Eyes of Certain Peruvian Mummies," Lieut. Rising, R.N., Communicated by Sir Woodbine Parish, K.C.H.; with Notes by F. Galton, Esq., E.R.S., 1865 http://archive.org/stream/jstor-3014277/3014277_djvu.txt

There is a possibility that Curtis knew that the "eyes" were not human, but he told the Tiffany workmen that they were. No one blinked an eye at the practice of making jewelry out of human remains.

A different type of "corpse collector," but a possibly unique cemetery.

A CURIOUS GRAVEYARD

In Which Is Buried Only the Amputated Legs and Fingers of Railroad Men.

Denison, Tex., May 2. Denison has a most peculiar graveyard. In fact, it is probable that not another cemetery of the kind is to be found in the state. The burial ground is a small plot of land lying north and immediately adjoining the Missouri, Kansas and Texas freight depot, and is used for the interment of hands, legs, fingers and such other parts of human beings as are mashed and mutilated by the cars in such a manner as necessitates amputation. In the Missouri, Kansas and Texas yards in this city and among its hundreds of miles of track north, south and west of the city accidents are frequently occurring, and a large number of those injured are forwarded here for medical and surgical treatment. The right building is used for such purposes, and the vacant lot north of the platform is used as a depository for amputated substance. Two weeks ago the legs of little Johnny Wells were interred in this peculiar graveyard, and this morning the right foot of E.R. McCain found a grave at the same place.

Dallas [TX] Morning News 3 May 1891: p. 10 TEXAS

Undertakers sometimes embalmed unclaimed corpses and displayed them as specimens of their art. Mr. Levy McCoy, the notable embalmer of Memphis kept a corpse several years old at his establishment. A famous corpse named "Eugene," was displayed at the Littleton Funeral Home in Sabina, Ohio for many years. [See *Haunted Ohio III* for the story.] The outlaw Elmer McCurdy was embalmed after his death in a gun battle and displayed first at a Pawhuska, Oklahoma funeral home, then at a variety of carnivals, side-shows, and haunted house attractions. Such display might also be used as revenge or blackmail when families did not pay. This comic tale tells of the adventures of a corpse with several electrifying features.

COURTED BY A CORPSE

An Embalmed Body Utilized as an Advertisement.

A Speaking-Tube That Seemed to Make the Dead Talk

A Spinster Who Thought That a Pale Gentleman Was Making Love to Her.

Not a great while since there died in San Francisco a gentleman who was on a visit to this coast from the East. He was apparently a person who commanded sufficient means for all the ordinary purposes of life, but when he died, says the San Francisco *Alta*, only a small sum of money was found in his possession. His relatives were communicated with, and instructions came from his wife to have the body embalmed, preparatory to shipment to his old home in the East. This was done, and the bill, representing rather a steep figure, forwarded to the grieving widow. The sum so far exceeded her expectations that she indignantly refused to pay for it, and the corpse was left on the hands of the undertaker. This gentleman had read somewhere that in a similar case down in Arizona the conductor of funerals had utilized the corpse left on his hands as an advertisement for his trade. Acting upon this suggestion, he had the cadaver in question taken from the neat metallic coffin to which it had been fitted, and, dressed up in a Prince Albert suit, adjusted to a sitting position in an armchair in the back parlor of his establishment.

So perfectly had the embalming been accomplished that, with the exception of the grayish pallor which overspread the face, the dead man looked as natural as life. This circumstance suggested to an ingenious young man connected with the undertaking establishment the idea of utilizing the corpse for entertaining visitors. To this end, the chair in which it sat was placed against a thin partition, which had been previously pierced for the reception of a speaking-tube. This was so arranged that the tube rested against the coat-collar of the corpse. By speaking through this from the other side of the partition, in the dim light of the back parlor, to the casual observer it appeared as if the corpse was talking.

Fortunately, however, the upright position and graceful poise of the body of this interesting person led all who looked upon it to conclude that it was only a middle-aged gentleman sitting there at his ease. But this was not all. The undertaker's ingenious clerk had attached to the right arm of the corpse the wire of a galvanic battery, and, by the proper manipulation of the instrument, he could cause the arm to rise or fall or gently curve around any object near it.

One day a spinster lady of uncertain age came into the parlor to make some inquiries relative to a prospective funeral. As she entered, the corpse, which she supposed to be a well-dressed visitor, gracefully bowing, invited her to take a seat at his side, where a vacant chair was ready for her service.

"Take a seat, miss, sit here (indicating the chair). I am charmed to have the pleasure of seeing in this desolate apartment a lady of such fascinations."

"You are very polite, I am sure," murmured the flattered fair one.

"I make it a point, my dear," continued the corpse, "to note every beautiful face that comes into this room. You must know that I remain here all the time, night and day, and my only happiness consists in receiving and entertaining the occasional visitor."

"Why, how curious! You stay here all the time?"

"All the time, my dear, night and day. In fact, I never leave this chair," softly and sadly remarked the dead man.

"Are you doing a penance, sir?" inquired the lady.

"Oh, no; the undertaker is my jailer."

For a single moment the lady was frightened. The thought occurred to her that she was in the presence of a maniac, and a thrill of apprehension shot through her heart. But the calm, serene face reassured her, and when the corpse gently raised its right arm and calmly encircled her waist, she no longer doubted its sanity.

"You are very beautiful, my dear," sighed the middle-aged cadaver.

"Oh, sir, how strangely you talk," and the lady blushed to the tips of her pink-like ears.

"You see, my dear, to a lonely man like myself, condemned to sit day after day in this darkened chamber, such a lovely vision as yourself comes to me like a gleam of sunlight. I trace in your fair face some of the sweetest memories of my youth when in long by-gone years I was loved and was beloved in return. When you entered this dreary place a moment ago you seemed to bring me a vision of the beautiful world which lies beyond the threshold I am never allowed to pass, and my withered heart turned to you with an emotion of delight." It must not be supposed that the lady listened to these bold words without sweet and tender reflections upon the possibilities they might lead to. Nevertheless she deprecated the dead man's enthusiasm, and insisted that he was speaking unadvisedly. Still she turned upon him a tender glance, which would have had anything but a chilling effect upon the ardor of a veritable wooer. It seemed to send fire through the veins of the dead man. The arm tightened around her waist. His words grew musical and soft.

"I see in you, my dear," continued the corpse, "the embodiment of all my dreams of bliss. If I only had your sweet companionship in this desolate room its gloom would take the hue of radiant sunshine, and I should be content to sit here forever warmed by your smiles and gladdened by the tender glance of your eyes."

"Oh, sir," sighed the lady.

"Can it be possible," continued the enraptured dead man, "that you reciprocate my passion! That you will be mine?"

The fair head was gently inclining to the shoulder of the corpse when the undertaker entered. The lady screamed. The corpse sat upright.

"Why, how is this?" exclaimed the astonished dealer in coffins.

"Oh, sir," gasped the fair one, "this gentleman has been talking so very strangely."

"Talking?" shouted the undertaker. "Why, you must be mad! How can a dead man talk?"

"Dead!" screamed the lady.

"Why, yes; look at him. Lord help you! You have been courted by a corpse."

The astonished spinster cast one fond despairing look on the ashen face of her wooer, and flinging her arms above her head, cried piteously: "Heavens! Does my beauty charm the dead?" and fainted away.

Patriot [Harrisburg, PA] 20 January 1888: p. 3 CALIFORNIA

A few years later, we find this similar story of the wealthy Mrs. Bivins and her husband's electric corpse.

TWO HUSBANDS

A Live One and a Dead One in the House at the Same Time

Special Dispatch to the *Enquirer.*

Cordele, Ga., October 12. The death in this city of Mrs. Joseph E. Bivins, wife of the President of the First National Bank recalls a sensation as ghastly as it was realistic. Mrs. Bivins was formerly an old maid in Atlanta, where she had some little property. Dr. Marvin, a specialist, from Omaha, Neb., came to Atlanta, wooed the matured maiden and made her his wife. He engaged in some real estate speculations which made him worth nearly $1,000,000. He then moved to this city and erected a magnificent home, which was a dream in the eyes of the country people hereabout. The happy couple lived in this new palace but a few weeks when the doctor

SICKENED AND DIED.

Mrs. Marvin refused to be comforted. She forbade a funeral and telegraphed to New Orleans for an expert embalmer and an expert electrician. The result of their joint efforts was that Dr. Marvin was enabled to remain in his seat in the parlor and by electrical appliance would rise and bow to his widow and then take his seat again. Ridiculous as this may seem, there was no arguing the widow out of its continuance. After about a year of this kind of enjoyment the widow concluded to give her hand and heart to Mr. Joseph Bivins, who had become her business manager. After her marriage she

TOOK HIM TO HER HOME

And then it was that she gained the remarkable distinction of having two husbands in the house at the same time, one alive and the other dead.

She had Mr. Bivins look upon the body of her dead husband in the parlor, and it was only after urgent solicitation on his part that she consented to the remains being sent to Macon and buried in Rose Hill Cemetery.

Notwithstanding this very peculiar conduct Mrs. Bivins was a lady of great charity and many Christian virtues.

Repository [Canton, OH] 12 October 1896: p. 2 GEORGIA

A bowing electric corpse? Well, maybe not *quite* electric. Much as I long for this tale to be true, the following is more likely the real story and it is bizarre enough.

CASKET IN THE PARLOR

Georgia Woman Kept Her Husband's Body for Months.

Mrs. Joseph Bivins, of Cordele, Ga., died a week or so ago. That would not be an extraordinary announcement were it not for the fact that her death concluded a strange exposition of woman's caprice, as unexplainable as it was unheard of.

When Dr. George W. Marvin died in Cordele, Ga., three years ago, he left a grief-stricken widow. Her lamentations were long and her sorrow was inconsolable. She had married Dr. Marvin in Atlanta about ten years before. He practiced medicine and soon amassed a considerable fortune.

It was in the midst of this prosperity that the doctor died. Mrs. Marvin was almost heartbroken. Her relatives could not console her. The kind words of friends failed to soothe in the slightest her poignant grief. She wept bitterly and continuously.

In the meantime the arrangements for the funeral, which were under way in charge of some solicitous relative, were being made. So entirely helpless with grief was the chief mourner that it was thought both unnecessary and cruel to call her into consultation regarding the last ceremonies. So the minister was summoned, and when the services at the house were to begin Mrs. Marvin was quietly notified.

Her reply was a scream of anguish. She became almost hysterical. When she was able to articulate understandingly she informed the funeral guests that they were entirely out of place; that there was to be no funeral. She would not permit the body of her husband to be laid away in the ground she said, and no conspiracy of unsympathetic, cold-blooded, heartless persons should interfere. She announced that she intended to keep Dr. Marvin's body in her home—their home—and that it should remain there forever. She wanted to have him always in sight.

Finally, under severe pressure, Mrs. Marvin consented to a ceremony over the body, but refused to authorize the interment. She had the body embalmed, placed in a casket and stood it in an upright position in the parlor. A cut-glass cover, working on hinges, was on the elaborate and handsome coffin, which is said to have cost $10,000, and she exhibited it to a few intimate friends.

For three months the casket remained in the parlor, and during that time Mrs. Marvin was in a state of mind that bordered on hysteria. Every day she brought fresh flowers as an offering to the memory of her departed, and in the presence of at least one visitor she kissed the cold cheeks of her husband and wept in grief-torn sobs. Dr. Marvin looked almost life-like as he stood upright, and he held in one hand a handsome gold cane, valued at $150, while in his shirt front were not less than $30,000 worth of diamonds. None of these were removed, but all were laid to rest with the body at the end of three months.

As Mrs. Marvin's grief expended itself she listened more calmly to the advice of her friends, and, much to their delight, finally consented to a burial.

The body of Dr. Marvin laid to rest, his widow began to improve, and just ten months later married Mr. Joseph Bivins, of Cordele, Ga.

Jackson [MI] Citizen Patriot 28 November 1896: p. 3 GEORGIA

NOTE: Dr. Marvin was not, in fact, buried until January of 1894, when he was laid to rest in Rose Hill Cemetery of Macon, although there are no records as to the exact location of his grave. Mrs. Bivins died in October of 1896, leaving Bivins with a tidy fortune. He only enjoyed it for a few years longer, dying on their wedding anniversary, 27 December 1898 at Dr. Allen's private sanitarium, where Dr. Marvin had died. Mr. and Mrs. Bivins are buried together under a modest tombstone at Sunnyside Cemetery in Cordele.

For the full and lurid story of Dr. George W. Marvin, please see this fascinating account researched and written by Stephanie Lincecum, beginning with this page http://rosehillcemeterymacongeorgia.blogspot.com/2013/04/paging-dr-marvin.html

From black comedy we turn to a husband's grim and guilt-driven devotion to his wife's corpse.

DEVOTION
To His Suicide Wife
Leads Moon To Practice of Unparalleled Rites
Sorrowing Man Exhumes the Life-Like Body
And Dresses It Anew in Immaculate Linens.
Mammies With Fears of Ghosts Decline to Aid in Paying Strange Fealty To the Beloved Dead.
Special Dispatch to the *Enquirer.*

Caddo, Ind. Ter., December 11. As strange as fiction, and so bizarre and grewsome as to cause those most familiar with it to shudder when it is mentioned, is the story of W. J. Moon's remarkable devotion to his dead wife—a devotion which has caused him to ignore all conventions, the sentiment of the community and the pleadings of his friends, and practically to alienate himself from the society of his equals in the community where he ranks as one of the wealthiest and most influential citizens.

Moon's self-imposed ostracism is the result of his persistent habit of disinterring the body of his dead wife, bathing it and clothing it in fresh linens before consigning it back to the grave for another brief period.

When Mrs. Moon committed suicide two months ago the husband was away from home on a hunting trip. It was impossible to communicate with him at the time. Neighbors and friends of the family therefore prepared the woman's body for burial and interred it before the absent husband knew of the death.

Frantic With Grief.

When he returned and learned of his loss he was almost frantic. He appealed to some of the best women of Caddo to assist in exhuming the body and preparing it for burial to suit his notions. He stated that he wanted the corpse clothed in a black silk dress which he had given her as a birthday present, and which she had worn but a few times. The sympathetic ladies agreed to humor him, and the body was taken from the grave, where it had lain for four days. They bathed and reclothed it according to the wishes of the grief-stricken man.

The incident caused some discussion, but a few days later, when Moon appealed to certain ladies of the town to assist him in again exhuming and preparing the body for the grave, the community was shocked. Nevertheless Moon succeeded in persuading some respectable women to assist him. The body was once more taken from the grave, bathed, clothed in fresh linen and reinterred.

In a short time this procedure was repeated, and again and again did Moon disturb the grave in which his dead wife reposed to carry out his grewsome ideas of devotion. In the meantime Moon's friends tried by every argument within their power to dissuade him from his course, but he seemed to be unsusceptible to reason on the subject. He no longer could obtain assistance from white women of Caddo, and was obliged to employ two old colored mammies to take part in the periodic rites. Finally the negresses were frightened from the work by stories of "spooks" and spirits told to them by indignant white people.

Declares He Will Persist.

Moon now attends to the grewsome matter alone and unaided. On every other matter he seems quite rational, but he declares that so long as his wife's body resists decay—and it is said to be in a remarkable state of preservation, approaching almost to mummification—he will at intervals purify it and clothe it in clean linen.

Moon is rated as one of the wealthiest merchants in this section. He is worth over $100,000. He has built up his fortune himself and is known far and wide as a shrewd business man. Little is known of his relations with his wife, save that just prior to the death of Mrs. Moon they had some domestic troubles which led to the beginning of this story. Moon left home hurriedly. Before he left he and Mrs. Moon had talked over their differences and their future was apparently to be one of happiness. During his absence she drank from an ounce bottle of carbolic acid while in a fit of despondency, and when neighbors called they found the body stiff in death. She had removed her clothing and turned back the covers on the bed, evidently having planned to lie down after taking the fatal dose.

She had written a note in which she stated that she was in her right mind; that she believed that she was justified in the action she was taking and that God would forgive her and that she was willing for Him to be the judge between them. This probably referred to her husband.

Ordered Two Dresses.

While away Moon had ordered for her two magnificent dresses, two diamond rings and many other valuable things, including trunks and traveling impediments, planning to give her a long trip. But she had not waited. The presents were never unpacked, but were sent away, the husband preferring never to see them again.

For a time friends feared that the blow would prove too much for the husband. He seemed unable to keep his mind off his wife. He would sit and talk about her all day.

Recently Moon completed the construction of a massive steel vault, in which the casket containing his wife's body now reposes. The vault gives promise of endurance for centuries. It is 12 feet wide by 20 feet long and is 12 feet high. The walls are 18 inches thick and composed of brick and concrete. The floor is concrete and the roof is dome-shaped and solid concrete. There are small windows in the north and south walls, steel barred and shuttered. There are double steel doors, the inner one being of steel bars and the outer one solid steel. The vault is built so that air circulates freely. Within the vault are stone piers, upon which the coffin rests. The elaborate receptacle for the body of the woman cost $2,000 and required three weeks to build.

Moon has had the body embalmed three times, and it is said to be gradually hardening.

Evansville [IN] Courier and Press 13 December 1904: p. 1
INDIAN TERRITORIES [OKLAHOMA]

NOTE: William Judson Moon owned a large general store and hotel in Caddo. His wife Molly killed herself while he was on one of his frequent buying trips to St. Louis. He remarried, but the marriage lasted only six weeks. His third marriage lasted until his death in 1923, when he was buried in the vault beside Molly. See this page for more information: http://mem55.typepad.com/caddo_my_home_town/2007/08/index.html

The Moon vault is housed in a modest brick building. http://www.findagrave.com/cgi-bin/fg.cgi?page=gr&GSln=Moon&GSiman=1&GScid=239922&GRid=29105332&

Cremation was considered a crankish fad for much of the nineteenth century. In keeping with its somewhat dubious reputation, we find this intriguing story of a wife who truly believed that her husband was "flesh of her flesh; bone of her bone."

Cremation's Odd Phases

One Widow Reported to Have Eaten the Ashes of Her Husband

Complications That Happen

A good many queer things have happened in connection with cremation, but perhaps the strangest of them all was the case of Mrs.

Matilda Francefort. Matilda ate her husband, which sounds canni-
balistic, but isn't.

In 1896 Mr. Francefort left his sphere of usefulness in Brooklyn
and his soul, it is to be hoped soared to a better world. As for his body,
they took it to Fresh Pond and cremated it. Then his widow went after
the ashes and took them carefully home with her. All widows do not.
Some don't even buy a niche for them at the crematory or pay storage
for them in the cellar.

But Mrs. Francefort was different. She got the ashes of the late Mr.
F. and carried them home in a japanned tin box, like a tea canister or
a spice box. Perhaps that was what suggested to the sorrowing widow
the disposition she should next make of them.

At any rate she decided to eat them. There was much to be said
in favor of this plan. It was economical. She would save the expense
of an urn and niche and a monument by being all that herself. Then,
too, she and the dear cremated had lived together for 31 years and she
was lonesome without him. She was informed that the ashes would
enter permanently into her system and it seemed to be a clear case
of eating your cake and having it too. Anybody could see that under
the circumstances it was the only way of keeping the family together.

Having decided to eat her husband, the next question was the
manner in which he should be served. Mrs. Francefort went over his
qualities with a sorrowful heart. He had been a witty man; there was
always a spicy flavor in his conversation. Mrs. Francefort made a note:
"Spice."

Then she defied anybody to say that he had not been the salt of the
earth. Another note: "Salt." Still she had to admit that he had a bit
of a temper. Note number three: "Pepper." But then, he was always
sweet to her. Final note: "Sugar." Clearly Mr. Francefort's post-mortem
specialty should be in the condiment line. Mrs. F. determined to take
him as seasoning.

So she put a pinch of him in her coffee at breakfast and sprinkled
him lightly over the boiled shad. At luncheon he went into the tea, and
contributed distinction to the lamb stew. At dinner—well, at dinner
the supply of Mr. Francefort's ashes went down in more ways than one.
And whatever the gentleman may have done in life, there is one thing
sure, he never disagreed with his widow when he was dead, though a
little of him did perhaps go a long way.

The Cincinnati [OH] Enquirer 16 March 1901: p. 12 CONNECTICUT

NOTE: Fresh Pond, Long Island, was one of the earliest crematoria on the East coast. The tongue-in-cheek tone suggested that this tale was just a whimsical flight of fancy, but a satirical tone seems to have been *de rigueur* in stories about the oddities of cremation. Although I haven't located them in the census or grave records, the Franceforts were mentioned in other newspaper articles. In an article published in various papers in February, 1897, Mrs. Francefort was candid about her scheme for eating her husband's ashes, although she coyly admitted that she hadn't discussed her plan with *him* while alive.

While we can be kept abreast by the Internet about events at the Wellcome Collection, the Morbid Anatomy Museum, and the Hunterian Museum at the Royal College of Surgeons, reports of collectors of anatomical specimens and murderabilia thrilled Victorian newspaper readers. There were titillating stories of young lady collectors of skulls, Sarah Bernhardt's skull letter-holder, and gentlemen who wore shoes of human skin. There were also tales of Gothic horrors, like this entrail-collecting scientist.

Resting in a case at a museum in Florence, the table-top looks like an indifferent specimen of Renaissance *pietra dura/pietre dure*, the decorative art of hardstone inlay, or perhaps clever marquetry, made to look like polished jasper, carnelian, and sardonyx. It is, however, made of petrified pieces of human viscera, bone, and muscle, the creation of Professor Segato of Florence, who discovered a process to preserve human remains by turning them into a stone-like substance. *Dura mater* instead of *pietra dura.*

Here is the story of this macabre piece of furniture. I was initially skeptical as I read accounts like this:

An Extraordinary Table

According to *l'Universe* of February 22, 1886, an attempt has been made to secure for the exhibition of the Franklin Institute, of Philadelphia, a most remarkable table, at present in the Pitti Palace in Florence. Of this table, *l'Universe* says:

It was made by Giuseppe Sagatti,[more properly Girolamo Segato] who spent many years in finishing it. So far as one can see, it appears to be a curious work of marbles of various hues, for it looks like polished stone, and yet it is composed only of the muscles, hearts and intestines of human bodies. One hundred cadavers were required to make it. The table is round, one meter in diameter, with a pedestal and four clawed feet, the whole made of petrified flesh. The author of this work died fifty years ago. After having passed through the hands of three owners, the last of whom committed suicide and sprinkled the table with his blood, it reached the Pitti Palace. Sagatti succeeded in solidifying the bodies by plunging them into many mineral baths. He obtained the cadavers from a hospital. The intestines serve for ornaments of the pedestal; the claws are made of hearts, livers and lungs, and preserve the colors of those tissues. The table is made of muscles artistically arranged; around it are a hundred eyes and ears which produce the most strange effect. The eyes, it is said, seem to be alive, and they look at you at whatever point you place yourself. This was the most difficult work of the artist. He was satisfied with his achievement and communicated his methods to scientists. The last owner of this table, Giacomo Rittaboca, had placed it in the center of his salon and took pleasure in showing it to guests, saying that it was the work of an original sculptor; then in the evening he would explain its real origin.

One Christmas night he had gathered together some friends and they were playing cards on this table. Rittaboca lost, and the eyes of the table fascinated him, he became pale, agitated; at last he arose and walked about with hurried steps, then came and sat down again and lost still, disconcerted by the fixity of the looks which followed him. It was proposed to change their place, and the importunate eyes were covered over. 'It is useless,' said he, and he told his friends the whole story of the table made up of parts of human bodies. 'It is not marble,' said he, 'it is flesh, real eyes, real muscles, real hearts. See! They are still alive. The eyes speak to you. I can not endure them, they make me mad.' Then suddenly he seized a dagger, and before any one had time to stop his arm, he had stabbed himself to the heart, exclaiming to his friends: 'I am rid of them.' His blood poured over the table and his corpse rolled upon the floor. His heirs were glad to sell the piece of furniture to the government, and if the guardian of the Pitti Palace is willing to lend it to the exposition, Americans who are fond of strong emotions may be satisfied.—*L'Union Medicate.*

The Cincinnati Lancet-Clinic, J.C. Culbertson, M.D., editor, New Series, Vol. XVII; Whole Volume, LVI, 1886. ITALY

There were a number of articles about this strange artifact, but since the newspapers of the 1870s and 1880s were so enchanted by petrified corpse stories, it seemed likely that this was just a journalist embellishing a popular theme. Even if such a macabre piece of marquetry *had* existed, surely it had long ago been lost.

But the internet is a wonderful thing. Today you can see, at an online museum, Professor Segato's astonishing and disturbing handiworks. The pedestal and the border of eyes has disappeared, but the rest is still intact, although Professor Segato's method of petrification remains a mystery.

His grave, in Santa Croce Church, Florence, bears an epitaph that translates loosely as "Here lies Girolamo Segato—who would be intact, petrified, if the secret of his art had not died with him."

NOTE: See http://hauntedohiobooks.com/news/elbows-on-the-table-professor-segatos-petrified-corpse-furniture/, also http://www.unifi.it/unifi/anatistol/anatomia/segato/index.htm [Site is in Italian.]

Professor Segato's corpse-entrail table.

16.

The Museum of Death:
The Horrors of the Morgue

The pomp of the Victorian funeral was pervasive—if one moved in the right social circles. If not, the public Death House waited. Here is an unflinching look at The Horrors of the Morgue, often the fate of the poor, the lost, and the unwanted.

THE HORRORS OF THE MORGUE

The city reporters are trying their hands at showing up the horrors of the Morgue during the recent hot weather. The Morgue is the great receptacle in New York for the unrecognized dead and dying. The following is from the pen of the *World's* reporter:

THE MUSEUM OF DEATH

"Bring in your dead."

This has been the terribly dismal cry for five days outside of the charnel house in Twenty-sixth street, known as the Morgue.

"Bring in your dead."

All day long. In the night, too, with the shadows gathering on the hot, seething river, with bodies washing in and out against the docks, which have fallen from the death boat on its way for Ward's Island. Slapping to and fro against slippery piles and filling the mid-air with a horrible, blue-bottle stench, which makes the nerves fidgety and the system weak. Ah! These terrible five days will long be remembered in New York.

Since morning, and for five days, the lower end of Twenty-sixth street which juts out into the East River, and looks, with its stables, low-roofed manufactories and sheds, deserted enough, has been darkened by a stream of hearses and hacks to take away the bodies of the stricken ones who have found their last shelter above earth in the stone-flagged yard and on the marble slabs of the Morgue.

The Morgue is a two-story brick building, with crenellated windows and a lonely aspect, blinking from the hot bricks in its wharf. To the right of the Dead Wharf is another wharf, where prisoners destined for Blackwell's Island are confined in a square wooden edifice, with a bad, reeking smell, not at all controlled by the plentiful whitewash which adorns its walls. There is a crowd of curiosity seekers, of both sexes and of all ages, standing and lounging and gaping in the hot sun, around the wharf, in the street, at the doors of the Morgue, and before the opening in the Death-yard. A few are distressed and agonized, seeking to recognize friends among the festering corpses; but the majority were low-browed, scantily-dressed, and hard-looking specimens. The prisoners on the dock, drunken men and women, with dirty, soiled garments and hideous faces are engaged in violent contention among themselves, and one old and wretched hag continually bawls out, regardless of the close vicinity of death and terror:

"Oh-hoh nyo-Oh-hoh ayo-Oh-hoh ny-y-a-a!"

We enter the yard of the Morgue thro' the door cut in its fence, and before crossing the threshold, a burly form of a man, in the prime of life, bare headed and steel-bodied, blocks up the aperture, and asks what we want. "To take a look at the Morgue and its adjuncts and appurtenances." "All right; come in." This is the assistant, who removes and boxes up bodies for transportation. He is a man of huge build, a hard, horny-handed man, with an eye to business.

We are in the yard, which is paved with flag, about fifty by twenty. Piles of coffins all around us, with a narrow passage to walk in. Rough boxes of pine, painted red, marked "3-6," "5-6," "6-6," and so on, to show what sized body may be accommodated within their wooden walls. There are two or three stacks of these boxes, empty and waiting for bodies. The rest are full, reeking and horrible to look at, but far more horrible to smell. The flags of the yard are covered with a moving matter of maggots—white, disgusting maggots—the refuse of what was once the tenement of light and life, joy, hope and despair. The shells of human souls, stricken to nothing by the scorching blasts of the burning July sun.

Streams of water from short lengths of hose are playing on these coffins. Some of these pine coffins have their lids partly ajar, and heads covered with greasy, wet hair protruding from them, and sickening, blasted faces, some the color of verdigris, some like boiled meat, and some like untanned leather, look up at the sun, and the dead, still, glassy eyes frighten one with their steadfast gaze. From the seams of these coffins pour columns, platoons, brigades and divisions of slimy white maggots. The coffins are filled with ice, but the blood in the bodies was turned to fire by long broiling in the sun, before death came as a relief, and has placed the rotten flesh beyond the control of a million icebergs.

"Augh! This has been an awful week for us," says John O'Brien, the boxer-up of bodies. "Shure, I'd rather have cholera, or yalla favir, thin sunstroke to dale with. Ah, man, ye ought to have seen the hearses these four days."

"You must have had a busy week, Mr. O'Brien," said we.

"Yis, and I have plenty more bodies. I keep them here under the jurisdiction of Mr. Brennan. But the great difficulty is that whin the coroner sinds for the friends of the bodies, they won't come. And the stink is awful. Ye can't recognize a body at all, after two days."

"Have you had many bodies here, Mr. O'Brien, this week?"

"Well, I guess I have had seventy five or more. There's a great many of thim unknown. I put ice on thim, but they won't keep, and thin there are a great many of thim that are kept in cellars and places a long while before they are brought here. Here is some of thim."

And we stepped into a small room, out of the pile of hot, reeking coffins, where there was a cold, deathly air pervading the low chamber. The assistant lifted a coarse, wet blanket off a recumbent figure, and showed us the worm-eaten face of a dead man of the laboring class, with legs bare and with small lumps of ice strewed on them.

"You see that's quite hard," said John, digging his thumb and finger into the breast of the man. The ice had saved all but his face, which was of the color of a copper-bottomed keel that had long been in the salt water. Then we went through the yard again, passing between rows of hot, slimy pine boxes, and in under the shed on the wharf where the bodies are embarked for the Island for burial. The wharf is quite dark, the sides being open on the river, and it is some time before we can see objects distinctly, but the odor is awful. The water splashes and plays with the under timbers of the wharf, and steamboats pass up and down in the distance. There is a breeze on the river today, and the sun is tame in comparison with its efforts of the previous days of the week.

"We have lots of thim here," says the attendant.

Looking along the narrow wharf we can discern a number of dark objects covered with canvass bagging. These are the rotting bodies. A number of coffins, also, with small cards nailed upon them, giving the name and cause of decease of each victim.

"This is the rouller on which we roull them into the boat," says O'Brien, pointing to a rude platform with roller attached, on which the bodies are dumped in the boat. Very few of the bodies can be carried, so they are placed upon the roller, and so rolled into the flat boat.

The board is covered like a butcher's block with blood, slime, fatty grease, and putrefied matter from the numerous bodies which have been rolled over its surface into the floating tomb. The big toes on either foot of each body are tied together and from under the canvas coverings of many of these loathsome, bulky objects, these ghastly, blanched toes stick out, for strange to say, the extremities are the last to putrefy.

One object before us, within two feet of us, seems to move, and we look inquiringly at O'Brien, who lifts the canvass. Great God! What is this? It is a human body or was once, but now it is a sponge or fungus. Looking down, we behold the shape and outline of a corpse, but such a corpse! There is the faint outline of a body, the slight swell of the breasts of manhood, the swelling curve of the hips, a crayon of a head, neck and arms. But there is no flesh or integuments. But the outline swarms and is moving. There is nothing of mortality left. The body is all white maggots and seems to have power of locomotion. It is all maggots....A cast iron stomach could not stand it any longer, and we leave the dark, rotting wharf with the idea in our mind that the maggots will, if left to themselves, soon eat up the timbers down to the water.

Now we are in the ante-chamber to the Morgue proper. The bodies for identification are preserved in a glass museum. Fifty or sixty idlers, many of them half-grown children, are crowding up to the panes of glass, which are defended by iron railings and bars, and those who are tall and strong press forward as if they would break in to get near the naked bodies. The strongest and tallest get the best chance, and the short and weak ones, with heated faces frowsy hair and soiled garments, have to be content with a look from between the legs of the taller ones. The boxer of bodies, with an air of authority, takes out a huge key, opens the door admitting us into the Chamber of Death, and the crowd presses forward, hungry and athirst to get a look, and glaring, with envious eye, that they are not admitted. We are in a chamber about fifty feet long by twenty-five feet wide, with a strong odor of carbolic acid pervading everything. There were seven marble-slabbed tables in the room, and on every one of the seven tables was a naked body, that is, naked as far as the arm pits. Streams of water pour down from pipes in the ceiling on the faces of the dead men. The clothing of each of them is hung up opposite each table, and ticketed with the name of the deceased, if any name is known, and when the body was found. They are all men of middle age, staring in a ghastly manner, their mouths wide open, the eyes glassy, and the tongues sticking out, whitened with a white fur.

Their arms hang down in a stiff, silent position, like stiff pieces of gutta percha. The faces are bloated and swelled, but identification is possible to those who knew them in life. The bodies are in good condition, and the flesh and skin firm and natural, except where the red streaks show from the effects of the carbonic acid, used to keep them from corruption. O'Brien takes up a huge glass jar full of liquid, which, when shaken, looks like coffee grounds, and pours it on the faces of the dead men, saying.

"Ah! That's the fine stuff. It keeps them beautiful sure."

One of the dead men has a clear, white skin, and a fine body, he shot himself through the left breast two days before, and lay there now, poor fellow, very quiet. All the rest have died of sunstroke, and looking horrible in this quiet chamber, with the plash of the stream of water and the intense, sickening odor of carbonic acid. Some of them have been lying here on these slabs for forty-eight hours awaiting identification which will never come perhaps, for them, poor wretches, in this world. There are lots of flies humming around—great, big, juicy fellows, with round, jolly bodies. They have had a royal week of it, these fat lazy fellows; and when the bodies are exhausted they will of a certainty eat one another. Well, we have got enough of the horrors of this place, and pass out from the dread results of this week of the fire of Sodom and Gomorrah.

FROM ANOTHER EYE WITNESS

The Morgue was crowded yesterday with men, women and children. Many would gaze for hours, as if only to gratify a morbid curiosity. Mr. O'Brien, of the dead house, says that he has slept but little during the past week, for, night and day the place has been besieged with those anxious to get bodies admitted or removed. The rush has been so great that even the warden was to leave the hospital and help the Morgue attendants. The bodies, while lying on the marble slabs, are frequently drenched with carbonic acid, and a constant spray of croton water is kept running upon their breasts. The scene yesterday was enough to make the gayest sad. Men with large arms came and went with coffins and dead bodies. In a court between the deadhouse and shed, red coffins were piled up like cordwood. Here were little coffins

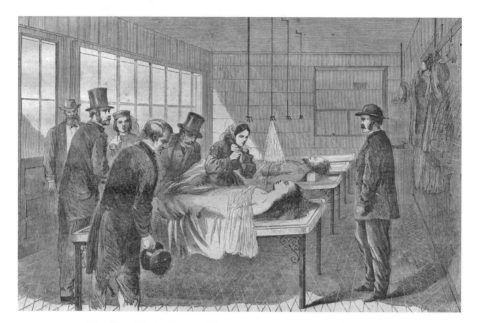

The New York City Morgue viewing room, Stanley Fox,
Harper's Weekly, 1866.

for children; in the corner was a blue coffin, while in the shed and
dead house, square boxes, cracked coffins and stretchers were lying in
all positions. Every two or three minutes some one wanted to see the
keeper who had charge of the dead. Among others was a spare woman
about 35 years of age. She was in search of her husband. Mr. O'Brien,
after listening to her description, went over to a coffin and wrenched
off the lid. Who ever saw such a sight! The stench was suffocating.
What the night before was a human being was now a bloated mass
of corruption. "Oh my God!" exclaimed the woman "my husband; oh,
my___" At this juncture another woman inquired for her son. She could
not find his body in the Morgue—was he dead or in the hospital? An
attendant swore that he knew nothing about the living, he could not
keep track of the dead. "Go through the wards," said he, "and may be
you can find him." More people came; some wept, others swore. The
woman first spoken of wrung her hands, and paced up and down the
Court in despair. At last she went up to the coffin, and, in a pleading
voice, she said: "Heavens above me, what shall I do? God of mercy, I
want him buried in Calvary." (She was a Catholic, and could not bear
the thought of having him buried in unconsecrated ground.) "What is
going to become of me? Last night poor John, poor John, you was at
work, why did you die before you bid me goodbye? My husband, since

last night here you are. My God, to think you have come to this."

Here she took hold of the green and putrid hand of her husband, shook it, and broke into a new paroxysm of grief.

Hornellsville [NY] Tribune 20 August 1868: p. 1 NEW YORK

It seems strange to think that 26th Street is still the location for the office of New York's Chief Medical Examiner and the DNA Forensic Biology Laboratory Building. The unwanted, lost and unidentified dead of New York are still buried in the same Potter's Field on Hart's Island. Modern descriptions of burials on Hart's Island are an eerie echo of the story below.

BURIED IN POTTER'S FIELD

The Grewsome Trips of the *Fidelity*

Her Daily Cargo of Pauper Dead

Scenes at the City Cemetery, Hart's Island.

Among the boats that may be seen on the East River any day is a small craft bearing the name *Fidelity*. People to whom the various vessels are only slightly known see nothing peculiar about the boat, because she is like hundreds of little vessels on the East and North rivers used for conveying freight and passengers between points where the larger vessels do not make landings. But to the river men and to the people who spend their time near the east waterfront the little boat is known as "the deadboat."

She belongs to the city, has a crew of four deckhands, besides a mate, an engineer and a fireman, and is commanded by Captain Edward McEvoy. This boat makes the tour of the city institutions on the East River daily and collects the bodies of the dead and takes them to the Morgue. Randall's Island, Ward's Island, Blackwell's Island and the Harlem Hospital all contribute to the grewsome cargo which is landed every evening at the Morgue, where the bodies of the homeless and the friendless are also taken.

"We have dull and busy seasons," said Captain McEvoy, "but we can usually count on about two a day from Randall's Island, about three a day from Ward's Island, and Blackwell's Island gives us about ten a day. The North Brother Island dead are taken care of by the Health Department; the Harlem Hospital, at One-hundred-and-twentieth-st., is good for about three a day."

THE *FIDELITY'S* CARGO

All the bodies as they come aboard are handled by the deckhands and are piled on the after deck, covered with tarpaulins, and when the *Fidelity* steams down the river with her load for the Morgue, passengers on passing vessels would never suspect the character of her cargo.

Twice a week in the winter months and three times a week during the warm season the *Fidelity* makes a trip to Hart's Island, where the bodies from the Morgue which have not been claimed or identified are buried in Potter's Field, or, as it is officially, the City Cemetery.

"It's all the same after you are dead," said a man who had made the trip, "but if you want to know the advantage of passing away among friends make a trip to Hart's Island on a burying day."

The boat's load, which varies in size from thirty to one hundred boxes, stands on the dock and in the hallways of the Morgue, ready to be taken away early in the morning. Every box is furnished with a card which contains the name, age, sex, cause of death, etc., of the subject, or, where the name is unknown, a number corresponding with the one on the Morgue records, by which everything that is known on the body may be ascertained. The marks on the box also show whether the person was a Catholic or a Protestant, when that fact may be ascertained.

"How many ye got to-day?" the deckhand asked one of the Morgue helpers who assist the regular attendants for their board and what they can pick up from undertakers in the way of tips for helping with the claimed bodies.

"Oh, it's a small day. Ten big and twenty-seven little ones." That meant that there were ten large coffins and twenty-seven coffins with children's bodies to be taken away. The cargo was taken on board with less care and ceremony than would have been devoted to a like number of boxes in the hands of a transportation concern marked "Handle with care," the boat moved away from the dock, which was littered with old and broken coffins, and the trip to Potters Field began.

AT HART'S ISLAND.

The distance to Hart's Island is about fifteen miles, past the City Hospital, Penitentiary, Almshouse, Maternity Hospital, Insane Asylum, House of Refuge, Idiots' Asylum, Infants' Hospital, North Brother Island and about six miles beyond Fort Schuyler, on Throg's Neck and Willets Point. At the landing there were several officials in the uniform of the Department of Correction and three men in convict's stripes.

"Didn't expect you to-day," one of the officers called in greeting to the captain, "you had such a big load yesterday."

The boat was made fast and the bodies, which had been transported by the Charities Department, were transferred to the custody of the Department of Correction. The three convicts loaded the boxes into a wagon and it started on its first trip to a trench about one hundred yards from the landing.

John Bopp, the Superintendent of Potter's Field, who has been in charge of the place for thirty years, and in spite of the nature of his work and the surroundings, retains a cheerful disposition, said:

"We have about fifty convicts here, who are detailed from the Workhouse, but some of them object to handling the coffins, so we select three men who are willing to take the job and give them a ration of whiskey after every load has been disposed of. These men have to do no other work, and, while they think they have 'a graft,' the other convicts, although they envy them the whiskey, call them ghouls."

The wagon brings the bodies to the open trench, which is 45 feet long, 15 feet wide and 7 feet deep, and into this the boxes are placed after Frederick Bartels, the assistant superintendent, who is serving his seventeenth year at the Field, has scratched the number on the box with an instrument called a scriber. The long ends of the trenches run east and west, and the bodies are placed in them facing north and south, heads to the edge. A row of twenty-five is placed at each side of the trench, and on this layer of fifty a thin covering of earth is placed until more bodies are received, when the trench is "tripped" by the convicts. This is the term for the process of taking the earth off the boxes before the next layer is put down. This is repeated until the trench holds three layers, or 150 bodies, when it is covered with earth, and built up about a foot. When this has been done a new plot for 150 bodies is laid out and numbered. A record is kept of the place occupied by every box, and the books which are kept by Mr. Bartels show all particulars necessary for identification in case a body should be claimed by friends or relatives.

All the coffins marked with a cross are buried in the Catholic plot, on the north end, and separate trenches are devoted to nameless children, unidentified bodies and boxes from the colleges, of which latter there are nine or ten every week.

The records show that since the City Cemetery was founded, in 1869, 110,751 bodies have been buried there. Last year's contribution was 4,377, of which 1,829 were credited to the "Outdoor Poor," 362 to

Bellevue Hospital and 435 to the Foundlings. There is a special plot for soldiers' graves, in which about forty bodies are buried, the last being two victims of yellow fever, who contracted the disease in Cuba and died at North Brother Island. This plot is marked by a handsome monument and is decorated every Memorial Day. Several attendants who died on the island are also buried in separate graves.

One enclosure contains the bodies of two little children whose mother asked that they might be kept separate from the others so that she might know where the little ones were laid away, and near the south end of the field is another child's grave, the existence of which is unknown to the little one's parents or friends. Some years ago, so goes the story, a man was going abroad with his family, and as they boarded the ship an attendant noticed the deathly pallor of the infant in the mother's arms. Examination showed that the child was ill, and before the vessel sailed the child was dead, and the body was left for burial. The story reached Potter's Field before the body arrived there, and in the hope that the names of the parents might be learned a separate grave was made of the body, but all efforts in that direction have failed....

"The men who work in the trenches where the bodies are laid away have a grewsome job," said an officer of the Department, "and one for which the 'drunk and disorderly' on the island don't envy them; in fact, being put in this gang is by no means a mark of distinction, and yet they see less mourning than the men who work in a private cemetery. There relatives and friends stand about the open graves and weep for those who have passed away. Here the bodies come, are carted to the trench, lowered and covered with earth, and that is all. No one knows, no one cares; a hundred and fifty make a trench full, and then a new hole is dug. Men grow accustomed to all kinds of work, and there's probably no convict gang in the New-York institutions where there is less of the blues than among the helpers at Potter's Field."

New York Tribune 1 April 1900: p. 6 NEW YORK

Further Reading: (The similarities to 1900 are striking.)

http://www.nytimes.com/2014/03/19/opinion/the-graves-of-forgotten-new-yorkers.html

http://www.nytimes.com/2013/11/17/nyregion/on-hart-island-new-yorks-potters-field.html?pagewanted=all&_r=0

http://hartisland.net/Home/tabid/36/Default.aspx

17.

"Death Never Could Gather a Fairer Flower:"

Deathbeds and Sorrow

There are fashions in emotions as well as funerals. The flowery sentiments of the Victorian courtship; the moralizing of the Victorian divine; the adoration of Victorian motherhood. These are as foreign to most of us as a faded daguerreotype. Yet stark sorrow at a death is unmistakable, no matter the century.

A MOTHER'S LOVE.

She Clings to Her Child in Death—Extraordinary Case of Superstition.

In the tenement house 173 Seventh Street, Jersey City, lives Mrs. Black, a widow. She had two children, one a girl five years old, the other a boy eighteen months old. The latter died at nine o'clock at night on Thursday, 15th inst. Friday passed, and the neighbors wondered why the woman did not make her appearance. Captain Van Riper, of the Second Precinct, was called on, and when he learned the child was dead he notified County Physician Buck. The latter called at the house and gave a permit for burial. The mother would not listen to such an order. Dr. Buck told her it was imperative. The poor woman threw herself on her knees and implored him for God's sake not to take her dear child away from her. She was convinced that after eight days it would come to life again. Dr. Buck consented to leave the lifeless child with her on condition that she would place it on ice. The poor woman answered, "Oh, no; it is cold enough without placing it on ice." Day after day passed, and the neighbors again appealed to the police. The distracted mother took the dead child to her bosom every night in the hope that life would return. She heated the poker and placed it to the soles of the infant's feet and when the child did not respond she groaned and cried so piteously that the neighbors were attracted to the place.

A second complaint was made to the police, and Captain Van Riper gave orders that the body be removed. In carrying out this order it was necessary to hold the frantic mother till the body was removed out of sight. After it was removed she cried and groaned in the most piteous manner. Some kind-hearted neighbors exerted themselves to console her, but in vain. She expects her brother, who is her sole support, to arrive to-day, and then she says everything will be right. Meantime the body lies at Brady's, and there is no sign of decomposition. The unfortunate woman, it is feared, has lost her reason. She will not admit any of her neighbors to sympathize with her, as she says she has been robbed of her child. Her cries at night are heartrending. To-day the body will be interred, and if the brother of the unfortunate woman does not appear it will be necessary to have her sent to the County Lunatic Asylum. Yesterday she acted in the most frantic manner and would not be comforted.

New York [NY] Herald 24 January 1874: p. 3 NEW JERSEY

Why He Bought the Dolls.

[*Dakota Bell.*]

A group of three little girls stood before the window of the toy store and gazed longingly at a display of dolls. A kind-looking man noticed them, and soon each little girl went merrily away with a doll in her arms, bashfully telling her thanks to the man. He lingered behind to say:

"The little ones like dolls, and when I see them looking at them, I can't help stopping and getting some for them. It gives me a sad sort of pleasure."

"Yes?"

"My little girl liked dolls—it seemed as if her whole soul was bound up in them, almost. And she was such a little thing, too. But she played with them almost continually, and took so much comfort with them, especially one small wax doll, with its hands broken off and one foot missing. Yes, and its nose was badly worn and its hair had been put up in the very height of fashion so many times that it was nearly worn out, too. All her dolls had names and this one she called 'Tatie'—she meant 'Katie,' but she wasn't old enough to talk very well. Every night when she went to bed she must have 'Tatie' in her arms, and she would take it so, all night. Then when she was taken sick 'Tatie' must lie in the little white bed beside her and nestle in her arms at night. And 'Tatie' must have some of the medicines, too, and part of the little delicate dishes the loving hands of her mother brought her.

"And as she grew worse she told us that 'Tatie' was weaker, and showed us how much paler her poor marred face and worn-off nose were. And every day she held 'Tatie' more and more closely in her arms. So we sat by her bedside and knew, hard as it was, that the little angel of our household was going away, and that the closer she hugged 'Tatie' in her slender, wasted arms, the faster she was slipping from us. And at last she grew so weak that she could scarcely move, but her arms clasped tighter if we tried to take her 'Tatie' away from her. One night I had lain down on the sofa, worn out with watching, and in a little while my wife woke me with a soft touch, and her tears fell on my face, and I knew what it meant. And when we went back in the bedroom our little girl lay there still and calm, and 'Tatie' yet in her arms with the scattering, half-worn hair pressed against her pale, wasted cheek. They put her in the little coffin, and when I looked 'Tatie' still nestled in her arms.

"So that is why I stopped and bought the little girls some dolls, though I never saw them before, and if they take half the comfort with them that my little girl did I will be more than repaid."

The Cincinnati [OH] Enquirer 11 June 1887: p. 10

The Shadows of Real Life

A gentleman witnessed the following piteous little drama in a market in Cincinnati last week. A lady richly dressed stood before a stall, and as she received a package from the pale, care-worn little market woman, said kindly: "How is your little girl today?" "She is dead," the woman answered.

"Oh, how sorry I am," with still greater gentleness: "when did she die?"

"This morning."

"And you__"

"Yes, Ma'am; I had to come or lose today's sales. I couldn't afford to do it—there are the other children to be provided for." The pale little woman laid her thin, toil-warped hands down on the rough boards with a pathetic gesture, and her sunken eyes wandered along the line of flaring lights. "It was a hard thing to do," she said simply. The poor are poor even in words.

The Boston [MA] Weekly Globe 26 June 1883: p. 6 OHIO

Measuring the Baby.

We measured the riotous baby
Against the cottage wall;
A lily grew on the threshold,
And the boy was just as tall;

A royal tiger lily,
With spots of purple and gold,
And a heart like a jeweled chalice,
The fragrant dew to hold.

Without, the bluebird whistled
High up in the old roof-trees,
And to and fro at the window
The red rose rocked her bees;

And the wee pink fists of the baby
Were never a moment still.
Snatching at shine and shadow
That danced on the lattice-sill.

His eyes were wide as bluebells.
His mouth like a flower unblown,
Two little bare feet, like funny white mice.
Peeped out from his snowy gown;

And we thought, with a thrill of rapture
That yet had a touch of pain,
When June rolls around with her roses,
We'll measure the boy again.

Ah me! in a darkened chamber,
With the sunshine shut- away,
Through tears that fell like a bitter rain.
We measured the boy to-day;

And the little bare feet, that were dimpled
And sweet as a budding rose,
Lay side by side together
In the hush of a-long repose.

Up from the dainty pillow,
White as the risen dawn,
The fair little face lay smiling,
With the light of heaven thereon

And the dear little hands, like rose-leaves
Dropped from a rose, lay still,
Never to snatch at the sunshine
That crept to the shrouded sill.

We measured the sleeping baby
With ribbons white as snow,
For the shining rosewood casket
That waited him below;

And out of the darkened chamber
We went with a childless moan —
To the height of the sinless angels
Our little one had grown.

-Emma Alice Brown, 1893

A Heart-broken Mother.

In 1864, notice was given that a boat-load of prisoners from Andersonville would be exchanged, and that they would be landed at Annapolis, Md. Men and women came from every part of the United States, each with the hope of meeting a friend whom they knew to be confined at Andersonville. Of course, among such a large number there could not be more than one in a hundred that could find the friend they came after. When the boat came up to the wharf there was a great crowd to welcome the forlorn creatures, and to inquire after others who did not come. Among the expectants was the mother of a soldier in the 12th Connecticut regiment, who rushed on board the boat, asking every soldier she saw, for her boy. From deck to cabin, in the cots and among the barrels she searched for him; but he was not there, and no one had heard of him. She had brought a cap, a shirt and a pair of pants, that he might have a clean change, and with these across her arm she wandered among the crowd saying, in a half-inquiring, vacant tone, "He has not come; he has not come." For a year after she went regularly to the wharf at sunrise from her lodgings, which nobody could find, and gazed for an hour down the bay, and murmuring "He has not come," would go to the post surgeon with the same cap, shirt and pants, and ask why her boy had not come. They shut the door in her face, and she wandered down to the wharf and was found the next morning stiff and cold, sitting upright behind some old barrels on the wharf, with her glassy eyes still gazing down the bay toward the point where steamers first came in sight.

"He had not come to her
But she had gone to him."

Jamestown [NY] Journal 15 October 1869: p. 2 MARYLAND

BIT OF CREPE

Upon His Arm Told Why the Little Man Gave Way to Grief

A bit of crepe encircled his tiny arm. His little knickerbockers were frayed at the knees and his wide collar was crumpled and very dirty. The front of it bore evidences of having been wet, and on the grimy little shirt front were spots where the dirt was washed away.

The little boy sat very still, with one hand on his valise, almost as big as himself. A half munched apple he held in the other hand, but it seemed to have lost interest for him. It was already turning brown at the bitten place. With his big gray eyes wide open he looked across the dark waiting room of the Union Depot, and out into the sunshine on the sidewalk. There were gathered several women with babies in their arms, chatting, and around played older children. The little boy looked and looked. Even his little legs, hanging over the edge of the seat, were motionless. His big eyes stared, and seemed growing bigger and bigger. Gradually, the edges of the long, thick lashes became moist. Higher and higher the moisture rose, and then in two big eyes it rolled down the cheeks, over the dirty collar, down on the little brown hands and the half-eaten apple. Two, three and four times they came, but the rosy cheeked face kept its grim look of determination. The children playing on the street, with a peal of laughter, ran in through the door and out again. One of the mothers raised her voice in sharp remonstrance at the noise.

The look of determination lost its stolidness, round the edges of the red, curving mouth came a suspicion of a pucker. The battle was fought, and lost. With one big sob the childish warrior against grief gave way. His soft cheeks, eyes and mouth seamed into a hundred wrinkles, and the tears flowed in a steady stream upon the little hands and the apple. Folding his arms around his face he leaned upon the valise beside him and cried, as only a child can cry.

It was hard to get him to talk. "Harry," he responded when asked his name—and that was all he could or would say.

His ticket, said the policeman, read to Topeka, from Leadville.

"Auntie'll meet me," was his explanation of his journey's purpose. "Oh, dear, dear! Papa said I must be a big, brave boy and not cry," and then sobs choked his voice.

The Cincinnati [OH] Enquirer 2 June 1900: p. 12

HAS SPENT NINE YEARS IN HIS WIFE'S TOMB

Devotion of Jonathan Reed Not Affected by the Incident of Death.

Every Day the Old Man Gazes Upon Her Face and Scours the Place.

With feeble, tottering steps Jonathan Reed made his way through Evergreen cemetery, Brooklyn, yesterday to the tomb in which rests the body of his wife, relates the *New York Herald*. There have been few days since she died, nine years ago, that he has not made the journey, but the sands of life are running low and his long pilgrimage is near an end.

It took all of his little strength to open the granite door yesterday and enter the vault. Then he walked to the hermetically sealed coffin in which his wife's body lies, and said: "Good morning, Mary; I've come to sit with you all day."

He spoke the words soft and low, as if soothing a child who was ill. Every morning it is the same. Never does he fail to greet her and talk to her just as he did in life.

Nearly every day he lifts the silk crazy quilt that covers the coffin and looks through the glass cover upon the face that has lain there still and dead for so long. Yesterday morning he looked at her face until the tears blinded him. Then he walked to the door of the tomb.

"She is just as pretty as ever," he said, sobbingly; "she was always the prettiest woman in the world.

"It's been forty-four years since we married, and we are still on our honeymoon. Yes, it's our honeymoon, and I love her as I did at first. You see her pictures here; I have them from the time she was a girl." Death will not be unwelcome to the old man who lives his life away there by the side of the woman he loved. He is 69. He says he will be with Mary soon. His coffin is ready for him by the side of the one in which she rests. He used to think there was nothing beyond the goal of the grave, and he had no hope of meeting his wife in another world. Lately he has come to believe he will see her in the spirit world and that she is calling him to her side.

For the nine years since they were parted by death he has made his home in her tomb. He would sleep there could he get permission, but this has been denied. Sometimes he remains with his loved one until nearly midnight. All the pretty things, all the trinkets she had, he has taken to the tomb. Rich tapestries and hangings, bought in the orient, swing from the beams. Paintings, curios, books and cushions fill nearly all the space not taken by the two coffins. Above the coffin of his wife, swinging in a little cage, is the canary bird that sang to her when she was dying. It was her pet, so he had it stuffed and put there with the other things dear to her.

Every day the old man cleans and scours the tomb, for he knows how particular she was that everything should be scrupulously neat. Feeble as he is, he carries the water from the lake. On bright days he sits outside in the sun, but when it is stormy and cold he goes inside and sits on a camp stool with his arms leaning on his wife's coffin. No matter how cold, he is always there. He says it would break his heart to be kept from her side, and that the three days of acute illness which he suffered recently were the saddest of his life because he could not be with her.

When he bids his wife good night and leaves the tomb he goes to a little room in a house at No. 153 North Fourth street. Early in the morning he starts back for the tomb. In the last few months he has been arriving later and later, for the spark of life in his frail body is growing dimmer and dimmer; his day is nearly done. Though his clothes are old and threadbare, he wears a large diamond—the one she loved to see him wear. He has never been without it since she died.

Omaha [NE] World Herald 4 May 1902: p. 19 NEW YORK

NOTE: Reed actually slept in the tomb for several years beside his wife's coffin until the cemetery authorities put a stop to it. In March of 1905 he was found on the floor of the tomb, struck down by a stroke. He joined his beloved Mary at last on 12 September, 1905, leaving a large endowment for the perpetual care of the tomb.

We finish this book, as we began, with a deathbed.

It has been suggested by some historians that high childhood mortality made parents indifferent to their infant losses. While nineteenth-century families tended to be large ones, few were untouched by the death of a child. This piece written by the Rev. John Todd, a Massachusetts minister and author, although slightly earlier than the Victorian period, poignantly expresses a universal anguish, which even at this remove, arouses our sympathy.

"Our dear little boy was born at sunrise, October 6th, 1827. Mrs. Todd had been remarkably well and active since our marriage, and probably his premature birth was owing to her over-exertion. At his birth, none seemed to think he could live but a short time; but with great exertions he was made to revive. He was small, but promised, humanly speaking, to do well. He soon opened his eyes, and began to notice sounds and objects of sight. For a week we had no fears concerning him, and enjoyed as much as parents could enjoy. When I went out, I hastened home to see my dear child lie in his mother's arms, and, at the sound of my voice, open his dark-blue eyes and turn them toward me. We began to talk of a name, and in my own mind I had begun to form many little plans concerning him...

"On Saturday, the little boy being a week old, we weighed him again, and found that he had lost. Here I first began to fear that he would not be spared to us. Still, he seemed well, and his nurse appeared to have no fears concerning him.

"In the afternoon of the same day he was evidently sick, and we began to be alarmed. Everything was done for him which could be. That night he rested pretty well.

"Sabbath morning he was evidently very sick—appeared to have something like fits—and during breakfast he turned so black as greatly to alarm his mother; but from this he soon recovered. I was obliged to leave at half-past ten o'clock, to go into the pulpit. I left the child in his nurse's arms, and tears in the eyes of his mother. I endeavored to conceal my fears and feelings, and went into the pulpit with a heavy heart. As soon as possible I was at home, and found the child worse, and his mother greatly distressed. It was then evident that he could not live. When I really came to the conclusion that he must die—our own sweet boy, our first-born, must die—it was almost insupportable. As we then came to the conclusion that he must leave us, we determined to give him formally to our covenant-God in baptism. I immediately wrote a note to our friend, Mr. Chaplin, requesting him to bring his venerable father down to baptize our dying child. Mrs. Todd's dressing-table was placed before her bed, the baptismal font was placed on it, and the family stood around the room. The child was in the arms of the nurse. The venerable old man, Doctor Chaplin, prayed with deep feeling and great appropriateness. I was kneeling by the side of the bed and holding my dear Mary's hand, while we both wept, and endeavored to give our child to God. The prayer ended, I took the dear babe in my arms and presented him to Doctor Chaplin. The old man was eighty-four years old, upward of six feet high, silver locks, and the most venerable person I ever saw. Our child was eight days old, fair, well-proportioned, and seventeen inches in length. Striking contrast, indeed! He was solemnly baptized into the name of the Father, and of the Son, and of the Holy Ghost, by the name of John William—the former name being his father's, and the latter that of his friend. The bell rang for meeting while the ordinance was administering, and I was obliged to go again into the pulpit, expecting to find my child a corpse on my return...

The audience felt for me, and very many wept. I preached as well as I could, hardly knowing what I was about, and again hastened home, and again found our dear child alive.

"It was now toward night, and he continued to have spasms, in which he would turn black, groan, and seem to be in great pain. I sent immediately for a physician, who put him in warm water, and he revived; but it was only for a time. During the whole afternoon the nurse held him in her lap without moving. In the evening, hoping it would endanger Mrs. Todd less, I had him removed into my study. He was carried out, and it was the last time his weeping mother ever saw him alive. I was in and out of the study during the evening, but was for the most part with my wife. At ten o'clock he had an awful spasm. I went in, and was told he was no more. I gazed at him: his beautiful little features were all composed and set, and it seemed as if Death had indeed now set his seal. All hope was cut off, all doubt removed. I returned to my dear Mary, and was obliged to tell her our first-born was no more. She burst into grief the most passionate, and it seemed as if her very frame would be crushed under the burden. We spake but little: it was, that God ruled; that our dear boy had gone to his bosom; that we trusted he would be among the angels, himself an angel; and that we should meet him again beyond the shores of mortality. I then knelt by the bed of Mrs. Todd, and we prayed, our right hands joined, and we committed and gave ourselves away to God.

"At eleven o'clock I left Mrs. Todd and went into the study; and here was the most severe trial I was called to undergo. I found the child was *not* dead: he had revived, and was now in great agony; it was the agony of death. He was in the arms of Miss Chaplin, his eyes open, his arms thrown out, his little fists clenched, and every muscle brought into intense action. They dared do nothing to relieve the little sufferer. I immediately gave him paregoric, and anointed his chest with warm olive-oil. His pains were less intense after that. As he lay with his eyes open, I spoke to him, called him 'John;' he turned his head and bright eyes toward me with an expressiveness that I shall never forget. I do not pretend he knew me or my voice; but it was such a look as a dying child might wish to leave with his father, if he could choose. I sat without turning my eyes from him for an hour, and then returned to inform his mother that he was still living. I did not see him again alive; for he ceased to breathe soon after the Sabbath was over. I never saw such suffering before; and it seemed as if God had indeed cursed our race, and had most awfully written his displeasure with sinners on the features of our dying boy. Mysterious system! that such a child should suffer so intensely! But 'clouds and darkness are round about Him,' which we trust will one day all be rolled away.

"Early on Monday morning I opened my study door. The room was solitary, the windows open, and the cold winds of a chilly morning were sighing through the shutters. The room was in perfect order. In a corner, near my book-case, were two chairs, and a white cloth between them. I went slowly and lifted the cloth, and there lay my sweet boy, pale as the cloth which covered him; the beautiful white robe of the grave was upon him; his little hands were folded on his bosom; he was dressed for the coffin. Never did I see a countenance so beautiful. Every part was well-proportioned and perfect. His dark-brown hair was parted on his forehead under his cap. It seemed as if death never could gather a fairer flower. I stood over him for a long time, and, if possible, loved my boy more in death than in life.

"For fear of injuring Mrs. Todd, we had rather a private funeral, that afternoon, at half-past three o'clock. There may have been fifty present, all of whom seemed to feel for us. The good old man was our pastor. He talked well to us: they sung a hymn, and he made the prayer. The little creature was put into a mahogany coffin, with a plate on the top with the following inscription: 'John W. Todd, who died October 15, 1827, aged nine days.' Without any parade or bell, he was carried in a chaise, and I rode alone in my chaise, and saw him softly laid in Doctor Chaplin's tomb, in the very spot where the good man himself expects to lie. When that event takes place, I intend to have him placed beside the old man's head, or on his breast, that in the morning of the Resurrection they may rise together. It seemed to be his wish to have him entombed there, and it was gratifying to us, for it seems as if even the grave would be sanctified by his remains."

Years afterward he wrote:

"I shall perish sooner than forget the feelings which I had clinging around our dear first-born. I know that we did not deserve him, and that it was all right; but my aching heart too frequently goes back to that dear lost one, and the gems of all the earth could not compensate for the loss of that one. Is he now alive? Shall we ever know him? Will that beautiful form ever come up again from the tomb? Oh, the agony of that moment when the little coffin-lid was actually closed! May God in mercy spare me from ever witnessing another such scene!"

John Todd: The Story of His Life Told Mainly by Himself, edited by John Todd [son], (New York: Harper, 1876) MASSACHUSETTS

Bibliography

Adams, Norman. *Dead and Buried? The Horrible History of Bodysnatching.* New York, NY: Bell Publishing, 1972

[Association for the Prevention of Premature Burial]. *Premature Burial, with Sir Benjamin Ward Richardson's Signs and Proofs of Death.* London, UK: H.W. Denton-Ingham, 1908

Bailey, Brian. *The Resurrection Men: A History of the Trade in Corpses.* London, UK: Macdonald & Co., 1991

Ball, James M., MD. *The Sack-'em Up Men: An Account of the Rise and Fall of the Modern Resurrectionists.* Edinburgh, UK: Oliver and Boyd, 1928

Barker, Felix. Highgate Cemetery: Victorian Valhalla. London, UK: John Murray Publishers, 1984

Bell, Michael E. *Food for the Dead: On the Trail of New England's Vampires.* Middletown, CT: Wesleyan Univ. Press, 2011

Bondeson, Jan. *Buried Alive: The Terrifying History of Our Most Primal Fear.* New York, NY: Norton, 2001

Brett, Mary. *Fashionable Mourning Jewelry, Clothing & Customs.* Atglen, PA: Schiffer Pub., 2006

Brooks, Chris. *Mortal Remains: The History and Present State of the Victorian and Edwardian Cemetery.* Exeter, UK: Wheaton Publishers Ltd., 1989

Burns, Dr. Stanley B. *Sleeping Beauty: Memorial Photography in America.* Altadena, CA: Twelvetrees Press, 1990

____ *Sleeping Beauty II: Grief, Bereavement and the Family in Memorial Photography, American & European Traditions.* New York, NY: Burns Archive Press, 2002

____ *Sleeping Beauty III: Memorial Photography, The Children: Selections from the Burns Collection & Archive.* New York, NY: Burns Archive Press, 2001

Cheroux, Clement. *The Perfect Medium: Photography and the Occult.* New Haven, CT: Yale University Press, 2005

Coates, James. *Photographing the Invisible: Practical Studies in Spirit Photography, Spirit Portraiture, and Other Rare but Allied Phenomena.* London, UK: Fowler, 1911

Colquette, Marian Patricia. "Graceful Death: The Use of Victorian Elements in Grace Episcopal Churchyard, St. Francisville, Louisiana and St. Helena's Episcopal Churchyard, Beaufort, South Carolina." Master's Thesis, Louisiana State University, 2003. Accessed 3 August 2014 http://etd.lsu.edu/docs/available/etd-1102103-142417/unrestricted/Colquette_thesis.pdf

Curl, James Stevens. *The Victorian Celebration of Death.* Stroud, UK: Sutton Pub., 2000

Dalton, Curt. *The Terrible Resurrection.* Dayton, OH: C. Dalton, 2002

Davies, Rodney. *Buried Alive: Horrors of the Undead.* London, UK: Robert Hale, 1999

DeLorme, Maureen. *Mourning Art & Jewelry.* Atglen, PA: Schiffer Pub., 2004

Dickey, Colin. *Cranioklepty: Grave Robbing and the Search for Genius.* Denver, CO: Unbridled Books, 2009

Doughty, Caitlin. *Smoke Gets in Your Eyes: And Other Lessons from the Crematory.* New York, NY: W.W. Norton & Co., 2014

Ebenstein, Joanna and Colin Dickey. *The Morbid Anatomy Anthology.* New York, NY: Morbid Anatomy Press, 2014

Farrell, James J. *Inventing the American Way of Death, 1830-1920.* Philadelphia, PA: Temple University Press, 1980

Faust, Drew Gilpin. *This Republic of Suffering: Death and the American Civil War.* New York, NY: Alfred A. Knopf, 2008

Frank, Lucy E., ed. *Representations of Death in Nineteenth-century US Writing and Culture.* Burlington, VT: Ashgate Pub., 2007

Frank, Robin Jaffee. *Love and Loss: American Portrait and Mourning Miniatures*. New Haven, CT: Yale University Art Gallery, 2000

Gettings, Fred. *Ghosts in Photographs: The Extraordinary Story of Spirit Photography*. New York, NY: Harmony Book, 1978

Gittings, Clare. *Death, Burial and the Individual in Early Modern England*. London, UK: Croom Helm, 1984

Habenstein, Robert W. and William M. Lamers. *The History of American Funeral Directing*. Milwaukee, WI: Bulfin Printers, Inc., 1955

Hartmann, Franz, M.D. *Buried Alive: An Examination Into the Occult Causes of Apparent Death, Trance, and Catalepsy*. Boston, MA: Occult Pub. Co., 1895

Harvey, John. *Photography and Spirit*. London, UK: Reaktion Books, 2007

Hillerman, Barbara Dodd. "The Evolution of American 'Widow's Weeds': 1865-1965 A Study in Social History." Master's Thesis, The Ohio State University, 1972

Iserson, Kenneth V. *Death to Dust: What Happens to Dead Bodies?* Tucson, AZ: Galen Press, 1994

Jackson, Charles O., ed. *Passing: The Vision of Death in America*. Westport, CT: Greenwood Press, 1977

Jacques, Janine. *Death and Mourning Culture in the American Civil War: The Experiences of Civilians, Soldiers and Nurses*. Norton, MA: Wheaton College, 2003

Jalland, Pat. *Death in the Victorian Family*. Oxford, UK: Oxford University Press, 1996

Jupp, Peter D. & Clare Gittings. *Death in England: An Illustrated History*. New Brunswick, NJ: Rutgers University Press, 2000

Kaplan, Louis. *The Strange Case of William Mumler, Spirit Photographer*. Minneapolis, MN: University of Minnesota Press, 2008

Kastenbaum, Beatrice and Robert Kastenbaum. *Encyclopedia of Death: Myth, History, Philosophy, Science—The Many Aspects of Death and Dying*. Phoenix, AZ: Oryx Press, 1989

Kete, Mary Louise. *Sentimental Collaborations: Mourning and Middle-Class Identity in Nineteenth-Century America*. Durham, NC: Duke University Press, 2000

Koudounaris, Paul. *The Empire of Death: A Cultural History of Ossuaries and Charnel Houses*. New York, NY: Thames & Hudson, 2011

____Memento Mori: *The Dead Among Us*. London, UK: Thames & Hudson, 2015

Laderman, Gary. *Rest in Peace: A Cultural History of Death and the Funeral Home in Twentieth-Century America*. New York, NY: Oxford University Press, 2003

____ *The Sacred Remains, American Attitudes Towards Death 1799-1883*. New Haven, CT: Yale University Press, 1996

Lesy, Michael. *Wisconsin Death Trip*. Albuquerque, NM: University of New Mexico Press, 2000

Lovejoy, Bess. Rest in Pieces: The Curious Fates of Famous Corpses. New York, NY: Simon and Schuster, 2013

Lynch, Thomas. *The Undertaking: Life Studies from the Dismal Trade*. New York, NY: W.W. Norton, 1997

MacDonald, Helen. *Possessing the Dead: The Artful Science of Anatomy*. Carlton, Vic.: Melbourne University Press, 2010

Marsden, Simon. *Memento Mori: Churches and Churchyards of England*. Swindon, UK: English Heritage, 2007

Martyn, Jolly. *Faces of the Living Dead: The Belief in Spirit Photography*. London, UK: British Library, 2006

May, Trevor. *The Victorian Undertaker*. Princes Risborough, UK: Shire Publications Ltd., 2000

McCracken-Flesher, Caroline. *The Doctor Dissected: A Cultural Autopsy of the Burke and Hare Murders*. New York, NY: Oxford University Press, 2012

Metcalf, Peter and Richard Huntington. *Celebrations of Death: The Anthropology of Mortuary Ritual*. Cambridge, UK: Cambridge University Press, 1979

Millian, Monica. *A History of Post-Mortem Photography and Contemporary Post-Mortem Photographers*. s.l.: sn., 2011

Mills, Cynthia J. *Beyond Grief: Sculpture and Wonder in the Gilded Age Cemetery*. Washington, D.C.: Smithsonian Institution Scholarly Press, 2014

Mitford, Jessica. *The American Way of Death Revisited*. New York, NY: Alfred A. Knopf, 1998

Morley, John. *Death, Heaven and the Victorians*. Pittsburgh, PA: University of Pittsburgh Press, 1971

Muller, Helen. Jet *Jewellery and Ornaments*. Princes Risborough, UK: Shire Publications Ltd., 2003

Needham, A.C. "Random Notes on Funeral Rings Compiled from Various Sources," *Old-Time New England: The Bulletin of the Society for the Preservation of New England Antiquities*. Vol. XXXIX July 1948-April 1949: 93-97

Nehama, Sarah. *In Death Lamented: The Tradition of Anglo-American Mourning Jewelry*. Boston, MA: Massachusetts Historical Society, 2012

Norfleet, Barbara P. *Looking at Death*. Boston, MA: D.R. Godine, 1993

Pike, Martha V. and Janice Gray Armstrong. *A Time to Mourn: Expressions of Grief in Nineteenth Century America*. Stony Brook, NY: Museums at Stony Brook, 1980

Prothero, Stephen. *Purified by Fire: A History of Cremation in America*. Oakland, CA: University of California Press, 2001

Quigley, Christine. *The Corpse: A History*. Jefferson, NC: McFarland, 1996

Ragon, Michel. *The Space of Death: A Study of Funerary Architecture, Decoration, and Urbanism*. Charlottesville, VA: University Press of Virginia, 1983

Rainville, Lynn. *Hidden History: African American Cemeteries in Central Virginia*. Charlottesville, VA: University of Virginia Press, 2014

Reeve, Jez and Max Adams. *The Spitalfields Project, Vol. 1 – The Archaeology, Across the Styx*. York, UK: Council for British Archaeology, 1993

Richardson, Ruth. *Death, Dissection and the Destitute*. Chicago, IL: University of Chicago Press, 2000

Roach, Mary. *Stiff: The Curious Lives of Human Cadavers*. New York, NY: W.W. Norton & Co., 2003

Robben, Antonius C.G.M. *Death, Mourning, and Burial: A Cross-Cultural Reader*. Malden, MA: Blackwell Pub., 2004

Robinson, David. *Beautiful Death: Art at the Cemetery*. New York, NY: Penguin Studio, 1996

Rose, Jerome C., ed. *Gone To a Better Land: A Biohistory of a Rural Black Cemetery in the Post-Reconstruction South*. Fayetteville, AR: Arkansas Archaeological Survey Research Series No. 25, 1985

Ruby, Jay. *Secure the Shadow: Death and Photography in America*. Cambridge, MA: MIT Press, 1999

Schantz, Mark S. *Awaiting the Heavenly Country: The Civil War and America's Culture of Death*. Ithaca, NY: Cornell University Press, 2008

Stannard, David E., ed. *Death in America*. Philadelphia, PA: University of Pennsylvania Press, 1975

Taylor, Lou. *Mourning Dress: A Costume and Social History*. Boston, MA: G. Allen and Unwin, 1983

Tebb, William, Edward Perry Vollum, and Walter Robert Hadwen. *Premature Burial and How It May Be Prevented*. London, UK: S. Sonnenschein & Co., 1905

Trostel, Scott D. *The Lincoln Funeral Train: The Final Journey and National Funeral for Abraham Lincoln*. Fletcher, OH: Cam-Tech Pub., 2002

Wescott, Daniel J., *et al*. "A Fisk patent metallic burial case from Western Missouri: An interdisciplinary and comprehensive effort to reconstruct the history of an early settler of Lexington, Missouri." Accessed 22 August 2014 http://www.academia.edu/199581/A_Fisk_Patent_Metallic_Burial_Case_from_western_Missouri_a_interdisciplinary_and_comprehensive_effort_to_reconstruct_the_history_of_an_early_settler_of_Lexington_Missouri

Whitenight, John. "Hair Work: 'Hair Today, Hair Tomorrow.'" In Under Glass: A Victorian Obsession. Atglen, PA: Schiffer Pub., 2013

Woodyard, Chris. *The Face in the Window: Haunting Ohio Tales*. Beavercreek, OH: Kestrel Publications, 2014

____ *The Ghost Wore Black: Ghastly Tales from the Past*. Beavercreek, OH: Kestrel Publications, 2014

_____ *The Headless Horror: Strange and Ghostly Ohio Tales.* Beavercreek, OH: Kestrel Publications, 2014

Worpole, Ken. Last Landscapes: *The Architecture of the Cemetery in the West.* London, UK: Reaktion Books, 2003

Wright, Roberta Hughes, Wilbur B. Hughes, and Barbara K. Hughes Smith. *The Death Care Industry: African American Cemeteries and Funeral Homes.* Cordele, GA: Hughes Wright Enterprises: 2007

Wright, Roberta Hughes, Wilbur B. Hughes, and Gina Renee Misiroglu. *Lay Down Body: Living History in African American Cemeteries.* Detroit, MI: Visible Ink Press, 1996

Websites and Blogs

The Art of Mourning. http://artofmourning.com/

Barts Pathology Museum. http://www.qmul.ac.uk/bartspathology/

Beachcombing's Bizarre History Blog. http://www.strangehistory.net/

The Chirugeon's Apprentice. http://thechirurgeonsapprentice.com/

The Farber Gravestone Collection. http://www.davidrumsey.com/farber/

Grave Addiction. www.graveaddiction.com

A Grave Affair: A selection of books and other materials about gravestones, graveyards, epitaphs, mourning & funeral customs of other times, and related topics. http://www.a-grave-affair.com/

Historic New England, "Not Lost But Gone Before: Mourning Jewelry." http://www.historic-newengland.org/collections-archives-exhibitions/online-exhibitions/JewelryHistory/themes/Mourning.htm

Morbid Anatomy Museum. http://morbidanatomymuseum.org/

Murder by Gaslight. http://www.murderbygaslight.com/

The Order of the Good Death. http://www.orderofthegooddeath.com/

Strange Company. http://strangeco.blogspot.com

The Thanatos Archive: Early Post-Mortem & Mourning Photography. http://thanatos.net/

Victorian Hairwork Society Website. http://www.hairworksociety.org/

Wellcome Collection. http://www.wellcomecollection.org/

General Index

Index by Location

Kestrel
Publications

Purchase copies of this and other books by Chris Woodyard at
your local bookstore or library, or ask them to order the books.
They are also available at Amazon or Barnes & Noble and
personally autographed copies may be purchased at
www.hauntedohiobooks.com

Please join us on Facebook at
Haunted Ohio by Chris Woodyard
and
The Victorian Book of the Dead
We're on Twitter @ hauntedohiobook

Chris writes two blogs: www.hauntedohiobooks.com,
which covers mourning, death, and international Fortean topics.
And www.mrsdaffodildigresses.wordpress.com,
about costume, history, and social ephemera.